Photoshop® 4 Artistry

A Master Class for Photographers, Artists, and Production Artists

New Riders

Barry Haynes
Wendy Crumpler

Photoshop® 4 Artistry
A Master Class for Photographers, Artists, and Production Artists

By Barry Haynes and Wendy Crumpler

Published by: New Riders Publishing
201 West 103rd Street
Indianapolis, IN 46290 USA

Printed in the United States of America   1 2 3 4 5 6 7 8 9 0

Library of Congress Cataloging-in-Publication Data available upon request

ISBN: 1-56205-759-6

WARNING AND DISCLAIMER

This book is designed to provide information about Photoshop. Every effort has been made to make this book as complete and as accurate as possible, but no warranty or fitness is implied.

The information is provided on an "as is" basis. The authors and New Riders Publishing shall have neither liability nor responsibility to any person or entity with respect to any loss or damages arising from the information contained in this book or from the use of the disks or programs that may accompany it.

Publisher:	*Don Fowley*
Associate Publisher:	*David Dwyer*
Marketing Manager:	*Mary Foote*
Managing Editor:	*Carla Hall*
Director of Development:	*Kezia Endsley*

TRADEMARK ACKNOWLEDGMENTS

All terms mentioned in this book that are known to be trademarks or service marks have been appropriately capitalized. New Riders Publishing cannot attest to the accuracy of this information. Use of a term in this book should not be regarded as affecting the validity of any trademark or service mark.

Adobe Photoshop® is a trademark of Adobe Systems Incorporated. Used with permission.

PRODUCT DEVELOPMENT SPECIALIST
John Kane

SENIOR EDITORS
Sarah Kearns
Suzanne Snyder

TECHNICAL EDITORS
Gary Kubicek
J. Scott Hamlin

SOFTWARE SPECIALIST
Steve Flatt

ASSISTANT MARKETING MANAGER
Gretchen Schlesinger

ACQUISITIONS COORDINATOR
Stacey Beheler

ADMINISTRATIVE COORDINATOR
Karen Opal

MANUFACTURING COORDINATOR
Brook Farling

COVER DESIGN
Wendy Crumpler and
Barry Haynes

COVER PRODUCTION
Barry Haynes and
Wendy Crumpler

COVER PHOTO
Barry Haynes

BOOK DESIGN AND PRODUCTION
Wendy Crumpler and
Barry Haynes

DIRECTOR OF PRODUCTION
Larry Klein

PRODUCTION TEAM SUPERVISORS
Laurie Casey
Joe Millay

PROOFREADERS
Linda Knose
Christy Wagner
Phil Worthington

INDEXER
Kevin Fulcher

NEW RIDERS PUBLISHING

The staff of New Riders Publishing is committed to bringing you the very best in computer reference material. Each New Riders book is the result of months of work by authors and staff who research and refine the information contained within its covers.

As part of this commitment to you, New Riders invites your input. Please let us know if you enjoy this book, if you have trouble with the information and examples presented, or if you have a suggestion for the next edition.

Please note, however: New Riders staff cannot serve as a technical resource for Photoshop or for questions about software- or hardware-related problems. Please refer to the documentation that accompanies your software or to the application's Help systems.

If you have a question or comment about any New Riders book, there are several ways to contact New Riders Publishing. We will respond to as many readers as we can. Your name, address, or phone number will never become part of a mailing list or be used for any purpose other than to help us continue to bring you the best books possible.

You can write us at the following address:

New Riders Publishing
Attn: Publisher
201 W. 103rd Street
Indianapolis, IN 46290

If you prefer, you can fax New Riders Publishing at:

317-817-7448

You can also send electronic mail to New Riders at the following Internet address:

jkane@newriders.mcp.com

New Riders Publishing is an imprint of Macmillan Computer Publishing. To obtain a catalog or information, or to purchase any Macmillan Computer Publishing book, call 800-428-5331 or visit our Web site at http://www.mcp.com.

Thank you for selecting *Photoshop 4 Artistry*!

ABOUT THE AUTHORS

Barry Haynes uses digital technology to print, show, and sell his photography. In addition to his love for creating photographs, Barry teaches digital photography, creates commercial special effects, and does digital image consulting. His books, *Photoshop Artistry: A Master Class for Photographers and Artists*, and *Photoshop 4 Artistry: A Master Class for Photographers, Artists, and Production Artists* are available in bookstores around the world. He has been teaching Photoshop courses since 1990 to clients including Apple, Oracle, Kodak, Nikon, Pacific Bell, Sony, Tandem, SuperMac, *The San Jose Mercury News*, and many others. He teaches regular digital photography workshops for the Photoshop Conference, University of California Santa Cruz Extension, The Palm Beach Photographic Workshops, and AD Vantage Computers in Des Moines, Iowa. He has given talks or workshops for the Photoshop Conference, the MacSummit conference, Seybold Seminars, MacWorld, the Center for Creative Imaging, the Digital Photography Conference, the American Society of Magazine Photographers, advertising agencies, design firms, and other organizations.

His articles have appeared in desktop publishing magazines, and his imaging effects can be seen in brochures, on the Web, and on magazine covers for companies including Apple, Netscape, and Tandem. Barry has a degree in computer science and spent 10 years, from 1980 to 1990, doing software development and research at Apple. There he did research involving desktop publishing, digital imaging, and high-speed networks, and before that he worked on Pascal and Object Oriented software development environments for Apple including Macintosh Smalltalk, MacApp, the Lisa Workshop, and Apple II Pascal.

Wendy Crumpler has been in advertising and design since 1980. She has worked in print, television, CD-Interactive, interactive television, and computer-based training. Prior to her discovery of the computer in 1981 and the Macintosh in 1986, she was an actress and teacher. Since her involvement in digital imaging she has done production, illustration, design, and training for a variety of clients using Quark, PageMaker, Illustrator, Freehand, Photoshop, and other applications. She has worked for Angotti Thomas Hedge, Boardroom Reports, Deutsch Advertising, J. Walter Thompson, TBWA Advertising, Wechsler Design, Manhattan Transfer, Wells Rich Greene, Canon, Parke Davis, IBM, and AT&T.

SAY YES TO THE UNIVERSE

In three days, we fell in love. In three months, we were married. In three years of marriage we've produced one remarkable son and two terrific books. A lot can happen when you say, "Yes!"

LET US KNOW WHAT YOU THINK

There's been a lot of student and reader involvement in the shaping of this book. Listening to people who use these techniques helps us to refine and dig deeper to find solutions to our clients' and students' problems. And, we get smarter in the process. We love what we do and invite you to become part of the digital revolution with us. Let us know what you think of the book, what was helpful, what confused you. We are committed to empowering people to use their computers and their software to advance their own artistic abilities and to make a difference on this planet.

SERVICES AVAILABLE FROM THE AUTHORS:

Besides creating our own artwork, producing commercial effects for clients, and teaching at digital imaging centers and conferences around the country, we also teach more personal Photoshop, Quark, and Illustrator courses in our own studios and courses tailored to your special needs at your business location. Check our Web site at MAXART.com for the latest information about the times and locations for our digital imaging courses, as well as book updates, and other useful information.

WE LOOK FORWARD TO HEARING FROM YOU!

Barry Haynes Photography
Wendy Crumpler Enterprises
820 Memory Lane
Boulder Creek, CA 95006
(408) 338-4569
fax (408) 338-6571

e-mail: Barry@maxart.com, Wendy@maxart.com, or just MAXART.COM

DEDICATION

For Max, bringer of joy, changer of lives.

ACKNOWLEDGMENTS

We assumed that rewriting a book would be a lot less work than writing the original. We were wrong. And so, there are a lot of people we'd like to thank for helping us through the process a second time.

First, we must thank John Kane, who simply has to be one of the nicest people in the world to work with as well as being organized and efficient. In fact, you could say pretty much the same thing for all the people at New Riders—they're great. We'd like to thank David Dwyer for making us believe that we have the very best Photoshop book on the market, Carla Hall for shepherding us through the production maze, Sarah Kearns for becoming Carla Hall for two weeks, Mary Foote and Gretchen Schlesinger for hammering out the cover details and easing our minds about marketing, Jennifer Eberhardt for standing in for John Kane during a critical vacation period, Kevin Fulcher for indexing and re-indexing, Brook Farling for being so accessible and easy to deal with, Gary Kubicek and Scott Hamlin for their very helpful technical edits and some PC screen grabs, Laurie Casey for being present for all those conference calls, Steve Flatt for putting the CD to bed, Christy Wagner and Linda Knose for following our proofreading instructions (probably against their better judgments), and finally, Phil Worthington for being everything you could want from an editor and for making us laugh.

Lisa Clark, Noli Farwell, Marguerite Meyer, and Andrea Schwartz for production assistance.

Bruce Ashley and Bill Atkinson for continuing to ask great questions and feed us great information every time they discover something new, and for the color management systems ideas. Bruce Fraser and Brian Lawler for help with color management questions. Dennis Gobets for first-rate assistance in answering our questions about printing,

Jim Rich, one of the smartest Photoshop gurus we know for the help, support, and friendship.

Frank Bevans for the great photography.

Tim Holt and Kurt Ellinger of Shepard Poorman for helping us through the printing process.

Brad Bunnin, our attorney, who has proven that lawyers can be divine.

Dr. Robert Bischoff, for keeping us sane and on-track, and for the Internet advice (also the jokes!).

Ken Harwell, our Airborne driver. Let's face it, Ken, without you we couldn't have done this.

Amy Romanoff and Kristine Plachy at Sybex for easing our transition to a new publisher.

Our friends Al Hoffman and Mary Cadloni, Bruce Hodge and Liz Weal, Steve and Sarah Clark, Bob Vallem and Sandy Pierson, Marcella Smith, Barry Demchak, Diane Wicks, Luke Neal, and Susan Merrie Hellerer. Your laughter, love, and e-mails have kept us feeling human when we were beginning to feel like machines.

Lynda Weinman and Ali Karp for convincing us that New Riders were the people to go with. And Bruce Heavin for signing our book.

The Staff at Children's Center of San Lorenzo Valley for their support, encouragement, and for loving Max, especially Lote Sanderson and Geri Lieby.

Denise Haynes, who is a mother to us both and one terrific G'amma.

Our son, Max, for lighting up our days with his sunny disposition and ability to spot a power shovel a mile off.

Our readers who've given us great feedback and comments.

From Wendy to Barry

Thank you a million times, Barry. You're the hardest-working, most organized person I've ever loved. It was your giving nature as a teacher that attracted me to you in the first place. Your stability, your support, your gentle heart, your stubbornness and ability to put up with mine, your love for our son, our animals, our earth, your art—there are so many things that I love about you, I just hope that all of the readers of this book get a glimpse of what a wonderful human being you are. Thanks for helping me grow and letting me sleep.

From Barry to Wendy

I couldn't do this book and many things in my life, without your love, your advice and all your help. Thank you, Wendy, we did this together and you added your design, and creativity, your patience with me, your friendliness on the phone with everyone, and most importantly, your love for Max and me. We look forward to all the other creations we will make together in this life.

Finally, and most importantly, our personal thanks to the Divine Creator who continues to walk this path with us.

TABLE OF CONTENTS

Foreword   xvii

A Photoshop book for photographers, artists, production artists, and people who deal with images. Here's what makes this book and CD different from all the rest. Read this section to decide if *Photoshop 4 Artistry* is the book for you.

Taking Advantage of Photoshop 4   xx

An overview of the new Photoshop 4 features and some quick tips about using them. A reference guide to where the new features are documented within the rest of the book. Getting through the Photoshop 3 to Photoshop 4 conversion.

An Overview of Digital Imaging   xxvii

For those new to digital imaging, a brief glimpse of the different types of input and output devices that are possible, a diagram of these possibilities, and a discussion of where digital imaging and the digital world is headed. (More advanced users may find they are familiar with most things in this chapter.)

THINGS YOU NEED TO KNOW   1

This section of the book contains overview information about Photoshop that all users should learn. Everyone should read the chapters, "How to Use This Book," "Navigating in Photoshop," "Automating with Actions," "Setting System and Photoshop Preferences," and "Using the Photoshop 4 Artistry CD." More advanced users, or those who want to play first, should read the other chapters in this part of the book when they want to pick up extra information.

How to Use This Book   2

A guide to help you learn Photoshop and enjoy this book. A must-read for everyone. This chapter also summarizes the minor Photoshop differences for Mac and Windows users.

Navigating in Photoshop   5

Organizing your screen, windows, palettes, and working environment to access and use Photoshop's features most effectively.

Automating with Actions   12

Using the Photoshop 4 Actions palette to automate your tasks. Creating, enhancing, and editing actions, including adding breakpoints and prompts, and getting user feedback during an action, as well as batch processing large groups of files automatically. Loading the ArtistKeys set of predefined actions, which you'll use with this book to speed your Photoshop tasks.

Setting System and Photoshop Preferences   17

Setting up your system and Photoshop's preferences for the most effective use of Photoshop, for better RGB to CMYK conversions, and standardizing Photoshop preferences and systems within an organization.

File Formats and Image Compression   30

Understanding the different file formats (Photoshop, TIFF, EPS, GIF, JPEG, and so on) and when, how, and why to use each. The options for image compression are also explored.

Using the *Photoshop 4 Artistry* CD   36

Using the images and steps on the CD to do all the step-by-step examples yourself and then compare your results with ours. Using the regular Photoshop set of images, for today's fast computers, versus the small JPEG set for less-powerful computers and teaching situations.

The Tool Palette   39

The many, and sometimes hidden, features of the Tool palette. Many selection, cropping, painting, and gradient shortcuts and techniques to speed up your work! A must for anybody who does a lot of painting and retouching. It's a useful chapter for everyone to read.

Picking and Using Color   56

A look at the RGB, CMYK, HSB/HSL, and LAB color spaces, what they are, when to use each, and how to access them from Photoshop; includes a discussion of the Photoshop Color Picker as well as the Color and Swatches palettes.

Color Correction Tools   61

An overview of Photoshop's many color correction and gamma adjustment tools; namely, which ones are most useful for what and why, and which ones are fairly useless if you are a professional Photoshopper. Using the Info palette versus the Color palette to measure color while correcting.

Selections, Masks, and Channels   68

An overview discussion of the differences between and uses of selections, masks, and channels to help you feel comfortable with these concepts. If you have any confusion about the differences between selections, masks, and channels and how they relate to layers, adjustment layers, and layer masks, you need to read this chapter and the next chapter.

Layers, Layer Masks, and Adjustment Layers   74

An overview of the functionality, features, and usage of layers, layer masks, and adjustment layers. Learn when to use each of these, the differences between them, and see an overview of their various options. To understand how they are different from, yet work along with, selections, masks, and channels, read this chapter and the previous one.

PHOTOGRAPHY AND OVERALL COLOR CORRECTION   81

This section shows you what technically constitutes a good photograph— both from a traditional perspective, which uses the Zone System, and digitally, which entails evaluating histograms and doing overall color correction. Seeing how to bring traditional photography skills into the digital realm gives you better scans, calibration, and overall color correction for the best possible output.

Digital Imaging and the Zone System   82

Professional photographers have used the Zone System, popularized by Ansel Adams, as a means of fine control and calibration in the traditional photographic world. This section explains how the Zone System's concepts carry over to the digital world, which gives you even more of that precise control for professional output and prints that well-known photographers like Ansel Adams, Bret Weston, and Charlie Cramer have had in the traditional world.

Calibration   88

Here, we explain one of the most essential parts of digital imaging, the calibration of your output devices themselves and the calibration of images on your monitor so that they look as close as possible to the printed results on those devices. We show you how to use our calibration images and how to create your own to calibrate with the tools and software that come standard with Photoshop. We also discuss color management systems.

Scanning, Resolution, Histograms, and Photo CD   99

Getting the best scan for the size and type of output you require. Simplifying bits, bytes, resolution, dpi, percentage, and all the scanning jargon. Using levels and histograms to evaluate and improve your scans with any scanner. Getting the best results from Photo CD scans.

Color Correction and Output   110

An overview of the optimal steps and color correction techniques for moving an image from initial scan to final output. Here, we focus on overall color correction and sharpening of your scan or Photo CD. Read this for the big picture and a detailed understanding of the entire process.

The Grand Canyon   117

The first things you do to a normal image after scanning it: using Levels for overall color correction to set highlights and shadows, overall brightness and contrast, and to correct for color casts; using Hue/Saturation to saturate overall and adjust specific colors; and using Curves to learn the art of tweaking certain color and brightness ranges. This chapter includes a complete introduction to Levels and Curves.

Kansas   129

Overall color correction using Levels and Hue/Saturation on a problem image that has unbalanced colors and lacks a good highlight or shadow position.

Burnley Graveyard   133

Using the Duotone features in Photoshop with custom curves, looking at separate duotone and tritone channels, printing duotones as EPS, and converting duotones and tritones to RGB and CMYK for final output.

After you finish overall color correction, you will want to use selections, layers, adjustment layers, and layer masks to isolate specific areas of your image and change their color or make them lighter or darker. Many of these techniques, including color matching different color objects, making a fine black-and-white print, and changing the color of objects, demonstrate the finer artistic control that digital photography gives you.

The Car
138

Selecting a complex object within an image using the Magic Wand, Lasso, and Quick Mask tools and changing its color using Hue/Saturation to create an advertising quality final hi-res image.

The Grand Canyon—Final Tweaks
143

Now that overall color correction is complete, fine-tune the GrandCanyon image using selections and adjustment layers with Curves to burn and dodge light and dark areas, then sharpen the image and remove the spots and scratches.

Kansas—Final Tweaks
149

Make final improvements to specific off-color and dark areas using selections and masks, dealing with out-of-gamut colors when converting to CMYK, and the details of using the Unsharp Mask filter to sharpen an image.

Yellow Flowers
155

Using Color Range and Replace Color to easily isolate all the yellow flowers and change their colors. Using Selective Color to fine-tune those colors after RGB to CMYK conversion. Moving Replace Color or Color Range results into an Adjustment Layer layer mask so you can soften or edit the mask, as well as change the color as many times as you like, without degrading the image.

Buckminster Fuller 161

Making a fine black-and-white print, with detailed dodging and burning, darkening the edges of the print using Curves with a feathered oval selection, doing detailed retouching to remove unwanted blemishes and facial objects, and colorizing the final image.

Color Matching Cars 166

Using Hue/Saturation, Levels, and Selective Color along with the Color palette to make sure the colors, tones, and moods match between several photos of the same object(s) on a multi-page spread. How to make a series of studio photos match even if they start out as different colors.

Color Correcting Al 169

Doing overall and final color correction and retouching of an image that has serious saturation and color problems in facial shadows, using one good channel to fix the others, using layer masks and adjustment layers to tweak color between several layers, retouching using blend modes to balance facial colors, sharpening, and final spotting.

Bryce Stone Woman 173

Advanced digital darkroom techniques are more than just filters and cyberspace. Threshold, layers, adjustment layers, and layer masks are used to combine Red, Green, and Highlight Bryce Stone Woman versions creating a final image with a great red canyon as well as wonderful green bushes and trees. These layers are then merged, sharpened, and spotted for the final look.

COMPOSITING MULTIPLE IMAGES WITH
LAYERS, ADJUSTMENT LAYERS, AND LAYER MASKS

The examples in this part of the book show you many possibilities for intricate effects and more accurate color correction by combining images using layers, adjustment layers, and layer masks. These chapters also show you how layers can be a great prototyping tool.

Bob Goes to...   180

After an introduction to the Pen tool and Paths, we use them to trace the outline of Bob, and then convert to a selection and layer mask to create a knock-out of Bob. We then use Free Transform to send Bob on journeys to Las Vegas, Miami, and other locations as we look into using Threshold and hand editing with the Paintbrush and Airbrush tools to fine-tune his layer mask.

Bob and the Kestrel   188

Automatically creating a knock-out of the bicycle using Threshold on a channel then editing that mask and adding a blend using the Gradient tool. Using this knock-out as a layer mask to place Bob behind the bicycle and seamlessly blend the two together.

Versailles   192

Using layers and layer masks to seamlessly combine two different scans of the same high-contrast original (one to get shadow detail and the other to get highlight detail), color correcting this difficult yet exciting image with multiple adjustment layers, and finally, using several effects layers, each with its own opacity and filter effect, to achieve a dramatic result.

The Band 200

Combining images using gradient layer masks, blending color channels to correct a badly exposed image, color correcting after compositing, then using adjustment layers to increase final color correction flexibilities.

The McNamaras 210

Try the ultimate retouching and color correction challenge as you move six smiling heads from other exposures into this family portrait to end up with everyone smiling. Resizing the heads with Free Transform, blending them together using layer masks, and using adjustment layers so you can continue to tweak the color of each head and the original group shot until they all match.

Night Cab Ride in Manhattan 215

Using layers to set up your Photoshop files to show yourself, or your clients, unlimited variations of a composite or effect quickly, without losing any of those variations. Using the Layers palette and Layer options, including clipping groups, layer masks, Blend modes, opacity, and drag and drop; reordering layers, and understanding when to Save a Copy, Merge Layers, and/or Flatten as you create a final composite with 11 layers and 7 original images.

CALCULATIONS, PATTERNS, FILTERS, AND EFFECTS 225

The examples in this section use Blend modes, filters, bitmaps, calculations, and layers in combination with each other to achieve a variety of special effects, including motion simulation, drop shadows , pattern creation, glowing text, text with shadows, line drawings, and many others.

Blend Modes, Calculations, and Apply Image 226

Detailed explanations and examples of using the Blend modes in all the tools (painting tools, the Fill command, Layers, Calculations, and Apply Image); the many variations and uses of the Apply Image and Calculations commands demonstrated and demystified.

Bike Ride in the Sky!

242

Combining positive and negative versions of the same image using Multiply, creating neon text with the Blend modes and placing it using Layer options, combining Illustrator text with Photoshop drop shadows, and saving as EPS from Illustrator for more creative control and higher-quality PostScript text output.

Posterize, Bitmaps, and Patterns

250

Creating texture and pattern effects using Posterize, Diffusion Dither bitmaps, layers, Layer options, Mezzotint, and Streak Patterns, and 3-D color embossed effects—cool stuff!

Filters and Effects

254

Getting the most from the standard Photoshop filters by combining filters and effects using layers, layer masks, opacity, Blend modes, levels, and other techniques to get many more combination effects. Demonstrating great uses of some more complex filters like Wave, Displace, Lighting Effects, Emboss, Find Edges, Minimum, Maximum, and others. Techniques to turn photographs into line drawings and get painterly effects, using a 50% gray layer for burning and dodging, the Fade command, and the new Photoshop 4 filters.

The APDA Magazine Cover

266

Using studio shot components to create a magazine cover canvas with Guides to show you the bleed size, trim size and live area, placing objects as layers in correct position on the canvas, creating motion blur and wave effects, fading objects during a blur, linking layers to move them together, selecting objects with the Pen tool, and creating a new background without losing existing shadows.

Creating Shadows 280

Different techniques using layers, blend modes, opacity, and painting tools to create drop shadows and cast shadows against both white and colored backgrounds and properly blending them into RGB and CMYK images.

IMAGES FOR THE WEB AND MULTIMEDIA 287

Creating the highest quality 8- and 24-bit GIF, JPEG, and transparent GIF images for Web sites and multimedia projects. Understanding 8-bit and smaller color palettes and creating small fast images that look good on both the Mac and PC and will work across the Web.

Differences in Creating for the Web and 8-bit Color 288

  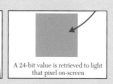

Understanding the differences in creating images for the Web and multimedia. Knowing why 8-bit color is important and understanding how it works. Working with JPEG and GIF files and knowing when to use each. Creating the images for your site so they look best to the users you care about most.

GIFs, JPEGs, and Color Palettes 292

Creating and comparing GIFs and JPEGS and seeing how they look on 8-bit versus 24-bit systems. Choosing between system palettes, the Web palette, and adaptive palettes. Creating adaptive palettes that work for a group of images.

Creating Small Transparent GIF Composites 296

Scanning images at a larger size and then color correcting, sharpening, and creating knock-outs using that larger image. Compositing a jacket with a separate collar image to create the "invisible man" look. Resampling the image down, sharpening again, and creating transparent GIFs using the GIF89a Export filter. Testing and correcting your transparent GIFs with various sample Web page background colors. Learning when to have aliased versus anti-aliased edges on your transparent GIFs and how to convert between the two.

Bibliography   301

Index   302

Colophon   313

FOREWORD

Ansel Adams, discussing the decision to make his original negatives available for future photographers to print, wrote in his autobiography that

> "Photographers are, in a sense, composers and the negatives are their scores. ...In the electronic age, I am sure that scanning techniques will be developed to achieve prints of extraordinary subtlety from the original negative scores. If I could return in twenty years or so I would hope to see astounding interpretations of my most expressive images. It is true no one could print my negatives as I did, but they might well get more out of them by electronic means. Image quality is not the product of a machine, but of the person who directs the machine, and there are no limits to imagination and expression."

Ansel Adams had a good vision for the future that we are now living. We hope this book will help you experience that vision in your photographic work.

Seeing an image on the computer screen is a beautiful thing. You bring it up from the scanner and you begin to think, "Now what do I really want this to look like?" If you know the Zone System, developed by Ansel Adams in traditional photography, then you know the type of control you can have while taking a photo or printing it in the darkroom. On the computer screen, you can have this control and much more. You can try numerous variations, making extreme or subtle changes easily and quickly. The computer is a new tool that enables the photographer to get precisely what he or she wants.

Many people think of using computer imaging for its proven ability to create special effects and image composites. It is very good at this, and we will show you how to create images that you cannot do optically in the darkroom, but I often use my computer darkroom to make a print of nature because it gives me much finer control in making that print. Realistic photography is another area in which we will show you things that you can do on the computer that you can't do easily or at all in the darkroom.

This book has developed from Photoshop courses I started teaching in 1990. It's not an exhaustive book that goes through each menu bar and each feature and lists them in order. The examples in *Photoshop 4 Artistry* teach you how to use Photoshop 4 by working with typical situations that you encounter as a photographer, artist, or production artist. This is Photoshop for creating fine images that are sometimes high-quality reproductions of reality and sometimes fine renditions of composites and effects.

We not only show you valuable techniques, but we give you a strategy for managing your digital images by creating an RGB master file for each image, which you can then use (maybe even using actions) to create different RGB files for color transparency, digital laser, dye-sub or inkjet printers, multimedia, or Web images and icons. These files, used with other actions, can create custom CMYK files for each of your printing situations.

For each situation, we spell out the detailed, step-by-step process. You can practice the technique yourself because the original images, masks, and progress steps, as well as the final images for each example, are included on the *Photoshop 4 Artistry* CD that accompanies the book. We have taught these examples over the past seven years to thousands of students across the country. Their feedback has helped us refine these exercises to make them easy to understand, concise, and full of special tips for more advanced users. All the the exercises have been updated and changed so that you can take advantage of the latest features, such as the new Photoshop 4 capabilities, and deal with current trends like making images for the Web. In addition to student tested, step-by-step instructions, *Photoshop 4 Artistry* includes explanations of concepts like color correction, calibration, 24- and 8-bit file formats and compression, duotones, selections, masking, layers, layer masks, adjustment layers, and channels, so you really understand what you are doing and are not just blindly following directions. Understanding allows you to expand the ideas in this book as you apply them to your own situations and creations without wasting your time on unnecessary issues.

We start with simple examples like cropping and color correcting a photograph. We cover color correction in great depth, and then move into things that you normally would do in the darkroom, like changing the contrast, burning and dodging, removing spots and scratches, and making a nice photographic print. Before we get into compositing and special effects, we talk about the importance of having absolute control over the colors in your photographs. The masters of color photography use contrast reduction masks, shadow, highlight, and color masks in the darkroom to make very fine Ilfochrome, C and dye transfer art prints. Using these techniques, you can make specific colors pop by increasing their saturation and changing their relationship to the rest of the photograph. *Photoshop 4 Artistry* shows you how to do all these things digitally using adjustment layers, layer masks and multiple layers of the same image, and how to generate art quality output to dye sublimation, laser or inkjet printers, or to the Web. We also talk about enhancing an image for output back to 4x5 and 8x10 film as well as for output to separations for printing on a press. We also show you how to use the above techniques along with sharpening to get great quality prints from Photo CD and Pro Photo CD scans.

After we explain how to make a fine color print using Photoshop, we make extensive use of layers, layer masks, and image compositing techniques. You can do most commercial compositing techniques easily using Photoshop. We present step-by-step examples for some simple compositing jobs and then move on to some more complex examples that involve using hard and soft edge masks as well as a variety of shadow and drop shadow effects and all the features of Layers, Adjustment Layers, and Layer Masks. The Apply Image and Calculations commands, as well as the many Blend Mode variations are explained in detail along with examples of where to use them in both still photography and motion picture situations.

Photoshop 4 Artistry also includes many tips and techniques on getting the most from the Photoshop filters, including some of the more obscure ones, like Displace, Wave, and Lighting Effects, and the new Photoshop 4 filters. We explain layer options and also get into creating duotones and bitmaps, adding textures to images, and other fun things.

Photoshop is great fun! And the more you know, the better time you will have and the easier it will be to turn the images in your mind into reality. We hope *Photoshop 4 Artistry* helps you have more fun than ever before with photography and digital imaging.

Happy Photoshopping!

P.S. Those of you who already have *Photoshop Artistry* will notice that the techniques in all the *Photoshop 4 Artistry* examples have been heavily changed to take full advantage of the new software. You can compare this book to the Photoshop 3 version and quickly see how to use the new features. Use our "Taking Advantage of Photoshop 4" chapter to quickly get up to speed on the new features and get through the transitions to the new Photoshop 4 Command keys. We also have added new chapters to help you create images for the Web and multimedia, retouch faces, and use the new Actions and Navigator palettes. The CD has ArtistKeys for the Actions palette to give you a great set of function keys and automated sequences for creating drop shadows and vignettes, converting file formats, and doing other useful but repetitive tasks.

TAKING ADVANTAGE OF PHOTOSHOP 4

*Easing the conversion from Photoshop 3 to 4;
making sure you are taking advantage of
the important new features in Photoshop 4.*

The new features in Photoshop 4 will be most useful to people doing detailed color work, advanced power users, and people who use Photoshop all the time. This type of user really needs Photoshop 4. *Photoshop 4 Artistry* has been completely rewritten to take full advantage of the new Photoshop 4 features. The new features are described and used throughout the book. This chapter is a summary of major new features and it will point you to the chapters in the book that make use of those features. In this chapter we mention the features you are most likely to use. Each feature mentioned herein is explained in great detail in the appropriate chapter of *Photoshop 4 Artistry*. To find more detail about a feature, follow the references mentioned here or look it up in the index or table of contents. References here to the Option key should be translated to the Alt key on Windows systems and the Command key here is the Control key in the Windows world.

CHANGES TO SELECTIONS, CHANNELS, AND LAYERS, AND THE NEW LAYER MENU

In version 4, you use the Option key instead of the Command key to delete from a selection because the Command key now switches you to the Move tool. Conversely, in version 4 you Command-click on a channel (instead of Option-click as you did in version 3) to load a selection from it. Command-Shift-click adds, Command-Option-click deletes, and Command-Option-Shift-click does an intersect of the channel's selection with the current selection. These selection keyboard shortcuts also work when you click on layer masks and adjustment layer masks in the Layers palette and on Paths in the Paths palette. The great thing about the new icons and features is that they are consistent across all the palettes that use them (Channels, Layers, Paths, and Actions).

Instead of just one icon at the bottom left of the Channels palette for both Load Selection and Save Selection, version 4 offers two, with the Load Selection icon being the left-most at the bottom of the palette and the Save Selection directly to the right of it. This is sort of like the decision of whether it is easier for people to get used to having just one button or two on their mouse. In some ways the Photoshop 3 single icon was more powerful and less confusing. To first save a selection in version 4 you need to remember to click on the icon that looks like a little mask, not the one that looks like a selection. To load a selection in Photoshop 4 you can click on a channel and drag it to the Load Selection icon but you can no longer click on the Save Selection icon and drag to an existing channel to update your changed selection to

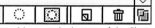

The Photoshop 4 icons at the bottom of the Channels palette. From left to right they are the Load Selection, Save Selection, New Channel, and Trash icons. The Load Selection icon also occurs in the Paths palette. If you drag a path to it, the path will be converted to a selection. The Save Selection icon is used to create layer masks in the Layers palette. The Channels, Layers, Actions, and Paths palettes all use the New icon to create a new item in their palette. Command-clicking on the New Layer icon in the Layers palette creates a new adjustment layer. These same four palettes also have a Trash icon for removing items from that palette. To remove an item, click on the item and either drag it to the Trash icon or click on the trash. Option-clicking on the Trash icon deletes without giving you the warning message.

that existing channel. This was very useful in Photoshop 3 when creating a complicated selection to update to the same channel over and over again. If you want that feature back, you should lobby with Adobe because you are not alone in missing it. Using the new 4.0 Actions palette, however, you can get similar capability. First record an action, using Select/Save Selection, to save your selection to a channel called Work-Channel whenever you press, say, Shift-F14. Now use Select/Save Selection again to record a second action that does a Replace Channel to replace the existing contents of Work-Channel. Set this action to happen when you press F14. Now pressing Shift-F14 the first time, followed by F14 for future times, gives you the functionality you had in Photoshop 3.

When you have a selection in Photoshop 4 and then create a layer mask or adjustment layer, Photoshop assumes you want that selection to be the visible area defined by that mask. That would be the adjustment layer's mask when creating an adjustment layer. The quick way to create an adjustment layer is to Command-click on the Create Layer icon in the middle at the bottom of the Layers palette.

The quick way to create a layer mask is to click on the Add Layer Mask icon, which is the left-most icon at the bottom of the Layers palette, which reveals the selected area with the layer mask. Option-clicking on this Add Layer Mask icon reveals the area not selected. Photoshop 4 has added a new Layer menu to the main menu bar. I don't use it that often because it is faster to use the keyboard and Layer palette icon shortcuts that are available for most of the Layer menu's choices. You can also create a layer mask by choosing New Layer Mask from the Layer menu, in the Main Menu Bar, and doing it that way allows you to choose to Reveal All, Hide All, Reveal Selection, or Hide Selection. Clicking on the Add Layer Mask icon is much faster. Photoshop 3 did not have all these shortcuts for going back and forth between selections and layer masks. Another thing that has changed is that in Photoshop 3 you would Command-click on a Layer Mask's icon to turn it off and now in Photoshop 4 you Shift-click, which also works for adjustment layer masks.

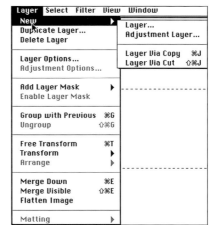

In Photoshop 4, Adobe added the Layer palette to the main menu then took some items from the Layer palette plus some new items and moved them up here. I usually use keyboard and icon shortcuts with the Layers palette instead of actually using the Layer menu. I use this menu mainly for doing transforms other than Free Transform which has the keyboard shortcut Command-T.

The Photoshop 4 Layers palette with its Icons at the bottom and keyboard shortcuts allows you to do most layer, adjustment layer, and layer mask functions.

When editing a layer in 4.0, you see the Paintbrush icon to the right of the Eye icon and the Layer icon has the dark highlight.

When editing a layer mask, you see the Mask icon to the right of the Eye icon and the Layer Mask icon has the dark highlight.

Notice the new Chain icon between the Layer icon on the left and the Layer Mask icon on the right. When it is present, which is the default, the Layer and Layer Mask are locked together and if you move one with the Move tool, the other will move at the same time. If you click on the Chain icon, it goes away and you can now move either the layer or layer mask independently. Double-clicking on the Layer or Layer Mask icon or the name of the layer brings up the Layer Options dialog box. Option-double-clicking on the layer mask brings up the Layer Mask Display options, which allows you to adjust the overlay color. To see an overlay of a layer mask while working on it, turn on the Eye icon for that mask in the Channels palette.

ADJUSTMENT LAYERS

One of the most important Photoshop 4 features for photographers is the new concept of adjustment layers. You can create an adjustment layer of Type Levels, Curves, Brightness/Contrast, Color Balance, Hue/Saturation, Selective Color, Invert, Threshold, or Posterize, which enables you to make any one of these types of color adjustments. Although an adjustment layer acts sort of like another layer, it does not make you pay the price of adding another set of RGB channels for that new layer. The color correction adjustment you make in an adjustment layer applies to all the layers below that adjustment layer. You can turn this correction on and off by just turning the Eye icon on or off for that particular adjustment layer. This allows you to try out variations of color correction by adding a new adjustment layer for each variation and then turning on the Eye icon(s) for the one(s) you want to see. If you double-click on the name of the adjustment layer, you can actually change the adjustment as many times as you want without degrading the color data in the file. Adjustment layers have only a Layer Mask icon, they don't have Layer icons because they don't have any RGB or CMYK data associated with them. You can move an adjustment layer up or down in the Layers palette to change which layers below it that it adjusts. You can also group it with the layer below for the color change to effect only that one layer: just check Group with Previous Layer in the New Adjustment Layer dialog box or Option-click on the line between the adjustment layer and the layer below it.

When editing an adjustment layer in Photoshop 4, you always see the Mask icon to the right of the Eye icon because there is no RGB data to edit. The Layer Mask icon is the only icon and it is always present. The white parts in the layer mask are the only areas of below layers that will be affected by this adjustment. You double-click on this icon to bring up the Layer options. Double-clicking on the name of the adjustment layer brings up the color adjustment tool (Hue/Saturation here) allowing you to change the settings in that tool as often as you like. Option-double-clicking on its Layer Mask icon brings up the Layer Mask Display options for changing the overlay color.

When you first enter a grouped levels adjustment layer, you may notice the Photoshop 4 bug that shows you a histogram of all the layers below it. Just choose OK in Levels, doing nothing, and then double-click on the new Adjustment Layer's name in the Layers palette. Now you will see the correct histogram of just the grouped layer below. Photoshop 4 seems to have several bugs in the initial viewing of Levels Adjustment Layer histograms. When you suspect a problem on the initial viewing, just choose OK in Levels, then double-click on the adjustment layer name again to go back to the now correct histogram. These bugs have been fixed in version 4.0.1 of Photoshop.

Another issue when viewing histograms in version 4 is that Photoshop defaults to using the Image Cache in creating the histogram. This can be quicker, but can also give less accurate histograms. Turn off the Use Cache for Histograms check box in the File/Preferences/Image Cache dialog box to get the most accurate histograms. To learn more about the feature changes and new features with selections, layers and adjustment layers, see the "Selections, Masks, and Channels" and "Layers, Layer Masks, and Adjustment Layers" chapters for overview information, and then see the entire "Improving Color and Mood with Selections, Channels, Layers, Adjustment Layers, and Layer Masks" and "Compositing Multiple Images with Layers, Adjustment Layers, and Layer Masks" sections of the book for detailed hands-on exercises.

THE ACTIONS PALETTE

You can use the new Actions palette to re-create all the single menu item functionality of the 3.0 Commands palette and much more. To have an action record a single menu item, create a new action by clicking on the New Action icon at the bottom of the Actions palette, then immediately choose Insert Menu Item from the Actions palette menu. This allows you to choose any menu item from any of Photoshop's menus, including the Palette menus. You then end your action by clicking on the Stop

My current Actions palette with the Actions palette menu items. Notice that you can load and save actions, allowing you to share your favorite actions with your friends. Replace Actions changes the entire set, whereas Load Actions just adds new ones to your existing set. I have defined actions to bring each palette up and down and to run my favorite menu items that have no keyboard alternatives. The ones toward the bottom do common sequences like creating drop shadows, and more. These are available as a loadable set on the CD that comes with this book.

Recording icon in the Actions palette. You can also use Insert Menu Item while creating an action whenever you want to force the user to enter the parameters of a dialog box when later playing that action. The Actions palette is one of Photoshop 4's most powerful new features, because it enables you to automate entire sequences of events and then play them back later over and over again. You can even play those events on a whole folder of files using the Batch menu item in the Actions palette. To learn more about Actions and the Actions palette, see "Automating with Actions."

FREE TRANSFORM

When I first learned that Adobe had changed Command-T from being the 3.0 shortcut for Threshold to being the Photoshop 4 shortcut for Free Transform, I was frustrated because I use Threshold a lot. Now I agree with the change because Free Transform is such a powerful tool. When you have to composite several objects together and you are not sure of their relative sizes and angles, just put each object in a separate layer surrounded by transparency by selecting the object, doing a Copy, and then doing a Paste in your layered document. Click on one of those object layers to activate it and then press Command-T for Free Transform. You can now scale, rotate, skew, distort, add perspective, and move the object in that layer while seeing these changes relative to the other objects in your other layers. In Photoshop 3, each of those steps was a separate menu command that you had to execute one at a time and you couldn't move the object while in the middle of executing any one of them. This made matching objects in scale and rotation a long iterative process in which the image was potentially degraded for each iteration along the way. Free Transform solves these problems and makes your production much faster. Whenever you are transforming any object, the Info palette will show you the current position, angle, and scale values. Command-Shift-T now gives you Numeric Transform, which allows you to scale, rotate, skew, and position an object numerically to exact and repeatable values. To learn more about Free Transform, see "Bob Goes To…," "The McNamaras," "Night Cab Ride in Manhattan," "The APDA Magazine Cover," "Creating Shadows," "Images for the Web and Multimedia," and the index.

THE CONTROL CONTEXT-SENSITIVE MENUS

One of the great new features in Photoshop 4 is the ability to hold down the Control key then click on the mouse to bring up a context-sensitive menu. On Windows systems, you can get these by clicking on the right mouse button. These menus show you useful things you can do, based on the current tool you are using and where you actually click on the screen. For example, when using the Move tool on a layered document, Control-clicking brings up a list of the layers that have pixels at the current location. You can then drag to activate the layer you want without having to bring up the Layer's palette and remember which layer to click on. If you were in the Marquee tool instead at that point, you would get a different menu of options having to do with the current selection. To learn more about these features see "The Tool Palette," "Navigating in Photoshop," "Layers, Layer Masks, and Adjustment Layers," and the hands-on examples.

GRIDS AND GUIDES

Photoshop 4 now has very useful Grids and Guides. These will be especially helpful to Web page developers and designers of multimedia applications where

The Navigator palette allows you to zoom to any zoom factor and also has the red box which defines the part of the image you see on the screen. You can click inside the red box and drag to move it and you can also Command-click and drag to resize the box.

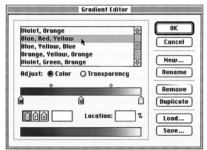

The View menu for creating a new view of a window that is already open, choosing your zoom factor, and controlling Grids and Guides.

The new Gradient Editor allows Photoshop to create much more interesting gradients, having many different colors and varying opacities. You will like this!

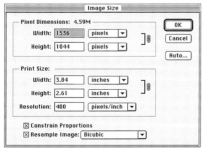

Check out "Scanning, Resolution, Histograms, and Photo CD" to learn how to use the improved Image Size dialog box.

buttons and other screen elements have to line up exactly. You can set up your grids and guides as you need for a particular project and then choose Snap-To for either of these to help in alignment of items. For more information on their use see "Navigating in Photoshop," and "The APDA Magazine Cover."

NAVIGATOR PALETTE, VIEW MENU, AND NEW ZOOMING

Getting around with your image on the screen is much easier in Photoshop 4. From anywhere you can use Command-0 to fill the screen with your image and Command-Option-0 to zoom in to 100% (this used to be called 1:1 in older versions of Photoshop). The Navigator palette allows you to type in any zoom factor whatsoever or to control the zoom with a slider. This palette, which can also be resized, shows you a red box within which is the currently visible part of your image. This box can be moved and sized in the Navigator palette to instantly get to parts of your image that you can't even see on the screen. The new View menu houses the menu items for zooming as well as some of the controls for Grids and Guides. For more information on zooming and navigating see "Navigating in Photoshop."

THE GRADIENT EDITOR

The Gradient Editor now allows Photoshop to create and save gradients of many different colors and opacities. This is similar to the gradients you can create in Illustrator 6 and 7. To learn all about this feature, check out "The Tool Palette."

CHANGES TO IMAGE SIZE

The Image Size command and its dialog box have been improved to show you both the Pixel Dimensions and Print Size. This makes Image Size easier to understand and use. It also allows you to change the resampling algorithm from within the Image Size dialog box instead of having to go to Preferences. To learn more about using Image Size, refer to "Scanning, Resolution, Histograms, and Photo CD," and also to the index.

TOOL PALETTE CHANGES

There have been many changes to the Tool palette although a lot of them are cosmetic and part of Adobe's effort to standardize tools and command keys across all their applications. Almost all the tools have been moved to new locations and the tools with more than one variation, like Blur and Sharpen, now have a Pop-Out menu similar to Illustrator's, allowing you to select any variation instantly. The Pen tool has been moved to the Tool palette although the Paths palette still exists in a modified and better form. The Lasso and Text tools work in a slightly different way and also each have new variations. For all the features of the Tool palette, even the hidden ones, see "The Tool Palette" and check out all the step-by-step exercises to really learn to be a power user with these tools. Most references to tool access in the hands-on sessions also give you the power user shortcut to get to the tool you are using. We show you how to work without having to bring up the Tool palette or even move your mouse over to it to change tools or tool options. These shortcuts are summarized in a table at the beginning of "The Tool Palette." To find exercises that use a particular tool, use the index.

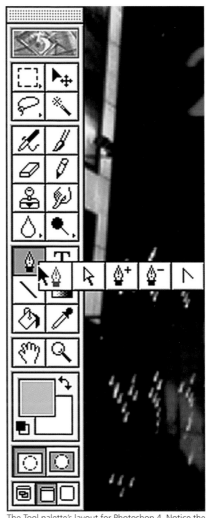

The Tool palette's layout for Photoshop 4. Notice the new pop-out menus for tools that have variations.

NEW FILTERS AND BLEND MODES

Adobe has improved some of the existing filters and added the Aldus Gallery Effects filters to the standard Photoshop 4 set. There are also three new Blend modes available. See "Filters and Effects" to learn how to get many more variations from all the filters by combining them using layers and the Blend modes. "Blend Modes, Calculations, and Apply Image" explains what each of the Blend modes actually does and gives examples of how and where to use them. The Blend modes and their proper usage are one of the main features that make Photoshop more powerful than other imaging applications. To learn more about a particular filter or Blend mode, look it up in the index.

GOODBYE TO THE MODE MENU, HELLO 16 BITS/CHANNEL

To make room for the new Layer and View menus, Adobe moved the Mode menu inside the Image menu. This makes accessing things like CMYK conversions a little harder, but you will probably be doing some of them with Actions now anyway. Photoshop now has limited support of 16-bit color, that is, 16 bits of color per channel instead of 8. This allows for the possibility of keeping data from scanners that scan more than 8 bits of color per channel. Your scanner software would have to

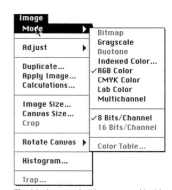

The Mode menu has been moved inside the Image menu and the items that used to be in Image/Map are now inside Image/Adjust. Notice the new 16 Bits/Channel feature!

allow you to save this extra information. Only a limited set of commands in Photoshop, mainly Levels and Curves, work with 16 bits/channel images, but you can open them and adjust them without throwing out the extra 8 bits of data. For information on using and converting between modes in the Mode menu, see "Scanning, Resolution, Histograms, and Photo CD," "Color Correction and Output," and the "Photography and Overall Color Correction," and "Improving Color and Mood with Selections, Layers, Adjustment Layers, and Layer Masks" sections. Check out the index for references to a particular menu item.

DIGITAL COPYRIGHT PROTECTION

Adobe has added support for the Digimarc watermark filters that allow you to put digital copyright information into your images. See "Filters and Effects" and the Photoshop 4 manuals for more information on this filter.

When Tool Tips is turned on, you see little yellow information boxes that appear when the cursor is on top of something in Photoshop's interface. These boxes tell you what that icon or tool does and sometimes other useful information like keyboard shortcuts to get that tool.

TOOL TIPS

For people first learning Photoshop, these are great! When you put the cursor over a tool or icon, you get a little yellow message box telling you what that tool or icon does. On the Tool palette, you also get the keyboard shortcut to access that tool. Power users may want to turn this off because it can slow down cursor feedback a bit. You can do this using File/Preferences/General (Command-K). For more information on this feature and all your preferences see "Setting System and Photoshop Preferences."

AN OVERVIEW OF DIGITAL IMAGING

*For those of you new to the digital world, this is
a quick introduction to the possibilities.
More advanced users may find they are familiar
with many things in this chapter.*

It's the year 2007 and you're on location in the Amazon jungle taking photos of a bambleberry plantation for tonight's issue of *Earth Survival News*. Since the discovery that the rain forest bambleberry cures AIDS and the teetee bush cures cancer, all countries have agreed to stop old-growth forest cutting. You're sitting high on top of a 90-foot bambleberry tree looking at the electronic layout of the article on the screen of your 17" color, 1024 by 768, fold-out, wristwatch Mac Decca. From the layout, you can see they need a 5x7 still photo for the cover and a five minute movie slot for the rest of the article on screen 10. Now you're taking the photo they will need; gee, this is going to look great in the layout! The 20 megabyte file is transmitted directly from your Nikon F10 digital camera into the layout on the Mac Decca. Now you're using Photoshop 9.1 to crop and edit the photos for final transmission. It's now 4:50 P.M. in Manhattan, so you have only five minutes to finish working with the photo. It is transmitted via satellite from your Mac Decca directly into the page layout. This gives the editorial team five minutes to make final approvals and adjustments for the 5:00 P.M. transmission. Readers around the world now see *Earth Survival News* and get most of their news and information on their wristwatch Mac Deccas and PC communicators. Think of all the trees this digital transmission technology is now saving. With the street prices for entry-level Mac Deccas dropping to $100, newspapers, magazines, and catalog advertisers across the world have either converted to digital transmission or gone out of business. Paper is no longer the medium of choice. Aren't you glad you stuck with digital photography when it was so frustrating in the early years?

BACK FROM THE FUTURE

Now it's back to reality in 1997. Here I am with my $20,000 Macintosh digital photography system. When I set out on my own in 1990, after 10 years doing software development and imaging research at Apple Computer, I wanted to return to my love for photography. I planned to set up a self-sufficient business that I could run from my home using my own equipment and without the need for partners or outside investors. It cost me under $10,000 to purchase a 4x5 camera system and a traditional color darkroom that can make professional-quality 16x20 color prints. This traditional color darkroom now sits idle most of the time because I'm in front of the computer screen playing with my *digital* darkroom. With Photoshop on the Mac or PC, you can do anything to an image that you can do in a traditional darkroom, only much more easily. It is easy and fast to try something or to try 20 different variations and pick the one you like most. With complete personal control and much more creative software on your own computer, you can do anything a high-end Scitex retouching station can do and much more. The possibilities for creativity in a digital darkroom are endless.

I'm sure that many of you have been wondering about digital photography. It is possible today to produce the highest-quality digital images using a desktop system. This includes going out to original-quality color transparency film or black and white negatives, making the highest-quality professional color laser, inkjet and dye sublimation digital art prints, making 24- and 8-bit images for the Web and multimedia, and also converting to CMYK for print on a press.

THE OPTIONS FOR DIGITAL PHOTOGRAPHY

You may be wondering if digital photography is worth the cost and effort. In this introductory discussion, I divide digital photography into three functional areas:
- Capturing the image
- Adjusting and manipulating the image
- Outputting the image

CAPTURING THE IMAGE

In most cases, film is still the highest-quality medium for image capture, especially if you are talking about short exposures on 4x5 or larger film. There are certain situations in which using a digital camera makes sense which we will discuss in later chapters. Once you capture an image on film, there are various ways to scan it into a digital version for your computer. You can take your original to a traditional color house and have it scanned with a quality drum scanner, or you can take your film to a desktop service bureau and have it scanned with a desktop scanner. With either of these alternatives, you often have little or no personal control over the quality of the scans. This book will help you learn what to look for in a good scan and how to make better scans yourself.

SCAN IT YOURSELF

A third alternative for scanning is to rent or purchase a desktop scanner and do the scans yourself. Doing your own scans is a great way to learn about scanning. There are desktop scanners that scan film and there are flatbed scanners to scan prints and artwork. Some flatbed scanners have optional attachments that allow you to scan film. Scanning original film gives you the best quality. I did extensive testing with a Leafscan-45 which enabled me to do my own high-quality scans on 35mm, 2¼, and 4x5 film. This is a great scanner! If you can afford your own scanner, it makes it much easier to prototype image creations and publishing projects. Before you buy a scanner, you ought to read the latest articles comparing the newest scanners because they get better and cheaper all the time.

THE KODAK PHOTO CD SYSTEM

An exciting alternative for scanning is the Kodak Photo CD system, which allows the masses to get high-quality scans quickly and in bulk for very little expense—about $1 to $2 per scan in most places. With Photo CD, you bring your film to get it processed and at the same time the images can be scanned and placed on a digital Photo CD disc. You can also send in any 35mm original (positive, negative, color, or B&W) that has been previously taken and get it put on Photo CD. The Photo CD discs can hold 100 images on the average. The quality of these images after color correction is high enough for most publishing output. What I have done is get over 600 of my best photographs put on Photo CD, which lets me use these images in brochures, this book, advertising, and other promotions. For publication at 150 line screen, regular Photo CD images usually are good for sizes of about 7x9 or smaller. Sometimes you can go bigger than this; it all depends on the image and the quality of the scan. I have some great-looking 11x17 dye sublimation prints from Photo CD scans. The maximum image size for a regular Photo CD scan is 18 megabytes. Photo CD Pro will allow scans of up to 70 megabytes from originals that are 35mm, 2¼, or 4x5. These are a bit more expensive, about $20 each, but are still much cheaper than high-end drum scans. If you give the CD processor a high-quality original, and the shop you choose knows what it is doing, the quality of these scans can be excellent. See the chapter, "Scanning, Resolution, Histograms, and Photo CD" for more information on how to get great scans from any scanner and also get the most from your Photo CD scans.

THE DIRECT DIGITAL METHOD

For certain applications, it makes sense to capture your images using a direct digital method. This makes your work much simpler because you process no film and do no scanning. Several technologies are available for capturing images. One of the earliest offered, still video, uses a 35mm type camera that you load with a small, still video disk. You can also get a card for your computer, called a video digitizer, that allows you to get digital still frames from any video camera or player. The problem with video digitizing and still video is that the quality of the digital images is not high enough for most print production.

For significantly better than video quality in a compact filmless camera, you can use the Kodak Digital Camera System (DCS). DCS is a series of digital backs that attach to Nikon, Hasselblad, and other cameras. DCS comes in various models and prices. Nikon also makes a high-quality digital camera called the Nikon E2. For studio work, there is the Leaf Catchlight Digital Back and the Dicomed Camera Back system. These systems act as digital backs for 2¼ and 4x5 cameras. The quality of the digital files captured with these systems can be very good. Digital cameras make a lot of sense for studio work because, while you are shooting the picture, you can bring the file directly into the Mac or PC and make sure it meets your needs. With digital cameras, you don't get the cost, time, and environmental problems associated with film processing. You also don't have the cost or time lag required to get scans done. For studios that do a lot of catalog work, especially with small to medium size images, digital cameras could save a lot of time and money and allow the photographer to shoot the images and provide digital separations. Stephen Johnson, a well-known landscape photographer, uses the Dicomed digital camera insert on his 4x5 camera and is very happy with the results he is able to get. This digital back is not able to do fraction of a second exposures but it produces very large accurate files, over 100 megabytes, and is great for still camera work where much detail and dynamic range is required. Steve has mentioned to me that in most lighting situations he can actually capture more detail using this setup than he could using even 4x5 film. His Dicomed prints are very beautiful. Using this type of camera setup, he actually sees the image on the computer screen of his Mac portable in the field, like on site in Yosemite.

Another advantage to direct digital capture with smaller images is that the images are in a form in which they can be easily compressed and transmitted over a phone line. Newspapers and magazines use this feature in highly time-sensitive situations. Pictures can be shot and sent compressed over the phone and literally be on a press minutes later. If you use a digital camera and want to learn how to use it to create automatic knock-outs, see the Difference blend mode in "Blend Modes, Calculations, and Apply Image."

Adjusting and Manipulating the Image

Once you have converted an image into digital format, you can more easily perform standard darkroom techniques like spotting, cropping, dodging, burning, changing the color balance, contrast, and so on. You can use a variety of adjustment layer, selection, and feather techniques to isolate portions of an image for change without affecting the rest of the image. You can do all these things in such a way that you can show many variations and always undo or change any effect. Not only are digital images easier to create, they are much easier to change and show variations in technique. Check out "The Grand Canyon," "Color Correcting Al," and "Bryce Stone Woman."

In addition to standard darkroom techniques, there are thousands of special effects, like posterization, rotation, skew, solarization, stretching, perspective, edge effects, sharpening, distortions, applying patterns and textures, blending, and far too many others to even list. Take a look at "Filters and Effects" and "Blend Modes."

You can use layers, adjustment layers, layer masks, channels, and other techniques to create knock-outs, drop shadows, and special lighting effects, and to combine images in any way you want. These changes are easy to set up so you can turn them on and off and show your client many variations. See "The McNamaras" and "The APDA Magazine Cover."

You can use Adobe Photoshop's painting tools to retouch, colorize, add to, and modify your images. The real world examples in this book show you how to do all these things. Any manipulation or effect that you can do on a Scitex or other high-end imaging workstation, you can do in Photoshop more easily. You can actually do far more in Photoshop, and Photoshop is fun to use, too.

Making Color Separations

If you are going to output your digital images to color transparency film, the digital files need to be in RGB (Red, Green, Blue) format. Most desktop scanners currently scan in this format. If you are going to print your final images on a press, you need to convert the images into CMYK (Cyan, Magenta, Yellow, Black) format. Photoshop and many other desktop applications do the conversions from RGB into CMYK format. This conversion process, called *making color separations*, has many variations depending on the type of printer and paper you will be using.

Creating Your Own Books

One of the advantages of using digital photography is that the computer equipment also gives you the required tools for doing your own publishing. If you want to create a brochure, poster, or even a book, you can learn the necessary skills to design and create the entire project yourself. Photographers and artists can publish their own books. This entire book—including the design, layout, color correction, compositing and effects, as well as the final color separations and the cover—was created by Wendy and me in our home studio in the Santa Cruz mountains using desktop equipment. The scans are mostly Photo CD, which we color corrected and separated using the techniques taught in this book. A few of the scans were done using the Leafscan-45 and several scans were done on a Howtek drum scanner, also attached to a Mac, at Robyn Color in San Francisco. Using this technology, you can create your own book like we did!

OUTPUTTING THE IMAGE

The choices available for output of your digital image are improving and getting cheaper on a month-to-month basis. Black-and-white laser printers now cost $\frac{1}{20}$ the price of 15 years ago. The same price drop is happening with color printers. There are many types of digital printers. Here, I am sticking to the ones that make prints of photographic quality or close to it.

DYE SUBLIMATION PRINTERS

A common type of digital printer is the dye sublimation printer. On images that are properly color corrected and sharpened, one can make dye sublimation prints that look close to or sometimes better than Ilfochrome quality. These printers can make prints of sizes up to 12x18 inches. These prints are beautiful and also big enough to frame and hang on the wall. I have a ProofPositive printer and find that it makes excellent prints. Most people cannot tell the difference between these and color photographs. I like the dye sublimation prints better than photographs because of the amazing control I have over color, effects, and sharpness using Photoshop. Many dye sub printers come with Level 2 PostScript so you can use them to proto-type any publishing project up to tabloid size. Many companies make dye sublimation printers, including Kodak, Tektronics, Fargo, and 3M. You can usually make dye sub prints at a service bureau, but having a photographic-quality digital printer in your studio is the final component that really makes a digital darkroom complete. Having it attached to your own computer allows you to work in the iterative way a photographer works in the darkroom. Make a print, tweak the colors and contrast a bit, make another print, and so on, until you get exactly what you want. I love it! Having your own printer in your studio gives you the control and ease of use that is essential for the artist and high-quality image maker. Dye sublimation printers that make prints from 8½x11 up to tabloid size cost from $1,500 to $15,000. Make sure you check out the market well before purchasing one. There are new products every day. To accurately compare them, you should print the same digital image on each printer you are considering purchasing. Different printers have various resolutions and quality; you need to carefully compare before you buy. For the best quality on most of these printers, you need a 300 dpi original. I use files of about 50 megabytes in size to get the best quality 11x17 prints on my ProofPositive.

IRIS PRINTERS AND CANON COPIERS

Iris makes a series of printers that produce art-quality work from digital images, in sizes up to 30x40 inches. These Iris printers can print on many types of standard art paper, including parchment. Unfortunately, Iris printers are out of the price range that most individual photographers can afford. Many specialized service bureaus do quality Iris prints and provide high-quality duplications of color and control. Among these service bureaus are Digital Pond in San Francisco and Nash Editions in Los Angeles.

Another very interesting set of devices is the Canon full-color copiers. With PostScript controllers, like the EFI Fiery and the Xerox Splash, desktop computers can send color images directly to the copier. I have seen some impressive prints from these machines in sizes up to tabloid, which makes them very useful for prototyping print work. Since the copiers are quite fast, they also are useful for short-run color printing. Speaking of short-run printing, the bookstore of the future will have many books stored digitally. You will call ahead and let them know what books you want and they will print and bind them to order. This is another digital development that will make it much easier for individual photographers to publish their own work. You won't have to pay the setup and material costs for large press runs.

THE FUGI PICTROGRAPHY PRINTERS

The desktop size printer that appears to me to do the closest to photographic quality is the Fugi Pictrography 3000. This RGB printer actually prints on a paper with a photographic-type emulsion and the maximum image area is 8½x11. These prints look like photographic prints even when you look at them with a loupe. I believe they are planning to come out with a tabloid size print version sometime in 1997. This printer is worth checking out.

LARGE PRODUCTION COLOR LASER PRINTERS

The Durst Lambda 130 Digital Photo Printer and the Cymbolic Sciences' Lightjet 5000 digital printer are both RGB devices that print on photographic-type papers and also transparet materials with prints up to 50 inches wide and with varying lengths. These things are in the quarter million dollar price range so most of us will probably have to go to a color house or service bureau to get prints. The color permanence of some of the materials are much better than the desktop dye sublimation type printers so you might want to consider these printers if you are creating art that needs to have color that is as permanent as possible. Just find a color house that is well calibrated and can give you repeatable results once you arrive at a final print. Two that I would recommend in Northern California are Robyn Color in San Francisco, which has the Lightjet 2000 film recorder and the Light 5000 digital printer, and Custom Color Lab in Palo Alto, which has the Lambda 130 digital printer.

PROTECTING YOUR PRINTS

One thing to watch out for when you make digital prints is that they may not have the color permanence of a Ilfochrome or C print. I mount my ProofPositive prints behind UV protective True-View glass and also UV protective plastics. They seem to do fine as long as I don't hang them where the sun hits them directly. Still, I've only had these prints for three years. You should contact Henry Willhelm at Preservation Publishing to get the latest independent test results on digital prints. Henry wrote the book, *The Permanence and Care of Color Photographs,* and is in the process of testing digital prints.

OUTPUT TO FILM

Various companies make film recorders across a wide variety of prices and quality. These recorders take a digital file and output it back to an original piece of film. You can create original-quality film with the best of these. The film recorders I have seen that seem to create the best-quality film are the Kodak LVT (Light Valve Technology) and the Cymbolic Sciences' Light Jet 2000. These are both very expensive devices, so output to film of original quality will probably have to be done at a service bureau for now. If you want to create a piece of film that has the same quality as an original, you need about 90 megabytes for a 4x5 transparency and much more for an 8x10. Many photographers who do successful commercial work use files in the 30Mb range for 4x5 film output. If you look at the film with a loupe, it won't be quite as sharp as a properly focused original, but it is good for many commercial purposes. You will have to run tests at your service bureau to determine the file size and image quality that works best for you.

PostScript Imagesetters

It may be that the imagesetter is the most popular output device for digital systems. Imagesetters make halftone films for B&W and color printing. Imagesetters, and many of the other printers I have been talking about, use a computer language called PostScript. PostScript allows computer graphic data, like text and line drawings, to be represented generically within the computer and output in various sizes at the highest possible resolution that each printer or imagesetter allows. Some imagesetters print at over 3,000 dots per inch. Early PostScript imagesetters could not achieve the same quality halftones as their traditional counterparts. These problems have now been solved, so it is possible for PostScript imagesetters to make halftones and color separations of the best quality. When printing color to a PostScript imagesetter, you will get better results if it has a Level 2 PostScript RIP. (RIP stands for Raster Image Processor, and RIPping is a computer process that converts a digital file from computer byte values into halftone screen dots and patterns.)

I have recently seem some amazing black-and-white darkroom prints by Huntington Witherill of Monterey, California. These were made as contact prints from large imagesetter output. These prints looked better than the traditional black-and-white prints he made from the original negatives and all of Huntington's prints are excellent. The technique used is described in the book *Making Digital Negatives for Contact Printing* by Dan Burkholder from Bladed Iris Press (bladediris@aol.com). Burkholder uses the technique to make platinum prints whereas Witherill makes larger silver prints up to 20x24 in size. The advantage of this technique is that instead of spending hours burning, dodging, and spotting each print in the darkroom, you spend the time creating a dodged, burned, spotted, and corrected digital file which you then output as a series of very small black dots, about 3,600 per inch, onto the imagesetter film at the full size of the print. You can then use this film to make contact prints in the darkroom that are just exposed and processed the same way each time. Once you get the system down, you get a perfect print every time. One of the difficult parts, according to Witherill, is getting the imagesetter output to create perfect dots across the entire print area. The dot patterns used in this process are not halftone screens.

The Digital Deliverable

The day when most deliverables are digital draws nearer. The Communications Superhighway that we keep hearing about is actually happening. From our home studio in the Santa Cruz mountains, which is 20 minutes by car from the nearest town, we can get 200 TV channels on a small radio dish pointed toward a satellite. One day we'll be able to transmit back. Over our phone lines we can get and receive ISDN digital services. The speeds of digital access to the home or business can be orders of magnitude faster than what we have. The technology exists in some areas to send hundreds of megabits per second over fiber-optic phone lines, called *broadband ISDN*. The technology exists for a photographer to quickly send an entire book digitally over these high-speed broadband ISDN lines to a printer or, better yet, to a customer who wants to read and interact with a digital book on their computer screen. Although the technology exists, both the artists and their clients must have easy access to it before it can become usable.

For some photographers, it will still be easier to output a digital creation to film and deliver that to the client. Art directors are used to film, and using film frees the photographer from responsibility for color separations and other possible reproduction problems. More and more photograhers I know are also delivering digital files and even separations to their clients, which gives them an extra billable service and also gives them more control over the final printed piece. More and more clients are seeing the advantage of this digital system. In creating this book, we sent digital files, mostly from corrected Photo CD scans, to our printer, Shepard Poorman, on removable 100Mb Zip disks. We sent a few JPEG compressed files over the phone line too. Maybe you will send your next book or art piece from your studio to your client or output center digitally. We are now in the digital era!

THINGS

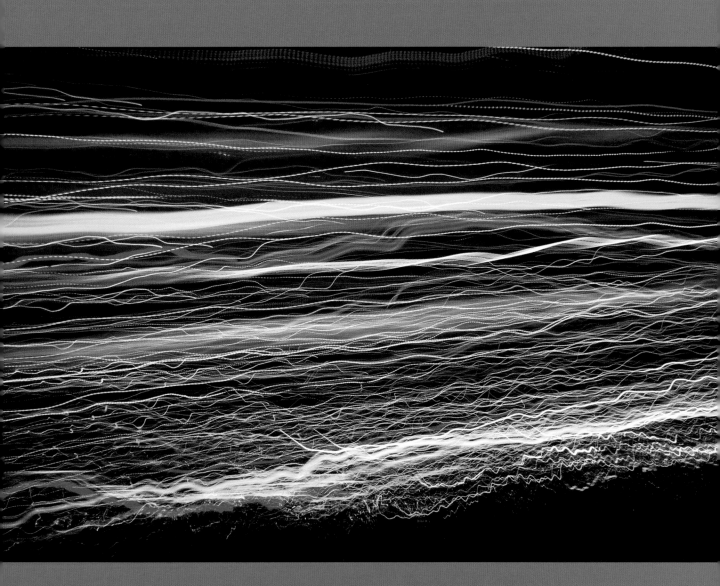

YOU NEED TO KNOW

HOW TO USE THIS BOOK

*This chapter gives you a quick preview of
what you'll find in this book and gives you some
valuable tips on the best way to use it.*

We believe that *Photoshop 4 Artistry* can help both new and advanced Photoshop users. If you read this book from front to back and do the hands-on sessions in order, it is an in-depth, self-paced course in digital imaging. If you're new to Photoshop and digital imaging, going in order may be the best way to proceed. If you are a more advanced Photoshop user more interested in learning new techniques, you may want to read the sections and do the hands-on that cover the skills you need to learn. Use the table of contents and index to find the areas you want to reference.

The book has two types of chapters: overview chapters, which contain information that everyone should learn, and hands-on chapters, where you learn by color correcting and creating images. The chapters are ordered beginning with the fundamentals and moving on to more advanced skills. All the chapters are in-depth, and we expect most users, even experienced Photoshoppers, to learn something from each chapter. Some of the chapters toward the end of the book are very detailed and assume you already have a lot of Photoshop knowledge. You need to know the foundation skills taught in the earlier chapters before you do the later, more advanced chapters.

The first part of the book, "Things You Need to Know," presents overview chapters that provide readers with a common base of knowledge. Everyone should read the chapters, "Setting System and Photoshop Preferences," "Calibration," "Scanning, Resolution, Histograms, and Photo CD," and "Color Correction and Output," so you can set up your system and Photoshop correctly, and calibrate your monitor for working with the book and doing color output. The rest of these overview chapters go into a lot of detail. If you are anxious to get your hands into the program, you don't need to read all of them before you start the hands-on. You should come back to these chapters later, however, to learn valuable information about the Zone System, picking colors, all the color correcting tools, and other matters. Before doing a hands-on chapter, it's a good idea to read any overview chapter in that part of the book.

The *Photoshop 4 Artistry* CD that comes with the book includes all the images you need (including the authors' before and after versions, Levels and Curves settings, masks, and so forth). It also includes sets of these images specialized respectively for Mac users and PC users. For the more powerful computers, it contains a full size set of images in Photoshop 4 and JPEG formats, and for teaching situations and smaller computers, includes compressed and smaller versions of the images. Each hands-on chapter has a separate folder on the CD with Essential Files and Extra Info Files subdirectories. The Essential Files subdirectory contains the original scan files you absolutely need for doing the hands-on. The Extra Info Files subdirectory contains the authors' versions of the exercise, including masks, steps along the way, and Levels, Curves, Hue/Saturation, and other tool settings. Use these files to compare your results to the authors' or to re-create the authors' results. For more information about using the CD, see the chapter "Using the *Photoshop 4 Artistry* CD."

IMPORTANT DIFFERENCES FOR MAC AND WINDOWS USERS

All Photoshop users, on both the Mac and the PC, will find this book beneficial. That's because in 99.9% of the cases everything in Photoshop is exactly the same for Mac and PC users. The contents of each of Photoshop's tool windows and menu bars is the same in a Mac window and a Windows window. Adobe has done an excellent job of making Photoshop cross-platform compatible in every way it can. Mac and PC users both have tested this book, and have found it valuable and easy to use. We have taught in classrooms where some of the computers are Macs and some are PCs and it works out fine.

The following sections discuss the few minor differences between Photoshop on the Mac and on the PC. I also point out any important differences that are relevant to the various topics I discuss.

MODIFIER KEYS

References in *Photoshop 4 Artistry* to keyboard modifier keys use the Option key and the Command key, which are the main modifier keys on the Mac. *Windows users need to remember that whenever we mention the Option key, you use the Alt key, and whenever we mention the Command key, you use the Control key.* In those cases where we actually mention the Control key, which we rarely do, you also use the Control key on the PC.

FUNCTION KEYS

Most PCs only have 12 function keys on their keyboards where the Mac extended keyboards have 15. *Photoshop 4 Artistry* includes a predefined set of function keys, called ArtistKeys, which we reference in the book. We have set these up so the ones used most often are within the first 12 keys. They will work the same for the Mac and the PC. We discuss this further in "Setting System and Photoshop Preferences."

PHOTOSHOP HELP

Mac users of Photoshop don't have a Help menu, which supplies Windows Photoshop users with the standard Windows online help system. Windows users access the Help system by pressing the F1 (Help) function key.

STATUS BAR

Windows users also have a Status bar that tells you what tool you are using and gives you additional information about what you are doing.

MEMORY SETUP

For Photoshop to work most efficiently, you need to set up the computer's application memory correctly. The process for setting up memory on the Mac is a little different than on the PC. Setting up memory for both types of systems is explained in "Setting System and Photoshop Preferences."

Gamma Calibration

You access the Gamma Monitor Calibration utility from a different place on the Mac than you do on the PC. These differences are explained in "Calibration."

Video LUT Animation

A few Macs and many more PCs don't have support for Video LUT Animation in their 24-bit video boards. If you don't have Video LUT Animation support, the way you use certain tools, like Levels and Curves, will change slightly. We explain this in "Setting System and Photoshop Preferences" and we also cover both uses throughout the book whenever Video LUT Animation becomes a major part of an exercise.

NAVIGATING IN PHOTOSHOP

How to most efficiently use the tools, palettes, and windows that Photoshop provides; make the most of big and small monitors; and use some general shortcut tips, like the Actions palette, that make Photoshop more fun.

Each digital image file you open into Photoshop has its own window. At the top of the window is the name of the file as it was last saved. This is a standard Macintosh or PC window with scroll bars and a grow box in the lower right corner, and all the rest of the standard fare. If other windows cover the one you want, you can find it in the list of open files in the Window menu. You can view any of these windows in any of three modes, which the icons at the bottom of the Tool palette denote. The left icon denotes the standard Mac window mode, shown here. The middle icon, which we call Full Screen mode, places the active, top window in the center of the screen in the middle of a field of gray.

Full Screen mode

Screen modes at the bottom of the Tool palette. Full Screen mode selected.

WORKING IN FULL SCREEN MODE

Working in Full Screen mode offers many advantages. If you are working on a small monitor, Full Screen mode does not waste the space that scroll bars normally take up. Also, accidentally clicking down in the gray area while in Full Screen mode doesn't switch you to the Finder or some other application. This gray area is especially useful when making selections that need to include the pixels at the very edge of the window. Using any of the selection tools, you can actually start or end the selection in the gray area, which basically just ensures that you have selected all the pixels along that edge. When using a typical Mac or PC window, the cursor often fluctuates between displaying as the tool you are using and the arrow cursor for the scroll bar when you move the mouse ever so slightly while at the edge of the window. Even if you are not using Full Screen mode, if you are making an edit along the edge of the image, you may want to make the window a little bigger than the image. Doing so adds Photoshop gray space between the edge of the file and the window's scroll bars so you can more easily make these edge edits. As you can tell, I am very fond of Full Screen mode. It removes all other distractions

Here we see the Photoshop desktop with three windows open. The active window, CamdenFogSailboat, is the window on top with its title bar striped. You will see a check mark beside this window in the Window menu. You can bring any window to the top, even a hidden one, by choosing it from the Window menu.

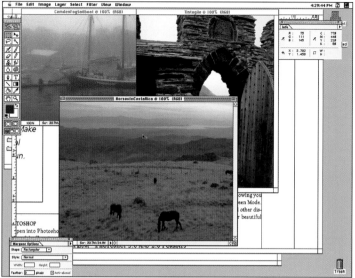

Here we see the Photoshop desktop in Standard Screen mode and how it can be cluttered by other applications in the background. It is easy to accidentally click outside a window and switch to another application on such a cluttered desktop.

Here we see Photoshop working in Full Screen mode with various palettes around the active window. We can still get to underlying windows by selecting them from the Window menu. A single press on the Tab key removes all these palettes and allows you to use the whole screen for your work. A second Tab press and all the same palettes are back in the same positions. This is a great way to see the big picture.

from your Mac screen and allows you to focus on your beautiful image surrounded by nondistracting neutral gray.

The right icon at the bottom of the Tool palette gives you a mode similar to Full Screen mode, but with the image surrounded by black instead of gray, and the menu bar removed. If you are a Photoshop power user, you can work without the menu bar by using command and function keys—but I generally use this mode only for presentations.

CONTROL KEYS FOR ZOOMING AND SCROLLING

There are certain control keys that I make everyone learn when I teach Photoshop. IT IS VERY IMPORTANT THAT YOU LEARN THESE THREE CONTROL KEYS! Even if you hate control keys and you don't want to be a power user, you have to learn these or you will find working in Photoshop a constant pain. I worked on the Lisa project at Apple. The Lisa was the predecessor to the Mac and much of the Mac's user interface actually was designed for the Lisa. Larry Tesler, who was head of applications software for the Lisa project, had a license plate on his car that read, "NO MODES." A mode is a place in the user interface of a program where you can't access the tools you normally use. Programs that have a lot of modes can be confusing, especially for the beginner. Photoshop is less modey than before, but it still has a lot of modes. Many tools in Photoshop come up in a modal dialog box; for example, Levels, Curves, Color Balance, and most of the color correction tools. When you use these tools, you are in a mode because you can't go to the Tool palette and switch to, for instance, the Zoom tool.

ZOOMING IN AND OUT

If you are inside Levels and you want to zoom in to see more detail, which I do all the time, you can't select the Zoom tool from the Tool palette the way you usually can. Holding down the Command key and the spacebar will show you the Zoom icon, which you can then click on to do a zoom in and see your image from closer up. Option-Spacebar-click will do a zoom out. When you zoom in and out using the Zoom tool or these control keys, Photoshop zooms by a known amount. If you are at 100%, where you see all the pixels, then you will zoom into 200% and then 300% and then 400%. You will find that the image is sharper at a factor of 2 from 100%. 50%, 100%, 200%, or 400% is sharper than 66.6%, 33.3%, and so on. In earlier versions of Photoshop, you used Command-+ and Command-– to zoom in and out at smaller increments; in version 4, they do the same thing as the Zoom tool. Don't forget that you can always zoom so

Again in Full Screen mode, here we have used Command-Spacebar-click to zoom in and fill the screen with our image, a more inspiring way to work. Learn to use Command-Spacebar-click to zoom in, Option-Spacebar-click to zoom out, and the Spacebar with a mouse drag for scrolling. Command-0 will fill the screen with your image and it fills the entire screen if you first press Tab to remove your palettes. Command-Option-0 zooms to 100%. This is the most efficient way to move around the Photoshop screen, especially when in Full Screen mode or using a dialog box like Levels.

Here we see a typical palette with its Options menu on the top right accessible by clicking on the black triangle icon. The Palette Options item shows you different ways to display the palette. You should check out the Palette Options on all the palettes that have them. Most Palettes have a close box on the top left and a similar box on the right for collapsing or opening the palette. The icons at the bottom of the palette are shortcuts for various functions associated with that palette. The name at the top is the palette's name tab. Here are some standard icons and what they mean.

Load Selection from Channel or Path

Save Selection to Channel or Path

New Channel, Path, or Layer

Throw Channel, Path, or Layer away

the entire image fits in the screen by pressing Command-0. If you press Command-Option-0, the image zooms to 100%.

SCROLLING WITH THE HAND ICON

Just holding the spacebar down brings up the Hand icon, and clicking and dragging this icon scrolls your file.

PALETTE MANAGEMENT

Photoshop contains a lot of different palettes, each of which controls a different set of functions. The Tool palette is the main palette. Its functions are discussed in "The Tool Palette." The different color picking palettes are discussed in "Picking and Using Color." Palettes include the Channels, Layers, and Paths palettes, which are discussed in "Selection, Masks, and Channels," and "Layers, Layer Masks, and Adjustment Layers." What we discuss in this chapter is how to most efficiently use all the palettes on the Photoshop screen.

ACCESSING PALETTES

All palettes are accessed from the Window menu. You can use this menu to open or close a particular palette. We recommend using the Actions palette to define function keys to bring up and close the palettes you use most often. The chapter, "Setting System and Photoshop Preferences," explains how to do this. Pressing the Tab key makes the Tool palette—and all other visible palettes—disappear. Pressing Tab again brings all these palettes up in the same locations. Pressing Shift-Tab opens or closes the other palettes without changing the status of the Tool palette. You can close any of the palettes, except the Tool palette, by clicking on the close

If you are working in Windows on the PC, use the Alt key where we specify the Option key and where we specify the Command key, use the Control key.

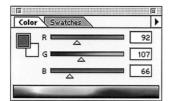

Here we see a group of palettes with the Color palette currently active. The Palette Options menu would now bring up the Color palette's options.

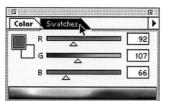

To switch to the Swatches palette, click on its name tab and when you release the mouse, the palette group will look like the group to the right.

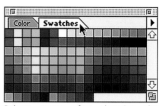

Palette group after choosing the Swatches palette. Now the Swatches Palette options show in the Swatches Palette Options menu.

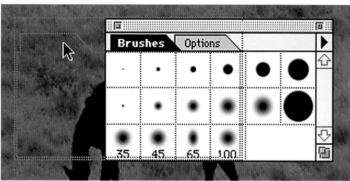

Click on a palette's name tab and drag it outside the group window to put that palette within its own window.

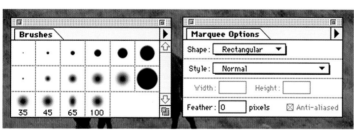

Here we see the Brushes palette after it has been removed from grouping with the Options palette. To regroup these palettes, click on the name tab of one of them and drag it on top of the window of the other. The palette that is within a group window first will have its name tab on the left. New palette tabs are added to the right.

Clicking the first time in the grow box, at the top right, resizes the palette so that it just holds the things within it, like the palette on the right.

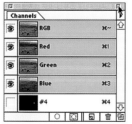

Clicking a second time in the grow box resizes the palette to show just name tabs, like the palette on the right, and will also send it to the top or bottom of your monitor.

Clicking again in this palette's grow box expands it to the size to the immediate left. The compacted size shown here can be left at the bottom or top of your monitor without taking up much screen real estate until you need it again later.

box in the top-left corner of the palette. You can use the Tab key or define an action to open or close the Tool palette or any palette. We have done this for you as explained in "Automating with Actions."

PALETTE OPTIONS

Most palettes also have a menu that you can access by clicking on the Menu icon at the top right of the palette (see illustration on previous page). You can move palettes around on the screen by clicking on the title bar at the top and moving the palette to a new location. Photoshop opens the palettes in the same location at which they were last used unless you turn off the Save Palette Positions option within Photoshop's Preferences (which you reach by choosing File/Preferences/General).

GROUPING AND SEPARATING PALETTES

In Photoshop 4, you can group several palettes in the same palette window. You then switch between palettes in the group by clicking on the name tab of the palette you want or by choosing the palette from the Window menu. If you hide any of the palettes within the group, the whole group gets hidden. Therefore, you are better off grouping only palettes that are used together. Sometimes you want to see two palettes at the same time that are usually used within a group. I do this often with Layers and Channels. When I'm working on a complicated layer document that has a lot of mask channels, I separate them to see both at the same time. To do this, click on the name tab of the palette you want to separate and then drag it out of the group window to a new location by itself. To move more palettes into a group, click on the name tab of the palette you want to add and then drag it over the group window. New palettes in a group are added to the right. If you have a small monitor, you may want to group more of your palettes together to save screen space. You can also compact and collapse your palettes by clicking in the grow box at the top right.

More Than One Window per File

You can have more than one window open at a time for the same Photoshop document. To do this, first open a Photoshop file that will give you your first window. Next, go to the View/New View command to open a second window of the same file. Utilizing this capability, you can, for example, have one window of a section of the file up close and the other window showing the entire file. You can also use this technique to have one window display a particular channel or mask of the file while another window shows the RGB or CMYK version. There are many uses of this feature.

Using the Info Palette

The Info palette is one of the most useful tools in Photoshop. Not only does it measure colors like a densitometer (which we will do extensively in the color correction exercises in later chapters in this book), it also gives you important measurements any time you are scaling, rotating, making, or adjusting a selection. The top-left location, the size of the box you are drawing, the degree of rotation, and many other useful measurements are always present in the Info palette. This is a good one to keep up on the screen most of the time.

Rulers, Guides, and Grids

Photoshop has always had rulers, but now version 4 also has guides and grids. Guides and grids are very helpful for creating composite images where you need to place objects in exact locations. They are also great for Web and multimedia projects to control the alignment of buttons and action objects. The controls for Rulers, Guides, and Grids are all located on the View menu. As you can see in the diagram on the next page, there is a different command key to turn each of rulers, grids, or guides on and off, as well as a different key to snap to each of grids or guides. You can also lock guides to prevent accidentally moving them.

Command-R turns your rulers on, at which point you can set the zero-zero location of the rulers (by default the top left of the image), by clicking in the top-left ruler box and then dragging to the point in your image that you want to be zero-zero. To return it to the top-left position again, just double-click in the top-left corner of the ruler display. You set up the ruler unit preferences in the File/Preferences/Units and Rulers.

To create a guide, just click in the horizontal or vertical ruler and drag the guide to where you want it. Clicking in the horizontal ruler will drag out a horizontal guide and clicking on the vertical ruler will drag out a vertical guide. You can move a guide, if Lock Guides is not turned on, by using the Move tool (V or the Command key) and just dragging the guide to its new position. Option-dragging a guide will toggle it from vertical to horizontal or vice versa. Take a few minutes to play with these options and you will find rulers, grids, and guides easy to learn. When working on projects where I need to measure the sizes and placements, I usually have at least

Here we see two views of the same file. The one on the top-left is a closeup of the inscription on the stone above the door at Tintagel Castle, England, the supposed castle of the Knights of the Round Table.

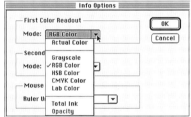

Here we see the Info palette during the Free Transform command. The contents of the right and bottom two sections change to show you information about your transformation.

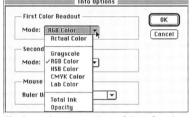

Check out the many options of the Info palette accessed from its Palette Options menu.

You use File/Preferences/Units & Rulers to set up the types of rulers you have.

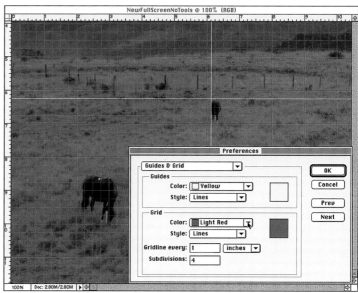

File/Preferences/Guides & Grid will bring up this Preferences dialog box which allows you to set the color and appearance of your grids and your guides. You can also specify how often you have gridlines and subdivsions.

Using the View menu, you can use Command-R to turn rulers on and off, Command-; to turn Guides on and off and Command-" to turn the Grid on and off. To snap to the Grid or Guides you use Command-Shift-" or Command-Shift-;.

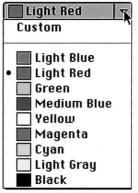

Here you see the choices you get for either Grid or Guide colors. Each can have a different color and choosing Custom brings up the Color Picker, where you can pick any color you want.

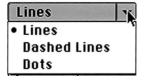

Here you see the options for Grid styles. Guides can be in either the Lines or Dashed Lines styles.

rulers on. When you are drawing a selection, you can actually see the starting location as well as the current location of the mouse by following the dotted lines that show you the current mouse location along each of the rulers. For faster positioning, turn on the grid as well as Snap To Grid; then you will know that things are exactly placed. To set your own specific locations, create guides anywhere you want. You can then line up objects along these guides. When I am just color correcting a photograph, I usually turn off Rulers, Guides and Grids and put the image into Full Screen mode so that I can see it unobstructed.

THE NAVIGATOR PALETTE

Photoshop 4 has a cool new Navigator palette (Window/Show Navigator or Shift-F2 with ArtistKeys) that allows you to zoom in and out to quickly see where you are in an image and more efficiently move to a particular spot in that image. This palette contains a small thumbnail of your entire image with a red box, called the view box, on top of the thumbnail that shows you the part of the image you can currently see in your window. As you zoom in, you will notice this box getting smaller because you are seeing less and less of the image area. You can click and drag this box, in the Navigator palette, to a new location and then your window will display what's inside the box. This is much faster than doing large scrolls with the Hand tool on the actual image window, because in the Navigator palette you always see the entire image. You do not need to guess where you want to scroll to; just click on the red box and move it there. It is even faster if you don't drag the box there, but instead just click down in the Navigator palette where you want the box to be then the box will instantly move there. To change the size and location of the red box, just Command-drag a new box over the area you want to see. You can change the size of the Navigator palette and its thumbnail by clicking and dragging in the grow box at the bottom right corner of the palette. Making the palette bigger gives you more exact positioning within your file using the bigger thumbnail. You can use the slider on the bottom right to drag the zoom factor smaller or bigger. You can also click on

Navigator palette and red view box when image is zoomed to 100% and all is visible in the image window.

Navigator palette and red view box when zoomed to 300%. Now only the area in the red view box is visible in the image window.

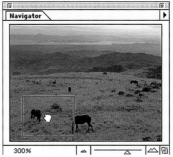
Dragging on the red view box to change what is visible in the image window.

the smaller or bigger icon on either side of the slider to zoom in a similar way to Command-Spacebar-clicking and Option-Spacebar-clicking. In the bottom left of the Navigator palette is a numeric text box where you can type in the exact zoom factor that you need. If you hold down the Shift key while pressing Enter after typing in a new zoom factor here, you will zoom to the new factor but the text percentage number will remain highlighted so you can enter a new value without having to click on the text box again. I have found that some images are a little sharper on the screen when zoomed to an even multiple of 100% (25%, 50%, 100%, 200%, 400%, and so on). You can change the color of the view box from red to another color by choosing Palette Options from the Navigator Palette menu.

Command Dragging a new box to view just the large horse at the bottom center. When the mouse button is released, we will zoom so this box fills the window.

Here is the small default size Navigator palette.

THE ACTIONS PALETTE

Check out the next chapter, "Automating with Actions," to learn how to use the Actions palette with my ArtistKeys command set to quickly set up function keys to show and hide any palette. You may notice, throughout the book, references like (F11 with ArtistKeys) or just (F11). These show you places where I have created shortcuts for you using the Actions feature. Actions can be used to automate a single menu choice, like bringing up a palette, or a whole sequence of events, like creating a drop shadow. Please check out actions, they are very powerful!

CONTROL KEY FOR CONTEXT SENSITIVE MENUS

Photoshop 4 has a great new feature using the Control key and the mouse! At any time, you can hold down the Control key then press the mouse button to bring up a set of context sensitive menus. What shows up in the menu at a particular time depends on the tool you are currently using and the location where you click. If you are in the Marquee tool, for example, you will get one name if there already is a selection and a different one if there is not. If you are in the Move tool, you'll get a menu showing all the layers that currently have pixels at the location where you click. These are a great set of time saving features. To learn more, see "The Tool Palette" and the step-by-step examples.

You can use the grow box in the bottom right corner to change the size of the Navigator palette. Here is a big Navigator palette.

AUTOMATING WITH ACTIONS

*Using the Actions palette to add function keys
for frequently used menu items and to
add sequences of keys and events to automate
your Photoshop production.*

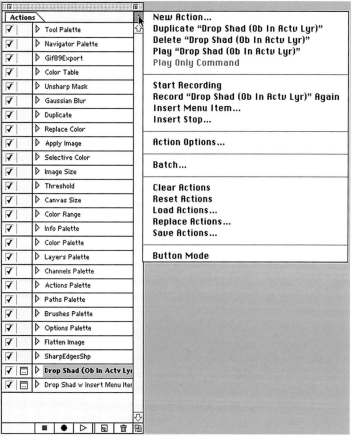

The Actions palette with Button mode turned off. This allows you to edit the actions in many ways. The Actions menu bar shows you all the things you can do with actions. We discuss each of these in this chapter and explain how they work. Notice the icons at the bottom of the palette that, from left to right, stop recording, start recording, play current action or command, create a new action or command, and allow you to throw an action or command into the trash.

Actions are one of the major improvements in Photoshop 4. They allow you to record and even edit single menu items or very complicated sequences of events. You can then run that menu item or series of events over an entire folder full of files. You can execute these events with the press of a function key on the keyboard or a click of a button on-screen. You choose Window/Show Actions (F11 with ArtistKeys) to bring up the Actions palette. To create new actions, you want to turn off Button mode from the Actions Palette menu. After you define all your actions, you can turn on Button mode, which turns the actions into buttons that you can play by clicking on them.

Photoshop 3.0 had a palette called the Commands palette that would let you define single menu choices as function keys or buttons that could be pressed in the palette to execute a single menu item. This Commands palette has been replaced in Photoshop 4 by the Actions palette. If you were using the Commands palette before, you will have to reprogram your commands as actions.

ARTISTKEYS TO SET UP YOUR ACTIONS

In the Preferences folder of the *Photoshop 4 Artistry* CD, we have given you a predefined set of actions, called ArtistKeys. You can load this Actions palette by choosing either Load Actions or Replace Actions from the Actions Palette menu bar. Choosing Load Actions adds the ArtistKeys actions to the set you already have and Replace Actions completely replaces any existing actions with the ones in the ArtistKeys set. You should load these actions now using either Load Actions or Replace Actions. This set of actions replaces the ArtistKeys set for the Commands palette, which we provided for Photoshop 3 on the CD that shipped with the previous edition of this book.

What we did with ArtistKeys is go through all of the menu items in Photoshop 3 and set up as function keys the ones that you will use most often. For example, F9 through F12 will bring up and close down the palettes you use most often. We tried to do this logically, so F9 is the Info palette and Shift-F9 is the Color palette. Both of these palettes deal with measuring color. F10 is the Layers palette and Shift-F10 is the Channels palette. You often use these together. Those of you who used the Photoshop 3 ArtistKeys will notice that I have changed some of them around. I found that some of the menu items that didn't have keyboard alternatives in Photoshop 3 now have them in version 4 so I didn't set up function keys for them. I also use Photoshop 4 differently, so I tried to use the keys that were most important. I use F2 through F12 to implement single menu items (and we do mention these quite often in the book, so you will find them quick to learn). I mention these keys in context as alternatives so you don't have to learn them if you would rather not. I consider F1, as well as F13 through F15 optional so you can use them to reprogram other actions. We may have used F1 or F13–F15 in ArtistKeys but the book doesn't mention these heavily.

To Record a Single Menu Item Action

Create a new Action or Duplicate Current Action or Command.

Stop Action Recording or Playback.

Play Current Action or Command.

If you want to set up an action with a function key to do any menu item, even the palette menus, here are the steps to take. Make sure the Actions palette is not in Button mode (Button Mode unchecked), by using the Actions Palette menu. Create a new action by clicking on the New Action icon at the bottom of the Actions palette or by choosing New Action from the Actions menu. Either way, the Action Options palette opens, enabling you to name your action as well as pick a function key and color for it. You do not need to pick a function key or color. When you click on the Record button, you can record a single menu item simply by choosing Insert Menu Item from the Actions menu. Doing so opens the Insert Menu Item dialog box shown here. Now just choose the menu that you want to automate and its name fills the text box. Choose OK and then click on the Stop Recording icon at the bottom of the Actions palette or choose Stop Recording from the Actions menu. To play the action you just recorded, press the function key or click on the action in the Actions palette and choose Play from the Actions menu, or click on the Play icon at the bottom of the palette. In Button mode, clicking on an action plays it. When we beta-tested Photoshop 4, the software came without a manual. We had not seen actions before and I must admit that it took me a while to figure out how to record a single menu item (something I could do easily using the Commands palette in Photoshop 3). The good thing about Actions is that even though recording a single menu item is a bit more work, you can now record, and even edit, highly complicated sequences of events and then run them over an entire folder full of files.

Recording Actions with Multiple Commands

To record an action with a sequence of events, you start the same way, by choosing the New Action icon or menu item. Name your action, press the Record button, then go through the sequence of events on the open file. Each recorded menu item in the sequence is now called a command. Since you want to run this

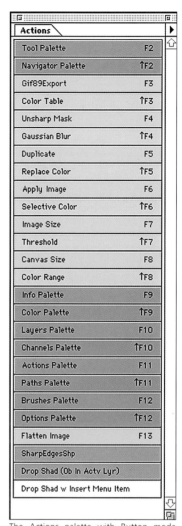

The Actions palette with Button mode turned on. In Button mode, you can click on an action to play it, even if it doesn't have a function key alternative.

The New Action command, or double-clicking on an existing action, brings up the Actions Options dialog box, where you can name your action, choose a function key for it, and also a color which will show up in Button mode.

Use this to create an action that plays a single menu item. You can pick any menu item from anywhere within Photoshop. Also use this when you don't want the action to insert any values into the command for you.

Left column images and captions

(Top action palette image)

Drop Shad Before Editing
- Duplicate
  - layer target
- Fill
  - Using: black
  - Opacity: 100%
  - Mode: normal
  - With Preserve Transpar
- Move
  - layer target
  - To: layer backward
- Offset
  - Horizontal: –10
  - Vertical: 10
  - Fill: repeat
- **Gaussian Blur**
  - Radius: 10

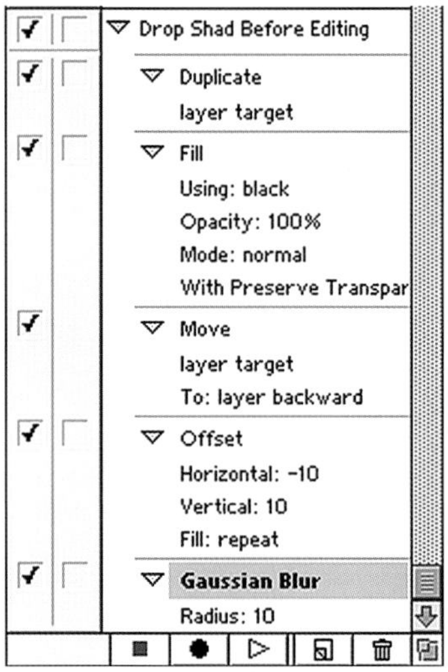

Here we see the Drop Shadow action prior to editing. If you play this action, the Offset command always offsets your shadow by –10 horizontal and 10 vertical. The Gaussian Blur of your shadow will always have a Radius of 10. This will not create the correct drop shadow in most cases because the size of the object will be different and the light may be coming from a different direction. You need to edit this to make it user-friendly and object-specific.

(Second action palette image)

Actions
- SharpEdgesShp
- Drop Shad (Ob In Actv Lyr)
  - Stop
    - Message: "Make sure the object
    - With Continue
  - Duplicate
    - layer target
  - Fill
    - Using: black
    - Opacity: 100%
    - Mode: normal
    - With Preserve Transparency
  - Move
    - layer target
    - To: layer backward
  - Stop
    - Message: "Enter the offset value
    - With Continue
  - Offset
    - Horizontal: –10
    - Vertical: 10
    - Fill: repeat
  - Stop
    - Message: "Enter the Ammount of
    - With Continue
  - Gaussian Blur
    - Radius: 10

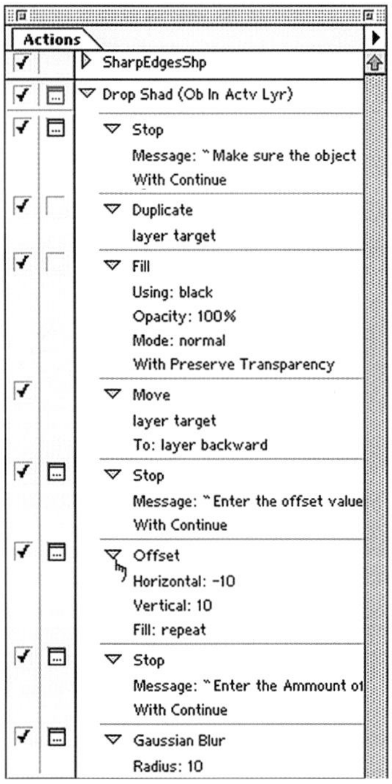

Here is the Drop Shadow action after editing to add the Stop commands as well as the breakpoints in the Offset and Gaussian Blur commands.

Enter the message you want displayed to give the user information about the action that is playing. Turn on Allow Continue so the action will continue when the user clicks on OK.

Main body

sequence on many other files, you need to be aware of the state of the file when you start recording. All subsequent files will have to be in the same beginning state for the action to work properly. Actions are like computer programs, they have no intelligence to pick the right layer within the file or make sure the file was saved before you start. Take a look at the first multiple command action within ArtistKeys. It is called Drop Shad (Ob In Actv Lyr) and is meant to add a drop shadow to an object on its own layer surrounded by transparency. Open the file called Ball from the Actions folder on the *Photoshop 4 Artistry* CD. You will notice that the layer called Ball is currently the active, grayed, layer and the ball within this layer is surrounded by transparency. Any file that you run the Drop Shad Action on will have to first be in this state for the action to do the right thing. If you have programmed before, this will be obvious but I know that many of you have not.

Why not get your feet wet now? Start out with a file in this state (you can use the Ball file, you have it open anyway) then create the action as described above. Click on the Record button and go through the simplest sequences of events to create a drop shadow. The Actions feature records these events as you do the work. If you have the Actions palette open, you can see the events recording as you work. Do absolutely nothing except this sequence of events; otherwise, you record that too. After you finish your sequence of events, choose Stop Recording from the Actions Palette menu or click on the Stop Recording icon at the bottom of the Actions palette. You are not done! Now you need to look at the sequence of actions and edit it to make sure it does the right thing when you play it back. Think about it; will you always want all the parameters to each command to be the same or will some things be slightly different for each instance? The great thing about actions is that you can customize them easily.

EDITING ACTIONS AFTER RECORDING

I wanted to create a drop shadow action that would work for most people most of the time. I wanted people to figure out how to use it without any directions. The unedited drop shadow action is shown here to the left at the top of the page with the edited one below it. We added a Stop message by clicking on the Drop Shad (Ob In Actv Lyr) line to activate it, and then clicking on the arrow to the left of the name, which opens up the action and displays the list of commands in it. Now, choose Insert Stop from the Actions menu to open the Record Stop dialog box. Enter the text of the message you want the user to see. The message I entered just explains that to use this action you need to start with an active layer that has an object surrounded by transparency within it. The Stop command now happens before the Action starts so that the user can click on Cancel if the file he is running it on is not in the right state. If the user clicks Continue, the action then goes on to make a copy of the target layer, fill that copy with black using preserve transparency, and then move this new black layer below the original target layer. To turn this new black layer into a shadow, we need to now offset it from the original and then blur it to make its edges soft. I added another stop message before the Offset command, this one explaining that the user needs to adjust the offset numbers to fit the object in question. The direction and amount of the offset will depend on the lighting on the original. To allow the user to change these values, I put a break point on the Offset command by clicking in the middle column to the left of this command in the Actions palette. Finally, I added another stop to explain that the Gaussian Blur amount also requires editing to make sure the shadow looks right for this situation. Then I added a break point on the Gaussian Blur again by clicking in the column to its left.

Throw Action or Command away.

FURTHER EDITING REFINEMENTS

The preceding exercise illustrates the types of editing you can do to actions. After you understand how this action works, you could turn off the Stop commands by clicking on their check marks to turn off each check in the leftmost column next to each stop command. You could also throw away the Stop commands as you can any command or action, by dragging it to the Trash icon at the bottom of the Actions palette. If you're using Batch mode to run the action on a bunch of items that all have the same offset and blur values, you can turn off the breakpoints on Offset and Blur by clicking in the middle column next to each of them. You can change the actual value of the default offset or blur by clicking on that command line and then choosing Record "that command" Again from the Actions menu. It will play that one command line and allow you to change its default value within the action. If you want the user to always enter the values for a particular command when he uses the command, you need to use the Insert Menu item from the Actions menu when recording the command, and choose that command. It doesn't actually execute the command until the action is played, so the user has to enter the values at that time.

Start Recording.

Here we have the Drop Shadow action where the Offset and Gaussian Blur were created using Insert Menu Item. These will automatically stop and allow the user to specify the parameters each time. There are now default values if you do it this way.

ADDING TO ACTIONS

After you record an action, you can add to it by selecting a particular command within the action and choosing the Start Recording menu from the Actions menu bar, or by clicking on the Start Recording icon at the bottom of the Actions palette. New commands are recorded right after the command you select. You can click on an existing command and drag it to the new action/command icon to make a copy of that command. You can then drag that copy, or any command, to another location in the current action or in another action. If you want to start playing an action in the middle, just click on the command at the point at which you want to begin and choose Play From (command) from the Actions menu to play the action from that point forward. You can also choose Play Only "that command" to just play the one command. You can also play an action or command by clicking on the Play icon at the bottom of the Actions palette.

THINGS THAT ACTIONS DON'T SUPPORT

Some menu items in Photoshop, like the Preference menus, are disabled during the recording of an action. Adobe probably didn't have time to include action support for those commands. If you want to include any of them as part of an action anyhow, you can choose Insert Menu Item, which will choose the menu to play when the action plays. You can't put default values into these commands, but at least you can get the user to respond to them. Notice that the Set Preferences action was done this way. It brings up most of the preference items that I recommend you change from defaults. (You need to read "Setting System and Photoshop Preferences" for the values to enter.) I could not find any way to record certain things into an action, such as setting the Eyedropper preferences to read a 3 by 3 average instead of a single pixel—I decided to do it as a Stop message so that you know that it needs to be done.

RUNNING THE SAME ACTION ON A WHOLE BATCH OF FILES

The Actions Palette menu contains an item named Batch which enables you to specify an action along with a source and destination folder for that action. If you specify a source folder and a destination folder, Photoshop opens each file in the source folder and runs the action on the file and then saves that modified file in the destination folder. You do not have to put Open or Close commands in your action; the Batch command automatically adds these at the beginning and the end. If your action does have any Open commands in it, a check box in the Batch dialog box allows you to tell it to ignore those commands. Another check box lets you tell the Batch command to ignore any Save commands. You select the action you want to perform by using the Action pop-up menu in the Batch dialog box and you choose the Source and Destination folders by clicking on their respective Choose buttons. If you choose None for Destination, Photoshop leaves the modified files open. If you choose Save and Close, they are saved back in the folder in which they started, under the same name. You can also create a Multi-Batch action that records more than one Batch command. You can then play this Multi-Batch action which allows you to batch one action after another on the same files or to batch the same action over different files in more than one folder. Let's get some action into our lives!

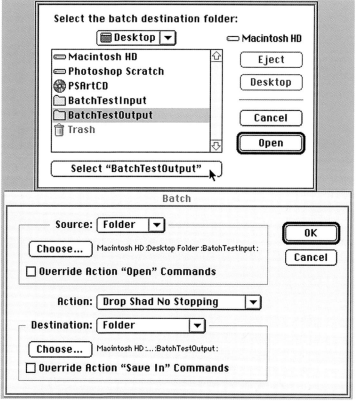

On the top we see the action that will break with each Stop command and also on the Offset and Gaussian Blur commands. On the bottom we have removed the Stop commands by clicking on their check marks in the check mark column to the left, and we have taken away the break points on the Offset and Gaussian Blur by clicking on them in the break column. This is the kind of thing you might want to do to an action to prepare it for automatically running in Batch mode over a lot of files.

Here is the dialog box for Batch where you can choose the Source, Action, and Destination for your Batch. When you use one of the Choose buttons that brings up the dialog box at the top here, the trick is to click on the Select "Folder Name" button as shown above, rather than the Open button, when you find the folder you want.

SETTING SYSTEM AND PHOTOSHOP PREFERENCES

Setting up your system and Photoshop's preferences to make Photoshop run more efficiently and make your work easier.

If you are new to computers or Photoshop, some of the discussions and settings here may seem a bit confusing to you. You should still read this chapter and set up your preferences as it recommends. Your Photoshop will run more efficiently and give you better results with your color corrections and separations. Your understanding will grow as you do the exercises and read the rest of the book, especially the chapters, "Calibration," "Scanning, Resolution, Histograms, and Photo CD," and "Color Correction and Output."

SETTING UP YOUR MAC

You may want to read this section with your Macintosh turned on so you can refer to your screen as you follow the steps outlined here. In the System 7.5 Finder, choose About This Macintosh from the Apple menu. An information window opens, giving you the total memory available on your Macintosh and how much memory each application currently running is using. If you check this when no applications are running, Largest Unused Block tells you the amount of space available for all your applications in multiples of 1,024 bytes. An abbreviation for 1,024 bytes is the expression One K. 1024K (1,024 x 1,024 bytes of memory) equals 1 megabyte (Mb) or 1,048,576 bytes of memory. If you had, like I do, 112Mb of Total Memory (114,688K), and your system software used about 5Mb (5,120K), the Largest Unused Block would display about 107Mb (109,568K). Your system can use this 107Mb for the applications that you want to run concurrently.

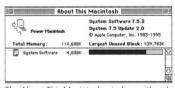

The About This Macintosh window with only the System running. The space for System Software and Largest Unused Block don't add up to exactly Total Memory because the system constantly borrows small amounts of memory for various purposes.

If you are going to use only one application at a time, then you can let Photoshop have most of this remaining memory. You want to leave at least 2–3Mb of space free for desk accessories to run. I often use Photoshop and Quark at the same time, so I assign 80Mb to Photoshop and 16Mb to Quark, which leaves about 10Mb for other applications. If I were working on a really large Photoshop project, I would assign all available memory to Photoshop. Still, I would leave a megabyte or two for desk accessories. If you don't leave enough room for the desk accessories, you can end up getting a message that there isn't enough memory to run a particular desk accessory. When the system barely has enough room to run a desk accessory, it becomes more prone to crashing.

About This Macintosh on my Mac with the system, Photoshop, and Quark running.

To tell the system how much memory to assign an application, you first select the icon for the application from the Finder. You select an application icon by opening the folder that contains that application and then clicking (just once) on the application file. You need to do this when the application is not currently running, so don't click twice because that starts the application. Next, choose Get Info from the File menu in the Finder. An information window about that application will appear. For every application, a suggested size and a preferred size appear at the bottom of the information window. Suggested size usually refers to the minimum size that the application developer recommends to allow the application to operate efficiently. Preferred size refers to the amount of memory this application will actually be given when it runs. Some applications will still operate if you set preferred size to less than suggested size and some will not. I would recommend an absolute minimum of at least 16Mb of memory for Photoshop 4.

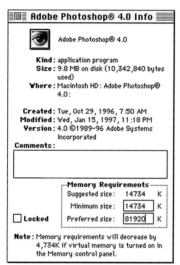

The Get Info window for Photoshop.

You can always set Preferred size to more than Suggested size, and that usually improves the application's performance level. Photoshop usually requires three to five times the amount of temporary space as the size of the file(s) you currently have open. It is much faster if Photoshop can put all of this temporary space into real memory. If Photoshop doesn't have enough real memory for the temp space, it allocates a temp file on the disk and uses it as virtual memory for its temp space needs. When this happens, Photoshop runs much slower than when everything is in real memory. Photoshop comes with its Preferred size set to a default of about 14Mb. If you try to work on large files with so little memory, Photoshop operates very slowly. If you increase Photoshop's memory on your Macintosh, you should notice a great improvement in performance.

Several settings in the Memory control panel (Apple menu/ Control Panels/Memory) that important to Photoshop's performance.

Disk Cache

Photoshop runs faster if you set the Disk Cache size to 32K—making it any larger just slows Photoshop down.

Virtual Memory

Photoshop has its own virtual memory system that is much more efficient for Photoshop than System 7.5's Virtual Memory. Therefore, you really need to turn off Virtual Memory in the Memory control panel. Power Mac owners get a message that system RAM requirements decrease by "x" if they use virtual memory. Still, Photoshop runs better on Power Macs with Virtual Memory turned *off*.

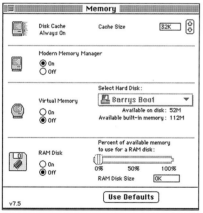

The Memory control panel and how it should be set for Photoshop.

32-Bit Addressing

Keep 32-Bit Addressing on.

RAM Disk

Giving more memory to Photoshop using the Get Info procedure we just described makes Photoshop faster than allocating that same memory as a RAM Disk, so keep the RAM Disk off.

Setting Up Your PC

When using Photoshop on a Windows-based machine, setting up your Photoshop memory usage is less complicated than on the Mac. Choose File/Preferences/ Memory & Image Cache from Photoshop and make sure that the Memory Usage setting is 75% (which should be the default). Next, click on OK in the Memory

Preferences dialog box. You need to quit Photoshop and then restart it for these changes to take effect. When Photoshop starts up, it calculates the amount of available RAM in your system. Photoshop measures this RAM by taking the amount of installed RAM and subtracting any that is used by disk caching software, RAM disks, and other software that permanently reserves RAM (including the Windows OS). Photoshop will allocate 75 percent of the available RAM for its own use. You should have a minimum of 12Mb of RAM available for Photoshop to use on a standard PC and a minimum of 16Mb available for Photoshop on a Pentium-based machine. Check the Scratch Size and Efficiency box at the bottom left of your open document to see how much RAM is available and how Photoshop is using it. See the "Plug-ins and Scratch Disk," section later in this chapter for more information on these.

Here is the Memory Preferences dialog box from the Windows version of Photoshop. Use it to set up how Photoshop will use memory on your PC.

SETTING UP THE PHOTOSHOP PREFERENCES

You access most Photoshop preferences from the File/Preferences or File/Color Settings menus. I go through the preferences in order and talk about the ones that are important for working efficiently with photographs. For a description of Photoshop preferences that I don't talk about, see the Photoshop 4 manual. If you are new to Photoshop, pre-press, or photography, you may not know some of the concepts or Photoshop functions mentioned in this chapter. If so, just set the preferences as we recommend for now, and then reread this chapter after you study the rest of the book.

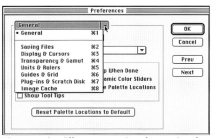

These are the different categories of general preferences. You can go to any one of them using this pop-up menu or by clicking on the Next and Prev buttons. You can also use Command-1 through Command-8 to get to a particular dialog box. Command-K brings up the General dialog box and Command-Option-K brings up the last preferences dialog box you were working on.

GENERAL PREFERENCES (COMMAND-K)

COLOR PICKER

You usually want the Photoshop Color Picker, because it gives you more options than the Apple Color Picker.

INTERPOLATION

Bicubic interpolation is the most accurate way to resize images, so select it for the best quality. If you are prototyping ideas and speed is more important than image quality, you might try one of the other choices. Nearest Neighbor is the fastest, and poorest quality.

These are our recommended settings in the General Controls dialog box.

ANTI-ALIAS POSTSCRIPT

Check Anti-alias PostScript if you are importing PostScript artwork from Illustrator or FreeHand; otherwise, your PostScript imports end up having jaggy diagonal and circular edges.

EXPORT CLIPBOARD

Have you ever seen the message "Converting Clipboard to Pict Format" while you impatiently waited to switch to the Finder or some other application? Turn off Export Clipboard to make switching between Photoshop and other applications much faster. You can still cut and paste inside Photoshop, just not between Photoshop and other applications.

Short PANTONE Names

Check Short PANTONE Names if you're exporting a PANTONE color as a Duotone EPS or in some other way to Quark, PageMaker, or Illustrator. Make sure those other applications use the exact PANTONE names you used in Photoshop.

Show Tool Tips

This is a new feature of Photoshop 4 and when it is on, you get a small yellow line of information that explains what each tool does when the cursor is on top of that tool. Displaying these tips can slow Photoshop user response down, so you can turn it off here.

Beep When Done

Setting Beep When Tasks Finish is useful if you have a slow computer or are working on exceptionally large files. It lets you go cook dinner while Unsharp Mask finishes up, for example. I used this feature a lot back when I had a Mac IIx. With my Quadra/PowerPC, 112Mb of memory, DSP accelerator, and fast hard disk, I don't need the beeps much anymore.

Dynamic Sliders in Picker

Dynamic Sliders in Picker allows the Picker palette to show you all the possible colors, for future changes, on the fly, as you are changing one color. It is very useful to have this on when you're color correcting.

Save Palette Locations

Save Palette Locations remembers where you had all the palettes last time you shut down and restores them next time you power up.

Reset Palette Locations to Default

This button restores all the dialog box and palette locations to the default locations on your main monitor screen. It comes in handy if you cannot find a particular palette. Some bugs in Photoshop 3.0 made the Tool and Color palettes partially disappear above the menu bar, so you couldn't move them down. Using this button is a good way to overcome such bugs in Photoshop. So far, though, I haven't encountered this problem in Photoshop 4.

Saving Files

Image Previews

I like to decide whether to save an icon whenever I save a file. You also can choose to always save an icon or never save one. Icon refers to the icon you see when you are in the Finder. Thumbnail refers to the preview you see in the Open dialog box. Full Size saves a 72dpi full size preview for applications such as Specular Collage. In the Windows version of Photoshop, icons are not an option, but you can create a Thumbnail when saving an image.

Append File Extension

If you turn this on (either Always or Ask When Saving), Photoshop will append the correct three-character file extensions to files so they can be understood and opened on the Windows platform. The Mac knows the type of file you have without the extension. On the PC, the extension tells the software the type of file. Before Windows 95, windows format files could have only eight characters in their file

Here is the Windows Saving Files dialog box

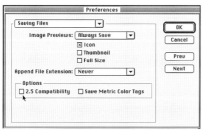

These are our recommendations for the Mac Saving Files Preferences dialog box.

names before the three-character file extension (often called the 8/3 file format). If you want to make sure your file will be recognized correctly on any platform, use the 8/3 file name convention and use only lowercase letters without special characters.

SAVE METRIC COLOR TAGS

You don't need Save Metric Color Tags unless you are using the EFI color system and you want color information forwarded to Quark or some other application.

2.5 FORMAT COMPATIBILITY

2.5 Format Compatibility allows applications that can read Photoshop 2.5 file format to open Photoshop 4 files. If you have layers in your Photoshop 4 files, Photoshop 2.5 cannot see the layers but it can open a flattened version of the layers whose Eye icons were on when the file was last saved. There is a space cost for this convenience though. Every time the file is saved, Photoshop 4 must save a flattened version of the file in addition to all the layers. Turning off 2.5 Format Compatibility saves disk space and time when you are working on files that have more than one layer.

DISPLAYS AND CURSORS

CMYK COMPOSITES

If you are working in CMYK color, you should choose Faster for the CMYK Composites option. Smoother is a little more accurate but it usually is very hard to see the difference. If you want or need to see CMYK gradients more accurately, however, do turn on the Smoother option.

COLOR CHANNELS IN COLOR

Turn off Color Channels in Color—it displays your Red, Green, and Blue, or CMYK channels, with a colored overlay that makes it very hard to see detail. Viewing individual channels in grayscale gives you a more accurate image.

Above, the Display & Cursors preferences. These are our recommended settings. Setting the Painting Cursors and Other Cursors settings to Brush Size and Precise is particularly important.

SYSTEM PALETTE

If you are working in 8-bit color, you don't usually want to use the System palette. You usually want a custom adaptive palette for each image. Having a custom palette for each image makes the image display more accurately, but also makes the screen flicker when you switch from one image to another in the 8-bit mode.

DIFFUSION DITHER

When working on an 8-bit system, the Diffusion Dither option makes smoother transitions on colors that are not in the current palette. I like the Use Diffusion Dither option to display 24-bit images on an 8-bit screen. I recommend leaving this option on.

VIDEO LUT ANIMATION

Unless you have a very old video board, you want to have Video LUT Animation on. It allows you to see many color and contrast changes instantly by tweaking the monitor display through the video card. A few old or poor video circuits don't support this, and you only want to turn this feature off if you have one of those displays. Video LUT Animation is not available on some PCs, because some PC-video cards don't support it. PC users should ask their video board supplier if Video LUT Animation is supported and turn it on only if it is. Another way you can see if your computer supports Video LUT Animation is to turn the option on and then go through the steps in the Grand Canyon exercise, which uses Video LUT Animation. If it is supported, leave the option on here. If not, turn this option off.

TOOL CURSORS

The Tool Cursors settings are important! If you set Painting Cursors to Brush Size, you will paint with a circle outline the size of your brush. This setting even takes into account the current zoom factor. I recommend Brush Size. Using the Precise option is like using the Caps Lock key, in that you paint with a cross-hair cursor. Standard uses the standard Photoshop cursors, a different cursor for each tool. I find that the standard cursors usually get in the way of seeing what I am painting. For the Other Tools option, I recommend the Precise setting.

PLUG-INS AND SCRATCH DISK

The Plug-ins preference tells Photoshop where to find its Plug-in filters. Usually these are in a folder called Plug-ins within the Photoshop 4 folder. You can easily interpret this dialog box wrongly, or click on the wrong button. When you find the folder that contains the plug-ins, you need to click on the Select "Plug-Ins" button at the bottom of the dialog box. Don't click on the Open button at that point like you would for most other uses of an Open dialog box.

The Scratch Disk preference tells Photoshop where to store temporary files on disk. Even if you give Photoshop plenty of memory, it often also stores things on a scratch disk. In fact, Photoshop requires more scratch disk space than the amount of memory you assign to it. Use the largest, fastest disk drive you can afford for your primary scratch disk. If you purchase a Mac that has a built-in drive, then later go out and purchase a very large high-performance external drive or a disk array, you probably should specify that disk array as your primary scratch disk since it may be faster than your built-in original drive. You can also specify a secondary drive on which Photoshop can store temp files when it runs out of space on the primary drive. Try to leave at least five times the scratch space the size of the file you are working on and certainly leave more space on the disk than the amount of memory you assign to Photoshop.

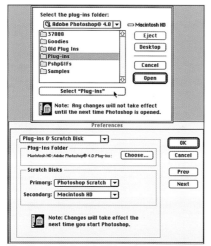

The Plug-ins & Scratch Disk preferences with the choosing Plug-ins dialog box above, which we accessed using the Choose button. Make sure you click on the correct Plug-Ins folder and then click on the Select "Plug-ins" button. Setting the Primary Scratch disk to your largest, fastest disk is also important for Photoshop performance.

Photoshop 4 has a scratch disk efficiency indicator. To access it, select the pop-up menu at the bottom left of the image border and choose Efficiency. The efficiency rating changes depending on the amount of time Photoshop spends swapping image data in and out of RAM from the disk. If your efficiency rating is less than 100% for most operations, you are using the scratch disk instead of RAM. You might want to add more RAM to your system to get better performance.

If the "*" character follows the percent display, your primary scratch disk is operating with asynchronous I/O

If the Efficiency is at 100%, Photoshop can do all its operations on this file without using the scratch disk. If Asynchronous I/O is working with your primary scratch disk, you should see the * character to the right of the efficiency percentage, as shown here.

The Document Sizes option in this same pop-up shows you the flattened image size on the left (if you saved the file with no channels or layers) and the actual size including all the channels and layers on the right.

working. That is good for better performance since Async I/O allows the disk to read or write while Photoshop does something else. If you don't see the "°," check the folder within the Adobe Photoshop® 4.0/Plug-Ins/Extensions folder called "¬ Enable Async I/O." If this folder *has* the character "¬" in front of it, remove that character and restart Photoshop. This turns on asynchronous I/O for Photoshop's primary scratch disk. If you still don't see the "°" character, read the ReadMe document that comes with Photoshop to learn how to set up the correct disk drivers for Async I/O.

The Document Sizes option in this same pop-up shows you the flattened image size on the left (if you saved the file with no channels or layers) and the actual size including all the channels and layers on the right.

The Scratch Sizes option gives you the amount of image data space Photoshop is using for all open images on the left and the amount of scratch memory space available to Photoshop on the right. If the number on the left exceeds the number on the right, you are using the hard disk for scratch space and likely are slowing Photoshop down. See the ReadMe file that comes with Photoshop 4 for more information about improving Photoshop performance.

TRANSPARENCY AND GAMUT

The Transparency and Gamut preferences settings allow you to change the way transparent areas of a layer look and how gamut colors look. The default settings work fine for us, but do check them out if you want to play around some.

GUIDES & GRID

The Guides & Grid preferences allow you to change the way Photoshop guides and grids appear on-screen. You can change the color as well as the types of lines (you can choose between Lines, Dashed Lines, and Dots). You can also specify how often the gridlines occur and how many subdivisions each major gridline has. When working on Web and multimedia projects, I use the grid and guides to help place objects precisely. When you're in the Move tool (V or Command key), you can double-click on a guide to bring up the Guides & Grid preferences and then easily change the colors and styles and view these changes as you make them.

You should set the Guides & Grids preferences according to the colors of objects in the project files you are currently working on.

IMAGE CACHE

The Image Cache increases Photoshop 4's efficiency when working with larger files. It makes several copies of the file in different sizes and uses the smaller versions to update the screen quickly when working with layers and doing complex tasks. When working with smaller files, set the Cache to about 2 or 3 and when working with larger files, set it to 4 or higher. The larger the image cache setting, the more RAM and disk space Photoshop uses when you open a file. We recommend leaving the Use Cache for Histograms setting off; it sometimes gives you slightly inaccurate histograms. The histogram you get with Use Cache for Histograms on depends on the current zoom ratio of your file. Leaving it off slows creating a histogram slightly but ensures that your histograms always are completely accurate and consistent, regardless of your zoom ratio.

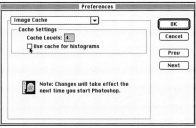

Turn off the Use cache for histograms check box to get more accurate Levels histograms. If you leave this on, the smaller cache image may be used to calculate the histograms. This will not be as accurate because the smaller file has fewer pixels being read. The default setting for Cache Levels is 4.

We usually leave the Ruler Units set to inches. When working on Web and multimedia projects, we change it to pixels to get very detailed measurements. The Units setting also controls the dimension display in the Info palette when selecting or drawing rectangles.

UNITS AND RULERS

The Ruler Units setting in the Units and Rulers Preferences dialog box controls the scale on Photoshop's rulers when you go to View/Show Rulers (Command-R). It also controls the dimension display settings in the Info palette and the initial dimension display when you enter the Canvas Size command. Changing the setting in the Info palette also changes it in Canvas Size. We usually leave it set at inches, but for very detailed measurements as well as for Web and multimedia projects, we change it to pixels.

COLOR SEPARATION SETTINGS

The File/Color Settings Photoshop preferences are the settings that can affect how Photoshop displays images on the computer screen as well as how Photoshop does color separations. You need to set these preferences settings correctly and should standardize on these settings if you have several people contributing Photoshop files to the same publication. Jim Rich and I have worked out these settings. Jim Rich is a color separation expert with a masters degree from RIT in Printing Technology and 20 years' experience doing color separations and setting up high-end scanners and color output systems for companies like *National Geographic* and Crosfield. Jim coauthored *Photoshop in Black and White* and several other great books about getting high-quality scans and purchasing desktop scanners. These color separation preferences give you good quality for web and for sheet-fed coated stock, without a lot of hassle and experimentation. These settings also work well for outputting RGB files to dye sublimation printers and film recorders. We recommend these settings as a starting point and will explain how to change them if you want to develop your own custom settings. We used these settings to create the color separations in this book.

MONITOR SETUP

Choose the selections here that match the monitor you use to display and color correct your Photoshop images. Photoshop 4 has built-in support for many monitors. If you don't find your monitor listed when you click down on the Monitor pop-up, you can also specify the Other setting and use the monitor manufacturer's suggestions for your monitor. If you don't have a hardware monitor calibration device, set the Gamma and White Point to 1.8 and 6500 and use the Gamma control panel that comes with Photoshop to calibrate your monitor. This control panel allows you to accurately calibrate your monitor to your own standard output proof, but that may not be an accurate measure of a particular gamma and color temperature. Adobe's recommended standards under those circumstances are 1.8 and 6500.

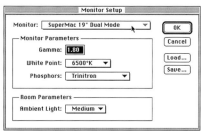

Set the monitor to the type of monitor you have. That also sets the phosphors for you. If your monitor is not listed, ask the monitor manufacturer what settings to use. Unless you have a hardware calibrator to accurately set your gamma and white point, leave them set at 1.8 and 6500. Set the ambient light based on the standard lighting in your room.

If you do have a hardware monitor calibration device (one of those suction cup things), you can set your monitor to other accurately measured color temperatures and gammas. In that case, you should enter the values you are using from your hardware calibrator. You should set the phosphors for the type your monitor has. Photoshop sets the phosphors for you when you choose one of the Monitors on the list in the Monitor pop-up. Set the ambient light for the lighting conditions in your room. The Monitor Setup settings effect how Photoshop displays images on the screen in CMYK mode and also the conversion from RGB to CMYK. See the later chapter in this book, "Calibration," to calibrate your monitor before you start the exercises. It provides more detail about these settings and how they influence what Photoshop does with color.

Eyedropper Tool Setup

Usually when you measure digital values in Photoshop, you want the Eyedropper set to measure a 3 by 3 rectangle of pixels. That gives you a more accurate measurement in a continuous tone image since most colors consist of groups of different colors. If you were to measure a Point Sample, the default, you might accidentally measure the single pixel that was much different in color from those around it. Double-click on the Eyedropper tool and set its Sample Size to 3 by 3 Average.

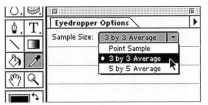

Usually you want the Eyedropper set to measure a 3 by 3 average when measuring continuous tone color.

Printing Inks Setup

INK COLORS: The settings I use for Printing Inks Setup are slightly different than the standard Photoshop settings. When you convert from RGB to CMYK, the actual CMYK values you get for a given RGB color depend on a combination of the preferences settings in Monitor Setup, Printing Inks Setup, and Separation Setup, along with the highlight and shadow preference values set in Levels or Curves. You want to set the Ink Colors setting in Printing Inks Setup for the type of output you are doing. For magazine-quality output to coated stock, you should start out using the SWOP Coated setting here.

DOT GAIN: The Dot Gain setting adjusts how dark Photoshop displays the CMYK image on the screen as well as how dense Photoshop makes each of the CMYK separation layers. The Dot Gain value represents how much the printing inks will spread when printed on certain papers. If you set the dot gain to 30%, Photoshop will separate each CMYK color with less density and display the colors on the screen darker than if the dot gain were set to 20%. You should start with a dot gain setting of 20%.

GRAY BALANCE: The Gray Balance controls the relationship between the amount of cyan, magenta, yellow, and black inks when you convert from RGB to CMYK. Our suggested setting is to leave cyan, magenta, and yellow all set to 1.0 and set black to .9 to generate a little less black and more color than normal.

USE DOT GAIN FOR GRAYSCALE IMAGES: We recommend that you leave the Use Dot Gain for Grayscale Images check box at the bottom of Printing Inks Setup off. When you display grayscale images, this setting adjusts your monitor's brightness depending on the dot gain setting, and also gives you the wrong 0..255 values in the Info palette when you measure a grayscale image. It adjusts these values to simulate the dot gain that you enter. I want to see the actual values. We recommend that you leave the setting unchecked and create a different monitor calibration setting in Gamma, calibrated to your grayscale image output device so you get accurate numerical readings in the Info palette.

Since we have changed all these Printing Ink settings, Photoshop will better remember them as defaults if we save them in a file. Click on the Save button, name this file C1,M1,Y1,K.9, and save it in your Photoshop folder.

To get these settings, first set the Ink Colors to SWOP Coated. Then change the black, K, value in Gray Balance to .9 instead of 1.0, to generate a little less black ink. Now choose the Save button and save these settings in your Adobe Photoshop folder. I like to call them C1,M1,Y1,K.9, because that's the modification we are making to the SWOP Coated settings. This will change the Ink Colors pop-up to C1,M1,Y1,K.9, an Other setting.

Separation Setup

The Separation Setup works in conjunction with Printing Inks Setup and Monitor Setup to control CMYK conversion values. It contains a curve diagram showing how Cyan, Magenta, Yellow, and Black are generated as the image goes from highlights on the left to shadows on the right. There is more ink used in the shadows, and black ink gets used only in the darker half of the color ranges. If you adjust the settings for Black Generation from Light to Medium, or Dark, you can see how the black setting effects the Cyan, Magenta, and Yellow curves. Changing the Black Ink Limit and Total Ink

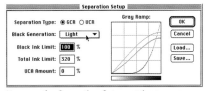

Here are the Separation Setup settings we recommend for output to coated stock. We are basing these settings more on the actual CMYK values we get when separating a gray stepwedge file. Measuring what you actually get, after influence from Printing Inks Setup and Highlight/Shadow settings, when making a separation is more accurate than just looking at the limits shown in this dialog box.

Limit also effects all the curves. Our recommended settings are GCR (Gray Component Replacement) on; Black Generation, Light; Black Ink Limit, 100%; and Total Ink Limit, 320%. These settings are based on the CMYK values we actually got when separating a standard grayscale stepwedge and from comparing the numbers to known good CMYK values for neutral colors and coated stock.

SEPARATION TABLES

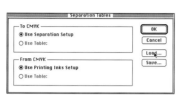

These are the settings for getting your separation and printing inks values from Photoshop's Separation Setup and Printing Inks Setup dialog boxes. Select Use Table only if you are going to get your separation tables from a file.

When using Printing Inks Setup and Separation Setup, you want the Separation Tables dialog box to match the choices shown here. You can create custom separation tables for each printing situation. If you do this, you would load these tables and then choose the Use Tables setting here.

HIGHLIGHT AND SHADOW PREFERENCES

The last preferences items that you need to set up for color separations are the Highlight and Shadow settings, which you can reach by choosing either Levels or Curves. Here, we show you how to get to them from Levels. Choose Image/Adjust/Levels and double-click on the Highlight Eyedropper (the rightmost one). The Color Picker opens. You want to set the CMYK values to 5, 3, 3, 0, which is a neutral color for highlights. If all your other preferences are set correctly, after you enter 5, 3, 3, 0 for CMYK, you should see 244, 244, 244 as your RGB settings. If this is not the case, double check your Monitor Setup, Printing Inks Setup, and Separation Setup. Even if you are using different settings than ours, you should always make sure your RGB values all equal each other so you get a neutral color. Click on OK in the Color Picker to return to Levels, double-click on the Shadow Eyedropper (the leftmost one). Set the CMYK values in the Color Picker to 95, 85, 83, 95, and check to make sure the RGB values are 2, 2, 2. If not, double check your Monitor Setup, Printing Inks Setup, and Separation Setup. Again, the RGB values should always be neutral. Click on OK in the Color Picker and then on OK on Levels. To learn more about these Highlight and Shadow settings and how you use them, turn to "The Grand Canyon," which takes you through all the basics of color correction.

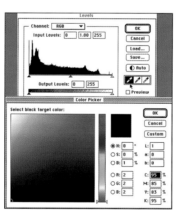

These are the highlight settings we recommend for CMYK coated stock, RGB output to film recorders and digital printers, and general overall color correction of a file. Double-click on the Highlight Eyedropper in Levels or Curves to change these settings. The RGB values here should always be all the same, a neutral color.

These are the shadow settings we recommend for CMYK coated stock, RGB output to film recorders and digital printers, and general overall color correction of a file. Double-click on the Shadow Eyedropper in Levels or Curves to change these settings. The RGB values here should always be all the same, a neutral color.

You now know how to set the correct separation settings for coated stock. These settings also work well for RGB digital printer output (like to a dye sublimation printer), film recorder output, and general overall color correction of a file for archiving. Using the technique discussed in the section "Creating Custom Separation Settings," coming up soon, you need to change these values and your other preferences for newsprint and maybe also for other types of output.

SAVING AND STANDARDIZING YOUR PREFERENCES

After you change your Photoshop preferences, you should quit from Photoshop immediately. When you leave Photoshop, it saves its current state (preferences, tool option choices, window locations, and so on) to a file named **Adobe Photoshop 4.0**

Prefs (on the Mac) or **PHOTOS40.PSP** (on the PC). Quitting at this point assures that Photoshop saves your preferences changes to this file. If you were to crash before quitting Photoshop, you would lose these latest preferences changes and they would revert to the preferences you had when you last successfully quit from Photoshop. On the Mac, this file is located in the Preferences folder in the System Folder, and on the PC, it is located in the Photoshop/Pref folder (directory).

It is a good idea for everyone in your company to standardize on a set of separation preferences, especially for the same publication, and vitally important to standardize separation preferences if you are doing color corrections and separations. You could copy a standard version of this file to the preferences folder on everyone else's machine, or print up a standards document and have your systems administrator make sure that everyone is using those settings.

CREATING CUSTOM SEPARATION SETTINGS

If you want to calibrate Photoshop separation settings for a newspaper, a particular type of Web press, or other custom CMYK output, you can do it, but it's a little tricky. First, you need to find out the correct CMYK values for the full range of neutral colors in a stepwedge file, like the one here. Your press person or printer manufacturer should know this information. Next, you adjust Monitor Setup, Printing Inks Setup, and Separation Setup, as well as the way you set highlights and shadows, until you get the CMYK values closest to their correct CMYK values for neutral colors in the stepwedge file. Using those settings in Photoshop usually gets you very close to the separations that you want. That's basically what we did to get our settings using the following table of desired values for coated stock.

	Neutral RGB 0..255 values			Target CMYK values to print these as neutrals			
	Red	Green	Blue	Cyan	Magenta	Yellow	Black
highlight	250	250	250	5%	3%	3%	0%
1/4 tone	190	190	190	28%	21%	21%	0%
midtone	128	128	128	62%	50%	48%	12%
3/4 tone	68	68	68	78%	68%	66%	45%
shadow	5	5	5	95%	85%	83%	80%

Actual CMYK values when separating the StepWedgeFile using our Photoshop Separation settings with the Highlight set using the Levels Highlight Eyedropper at 2% and the Shadow set at 98% using the Shadow Eyedropper

	Cyan	Magenta	Yellow	Black
highlight	5%	3%	3%	0%
1/4 tone	32%	22%	22%	0%
midtone	58%	45%	44%	4%
3/4 tone	75%	63%	62%	35%
shadow	80%	69%	69%	96%

The preference settings we chose don't exactly match the values in the target CMYK table, but they give the closest overall to these values, which also are the most useful starting point settings. For more information on calibration, see the chapter, "Calibration."

NEWSPAPERS AND OTHER CUSTOM SETTINGS

Our default values usually are good for most RGB output purposes including output to film recorders and also for CMYK separations to coated stock. If they are not working for you, use this process to change them. Newspaper presses tend to vary much more than web or sheet-fed presses for coated stock. If you are doing output for newspapers or some other special process, first get a set of correct values for printing neutral colors from your press person. It should look like the preceding table, but with different numbers. For newspapers, start out with Printing Inks set to SWOP Newsprint with a Dot Gain of 30%. Set the Separation Setup to GCR; Black Generation, Medium; Black Ink Limit, 100%; and Total Ink Limit, 300%. Set the highlight (5, 3, 3, 0) and shadow (95, 85, 83, 95) preference values in Levels initially as we have recommended for coated stock. If you want to change your coated stock settings, start with our recommendations earlier in this chapter and then use this same process to adjust them.

Bring up the StepWedgeFile, which starts out as a grayscale, and convert it to RGB. Click with the Highlight Eyedropper to set the highlight (using Levels as described in the Grand Canyon chapter) on the 2% gray wedge and set the shadow at the 98% wedge. For Newspapers, use the 5% and 95% wedges for Highlight and Shadow Eyedropper clicks. Bring up the Info palette and measure the RGB and CMYK values you get at different density areas along your stepwedge. Compare the CMYK numbers with the ones you got from your press person. Change the Dot Gain and Gray Balance settings in Printing Inks Setup and the Black Ink Limit and Total Ink limit settings in Separation Setup until you get values that are as close as possible to those your press person gave you. You can also change the Black curve between Light, Medium, and Heavy in Separation Setup as well as create a custom Black curve. Separation Setup doesn't give you direct control over the Cyan, Magenta, or Yellow curves, but you can affect them via changes you make to the Black curve. You can adjust the weight relationship between cyan, magenta, yellow, and black by using the Gray Balance settings in Printing Inks Setup.

A standard grayscale stepwedge file. We use this with the Eyedropper and the Info palette to measure what Photoshop actually does when making a separation. As you make changes in the Monitor Setup, Printing Inks Setup, and Separation Setup, as well as to how you set your highlights and shadows, you can see how those changes affect the separations by measuring this stepwedge using the Eyedropper. You can find this StepWedgeFile in the Calibration folder on the CD.

You will have to play with all these settings until you get a feeling for the relationship they have with each other. The settings we have recommended for coated stock have worked quite well in producing this book and for other projects that I have done. We don't recommend particular settings for newspapers since they tend to vary from paper to paper. For more help with newspapers, you might want to visit the *Mac Newspaper News* Web site. *Mac Newspaper News* is a monthly electronic newsletter pertaining to Macs and newspaper publishing. The Web site is just now being set up as this converts from a printed newsletter to an electronic one. The co-editors are Michael Kienitz and Ken Miller, and you can get the site address by contacting them at photo4u@aol.com. For more information on output to black-and-white halftones, you should get *Photoshop in Black-and-White: An Illustrated Guide to Producing Black-and-White Images with Adobe Photoshop Version 4.0* by Jim Rich and Sandy Bozek from PeachPit press.

Using the Separation Tables preferences settings, you can also load a custom table by clicking on the Load button. This custom table would decide for you how to convert from RGB to CMYK. When you load a custom table, you should select Use Table in both To CMYK and From CMYK. There are companies that sell custom separation tables for Photoshop. If you have another color separation system that you would like to import into Photoshop, like from Scitex or some other high-end system,

Adobe has a technical note called **SEP TABLES FROM OTHER APPS** which explains how to use Load Separation Tables to do exactly that. You can find this very useful technical note on the Photoshop 3.0 Deluxe CD-ROM in the Photoshop Tech Notes folder in the Technical Library folder. Anyone responsible for color separations should read this technical note. I have not found it on the Photoshop 4 CD set, but the technique should still work the same with Photoshop 4.

You should read the "Reproducing Color" chapter (Chapter 5) in the *Adobe Photoshop 4.0 User Guide*. It has some useful information about building color separation tables. It also talks about using the Apple ColorSync Manager on the Mac or the Kodak ICC Color Management modules for Windows to build separation tables based on custom profiles for different presses, digital printers, or proofing systems. This is a process where you first print a standard set of gray swatches and then measure them with a spectrophotometer to characterize densities on your printing device. You then use this information to create a standard color swatch test, which you also print and measure. These measurements allow ColorSync, or the Kodak system, to create an exact characterization of how density and color behaves on your device. These systems can then create custom color separations that promise to be the best possible for that particular device. I looked into doing this type of calibration and color separation in printing this book. The printer had not used this system before and neither had I. We were both very interested in trying it, but decided, because we have achieved excellent results so far without it, to wait for a smaller project to test the process (one where we have more control and less at risk than when doing direct-to-plate for a 350-page full-color book). I believe that ultimately this type of ColorSync exact calibration system will yield much better results with much less effort at the actual press or at a digital printer.

FILE FORMATS AND IMAGE COMPRESSION

When and how to use each of the important
file formats, and understanding Photoshop, TIFF,
and JPEG image compression.

OVERVIEW OF FILE FORMAT ISSUES

OPENING AND SAVING FILES

When you read a file into Photoshop, no matter what format it was in when you read it, the file will be in Photoshop's built-in format while you are working on it. Photoshop creates a temporary work file in memory and also, depending on the size of the file you are working with, in the free space remaining on your disk. Photoshop doesn't touch the original file that you opened on the disk until you do a File/Save. As you work on a project in Photoshop, it's a good idea to save often. Every time you have done enough work since your last save that you would be upset if your computer crashed and you lost that work, you should do another save. When you choose File/Save (Command-S) to save the file, Photoshop overwrites your original file on the disk. If you have just had a file scanned, or if you want to save the original before you change it in Photoshop, you should choose File/Save As to save the file you are about to modify with a different name. This leaves your original file unchanged. When you do a Save As, the name of your window changes from the your original file name to the new name you used when you did the Save As. Doing another Save later overwrites the file with the new name.

PHOTOSHOP 4 VERSUS OTHER FORMATS

While you are working on a project, you should normally save in Photoshop 4 format (just called Photoshop in the Save dialog box). When you first open a file in Photoshop, the first Save saves the file using the same format in which you opened it. If you open it as a TIFF, for example, Photoshop saves it as a TIFF. If you open it as a JPEG, Photoshop saves it as a JPEG. The first time you save the file, use Save As and change the format to Photoshop. Using Photoshop format makes Photoshop operate more efficiently because it's Photoshop's internal format and it supports everything that Photoshop can do, including layers, adjustment layers, channels, and paths. None of the other file formats support all of these features. You especially should avoid resaving JPEG files over and over again because every time you save a JPEG file it loses some information; more about this later in this chapter. If you open a file in TIFF format and add a channel to it, Photoshop still saves it in TIFF format because TIFF supports extra channels. If you were to add a layer to the same file, however, Photoshop would save it in Photoshop format because TIFF doesn't support layers. If the format changes automatically to Photoshop, it means you added a feature to the file that the format you were working with before doesn't support.

DIFFERENCES BETWEEN FILE FORMATS

What are the differences between file formats? After you open the file in Photoshop, it always resides there in Photoshop's own internal format. Saving the file into a different format is sort of like translating a book into a different language. In most cases, the raw data for the different formats is exactly the same; only how the data is stored or what additional information can go with the data changes. For example, an RGB file in format A may have all the red bytes stored together, then all the greens, and then all the blues. In format B, the storage might be a red, green, and blue byte for pixel 1, then a red, green, and blue byte for pixel 2, and so on. Some formats may use a simple type of compression called run length encoding, a lossless compression where, if there are say 50 bytes in a row that are exactly the same, these 50 bytes are stored using a special code so they take up only 4 bytes. Another format may specify a space at the beginning of the file where extra information can be stored. The EPS file format, for example, allows you to store clipping paths, preview picts, screen angles, and transfer function information within the file. In all these cases, the RGB or CMYK information in the file format remains the same. Only the packaging of the information changes from one format to another. If you save the file as a JPEG, this format does a "lossy" data compression. The lossy compression allows this format to save the file in much less space than in other formats. The lossy part means that when you read the file back in, or decompress the file, it will be the same size you started with but the actual data won't be identical. You need to be careful when using lossy compression not to lose important image data. We talk about this in the second part of this chapter.

INFORMATION ABOUT EACH FORMAT

Now let's discuss each of the formats that most of you will be using and when using that format might be best. The file formats you will probably use most often with Photoshop are Photoshop 4, Photoshop 3, Photoshop 2.5, and Photoshop 2, and TIFF, EPS, JPEG, GIF89, PICT, and Scitex CT. Photoshop supports other file formats too, but these here are the ones we recommend for the type of work you will be doing. If you need to know about some other format, the Photoshop 4 manual discusses all the formats that Photoshop supports.

PHOTOSHOP 4, 3, AND 2.0

When you are continuing to work on the same file in Photoshop between shutdowns of your computer, you should usually be working on that file in Photoshop 4 format (just called Photoshop in the version 4 Save dialog boxes). It's the only format that supports all of Photoshop 4's features, such as adjustment layers, guides, and grids. If you need to exchange files with others that are using Photoshop 3 or 2.5, you can make sure every Photoshopper can open this file by saving it in Photoshop 2.0 format. Photoshop 2.0 and 2.5 formats do not support Layers. Photoshop 3 format (which you get automatically by saving from Photoshop 3) does not support adjustment layers or guides and grids but it does support regular layers, layer masks, and channels. Photoshop 4 can open any Photoshop 3, 2.5, or earlier format, but Photoshop 3 cannot read adjustment layers or guides and grids in a Photoshop 4 file and if you resave this file in Photoshop 3 format, from Photoshop 3, these features are stripped from the file. If you are working with Photoshop 4 and you have the 2.5 Format Compatibility option set from File/Preferences/Saving Files, then people using Photoshop 2.5 can open your layered files and see a composite of the layers for which the Eye icons were on when you saved the Photoshop 4 file. If the file has multiple layers, those users can't modify the file's different layers and the cost of this 2.5 compatibility is an extra RGB layer the size of your Photoshop 4 canvas. You can save a lot of disk space by turning off the 2.5 Format Compatibility option. Most page layout applications and many other programs can't read any Photoshop format. Some applications can read Photoshop 2.5 format but not the newer Photoshop formats; the main purpose for the 2.5 option is the capability to open files into those applications.

Photoshop file formats do some compression, especially on mask channels. Consequently, files saved in Photoshop format are smaller than their corresponding TIFF files, especially those that have a lot of mask channels. Photoshop 4 does a great job of compressing simple masks; they are often in the same size ratio as JPEG. The RGB and CMYK components of Photoshop files are also compressed, although this compression does not make the file much smaller unless large areas in the file have the same color. The advantage of using Photoshop 4 format to compress is that it's a fast lossless compression.

TIFF

It seems like the most common file format that popular imaging applications support is TIFF. You can save both RGB and CMYK files in TIFF format and TIFF is supported on both the Mac and the PC. I often save grayscale and RGB files in TIFF format so I can go back and forth between Photoshop and Quark. TIFF format will also saves your mask channels. If you want to save a TIFF file but not the mask channels, use File/Save a Copy and choose the Don't Include Alpha Channels option.

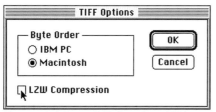

The normal choices available for saving a TIFF image. To save TIFF without the mask channels, use File/Save a Copy and choose Don't Include Alpha Channels.

When working on the Mac, you should set the byte order to Macintosh. If you set the byte order to IBM PC, both Photoshop and Quark on the Mac can still open the TIFF file. Some applications on the PC probably can't open the Mac byte order TIFF files.

The TIFF dialog box lets you choose LZW compression. LZW compression is a standard TIFF form of compression that typically takes longer to open and close than JPEG or Photoshop compression. TIFF LZW compression is a lossless compression. When you use LZW, you usually get a file that falls somewhere between ⅓ to ⅔ as large as the original, depending on the image details in the original. Some applications that use TIFF files do not support LZW-compressed TIFF. If you run into problems, resave your TIFF file without compression.

ENCAPSULATED POSTSCRIPT (EPS)

Victorians.eps

Victorians.C

Victorians.M

Victorians.Y

Victorians.K

The EPS.DCS option with 72 dpi preview gives you five files. The Cyan, Magenta, Yellow, and Black files need to be in the same folder as your Quark document when you send the job to the imagesetter. The eps preview file is used for placing and cropping in Quark.

The EPS format, now called Photoshop EPS, is the most versatile format. It's especially useful for communicating back and forth between Photoshop, Illustrator, and Quark. If you want to save a clipping path from Photoshop, you need to use the EPS format. The Path you choose will show up in the Clipping Path section of the EPS Format dialog box. For more information on saving paths from Photoshop to Quark and Illustrator, see the chapters, "Bike Ride in the Sky!" and "Bob Goes to… ."

After converting your file into CMYK using the Mode menu, you can save it into EPS format in several ways. If you leave the DCS (Desktop Color Separation) option off, all four components of your CMYK file stay together. Placing just the one CMYK file directly into Quark is less error prone, although it does create very large Quark files, because the same file that is placed is printed. The DCS option divides your EPS file into five smaller files; one file each for cyan, magenta, yellow, and black, and one preview file. Before you save any file for final output, make sure the dots per inch (dpi) setting is correct for that final output. For a 150 line screen, for example, the setting should be 300 dpi. If you set the dpi properly, the fifth preview PICT usually is smaller than the other four files and can read very quickly into Quark. Be aware, however, that all five of the files must be in the folder with the Quark document for the image to print correctly.

The big advantage of EPS/DCS is that you need to transfer only the preview PICT over the network (or, on removable media, to the desk of the person placing and cropping the pictures in the page layout application). It's much faster than transferring the entire CMYK file, which you would have to do with EPS composite or TIFF format. The tricky thing about EPS/DCS is that you need to be sure to include the other four CMYK files in the same folder as your Quark document and preview file when you print your layout to the image-setter; otherwise, you get a low-quality printout. Again, you should discuss this file format choice with your service bureau. Also, the Photoshop manual offers more information about the EPS file format.

The choices available for saving an EPS image. Here we show you the recommended Mac settings for EPS/DCS five file format. If you have chosen a clipping path, it should show up here. Leaving the flatness blank uses the printer's default setting for flatness. Don't check Include Halftone Screens or Transfer Functions unless you are setting these things in Photoshop. Discuss all of these settings with your service bureau before you send them any files.

GIF AND GIF89

The GIF format is used most often for images intended for use on the World Wide Web. The GIF format is a lossless compression format for images of up to 8-bit color. Photoshop can create GIF files from the Save dialog boxes if the file is in bitmap, grayscale, or index color format. Using File/Export/Gif89, you can create GIF format files from RGB Photoshop documents that have layers and transparent regions with much more flexibility and control. The GIF file format is discussed in great detail in "Images for the Web and Multimedia."

PICT

PICT format is an Apple standard file format supported by automatic compression and decompression in QuickTime. I have found this format to cause some problems when placed in Quark documents and don't recommend it for that purpose. It is, however, a commonly used multimedia format, as well as the format that is used by the system between applications when you copy an image from one and paste it into another. When you save in PICT format, the QuickTime compression you automatically get is lossless, but if you choose one of the JPEG options, you get a compression that isn't lossless—so beware.

SCITEX CT

Scitex CT format is sometimes used when saving CMYK files that will be processed on a Scitex imaging system. Again, your service bureau will tell you if you need to save in this format.

DISK SPACE AND COMPRESSION FORMATS

In today's world of color page creation, disk space is a commodity that can be used up quite quickly. Color photographs for print are the items that take up the most disk space. For the best quality, a color photograph has to be scanned at twice the dots per inch (dpi) as the line screen it will be printed. For a 5x7 color image in a 150 line screen publication, the required disk space would be: *(5x300) x (7x300) x 3 = 9,450,000 bytes for the RGB version of the file* (over 9 megabytes for just

After converting the Low JPEG compressed image to Lab color mode and looking at the A channel, you can see how JPEG compression breaks the image up into square areas and then tries to optimize each of these areas by representing it with fewer color and tone variations.

one copy of the file). Usually, by the time you finish production, you may need two or three copies of each file. That could be 30 megabytes of storage for just one 5x7 photograph. You might want to consider using compression to reduce the size of your image files. You also use compression for sending files to a client or printer electronically and in placing images on Web pages. To find out more about GIF and JPEG compression for Web and multimedia use, please refer to "Images for the Web and Multimedia."

LZW COMPRESSION

When you save a file in TIFF format from Adobe Photoshop, you can choose LZW compression. It saves the 9Mb uncompressed Victorians file in 5.5Mb. When you look at the amount of time LZW compression takes versus the minimum space savings you get, LZW compression often isn't worth the effort.

JPEG COMPRESSION

Using the Joint Photographic Experts Group (JPEG) compression software built into Photoshop with the quality setting on High, the 9Mb Victorians file was compressed to 640K. You can see a real savings in data space here—the compressed file is about 1/15 the size of the original! When you use JPEG compression, you can choose how much you want to compress a file. Using more compression gives you a smaller file but also more loss of image detail. A smaller amount of compression gives you less loss of image detail but the compressed file doesn't save as much disk space. Depending on your publication quality requirements, you can choose a compression factor that compresses files without any visible detail loss on the final printed page.

The uncompressed TIFF version of the Victorians image; 9 megabytes saved as TIFF and 6.5 megabytes saved in Photoshop format.

JPEG is an industry standard file format for image compression. Many companies sell JPEG software and hardware compression products. The hardware compression boards which contain DSP chips can compress and decompress images much faster than they could without the DSP. DSP stands for Digital Signal Processor, which is a chip that speeds up the mathematical operations used in many image processing filters and effects, including JPEG compression and decompression.

CHOOSING A COMPRESSION FACTOR

To show you the kinds of problems to look for when choosing your compression factor with JPEG compression, we have printed the same file with different degrees of compression. For printing on coated stock or for art prints, we would recommend not compressing your file at all unless you need to. If you do need to save space, use the Maximum Quality setting when possible, because it gives you the best image quality. If you can't see any data loss in your final printed image, then the loss may not be

The JPEG high compressed version of the Victorians image. This file is 640K.

important to you. On the other hand, if you archive a digital file for use in future printed pieces, slide productions, or multimedia presentations, you need to be sure that compression data loss won't show up in one of those future applications.

Another JPEG compression issue is that compressed files take longer to open and process when printing at the service bureau. Before you compress, talk to your service bureau about whether to use JPEG compressed files. Unless the service bureau owns a Level 2 PostScript imagesetter, they cannot download JPEG files directly. They have to re-open the file in Photoshop and save it to another uncompressed format. They may charge you more for JPEG compressed files if it will take them longer to process them on output. Other lossless compression options are DiskDoubler and StuffIt. Again, you should discuss these options with your service bureau before choosing one of them.

The original Victorians, 9Mb TIFF, uncompressed, is on the top left. Below that is the JPEG compression set to the maximum image quality, 1.2Mb. On the bottom right is the medium quality setting, 352K. Finally, on the top right you see the low-quality setting, 256K. All these JPEG compressions, except for the low quality, will work for printing. For printing, I would usually use the high or maximum quality to be safe, or better yet, not compress at all unless you really must. The Medium quality is good for sending a comp to a client over the Net, and for creating Web images. Avoid using the low setting. These files were compressed with the Baseline Optimized setting on in the JPEG dialog box, which should create higher color quality.

USING THE *PHOTOSHOP 4 ARTISTRY* CD

Using the Photoshop 4 Artistry CD *to create the examples in this book; choosing the right CD images to use for Macintosh or PC and for high-end or small workstations; and using these images in a classroom.*

The *Photoshop 4 Artistry CD* that comes with this book contains all the images for doing the examples in the book yourself. You can use this as a self-paced course or you can use it to teach a course at the college or professional level. When you put the CD in a Mac CD player, it will come up with the name *Photoshop 4 Artistry CD*, and it will look like a Macintosh directory with folders, files, and icons, as well as file names that are often longer than eight characters.

When you put the *Photoshop 4 Artistry CD* in a Windows machine, you will see a Windows directory named *Photoshop 4 Artistry CD* that contains files that have the same file names as in the Mac directory and the appropriate three-character suffixes that the PC requires.

WHAT'S ON THE CD

The directory on the *Photoshop 4 Artistry CD* opens up to show you a folder for each chapter that is a hands-on exercise. It also contains folders with files and images that you can use to enhance your knowledge about some of the overview chapters. Green folders are for hands-on exercises and blue folders are for overview sections. The folders are numbered in the order you should follow if you use this book as a self-paced course.

Each hands-on chapter's folder contains the images and other information you will need to complete that hands-on exercise and a folder called Extra Info Files. Extra Info Files contains the authors' intermediary and final versions of the images for that exercise, as well as masks, levels, and curves settings and other pieces of information that will help you compare your results to the authors'. We have tried to make the images printed in this book look as much like those on the CD as possible. The digital files on the disc, however, are more accurate comparisons of the progress that happens on each creation. To get the best

- 1.Automating with Actions
- 2.Photoshop Preferences
- 3.Tool Palette
- 4.Layers&LayerMasks
- 5.Calibration & Output
- 6.The Grand Canyon
- 7.Kansas
- 8.Burnley Graveyard
- 9.The Car
- 10.Grand Canyon Final Tweaks
- 11.Kansas Final Tweaks
- 12.Yellow Flowers
- 13.Buckminster Fuller
- 14.Color Matching Cars
- 15.Color Correcting Al
- 16.Bryce Stone Woman
- 17.Bob Goes To
- 18.Bob & Kestrel
- 19.Versailles
- 20.The Band
- 21.McNamaras
- 22.Night Cab Ride
- 23.Blend Modes Cals & Apl Im
- 24.Bike Ride in the Sky
- 25.Posterize Bitmaps & Patterns
- 26.Filters and Effects
- 27.APDA Magazine Cover
- 28.Creating Shadows

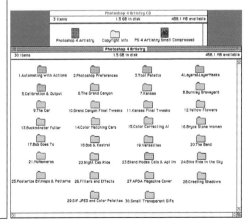

When you insert your *Photoshop 4 Artistry CD* on the Mac or Windows systems, the Photoshop 4 Artistry folder contains the best set of Photoshop 4 format images for doing the book's exercises. The PS 4 Artistry Small Compressed folder contains smaller versions of the images. Each hands-on chapter has a green folder that contains the before and after files, masks, and so on, necessary for completing that chapter. For each overview chapter, there is a blue folder, if that chapter has images or files that can add to the user's understanding. When you insert the CD on a Windows machine, you will see the directories and subdirectories shown above left.

results when viewing any of the CD files, you might want to calibrate your monitor to our course files as explained in "Calibration."

To Teach a Course

We certainly hope that other instructors will use this book to teach Photoshop courses around the world. Since 1990, Barry has been using these examples to teach many Photoshop courses at the University of California Santa Cruz Extension, the Photoshop Conference, the Palm Beach Photographic Workshops in Florida, Ad Vantage Computers in Des Moines, and many other places around the country, including the famous but now defunct Center for Creative Imaging in Maine. Having a professional course where the students can take home the images and exercises to practice them again later has been a main factor in making Barry's Photoshop courses so well received. We hope that you can take advantage of his years developing these exercises by using this book as the text for your Photoshop courses.

If each student purchases the book, they will have copies of all the images and step-by-step exercises for each example. The main images on the CD, in the Photoshop 4 Artistry folder, along with the extra info files, are in Photoshop 4 format and take up about 470 megabytes of information. Most images open to about 4 megabytes in size and can grow as the exercise progresses. For a professional course, I have discovered that using images large enough to see the kinds of details students will be working with when they are doing real projects for their art, magazines, film output, and publications works best. These 4Mb Photoshop files from the Photoshop 4 Artistry folder are the easiest to use and give the students the most information for doing the course. If your course machines each have CD players, each student should access the images directly from his or her own CD within the Photoshop 4 Artistry folder.

If you plan to use *Photoshop 4 Artistry* to teach a class, please contact the authors at MaxArt.com to find out about school discounts and also to get complete information regarding purchase and distribution of books and images.

Using the Small Compressed Images

If you are working on Macs other than Quadras or PowerPCs, or on Windows systems that are less powerful (especially if they have little memory or small hard disks), you may want to use the PS 4 Artistry Small Compressed images set. This is a second set of smaller images, about 145 megabytes, that comes on the CD and fits on two Zip disks or one of the larger 200+ megabyte Bernoulli or Syquest disks. These images open up to about one megabyte in size instead of four megabytes in size. These are more usable on less powerful computers. They don't, however, show as much detail as the standard *Photoshop 4 Artistry* images, which we recommend for users who have more powerful computers.

Because they don't show as much detail, use the PS 4 Artistry Small Compressed images only if you have an older, less powerful Mac or PC with little memory and/or a small hard disk. If you have a Mac Quadra 650, 700, 900, 950, or faster or any Power PC, with at least 32 megabytes of memory and at least 200 megabytes of free disk space, you should use the standard *Photoshop 4 Artistry* images. If you have a Mac IIx or IIci or Performa or other older, slower Mac that is not accelerated and also has little memory or free disk space, then you should be using the Photoshop 4 Artistry Small Compressed images. The total set of these small compressed images takes up about 145 megabytes of disk space so they are also easier

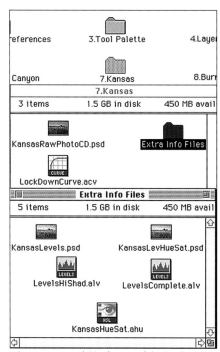

When you open a folder for one of the hands-on sessions, it contains the images and other files you need for completing the exercise. The Extra Info Files folder will contain things like the intermediate and final versions of the images and masks for that exercise, as well as levels and other settings we used along the way. You can compare these with your results if you have any questions about the way you are doing the exercise.

to distribute over a computer network. If you have a less powerful PC, you can also use the PS 4 Artistry Small Compressed images.

USING THESE IMAGES WITHOUT A COPY OF THE BOOK

We do not mind if teaching institutions or individual users use a copy of the *Photoshop 4 Artistry* images from their hard disk or over a network, as long as they have a copy of the *Photoshop 4 Artistry* book. Each person or student who uses these images to learn about Photoshop should have a copy of the book. If a school, company, institution, or person gives out copies of these images to any person who has not purchased the book, that's copyright infringement. If a school, company, institution, or person copies the step-by-step instructions or copies paraphrased step-by-step instructions and hands either of those out in class, especially when using them with the *Photoshop 4 Artistry* images, that too is copyright infringement. Please don't do this! Thanks.

THE TOOL PALETTE

An explanation of each tool in the Tool palette with tips for usage and discussions of helpful, hidden features. General information about selections, cropping, painting tools, and other good stuff!

This is not an exhaustive tour of every tool, all its possibilities and applications. Several other very fine books, including the Photoshop manual, go into more detail. We try to give you all the information that you need for working with photographs. This is actually a lot of fun for us and we hope you enjoy and take some time to play with these tools. As you begin to discover how the tools work, you can apply them to the type of images you have been creating and, perhaps, begin to discover new creative impulses. Open the Ceramic-Fruit, MenInBoat and TheLeaf images in the Tool Palette folder on the CD and play with the Tool palette features as you work through this chapter.

All of the tools have changeable options you can access through the menu bar from Window/Show Options or by double-clicking on the tool itself. If you choose a tool by using its shortcut character, pressing Return brings up the Tool options for that tool. This lets you change a tool's options without moving the mouse from your work. Additionally, some of the tools can have different brush sizes, which are available through the Brushes palette (Window/Show Brushes or F12).

Holding down the Control key and clicking brings up a menu of useful options you can do with a particular tool. This is a very powerful feature since the items in this Control menu may actually come from several different regular menus in Photoshop and are chosen based on Photoshop's state when you click on Control. We point these out as you go through this chapter.

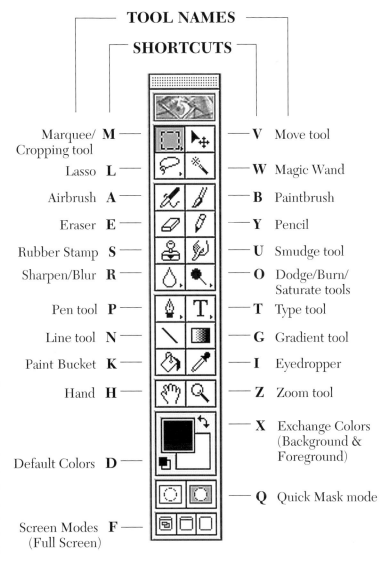

TOOL NAMES

SHORTCUTS

Marquee/ **M** — Cropping tool

Lasso **L**

Airbrush **A**

Eraser **E**

Rubber Stamp **S**

Sharpen/Blur **R**

Pen tool **P**

Line tool **N**

Paint Bucket **K**

Hand **H**

Default Colors **D**

Screen Modes **F** — (Full Screen)

V Move tool

W Magic Wand

B Paintbrush

Y Pencil

U Smudge tool

O Dodge/Burn/ Saturate tools

T Type tool

G Gradient tool

I Eyedropper

Z Zoom tool

X Exchange Colors (Background & Foreground)

Q Quick Mask mode

The Tool palette with corresponding keyboard commands. Copy this chart and paste it to the plastic side of your monitor for a quick reference.

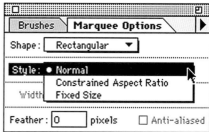

Styles available for Rectangular and Elliptical Marquees. Note that Anti-aliased is not available on rectangular because it is not needed on vertical and horizontal selection lines.

This is the menu that comes up when you Control-click and have no current selection loaded but you do have selections saved in mask channels.

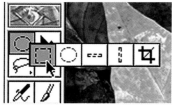

These are the tool choices available from the Marquee icon if you press down in the arrow at the lower right corner. This will currently select the Rectangular Marquee.

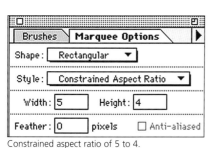

Constrained aspect ratio of 5 to 4.

To compute size of selection in pixels, multiply the width or height in inches times the number of pixels per inch of resolution in your image.

THE SELECTION TOOLS

The first three tools in the Tool palette concern making selections. In conjunction with items from the Selection menu and the Pen tool (which we discuss later) you can isolate portions of your image for editing.

MARQUEE TOOL

KEYBOARD SHORTCUT: Type the letter M, and if you type M again, the tool switches from rectangular to elliptical and back again.

You can use the Marquee tool to make rectangular or oval selections or to select a single row or single column of pixels. You can switch back and forth between these tools using Shape in the Options palette as well as set your selection to single row or single column.

CONSTRAINED ASPECT RATIO: The Style pop-up menu allows you to choose a constrained aspect ratio or a fixed size for either the rectangular or oval marquee. You would use a constrained aspect ratio if you were making a selection that you knew needed to have a 4x5 ratio, for example, or a 1 to 1 ratio for a perfect square or circle.

FIXED SIZE: A fixed size is useful when you know exactly the size in pixels of the print you want to make and want to crop to that size. Here, if you click down with the Marquee tool, you get a rectangular selection of the size that you specified. By keeping the mouse button down and moving the mouse, you can move the selection around the image to find exactly the crop you desire. Of course, you can also use this option simply to select and edit an area of a specific size.

FEATHER: The Feather option allows you to set the amount of blend on the edges of your selection. A larger feather radius will give you more of a vignette effect. The amount of feather is calculated in both directions from your selection border. For example, a 15-pixel feather measures both 15 pixels to the outside of your selection area and 15 pixels to the inside, giving you a total feather effect of 30 pixels. We rarely set a feather radius on our Marquee tool, preferring to make a selection and then use Select/Feather from the menu bar to set the feather. This way, we can change our radius if we are unhappy with the effect. Also, if you make a selection with the Rectangular Marquee and the feather is zero, you can later choose Image/Crop to crop to that selection. If you set the feather to a non-zero value, on the other hand, Image/Crop would be disabled.

ANTI-ALIASED: You may have noticed that the Elliptical Marquee has one other option, Anti-aliased. Anti-aliased subtly blends the edge of your selection with the surrounding area, so you usually want to leave it on. It's also available on the Lasso and Wand tools, but is grayed out on the Rectangular, Single Row, and Single Column tools. Keep Anti-aliased on when you want your selection edge to blend with the surrounding area. Making selections with Anti-aliased off gives you hard edges that are jagged on diagonal lines and curves.

MODIFIER KEYS: Holding down the Shift key while using either of these tools constrains your selection to 1 to 1; that is, you get a perfect square or a perfect circle. Make sure you release the mouse button before you release the Shift key. If, however, you already have a selection, the action is different. The Shift key causes Photoshop to add a new, unconstrained selection to your original selection.

Holding down the Option key while drawing forces the selection to draw from the center where you first click down. This can be extremely useful, as you will see in "Buckminster Fuller" later in this book.

Holding down the Shift and Option keys while dragging gives you a perfect circle or perfect square drawn from the center.

Be careful how you click in a file with an active selection. If you click inside the selection, you may inadvertently move the selection slightly. If you click outside the selection, you lose the selection.

If you press the Spacebar after starting a selection, you can move the selection while making it and then release the Spacebar again to continue to change the selection.

Some of the tools in the Tool palette have a little arrow in their bottom right corners. Clicking on it shows other tools that you can access from the same icon area. The Marquee area also houses the Cropping tool, Single Row and Single Column.

SINGLE ROW AND SINGLE COLUMN: Single Row and Single Column are just that. Single Row gives you a selection 1 pixel high all the way across your file, Single Column selects 1 pixel top to bottom. We rarely use these selection modes, but you can use them to draw straight lines or as a quick guide to make sure things are lined up. Generally, though, the Line tool is easier to use for both purposes. This option also is useful for selecting single row or column artifacts introduced by scanners or bad media and then cloning into the selected area.

LASSO & POLYGON LASSO TOOLS

KEYBOARD SHORTCUT: Type the letter L. If you type L again, the tool switches between the two Lasso tools.

You use the Lasso tool to make freehand selections. Although it's a little clunky to draw with a mouse, you'll find yourself using this tool a lot. You can always get a graphics tablet if you want to draw with a pen. Clicking and dragging gives you a line that follows the track of your mouse. After starting the selection, if you hold down the Option key and click, let go of the mouse button, then click in a new spot, you can draw with straight lines between mouse clicks. Continue clicking this way to make geometric shapes, or you can hold down the mouse button and draw freehand again. When you let go of the mouse and the Option key, a straight line will be drawn connecting the beginning and ending points of your selection, so be careful not to let go of the Option key until you finish your selection. Since the Option key in Photoshop 4 is now used for deleting from a selection, you have to press Option after starting the selection to get the straight line behavior. Version 4 also provides a Polygon Lasso tool that you get to by typing L, a toggle between the two tools. This tool draws

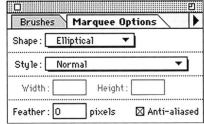

Anti-aliased is available as an option for the Elliptical Marquee.

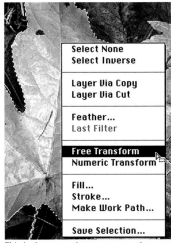

This is the menu that comes up when you Control-click when there is an existing selection.

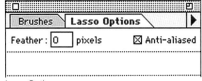

Lasso Options.

straight lines at every click, without using the Option key. In the Polygon Lasso tool, using the Option key after starting the selection enables you to draw in freehand. The Polygon Lasso tool requires you to click on the selection starting point again to complete a selection, as you also need to do in the Pen tool to complete a path. See the chapter, "The Car" for more information on how to use these Lasso features.

Magic Wand Tool

KEYBOARD SHORTCUT: Type the letter W.

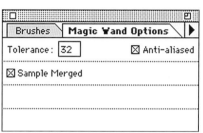

Magic Wand Options.

Whereas the Marquee and Lasso tools make selections based on physical proximity of pixels, the Magic Wand makes selections based on color values of adjacent pixels.

TOLERANCE SETTINGS: The tolerance that you set determines how close in value pixels must be before they can be selected. The lower the tolerance, the more similar the colors must be, and the higher the tolerance, the greater the range of colors.

SAMPLE MERGED: The Sample Merged option makes its selection based on a merged version of all the currently visible layers. Whether you want this option on or off depends on the type of image you are working with and the kind of selection you wish to make. If another layer affects the colors of the object you want to select, you probably want this option on. If all the colors you want to select are on only one layer, leave it off. But remember: Regardless of whether your selection is based on one layer or on merged layers, the edits that you make affect only the currently active layer.

THE GROW AND SIMILAR COMMANDS: The tolerance value that you set on the Magic Wand also affects which pixels you select when you use the Grow and Similar commands from the Select menu. The Grow command will select adjacent pixels that fall within this tolerance whereas the Similar command will select pixels throughout the entire image that fall within the tolerance range. You may also change the tolerance setting on the Magic Wand between uses of these two commands, to select a larger or smaller range of colors.

SELECTION TOOL TIPS

ADDING TO YOUR SELECTION: After you make a selection using any of these selection tools, you can hold down the Shift key and add to that selection.

SUBTRACTING FROM A SELECTION: If you hold down the Option key after you make your initial selection, you can take away portions of the selection. This is different than in previous versions of Photoshop, where the Command key subtracted from the selection. Confusing, isn't it?

MOVING A SELECTION MARQUEE: Once you have made a selection, you can move the selection marquee without affecting the underlying pixels by clicking and dragging within the selection. Previous versions of Photoshop used Command-Option click and drag.

MOVE TOOL

KEYBOARD SHORTCUT: Type the letter V or hold down the Command key.

You use the Move tool to move a selection or the contents of a layer. Click and drag on a selection or layer to move it to a new location within your document. You can also use the Move tool to drag and drop a layer from one document to another. If you are using any other tool, you can hold down the Command key to access the Move tool. The Pixel Doubling option in the Options palette makes moving selections move efficient.

CROPPING TOOL

KEYBOARD SHORTCUT: Type the letter C.

The Cropping tool is now a sub-tool of the Marquee and you can access it by typing a C or using the arrow pop-out menu at the bottom right of the Marquee icon area. Although we often use the Rectangular Marquee tool and the Image/Crop command to crop an image, the Cropping tool is more powerful and now easier to use in Photoshop 4. To use the Cropping tool, click and drag a box around the area you want to crop. Click and drag on one of the handles (little boxes in the selection corners and edges) to change the size of the crop area. To cancel the crop, hit the Escape key, and to accept the crop, hit Return or Enter.

MOVING AND ROTATING: Click in the middle of the selected area to move the crop boundary without changing its size. Click outside the crop box corners when you see the curved double arrow rotate icon and drag to rotate the crop boundary.

FIXED TARGET SIZE: With fixed target size on, click on the Front Image button in Cropping Tool Options to make the crop the exact dimensions and resolution of the currently active image, or you can set the width, height, and resolution of the crop manually. Whatever crop you make will be constrained to these proportions and it will be resampled to exactly these specs when you accept the crop by pressing Enter. Leave the resolution blank to maintain the specified aspect ratio. Photoshop resamples the file if necessary. For example, if you ask for your crop in inches, and the dimensions are larger than the area you selected, Photoshop lowers the resolution of the file after the crop but does not resample the crop area. However, if you ask for your crop in pixels and the crop is larger than the current file, it maintains the resolution of the image but adds pixels; in effect, it samples up the image. Make all entries blank, deselect Fixed Target Size, or choose Reset Tool from the Options triangle to restore the tool to normal, non-resampling cropping operation.

THE PAINTING TOOLS

The Pencil, Paintbrush, and Airbrush tools are the regular painting tools. The Rubber Stamp, Smudge, Blur/Sharpen, and Dodge/Burn/Sponge tools are more specialized painting tools. If you double-click on any of these tools or go to Window/Show Options, you get the specific options for that tool. Note also that the tool cursor options you set in your File/Preferences/Display and Cursors preferences control how your tool cursor appears. We use Brush Size for the Painting Cursors and Precise for the Other Cursors. Before we discuss each particular tool, we discuss the Brushes palette and some options that are pretty standard to all the tools.

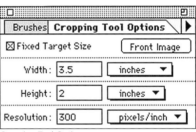

To access the Cropping tool from the Tool palette, press down the arrow at the lower right corner of the Marquee icon, then drag and choose the Cropping Tool icon. It is faster to just type a C.

Cropping Tool Options.

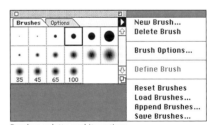

Brushes palette and its options.

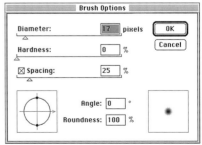

Double-clicking on any brush will take you to its Brush Options dialog box.

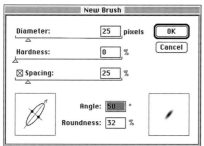

Custom brushes can be built using the New Brush option...

...or by defining a rectangular selection as a brush shape.

Lines drawn with the brush shape above and Spacing turned off.

THE BRUSHES PALETTE

All of the painting tools get their brush information from the Brushes palette. To see this window, choose Window/Show Brushes (F12 if you use ArtistKeys). The set of brushes is the same for all the tools except the Pencil tool, which has only hard-edged brushes. Each tool retains the brush and option set last used for that tool. You can add and save brushes or groups of brushes using the pop-up menu at the top right of the Brushes palette.

SETTING BRUSH OPTIONS: If you double-click on a particular brush, or an area where no brush is currently defined, you get the Brush Options window, in which you can change the diameter of the brush, up to 999 pixels, the hardness of the brush, and the spacing. When you set the hardness to 100%, you get very little or no blending between the color or image you are painting and the background. A hardness of 0 gives maximum blending with the background. Try the same large brush with different hardness settings to see how it can affect the stroke. The spacing affects how closely dabs of the paint tool are placed together on the screen (the default value for this is 25%, which causes a 75% overlap of each dab, so it looks like a continuous stroke). To learn about spacing, set it to 100% and then paint using the Paintbrush tool with a big, hard-edged brush. At 100%, the dabs will be tangent to each other on the canvas. Now try turning the spacing off (uncheck the Spacing box). With spacing off, the spacing is controlled by how fast you move the brush. Try it!

You can change the angle and roundness of the brush by typing in values in the dialog box or by using the handles and arrow on the brush definition area on the lower left of the palette. The lower right portion of the window illustrates what that brush will look like.

DEFINING A CUSTOM BRUSH: In addition, you can define a custom brush by drawing a rectangle around all or part of an image and pulling down the Brush Options to Define Brush. You can use a color or grayscale rectangular selection to define your brush, but the brush will appear as grayscale in your palette. Consequently, if your brushes are built in grayscale with a white background, your results will be more predictable. When you paint with any brush, it uses the density of the gray in the brush to determine the amount of foreground color to lay down. Once you have defined your custom brushes, you can use Save Brushes from the Brushes menu to give your new brushes distinctive names. You can save the brushes wherever you like, but if you've hit on something you think you're going to use again, save your brushes in the Photoshop folder inside the Goodies/Brushes and Patterns folder.

Photoshop includes several custom brush palettes inside this folder. You can load these palettes or any palette you create by using Load Brushes from the pull-down

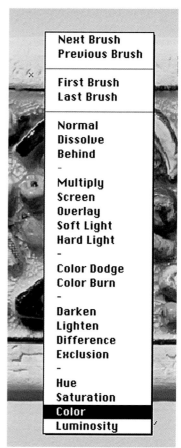

This is the type of menu that comes up when you Control-click while working with a painting tool.

options, or if you want to add those brushes to the current palette, choose Append Brushes. Reset Brushes restores the default Brushes palette.

The Options Palette

The following options work primarily the same way for all of the painting tools.

OPACITY: Note the painting mode and opacity settings at the top of the Options palette. The default painting mode is Normal and the default opacity is 100%. Try out the different painting modes and try painting with different opacities. You can change the opacity by typing in a number from 0–9 while using one of the brush tools. 1 = 10%, 2 = 20%...9 = 90%, and 0 = 100%. If you type two numbers quickly, like 25, you can set the opacity to that double digit percent. Also, please note that the tools do not all handle paint buildup the same way. The Pencil, Paintbrush, and Rubber Stamp tools paint only in strokes. That is, if you lay down a stroke of color or image at a certain opacity, holding down the mouse button and moving back over that stroke has no cumulative effect. You must release the mouse and paint a new stroke to build up the amount of paint. In contrast, the Smudge tool, Focus tools, and Toning tools add paint cumulatively. Holding down the mouse button and moving back and forth over a stroke increases the effect on each pass. Finally, the Airbrush and Blur tools produce a cumulative effect whether stationary or moving. Changes continue to be applied in the mouse location until you let go of the mouse button.

FADE: The Fade distance causes color painted with the tool to fade to transparent or the background color over the number of pixels you choose for the distance. If you leave the distance box empty—the normal setting—you get no fade-out.

STYLUS PRESSURE: You may vary the size, color, and opacity based on stylus pressure only if you have a graphics tablet instead of a mouse.

MODIFIER KEYS: If you hold down Shift when using any of the painting tools, you draw vertically or horizontally. Also, clicking once with the tool, letting go of the mouse button, and then Shift-clicking somewhere else, draws a straight line between these two points with the current brush.

Pencil Tool

KEYBOARD SHORTCUT: Type the letter Y.

When you use the Pencil tool, the edges of your drawing are jagged because there is no anti-aliasing here. Use the Pencil when you want to be sure to get a solid color even on the edge of the painted area.

BRUSHES: Note that when you switch from an anti-aliased paint tool, such as the Paintbrush, to the Pencil tool, the brushes in the Brushes palette switch to hard edge brushes.

AUTO ERASE: The Auto Erase option replaces any pixels that are currently the foreground color with pixels of the background color. You usually want to leave this option off.

Airbrush Tool

KEYBOARD SHORTCUT: Type the letter A.

The Airbrush nib looks similar to the Paintbrush except that it continues to add density as you hold down the mouse button and go over the same area again and again. If you click the Airbrush down in one spot and continue to hold down the mouse button, paint continues to be applied until you reach 100% opacity. Instead of the opacity setting, this tool has a pressure setting that controls how fast the density

COOL BRUSH TIP: *While you are painting, you can change the size of the brush by using the right and left bracket symbols, [and], on the keyboard. Pressing the right bracket moves you to the next bigger brush and pressing the left bracket takes you to the next smaller brush. If you set General Preference Painting Tools to Brush Size, you can change the brush size even as the brush sits over the area you want to paint. You'll see when you've reached the right size. Pressing Shift-] takes you to the last brush and Shift-[to the first brush.*

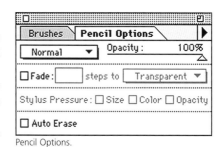

Pencil Options.

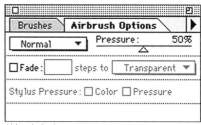

Airbrush Options.

increases. Using the Airbrush is like painting with an airbrush or a spraypaint can. For even more of a real airbrush effect, use the Brushes Options to set the spacing on your brush to 1 and then set the pressure to very, very low; about 5–10% or lower. You might also like the effect of turning the spacing off completely.

PAINTBRUSH TOOL

KEYBOARD SHORTCUT: Type the letter B.

The Paintbrush tool has anti-aliased edges that make the edge of where you paint blend more evenly with what you are painting over.

When painting with the Pencil or Paintbrush, the opacity setting from the Brushes palette will not be exceeded so long as you hold the mouse button down, even if you paint over the same area again and again.

WET EDGES: If you turn on this option, more color is laid down on the edges of your brushstroke. It's sort of a watercolor effect.

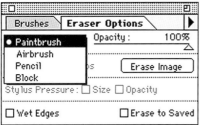

Paintbrush Options.

ERASER TOOL

KEYBOARD SHORTCUT: Type the letter E.

The Eraser tool erases to the background color in the background layer and to transparency in any other layer. The background color usually is white but can be any color. Erasing a layer to transparent allows you to see through the erased area to the layers below it. You can choose from four options for the type of eraser nib: Paintbrush, Airbrush, Pencil, and Block. The first three give you eraser nibs that act exactly like their painting tool counterparts in respect to style, so refer to the Paintbrush, Airbrush, and Pencil sections of this chapter, respectively. The Block option is most like the eraser from early versions of the program. It does not have anti-aliased edges and the size of the area you erase is determined not by brush size, but rather by the magnification of the image that you are working with. The higher the magnification, the smaller your erased area, until you reach the point that you are erasing individual pixels.

You usually use the Eraser tool when you want to completely remove something in a small area. If you hold down the Option key when erasing or click on the Erase to Saved option, you get the Magic Eraser, which erases back to the last saved version of the image. You also can click on the Erase Image option to erase your entire image—don't worry, you get a warning before the big zap! If you hold down the Option key and click on the Eraser icon, or if you continue to type the letter E, you cycle through the tool's painting options. The Stylus options work only if you have a graphics tablet attached instead of a mouse.

The four different erasers at 50% opacity.

RUBBER STAMP TOOL

KEYBOARD SHORTCUT: Type the letter S.

The Rubber Stamp tool is one of the most useful tools in Photoshop. It offers many different painting options. If you'd like to try some of the options that we show here, open the file MenInBoat in the Tool Palette folder on the CD.

CLONE (ALIGNED): Clone (aligned) is the option you will use most often. You use it to remove spots and scratches and also to copy part of an image from one place to another. To use it, pick a brush size from the Brushes palette then hold down the Option key and click at the location where you want to pick up the image (called the pickup location). Now, without holding down the Option key, click on the place where you want to clone the new information (called the putdown location). As long as you hold down the mouse, information copies from the pickup location to the putdown location. Both of these move correspondingly when you move the mouse. When you release the mouse button and then move it and click down again, the relative distance between the pickup location and the putdown location remains the same, but both move the offset distance that you move the mouse. Therefore, you can clone part of the image, stop for lunch, then come back and finish the job without worrying about misaligning your clone. This makes Clone (aligned) very good for removing spots. You can also clone from one image or one layer to another by Option-clicking in the pickup image or layer and then clicking down to clone in the putdown image or layer. See the chapter, "The Grand Canyon—Final Tweaks," for more information on removing spots and scratches with Clone (aligned).

CLONE (NON-ALIGNED): You would use Clone (non-aligned) to copy the same object into various places within the image. When you use this option, the pickup location remains the same when you move the mouse and click down in a new putdown location, which allows you to copy the same part of the image to multiple places within the image. When you want to change the pickup location, you need to Option-click again.

PATTERN (ALIGNED): Patterned cloning uses the current Photoshop pattern and copies it wherever you paint with the mouse. When different painting areas come up against each other, the patterns line up even if you have released the mouse button and started drawing more than once. This is the tool you want to use if you are painting wallpaper or some pattern that must match. To define a pattern, you select a rectangular area with the Rectangular Marquee and then choose Edit/Define Pattern. It

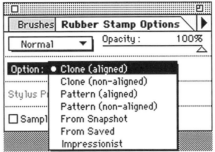

Rubber Stamp Options.

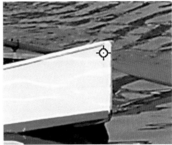

For Clone (aligned), Option-click at the pickup location...

then click with no Option key at the location where you want to put down the clone. Notice the + that shows you the current pick-up location.

With Clone (aligned) if you let go of the mouse and move to a new location, the Rubber Stamp remembers the original location of your Option-click and maintains the relative distance.

With Clone (non-aligned) if you let go of the mouse and move to a new location, the rubber stamp begins cloning again from the original location.

Select a rectangular area and then choose Edit/Define Pattern.

Pattern (aligned) clones the pattern in perfectly abutted regularity, even if you lift the mouse and begin a new clone.

Pattern (non-aligned) will clone over an existing pattern if you lift the mouse and begin a new clone.

A Snapshot taken after Filter/Stylize/Find Edges and Filter/Pixelate/Crystalize were applied.

File reverted to Saved and rubber stamped from the Snapshot in certain areas.

After more filtering, parts of the image Cloned from Saved at 30% opacity.

Impressionist rubber stamp over original file using a small brush and short strokes.

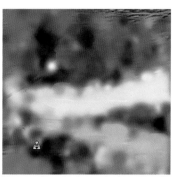

The same file using Impressionist mode with a large brush.

remains the current pattern until you define a new one.

PATTERN (NON-ALIGNED): Pattern (non-aligned) is the same as Pattern (aligned) except that the patterns do not necessarily match when different painting areas come up against each other. You would not want to use this option to paint wallpaper.

FROM SNAPSHOT: Clone From Snapshot allows you to clone from the last version of the file saved as a Snapshot. To use From Snapshot, you need to have previously used Edit/Take Snapshot. A Snapshot saves the current version of the image in a special buffer. Without using layers, you can therefore work with three versions of the image at the same time—the saved version, the snapshot version, and the current version—in your workspace. Cloning from the Snapshot is faster than cloning from the last saved version.

FROM SAVED: You can clone from the last version of the file that was saved, if you have not cropped the file since that last save. From Saved is very useful when compositing images and the need comes up to revert a small area back to the way it looked before a composite. You can also use it to remove mistakes made while using the other painting tools.

IMPRESSIONIST: This is not an option that we have used often, but it's fun to try some options if you have time. The Impressionist mode uses the brush size and hardness that you choose, as well as the direction and length of the strokes that you make to transform all or part of your image into a soft-focus Impressionist painting.

THE EDITING TOOLS

SMUDGE TOOL

KEYBOARD SHORTCUT: Type the letter U.

Open the file CeramicFruit from the CD to follow the next part of this chapter on the Tool palette. The Smudge tool turns your whole image into wet paint. You can click and drag to smear one color area into another. This blends the colors within the brush area, so the size of the blend depends on the size and softness of the brush you use. The pressure controls the amount of paint that mixes with each stroke and how far into the stroke the paint smears. At 100%, the color that you pick up will be laid down the whole length of the stroke. If you hold the Option key down when you start

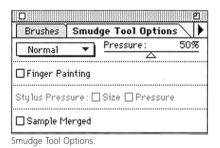

Smudge Tool Options.

Smudge tool in action.

Orange foreground color mixed with the image with Fingerpaint mode.

a paint stroke or click on the Fingerpaint mode, a dab of the foreground color mixes in with the rest of the colors being smudged.

BLUR/SHARPEN TOOLS

KEYBOARD SHORTCUT: Type the letter R. Type R again to toggle between Blur and Sharpen.

You can switch the Blur tool to a Sharpen tool by double-clicking on the tool and using the pop-up option menu. If you Option-click on the tool, it toggles between the Blur and Sharpen tools. You use the Blur tool to help blend jagged edges between two images being composited, as well as to remove the jaggies from a diagonal line, or just to soften selected parts of an image. You can use the Sharpen tool to locally sharpen an area without making a selection. Both tools work best when you try different levels of pressure (opacity) from the Options palette, and you should start out with a low pressure, as they can work quite quickly.

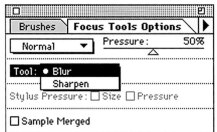

Blur and Sharpen tool options.

Blur tool after several applications.

Sharpen tool after several applications.

DODGE/BURN/SPONGE TOOLS

KEYBOARD SHORTCUT: Type the letter O. Type O again to toggle between the three options.

You can switch the Dodge tool to the Burn or Sponge tool by double-clicking on the tool and using the pop-up option menu. If you Option-click on the tool, it toggles between the Dodge, Burn, and Sponge tools. You use the Dodge tool when you want to make local areas of your image lighter, and the Burn tool to make local areas of your image darker. Both tools work best when you try different levels of

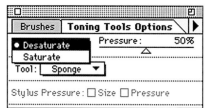

With the Sponge tool you can saturate or desaturate the colors.

The original image.

After dodging with the Dodge tool.

After burning with the Burn tool.

Several applications of the Saturate Sponge.

Several applications of the Desaturate Sponge.

exposure (opacity) from the Options palette. Start with a low value; about 30%.

When you use the Burn and Dodge tools, you need to specify the part of the image area you are working on. Set Highlights, Midtones, or Shadows depending on the part of the image you are dodging or burning.

We describe other techniques for dodging and burning, which we like better because they are more undoable and adjustable, in the chapters, "Buckminster Fuller," "Grand Canyon Final Tweaks," "Blend Modes, Calculations, and Apply Image,"and "Filters and Effects."

The Sponge tool allows you to saturate or desaturate the area you brush over. It is very useful for desaturating out-of-gamut colors (colors that you can see on-screen but are unprintable) to bring them back into gamut (printable colors).

TYPE AND TYPE MASK TOOLS

KEYBOARD SHORTCUT: Type the letter T. Type T again to toggle between the two type tools.

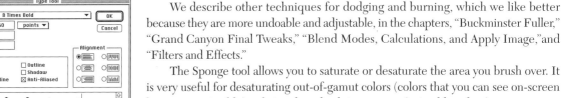

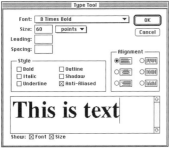

Type dialog box that appears after you click in your file with the Type tool.

When you use the Type tool, you enter text by clicking on the image in the location where you want to insert the text. Text looks better if you have Adobe Type Manager installed and the Anti-Aliased option on, except for very small type. Type is added to your image as a new layer with the type surrounded by transparency. The text comes in as the current foreground color at 100% opacity. You can access this new layer through the Layers palette, where you can modify the Opacity and the Paint mode. The Type Mask tool adds a selection of your type boundaries. For the highest resolution output and more control over type modifications, text often looks better if you add it using Illustrator or Quark. We show you how to do this in "Bike Ride in the Sky."

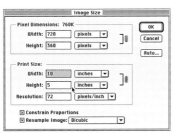

A 760K file at 72 ppi is 5 inches high.

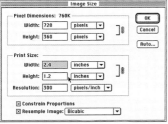

The same file at 300 ppi is 1.2 inches high.

FONT: Font is the name of the typeface that you will be using. Sometimes the name starts with a letter that categorizes the weight or cut of the font. In the example here, you select B Times Bold. If you're not used to dealing with typeface names, this can be confusing. Generally, you look for the name of the typeface, such as Times or Garamond, then select the weight of the face that you wish to use, such as light, book, bold, or italic. If you are using Adobe Type Reunion, the weights of each face are grouped together. If you are not using Type Reunion, all the bold fonts

Chapter 7: The Tool Palette

appear in the menu together prefaced by the letter B. All the italic fonts are grouped together prefaced by the letter I, and so forth.

SIZE: The size that text appears depends not only on the size you choose in the Type Tool dialog box, but also on the resolution and dimensions of the image you set using the Image/Image Size command. If you set the resolution to 72 ppi, Photoshop thinks the image is large, in this case, 5 inches high. 12 point type would look quite small in this file. If you change the resolution to 300 ppi without changing the file size, however, Photoshop then thinks that the image is 1.2 inches high. Your 12-point type will look considerably larger.

LEADING: Leading is the amount of vertical spacing between the baselines of the lines of text. A positive number gives you more space between the lines, and a negative number, less space. If you set type in all capitals, a negative number usually gives better spacing between the lines.

SPACING: Spacing refers to the horizontal letter spacing of the text. Use a larger number for more space between the letters. As in leading, a positive number gives you more space between the letters, spreading them out, and a negative number draws the letters tighter together.

STYLE: We rarely use any of the other type style options, preferring to use a typeface that renders as it is designed to render. If you use Bold or Italic (called machine styling), the type is merely fattened or slanted. It's not beautiful type, but you might find some useful effects.

ALIGNMENT: You can change the alignment of your text from flush left to flush right or centered, or even align the letters vertically.

SHOW FONT/SIZE: Click on either or both of these options if you want to see what the actual typeface looks like when rendered. Remember that size is relative.

PAINT BUCKET TOOL

KEYBOARD SHORTCUT: Type the letter K.

The Paint Bucket tool does the same thing as the Magic Wand, but it also fills the selection with the foreground color after the selection is made. We seldom use the Paint Bucket, preferring to make the selection first and then, once we have the right selection, use the Fill command from the Edit menu. The Fill command (Shift-Delete) also offers many more options than does the Paint Bucket. The Bucket is very useful, and faster than Fill, for colorizing black-and-white line drawings like cartoon drawings, animations, or solid color areas.

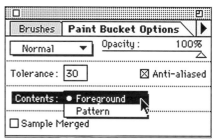

The Paint Bucket Options.

PAINTING MODES: We discuss the various painting modes in a later chapter, "Blend Modes, Calculations, and Apply Image."

OPACITY: Changes the opacity of the fill.

PATTERN: To access the Pattern option, you must first define a pattern. Use the Rectangular Marquee with no feather and choose a selection that you'd like to turn into a pattern. Now choose Edit/Define Pattern. You may define only one pattern at a time, so if you like to have lots of neat patterns available, you need to save these rectangular selections as separate files or together in one file.

SAMPLE MERGED: If you are using several layers, you can choose which layers you want the Paint Bucket to search for the color tolerance range. If you click on Sample Merged and have the Eye icon on in more than one layer, Photoshop samples the data in every layer currently visible. The Paint Bucket fills only the currently active layer.

Define Pattern in the Edit menu.

The TheLeaf file. Open this file if you want to play along with the Gradient tool. Now use Select/Load selection to load the Leaf Mask.

This file, called GrColOrPur, has an orange foreground and purple background. These are the colors we used to illustrate the Gradient tool. To use the same colors as you experiment, use the Eyedropper tool by itself to click on the orange square and set your foreground color, then hold down the Option key with the Eyedropper and click on the purple square to set your background color.

A blend across the selected area with the default setting...

gives a blend from foreground to background with 50% of each color at the midway point.

A blend that begins or ends before the selection boundaries...

will be 100% of the foreground color before the beginning of the blend and 100% of the background color after the blend line ends. When using the default settings, the midpoint, where color is 50% foreground and 50% background, will still be at the midway point.

Foreground to Background Color Only.

Foreground (Purple) to Transparent blend inside mask of the leaf.

Transparent to Foreground (Purple) blend inside mask of the leaf.

GRADIENT TOOL

KEYBOARD SHORTCUT: Type the letter G.

The basic function of the Gradient tool is to make a gradual blend in the selected area from one color to another color. A blend is accomplished by clicking and dragging a line the length and angle you want the blend to happen. The Gradient tool is often used in a mask channel to blend two images together seamlessly by making a blend from black to white. Black represents one image and white the other. We use the gradient tool for masking in "Bike Ride in the Sky," and "The Band." If you'd like

Chapter 7: The Tool Palette

to experiment with the tool, open the files TheLeaf and GrColOrPur from the Tool palette folder on the CD. You can use Select/Load Selection to load the Leaf Mask as a selection.

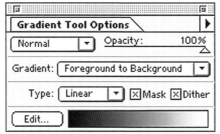
The Gradient tool default settings.

THE DEFAULT SETTINGS: When you set the Blend mode to Normal, the Type to Linear, and the Gradient to Foreground to Background, everything from the first click on the line to the edge of the selection will be solid foreground color. Everything from the mouse release to the other end of the selection will be solid background color. Along the line, there will be a blend from foreground to background color, and at a place 50% along the length of the line, the two colors will each be at 50% opacity.

BLEND MODES AND OPACITY: You can set the Blend mode and Opacity of the gradient you are about to create using these settings in the Gradient Options palette. We discuss the various blend modes in the chapter, "Blend Modes, Calculations, and Apply Image." However, you might want to try some of the modes, like Color, as you explore the Gradient tool.

THE DITHER OPTION: Leaving the Dither option on results in smoother blends with less banding. We recommend that you leave it on unless you want a banded and uneven gradient.

FOREGROUND TO TRANSPARENT/TRANSPARENT TO FOREGROUND: Use these Gradient options to blend the foreground color to transparent or vice versa.

RADIAL BLENDS: Setting the Type to Radial creates a radial blend done as a circle. If Gradient were set to Foreground to Background, the first click of the mouse will be the circle's center using the foreground color, the line length that you drag will be the circle's radius and the mouse release location will be at the outside edge of a blended circle using the background color.

THE GRADIENT EDITOR: Notice the different gradients in the Gradient pop-up menu within Gradient Options. Each of these was created by Adobe using the new Photoshop 4 Gradient Editor. To open the Gradient Editor, click on the Edit button in the Gradient Options palette. The Gradient Editor provides a list of the currently defined gradients. If you want to base your new gradient on an existing one, click on the name of the existing gradient and then click on the Duplicate button to make a copy of it. To create a new gradient from scratch, click on the New button and you'll get the default name Gradient 1, which you can rename if you like. To modify an existing gradient, just select it and start making changes. To rename or remove a gradient, select it and then click on Rename or Remove. You can also save and load gradient sets using the Load and Save buttons.

You can use the Adjust radio buttons to change either the color or transparency of a gradient. Here we see a gradient that has three colors, red to the left, purple in the middle, and green to the right. The bar below the Adjust choices, which is now colored, allows you to choose the colors of the gradient and where you want each color to appear along the gradient line that you draw. Each point below this color bar represents a different color. You can add a new point by clicking below the Color Bar and you can move this point by dragging from left to right. The Location box tells you the location of this color as a percentage of the length of the line you draw to create the gradient. You can set a point to a particular color by first clicking on that point and then

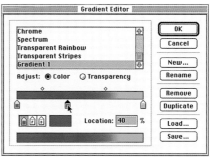
The Gradient Editor set up to adjust the color of the gradient. You access this by tying G to get to the Gradient tool, pressing Return to bring up the Gradient Tool Options palette, and then pressing the Edit button. Here the bottom transparency bar shows 100% opacity because we haven't edited the Transparency.

A gradient created with the Gradient 1 setting and Mask turned on.

A gradient created with the Gradient 1 setting and Mask turned off. There is no transparency here.

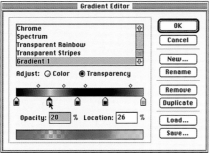

This is the Transparency mode where you move and change the the opacity of the points below the black-and-white bar to effect the opacity of the color preview at the bottom of the dialog. Here we have 5 different points and the one that is currently selected has an opacity of 20% and a location of 26%. Transparency is shown as the same checkerboard pattern used by transparent layers.

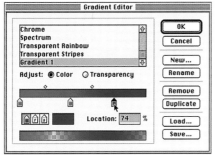

Here we are back in Adjust Color mode and we have changed the rightmost color point to the color blue and moved it from Location 100% to Location 74%. Notice that the Opacity bar at the bottom now shows the Transparency that you set up in the previous dialog box.

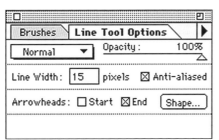

Line Tool Options with Arrowheads selected.

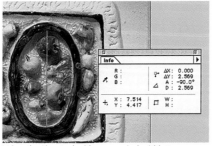

Using the Line tool with a zero pixel width to measure distance with the Info palette.

either clicking on the F point below and to the left to get the foreground color, the B point to get the background color, or in the color box below and to the left to bring up the Color Picker and pick a new color. The color point you are currently working on will have its triangle top highlighted in black. You can click on these points and drag them to any location along the length of the bar and the colors in the bar, and the transparency indicator below will change to show the effect of your movement. The little diamond points above the colored bar represent the halfway point between the color point below left and the color point below right of that diamond point. Click and drag on it to have the Location window show you the location relative to the percentage of distance between these two points. The default location of the diamonds is always 50% of this distance, but you can move them left and right.

If you click on the Transparency setting of the Adjust radio buttons, you can change the transparency of the gradient at each point along its length. You can turn off the transparency of any gradient by turning off the Mask check box on the Gradient Options palette. Try turning off Mask and then using the Foreground to Transparent option. You get just the solid foreground color. The bar that had color in it when you were adjusting the gradient colors now is black or white representing the opacity of the transparency. (Black represents 100% opacity and white represents 0% opacity.) The length of the bar again represents the length of the line you draw when making the gradient. You can place Opacity points anywhere along the bottom of the bar by clicking below the bar. When you click on a point, the top of it turns black, indicating that it is the point you are currently editing. The Location window will show you the location of this point relative to the total length of the line and the Opacity window shows you its opacity. You can see the effect of your changes in opacity by looking at the Opacity preview bar at the bottom of the dialog box. As when adjusting the gradient color, you can click above the Opacity bar to place diamonds that represent the midpoint between the opacity point to their left and the opacity point to their right. Bring the Gradient Editor up and play with it a bit and I believe it will become obvious how it works. I must admit that when I first saw this extension that it was not intuitively obvious how it worked. Hopefully, this description will get you along your way.

LINE TOOL

KEYBOARD SHORTCUT: Type the letter N.

The Line tool makes great anti-aliased lines in whatever thickness you specify. To make a line, you click where you want the line to start, drag, and then release where you want the line to end. You can also have arrows at the beginning or end of a line, and you can edit the width, length, and concavity of the arrows by clicking the Shape button. If you set the line width to 0 and turn off the arrows on both ends, you can use the Line tool, in conjunction with the measurements in the Info palette, as a ruler.

Eyedropper Tool

KEYBOARD SHORTCUT: Type the letter I.

You use the Eyedropper tool to choose the foreground and background color from within an image on-screen. You can click on the Eyedropper tool to use it and then click on the color that you want to make the foreground color. You can Option-click to get the background color. You can get to the Eyedropper tool by holding down the Option key when using any of the painting tools and then clicking where you want to pick up a new foreground color.

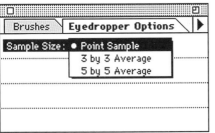

Eyedropper Options: Use Point Sample when choosing specific colors, 3 by 3 Average when color correcting.

This is the menu that comes up when you Control-click while using the Eyedropper tool.

AUTOMATIC EYE DROPPER: The Eyedropper tool automatically shows up whenever you are in Levels, Curves, Color Balance, or any of the color correction tools and you move the cursor over the image. This allows you to see the color values of any location in the Info and Color palettes while you are correcting and changing those values. As a preference setting, for this type of use with continuous tone images, you should double-click on the Eyedropper and set the sample size to 3 by 3 Average rather than the default Point Sample setting.

Hand Tool

KEYBOARD SHORTCUT: Type the letter H.

Use the Hand tool to scroll the image. Scrolling doesn't change your document; rather, it allows you to look at a different part of it. You can access the Hand tool more efficiently by using the Spacebar on the keyboard along with a mouse click. You can do that any time. If you double-click on the Hand tool in the Tool palette, the image resizes to the largest size that fits completely within the current screen and palette display.

Zoom Tool

KEYBOARD SHORTCUT: Type the letter Z.

Use the Zoom tool to magnify the image and, with the Option key, to shrink the image. The location where you click will be centered within the bigger or smaller image. Using this tool is like moving a photograph you are holding in your hand either closer to your face or farther away. The actual size of the photograph doesn't change, only how closely you are looking at it. It is best to access the Zoom tool using Command-Spacebar-click to zoom in closer, or Option-Spacebar-click to zoom out further. You can use these command keys any time, even when a dialog box, like Levels, is up. If you double-click on the Zoom tool within the Tool palette, the image zooms in or out to the 100% size. At 100%, the image may be bigger than the screen but you see every pixel of the part of the image you are viewing. Use this for detailed work. The Resize Windows to Fit option resizes your normal window to surround your zoomed size, if possible. I leave it off because I don't like my windows automatically resizing.

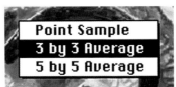

Arrow drawn using the options on the previous page.

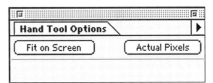

Hand Tool Options.

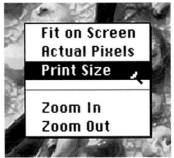

This is the menu that comes up when you Control-click when you are in the Zoom tool.

PICKING AND USING COLOR

*A look at RGB, CMYK, HSB, and LAB color spaces,
what they are, when to use each, and how to access them
from Photoshop; the Photoshop Color Picker and the
Picker, Swatches, and Scratch palettes explained in detail.*

There are different color spaces available in Photoshop that you can use for different purposes at different times. Instead of just working in one color space, like RGB or CMYK, it is a good idea to learn the advantages and disadvantages of the different spaces. There are various tools in Photoshop for picking and saving colors. We talk about these issues in this chapter. The rest of the book assumes that you are familiar with these tools and issues.

THE RGB COLOR SPACE

For overall color correction and ease of work, using the Red, Green, Blue (RGB) color space offers many advantages. I recommend keeping your final master files in RGB format. Red, green, and blue are the additive colors of light that occur in nature. White light consists of wavelengths from the red, green, and blue spectrums. All scanners, even high-end drum scanners, actually have sensors that originally capture the data in RGB format. You can use RGB for final output to computers, multimedia and TV monitors, color transparency writers, digital video, Web sites, and some digital printers because these are all native RGB devices. RGB files are smaller than CMYK files because they have only three components of color instead of four.

THE CMYK COLOR SPACE

Cyan, magenta, and yellow are the complementary colors to red, green, and blue. Red and cyan are opposites, so if you take away all the red from white light, cyan is what you have left. Cyan is formed by mixing green and blue light. Green and magenta, as well as blue and yellow, work similarly; that is, they are complementary colors. When you print on a printing press, the colors of ink used are cyan, magenta, and yellow. These are called subtractive colors, because when you view something that is printed, you actually see the light that is reflected back. When white light, which contains all the colors, hits a surface painted cyan, you see cyan because the cyan paint subtracts the red from the white light and only green and blue reflect back for you to see. To print red using CMY inks, you use magenta and yellow inks. Magenta subtracts the green light and yellow subtracts the blue light so what reflects back to your eyes is red light. The cyan, magenta, and yellow dyes that make up printing inks are not pure, so when you print all three of them at the same time, instead of reflecting no light and giving you black, you get a muddy gray color.

Because of this problem, the printing trade adds black ink (the K in CMYK) to the four color process so that dark areas are as dark as possible.

THE AMOUNT OF BLACK

The amount of black ink used in the printing process and the way that it is used depends on the type of paper and press that you are using. Newspaper presses typically use a lot of black ink and as little color ink as possible because black ink is cheaper. High-quality advertising color for magazines and other coated stock is printed with much more colored ink and less black. A skilled printer can create the same image in CMYK using a lot of black ink or very little black ink. There are many different ways to combine the colored and black inks to get the final result.

CONVERTING RGB TO CMYK

Because of these different choices, converting from RGB to CMYK can be a complicated process. Once an image is converted to CMYK, whether by a high-end scanner or by you in Photoshop, managing the relationship between the CMY colors and the black ink can be tricky. That's just one of the reasons you're better off doing your overall color corrections in RGB so that you are taking a correct RGB file and then converting it to CMYK. You then end up with a CMYK file that has the black in the right place in relationship with the final, or close to final, CMY colors. The main reason to use the CMYK color space is that your final output will be on a printing press or a digital printer that uses CMYK inks or dyes. We discuss color correction in both RGB and CMYK as we present the examples in this book. Because you want to customize the creation of your CMYK file to the type of printing you are doing and since colors can get lost when you convert to CMYK, you should keep your master file in RGB format, for the highest quality and versatility across all media.

THE HUE, SATURATION, AND LIGHTNESS COLOR SPACE

Another color space used in Photoshop is Hue, Saturation, and Lightness. You can no longer use the Mode menu to convert an image to HSL mode like you could in some older versions of Photoshop, but the many color tools allow you to think about and massage color using this color space. Instead of dividing a color into components of red, green, and blue, or cyan, magenta, and yellow, HSL divides a color into its hue, its saturation, and its lightness. The hue is the actual color and can include all the colors of the rainbow. A particular red hue differs from a purple, yellow, orange, or even a different red hue. The saturation is the intensity of that particular hue. Highly saturated colors are quite intense and vivid, so much so that they almost look fluorescent. Colors of low saturation are dull and subtle. The lightness of a part of an image determines how light or dark that part is in overall density. Lightness is the value in the image that gives it detail. Imagine taking a black-and-white image and then colorizing it. The black-and-white image originally had different tonal values of gray. The details show up based on the lightness or darkness of the black-and-white image. Removing the lightness value would be similar to taking this black-and-white detail part out of a color image. If you increase the lightness, the image starts to flatten and show less depth. If you increase the lightness all the way, the image loses all its detail and becomes white. If you decrease the lightness, the image may appear to have more depth and if you decrease it all the way the image becomes black. For working with the image using the Hue/Saturation/Lightness model, you use Image/Adjust/Hue/Saturation or Image/Adjust/Replace Color. The different color pickers allow you to work in the HSL color model and there is also a filter called HSL & HSB that allows you to convert RGB (Red, Green and Blue) into HSL (Hue, Saturation, and Lightness) and back. This filter does not install with Photoshop 4 but can be found on the Adobe Photoshop CD. Look for it in Other Goodies/Optional Plug Ins.

THE LAB COLOR SPACE

The Lab color space is used internally by Photoshop to convert between RGB and CMYK and can be used for device independent output to Level 2 PostScript devices. The Lab color space is quite useful for some production tasks. For example, sharpening only the Lightness channel sharpens the image without "popping" the colors. There also are some technical notes about the Lab color space in the Photoshop 4 manual.

Current hue

Click here to get the Color Picker and change the foreground color.

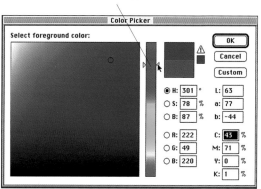

The Color Picker in Hue mode, which is the default. Sliding the color slider (shown with the arrow cursor above) up and down changes the hue in Hue mode. For a particular hue, purple here, click and drag the circle in the color box to the left to pick a particular color. As you move the cursor around in the color box with the mouse button down, left to right movement changes the saturation and up and down movement changes the brightness. You will see the values for saturation and brightness change in the number boxes to the right. You also see the corresponding RGB and CMYK values for each color. Hue is frozen by the color slider position.

USING THE COLOR PICKER

The main tool for picking colors in Photoshop is the Color Picker. You access the Color Picker by clicking on the foreground or background color swatch at the bottom of the Tool palette. You can use this picker in Hue mode, Saturation mode, Lightness mode, or Red, Green, or Blue mode. See the diagrams here for an explanation of each mode. In addition, you can set a specific color by typing in its Lab, RGB, or CMYK values.

The Custom button brings up the Custom Picker for choosing PANTONE, Trumatch, and other standard colors. You can actually use these as separate

Current saturation

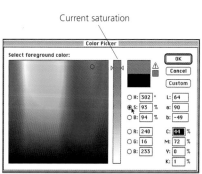

Put the Color Picker in Saturation mode by clicking on the S radio button. Now sliding the color slider up and down changes the saturation. Left to right movement of the cursor circle changes the hue and up and down movement changes the brightness.

Current brightness

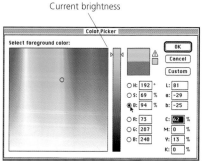

Put the Color Picker in Brightness mode by clicking on the B radio button. Now sliding the color slider up and down changes the brightness. Left to right movement of the cursor circle changes the hue and up and down movement changes the saturation. Brightness here is similar to Lightness, mentioned earlier in this chapter.

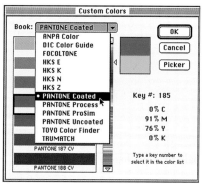

The Custom Colors picker with the different color systems that it makes available in the pop-up menu. Drag the slider or click on the up/down arrows to locate a color, click on a color to choose it, or type in the number associated with a particular color to choose that one. Choosing OK picks that color, and clicking on Picker returns you to the Color Picker where you can see and pick the RGB and CMYK equivalent to that color.

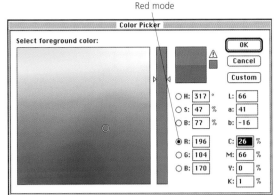

Red mode

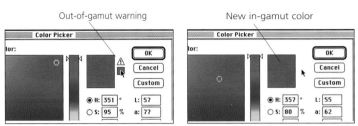

Out-of-gamut warning   New in-gamut color

Put the Color Picker in Red mode by clicking on the R radio button. Now sliding the color slider up and down changes the amount of red in your color. For particular blue and green values, click and drag the circle in the color box to the left. Left to right movement changes the amount of blue and up and down movement changes the amount of green. You will see the values for blue and green change in the number boxes to the right. Red is frozen by the color slider position. The values for cyan, magenta, yellow, and black also change as you move around in the color box. This is a great way to see how the RGB and CMYK components change for different colors. If you are not sure how to adjust a certain color, go into the Color Picker and visually see what will happen to it as you add or subtract different component colors from it.

The exclamation sign shows you that the current color may be out-of-gamut (not printable in CMYK). Click on the sign to change the chosen color to the closest in-gamut color (shown at right). See the chapter, "Kansas—Final Tweaks" for a discussion of out-of-gamut colors.

color channels within Photoshop's Duotone mode, or they automatically convert to RGB or CMYK depending on the active color space.

USING THE COLOR PALETTES

Besides the Color Picker that you access from the Tool palette, you can also access the Color palette and the Swatches palette from the Window menu. Normally these are grouped together on the desktop, but you can separate them by clicking on their name tabs and dragging each of them to some other specific location on the desktop. Since the big Color Picker is a modal dialog box that you cannot access on the fly when using the painting tools, the Color and Swatches palettes come in very handy for getting the colors you need quickly.

THE COLOR PALETTE

In the Color palette, you can move the RGB, CMYK, HSB, or other color sliders to create a color that you like. You pick this color for the foreground or background depending on which of the swatches is chosen in the Color palette. You change the display mode in the Color palette using its pop-up option menu. You can also pick colors from the color bar along the bottom of the palette. This color bar offers different display modes to choose from using the Color palette's options. The Color palette is also useful to have around while you're in Levels, Curves, and the other color correction tools. It remembers the colors at the last location where you clicked the Eyedropper in an image, and it shows you how the color adjustments you are making are changing that location. See the "Color Matching Cars" hands-on for more details.

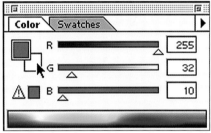

The Color palette shown as it is normally grouped with the Swatches palette. The foreground and background colors are shown to the left. You know that the foreground color is currently active because of the double line around it. If you move the sliders, you adjust the foreground color. The arrow cursor is over the background color. If you click on the background color, it becomes the active color and moving the sliders modifies it. This palette also shows you the Gamut Warning icon.

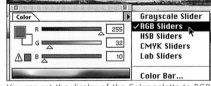

You can set the display of the Color palette to RGB, CMYK, HSB, Lab, or Grayscale.

The Color Bar choice brings up options for how to display the color bar at the bottom. You can choose the foreground color by clicking on a color in the color bar; Option-click for the background color.

THE SWATCHES PALETTE

The Swatches palette allows you to save and then later access your favorite set of colors. To pick a color from the Swatches palette and make it the foreground color, you just click on the color using the Eyedropper tool. Option-clicking picks a new background color. You automatically get the Eyedropper when the cursor moves over the swatches area. To save the current foreground color in the Swatches palette, Shift-click on the swatch you want to overwrite. If you want to add a new swatch without overwriting the ones there, Option-Shift-clicking on top of a swatch shifts it and all the other swatches one slot to the right, making room for the new swatch. Pressing the Command key gives you the scissors, and clicking over a swatch with them removes it. Using the pop-up options menu, you can load custom swatch sets into the Swatches palette, including sets for the custom colors, like PANTONE, that are supplied in the Color Palettes folder that comes with Photoshop.

If you have a continuous tone 24-bit color image that has many colors that you might want to use for other projects, there is a quick way to load 256 of these colors into the Swatches palette. First, choose Image/Mode/Indexed Color to convert *a copy* of your image into Indexed Color mode. (Be sure to use a copy so you don't destroy your original image.) Using the 8 bits/pixel color depth, Adaptive Palette, and Diffusion Dither settings in the Indexed Color dialog box gives you the 256 colors most common in the image. Click on OK in the Index Color dialog box, then choose Image/Mode/Color Table to see a table of the 256 colors you have created from the image. Click on the Save button in the Color Table to save these colors in a file. You can now use Replace Swatches in the Swatches palette to load all these colors. They are now easily available for painting projects in Photoshop. For more information on 8-bit color and creating images for the Web and multimedia, see the "Images for the Web and Multimedia" section of this book.

In the Goodies folder in the Photoshop folder there is a Color Palettes folder that contains swatch sets for PANTONE, Trumatch, and other standard color systems. Here we see all the PANTONE colors loaded into the Swatches palette. When the Eyedropper gets over a particular color, the Swatches tab changes to tell you which PANTONE you are about to choose. This may be a quicker way for you to find the custom color you want.

You can load and save different sets of swatches to files. If you have certain colors that you use for a particular client, you may want to save these in a file under that client's name. You can append swatches, which adds the swatches stored in a file to the ones you already have in the palette. Reset Swatches just goes back to the default set of swatches.

Converting a 24-bit color image to Indexed Color to create a color table for loading into the Swatches palette.

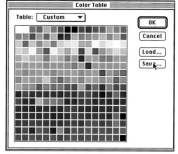

Saving your indexed color table using the Color Table editor. After saving this table, you choose Replace Swatches from the Swatches palette pop-up menu to make this the current set of colors in the Swatches palette.

COLOR CORRECTION TOOLS

Overview of Photoshop's many color correction and gamma adjustment tools; which ones are most useful, for what and why, and which ones are fairly useless for the professional.

There are many tools in Photoshop for adjusting color and modifying image gamma or contrast. This chapter clears up general confusion about what the different tools do and when to use each tool. The color correction tools are in the Image/Adjust menu. Levels, Curves, Hue/Saturation, Replace Color, and Selective Color are the ones we use most. Auto Levels, Color Balance, Brightness/Contrast, Desaturate, and Variations are the ones we don't use much. In later hands-on chapters, we actually go through the details of each tool's features and how they're used in real world examples. Invert, Equalize, Threshold, and Posterize are used more for effects and masking, which are covered in other parts of the book.

USING THE INFO AND COLOR PALETTES

When you use any of these color correction tools, it is very helpful to have the Info and Color palettes visible on-screen too. Use Window/Palettes/Show Info (F9 with ArtistKeys), and Window/Show Color (Shift-F9 with ArtistKeys) to bring up these palettes. While color correcting, you should also have the Eyedropper available for measuring colors in the image. Photoshop automatically selects the Eyedropper for you when you use any of the color correction tools. The Info palette shows you the RGB values and the CMYK values of the pixel or group of pixels you currently have the Eyedropper tool above. It shows you these values both before (left of slash) and after (right of slash) any changes you have made during the current iteration of the color correction tool you are now using. The Color palette has a subtle but important difference from the Info palette, in that it displays the values of the last place where you clicked with the Eyedropper. This allows you to click on a picture

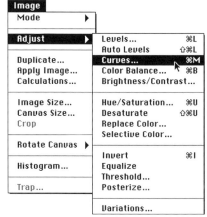

The color correction tools are in the Image/Adjust menu.

The Info palette with the before values to the left and the after values to the right of the slash.

tone or color area and see how the pixel values of that particular area will change as you make adjustments with the Color tool.

When adjusting a digital image, you want to make as few separate file modifications as are necessary to achieve the desired result. A file modification is when you click on the OK button for any of the color correction tools. Each file modification changes the original data, and too many

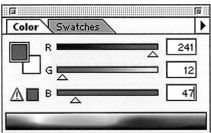

The Color palette remembers the values at the last location you clicked with the Eyedropper, then shows you how those values change when you make adjustments in a color correction tool.

changes can eventually degrade the quality of the data. Therefore, you don't want to constantly go from one color correction tool to the other frantically trying to get the effect you need. You want to use these tools intelligently, knowing what each one is good for and keeping the total number of uses down to the minimum required to do the final adjustments on a particular image. If you do your changes using Photoshop 4 adjustment layers, the actual image pixels do not change until the image flattens. Adjustment layers allow you to go back and change the color over and over again without suffering from this cumulative degrading effect on the digital values.

COMMON COLOR CORRECTION TECHNIQUES

All the color correction tools share a few things in common. When using Levels, Curves, Color Balance, and Brightness/Contrast on the entire image, you often want to have the Preview button turned off. When you have the Preview button turned off during these tools, Photoshop adjusts the color and brightness output of the video card controlling colors on the monitor, which gives you instant results on-screen when you make changes. This technique of adjusting the video card to preview color and contrast changes is called Video LUT Animation. The changes happen over the entire computer screen, not just in the active window. Also, when you have the Preview button off, you can click on the title bar of this color tool's dialog box and hold the mouse button down to see the image as it looked before you make the adjustment. Click and release the mouse on the title bar and you instantly see a before and after view of your image. This feature makes a difference when you are making subtle color adjustments, because when you stare at an image on the computer screen for more than a few seconds your eye tends to adjust to make the image look more correct. This quick before/after toggle stops your eye from having time to do this and you can better decide if you really like the color adjustments you have made. Video LUT Animation, with the Preview button off, gives a quick preview of your results no matter how big the file. It's usually fairly accurate and you should use it when possible when you make changes to the overall image in Levels, Curves, Color Balance, and Brightness/Contrast. After you make your changes, you may want to turn on the Preview button to force Photoshop to calculate all the changes and show you exactly how they will look, not just the approximation the Video LUT Animation gives you. When you use the Hue/Saturation, Replace Color, and Selective Color commands, the corrections are too complicated for Photoshop to simulate them simply by changing the video board, so you usually need to work with the Preview button turned on. Video LUT Animation also doesn't work with adjustment layers, so you need to use them with the Preview button on. Video LUT Animation doesn't work with a few Macs and with many PCs and compatibles. If your video board does not support Video LUT Animation, just always work with the Preview button on.

When working with a selected sub-area or comparing one window to another or adjusting an area in one layer to blend with non-adjusted items in other layers within Levels, Curves, Color Balance, or Brightness/Contrast, you usually work with the Preview button on so you can compare the changes you make to the selected area to the rest of the image. If the Preview button is on during a tool, clicking on the title bar doesn't give you the quick before/after toggle. Also, you can *never* get this quick toggle during the Hue/Saturation, Replace Color, or Selective Color commands.

In any of the color correction tools, you can Option-Cancel to stay in the tool but cancel any changes you have made in that tool so far. Many of these tools also let you load and save a collection of settings. This is useful when you have many very similar images in a production situation. You could carefully make your Levels setting for the first image and then use the Save button to save those settings in a file. If you have subsequent images in the group, you can use the Load button to automatically run the same settings. You can also use the Save and Load features to make Levels or Curves changes while looking at a layer with Video LUT Animation and then saving those changes and actually reloading them in an adjustment layer where you can't use Video LUT Animation.

LEVELS AND CURVES

The Levels and Curves tools have the broadest range of capabilities of any of the color correction tools. When you color correct an image from its original scan, you want to do so in a particular order. (We discuss that order in great detail in "Color Correction and Output," and you should read it for a better understanding of this overview.) The first step after you do a scan is to do overall color correction; that is, correcting the complete image without any selections. Levels is the best tool to use because it gives you a histogram of the data in the image. You can use the histogram to judge the quality of the scan and to fix many scanning problems. You also can use Levels to precisely adjust the highlight and shadow values, the overall brightness and contrast, and the color balance, while viewing the results on-screen and in the histogram. You make all these changes in one step and must choose OK only once for all these improvements. Levels is the color correction tool we use most often.

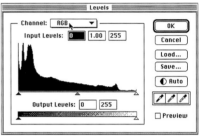

The Levels tool with its histogram is best for doing the overall color correction right after bringing in a scan.

You can also use the Curves command to do your initial overall color adjustments of the entire image. Curves enables you to do all the same adjustments that Levels does. The Curves command has a different user interface than Levels, however. Instead of furnishing a histogram, it provides the curve diagram shown here. The horizontal axis of the diagram represents the original image values with black and shadows on the left and white and highlights on the right. The vertical axis represents the modified image values with the shadows at the bottom and the highlights on the top. When the curve is a straight diagonal, as shown here, the image has not been changed. Moving the curve down in the middle darkens the image, and moving it upwards lightens the image. The endpoints of the curve are used to change the highlight and shadow values. Using Curves, you can measure individual colors, see the range of values they represent on the curve, and then change only that color range (and, that's one advantage of using Curves instead of Levels). The advantage of using Levels is being able to see the histogram as you make changes.

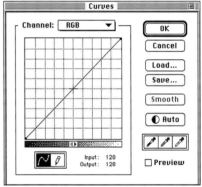

The Curves tool with a curve showing no adjustments to the image. The horizontal axis shows the original image values and the vertical axis shows these values as modified by the curve.

Levels and Curves are the most powerful color correction tools. See the chapters "The Grand Canyon," "Kansas," and "Color Correcting Al" for good discussions of using Levels and Curves in the ways for which they are best suited. Also read the chapter "Digital Imaging and the Zone System" to understand how Levels histograms relate to the original photograph.

THE HUE/SATURATION COMMAND

Hue/Saturation is often used to increase the saturation of all the colors by 10% to 20% after doing the overall color correction using Levels. This change is done with the Master button on. Using the Red, Yellow, Green, Cyan, Blue, or Magenta radio buttons, you can change the hue, saturation, or lightness of objects in the image that have one of these standard colors as their primary color without actually making a detailed selection. You should use Hue/Saturation when you want to change the color, saturation, or lightness of a particular object or color range without changing

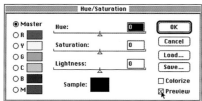

The Hue/Saturation tool. Usually you want the Preview button on when using Hue/Saturation.

its gamma or other characteristics. The first part of the process is to select the object(s) you want to change and use the Eyedropper to get a dab of representative color, which shows up in the Sample patch at the bottom of the Hue/Saturation window. This patch shows changes to your representative color as you make them. Unlike Levels and Curves, with this tool you need to use the Preview button to see your changes within a file on a 24-bit color monitor.

The Hue slider looks at hues in a circular fashion, sort of like the old Apple Color Picker. The initial hue value, 0, is the degree value where you find your initial color. To change just the color, slide the Hue slider to the right (like rotating counter-clockwise on the Apple Color Picker). If your initial color was red, then red would be your 0. A Hue change of 90 degrees would make the color green. A Hue change of –90 degrees would make your color purple. A Hue change of 180 or –180 would yield the opposite of red, cyan. Sliding the Saturation slider to the right makes the selected items more saturated and sliding to the left makes them less saturated. This is like moving further from the center or closer to the center on the Apple Color Picker.

Moving the Lightness slider to the right takes away gray values and moving it to the left adds gray values (similar to the sliding bar on the right side of the Apple Color Picker). See "The Grand Canyon," "The Car," and "Color Matching Cars" for more information on the Hue/Saturation tool.

THE REPLACE COLOR COMMAND

The Replace Color command allows you to make a selection based on color and then actually change the color of the selected objects using sliders built into the command's dialog box. The selections are similar to selections made with the Magic Wand, but this tool gives you more control over them. The Magic Wand requires you to make a selection by using a certain tolerance setting and clicking on a color, and then selects adjacent areas based on whether their colors fall within the tolerance value you set for it. If the selection is incorrect with the Magic Wand, you need to change the tolerance and then select again. This process takes a lot of time and iteration. The Replace Color command allows you to change the tolerance on the fly while viewing the actual objects or colors you are selecting.

The tolerance here is called Fuzziness. Increasing the Fuzziness, by moving the slider in the dialog box to the right, enlarges your selection, and decreasing it shrinks the selection. You see a preview of what is happening with the selection in a little mask window in the dialog box.

After you perfect the color selection, you then use the Hue, Saturation, and Lightness sliders in the Replace Color dialog box to change the color of the selected objects. You can see this color change in the image by clicking on the Preview button, and that allows you to make further tweaks on the selection while actually seeing how they're affecting the color change. Replace Color selects and changes color on these objects from everywhere within the part of the image that was initially selected when you first entered Replace Color. To learn more about using Replace Color, see the "Yellow Flowers" chapter.

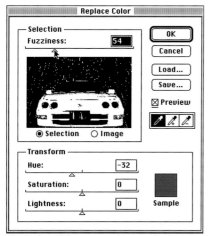

The Replace Color command has a selection capability based on object color and has some of the controls from Hue/Saturation built into it. Use it for quickly selecting and changing the color of objects. Use the sample swatch as a quick reference to see how your color will change, then use the Preview button to see the change happen within the file.

THE SELECTIVE COLOR TOOL AND CMYK

The Selective Color tool works great when you are working with CMYK images. It is a good tool for making final tweaks to CMYK colors after converting from RGB to CMYK. With this tool, you adjust the amount of cyan, magenta, yellow, or black ink within the red, green, blue, cyan, magenta, yellow, black, neutral, or white colors in the selected area. It's also a great tool for fine control over fixing color areas that fade a bit when converted to CMYK. For more information about using this tool, see "Yellow Flowers" and "Color Matching Cars."

COLOR BALANCE, BRIGHTNESS/CONTRAST, AND VARIATIONS

You will notice that we don't use Color Balance, Brightness/Contrast, and Variations tools much in this book. We consider them less precise than the other five color correction tools previously mentioned. We explain the advantages and disadvantages of using these three tools in this section. In general, they are more for color beginners and don't offer as much control as the Levels, Curves, Hue/Saturation, Replace Color, or Selective Color commands.

THE COLOR BALANCE TOOL

The Color Balance tool shows the the relationship between the additive colors (red, green, and blue) on the right, and the subtractive colors (cyan, magenta, and yellow) on the left. You move three sliders, the Cyan/Red slider, the Magenta/Green slider, and the Yellow/Blue slider, either to the left to get the CMY colors or to the right to get their complementary RGB colors. If you don't understand the relationship between RGB and CMY, this tool makes it a little easier to see. When you use Color Balance, you need to adjust your shadows, midtones, and highlights each separately, which can take longer than using Levels or Curves.

In general, the Color Balance tool is much less powerful than Levels or Curves because you can't set exact highlight or shadow values, and you don't have much control over brightness and contrast. If you were to use Color Balance to do the overall correction of an image, you probably would have to go back and forth between it and Brightness/Contrast several times, and that would break the rule of clicking on OK as little as possible—and you still have less overall control than with Levels or Curves. You also can't adjust where the breakdown happens between highlights, midtones, and shadows. Moreover, if you have a setting that you use all the time in Levels, Hue/Saturation, or Curves, you can save it in a file and load it later to use on a similar image, which is very useful when you want to save time and make a group of images have similar color adjustments—once again, the Color Balance tool doesn't have this option.

THE BRIGHTNESS/CONTRAST TOOL

The Brightness/Contrast tool allows you to adjust the brightness and/or contrast of your image using Brightness and Contrast sliders. Usually we adjust the brightness and contrast using Levels or Curves because those tools allow you to also adjust the color balance and highlight/shadow values at the same time. Like the Color Balance tool, I would say that Brightness/Contrast is more of a toy, an entry-level tool. Most professionals use Levels and Curves. The only time you might use Brightness/Contrast is when you don't need to make any color adjustment and need only a subtle brightness or contrast adjustment. We demonstrate an example of its use in the "The Band" chapter: in it, we do a subtle adjustment to match the brightness and contrast of two grayscale channels.

When using Color Balance and Brightness/ Contrast, you usually do your initial adjustments with the Preview button off, as you would when using Levels and Curves. Again, the exception comes when you want to see how the changes in a selected area blend with the rest of the image or when you want to compare changes happening in one window with other images that are on the same computer screen.

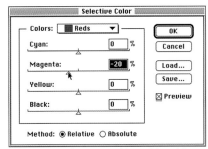

The Selective Color command is used for adding or subtracting the percentage of cyan, magenta, yellow or black inks within the red, green, blue, cyan, magenta, yellow, black, neutral, or white colors in the selected area of a CMYK image. These percentages can be relative to the amount of an ink color that is already there or they can be absolute percentages.

The Color Balance tool. Color levels of 0 mean that no adjustment has been made. Negative values mean adjustments in the CMY direction, and positive values are adjustments in the RGB direction. Preserve Luminosity is the only feature this tool has that can't be done with more precise control using Levels or Curves.

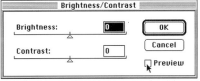

The Brightness/Contrast tool. Moving the sliders to the right increases the brightness or contrast, generating positive numbers in the respective boxes. Moving the sliders to the left decreases brightness or contrast and results in negative numbers.

Overall, I would say that the Color Balance tool is more of a toy for beginning color correctors and not the the tool I would recommend for imaging professionals. The one exception is that you can make adjustments in Color Balance with the Preserve Luminosity button on, which allows you, for example, to radically alter the color balance of a selected object toward red without the object becoming super bright like it would if you made such a radical adjustment in Levels or Curves. There are times when this is very useful.

THE VARIATIONS TOOL

The Variations tool is a neat idea, but it has several serious flaws. Variations is useful for the person who is new to color correction and may not know the difference between adding a little cyan and adding a little green to an image. When you use it, you see the current image surrounded by different color correction choices. The main problem with Variations is that you cannot zoom in on the current image or any of its new choices to see the details of what will happen when you make possible changes. If Adobe would add some way to zoom in and look closely at the changes, the Variations tool would be much more useful.

Variations works better on a 19" or 21" monitor, simply because the small images used to illustrate the changes are a little bigger on a larger monitor. Still, once you make the changes and say OK to Variations, you are often surprised by how the changes that looked cool in small size inside the Variations dialog box have adversely affected certain color areas. Like the Color Balance tool, you can't set precisely where the highlight and/or shadow values begin. You have to adjust highlight and shadow values separately using the radio buttons at the top right of the Variations dialog box. You can't set the highlights or shadows to known values like you can in Levels and Curves.

In Variations, you can also adjust the saturation by selecting the Saturation radio button. The saturation, highlight and shadow settings will show you out-of-gamut colors if you have the Show Clipping box checked. When shadows will print as pure black or highlights as pure white, these clipped areas show up as a bright complementary warning color. In Saturation mode, colors that are too saturated for the CMYK gamut show up the same way.

The Variations color correction tool shows you the original and current version of the image up in the top left corner. As you change the current image, you can easily compare it here to the original. The big box in the bottom left corner shows the current image in the middle surrounded by versions with more green, yellow, red, magenta, blue, or cyan added to it. You click on one of these surrounding versions of the image if you like it better. It replaces the current image in the middle of this circle (also at the top), and then another round of new color iterations surround this new current image. On the right hand side, the current image is in the middle with a lighter one above and a darker one below. Again you can click on one of these to make it the current image.

If you are not used to doing color corrections, Variations is a good way to prototype the corrections you want to make. Maybe you'll decide to add some yellow, darken the image, and increase the saturation a bit. After you make these decisions with the aid of Variations, you may want to go back to Levels, Curves, or Hue/Saturation and try to make the corresponding changes there. Then you can also set the highlights and shadows more exactly and see the details of the changes you are making as you make them. We do not use Variations in this book. For more details on Variations, see the Photoshop 4 manual.

The Auto Levels and Desaturate Commands

The Auto Levels command does an automatic color correction of your image. I would not recommend using it for quality color control, but it's okay for a quick color fix to an FPO proof. The Desaturate command completely desaturates your image, taking all the hue or color values out of it, leaving you with a black-and-white image in RGB or CMYK mode. Desaturate does not do exactly the same thing as doing Image/Mode/Grayscale; with Desaturate, the image appears flatter.

Where to Learn More

To learn more about the color correction tools mentioned in this overview, read the chapters "Color Correction and Output," "Digital Imaging and the Zone System," and "Setting System and Photoshop Preferences," and do the step-by-step examples in "The Grand Canyon," "Kansas," and "Color Correcting Al." The chapters, "Yellow Flowers," "Color Matching Cars," "The Band," "Versailles," and "Bryce Stone Woman," also have color correction techniques.

RGB to CMY Relationship

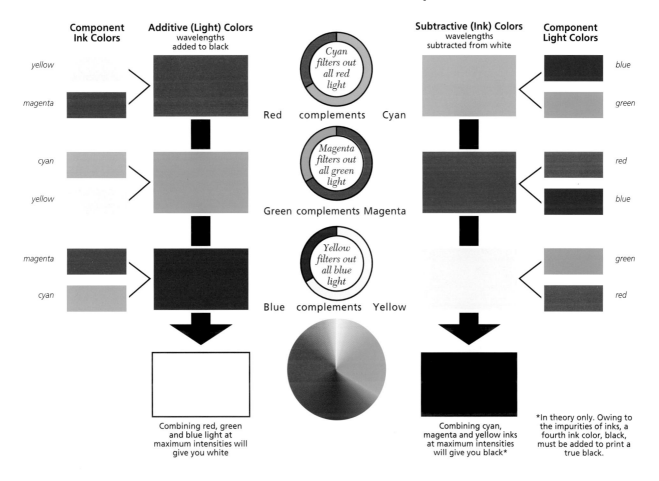

SELECTIONS, MASKS, AND CHANNELS

Terms and concepts for working with
selections, masks, and channels.

Before you can understand all the possibilities, we first need to explain several important concepts. You need to understand the concept of a selection and how to make a selection using the Photoshop tools. You need to understand what a mask channel is, how to turn a selection into a mask channel, and how to edit a mask channel using different tools to allow you to isolate the necessary parts of an image to achieve a particular effect. This includes understanding what a selection feather or a mask blur is and how these affect the edges of blended selections. We will discuss the concept of opacity, which also affects image blending. We also show you how to effectively use the Channels palette.

MAKING SELECTIONS

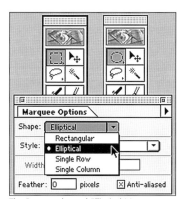

The Rectangular and Elliptical Marquees are the simplest selection tools. Double-click on the Rectangular Marquee, or type M, to change its option to Elliptical.

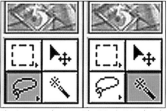

The Lasso tool.   The Magic Wand tool.

Let's start out by talking about the concept of a *selection*—an isolated part of an image that needs special attention. You may want to make this part of the image lighter or darker, or you may want to change its color altogether. You might also select something in an image that you wanted to copy and paste into a different image.

THE BASIC TOOLS

There are various tools for making selections. The simplest ones are the Rectangular and Elliptical Marquees, which allow you to draw a box or an ellipse around something by clicking at one side of the area you want to isolate and then dragging to the other side. This will create a box- or oval-shaped selection that is denoted by dotted lines around the edge. The next level of selection complexity is the Lasso tool, which allows you to draw a freehand shape around the selected objects. Using the Lasso in Photoshop, you can draw either freehand or straight line segments, or combinations of both. Another selection tool is the Magic Wand, which allows you to click on a certain color in an image and automatically select adjoining areas based on that color. There are ways to increase the size of this selection and also to select all objects of similar color within the image. To learn about the Selection tools, go to the "The Tool Palette" and "The Car" chapters.

Working with and Inversing Selections

Here you see the Paris Dog Image, in which we have selected the dog using the Lasso tool. When the Dog is selected, anything we do (painting, changing color, and so on) can happen only within the boundaries of the selected area. That is the purpose of a selection, to isolate your work to a particular object or area within the image. If you compare working on an image in Photoshop to painting a mural on a wall, selecting just the dog would be equivalent to putting masking tape everywhere else on the wall, allowing us to paint only on top of the dog. If we choose Select/Inverse, then everything except the dog becomes the selection. Now we have selected the background and not the dog. So, any time you have a selection of an object, you also have, via Select/Inverse, a selection of everything except the object. Returning to the wall analogy, using Select/Inverse would be like removing the masking tape from the background and putting tape over the area of the dog.

Here is the Paris Dog where we have used the Lasso to select just the dog.

The above selection after choosing Select/Inverse.

Changing a Selection

Changing a selection is a lot easier than moving masking tape. You can add to any selection made using any of the Marquees, Lasso, or Magic Wand selection tools by using any of these tools with the Shift key down when you create the new selection. You can subtract from a selection by having the Option key down when you define the area you want to subtract using these same tools.

Setting the Feather Value

Using most of the selection tools in their default mode is similar to placing masking tape along the edge of the selection, in that there is a defined sharp edge to the selection. Such a selection is said to have a feather value of 0. The selection feather is something that determines how quickly the transition goes from being in the selection to not being in the selection. With 0 feather, the transition is instantaneous. You can change the feather of a selection using the Select/Feather command. If you change the feather of the selection to 20, the transition from being fully selected to being fully unselected would happen over the distance of 40 pixels (actually, at least 20 pixels on either side of the zero feather selection line). If you used this type of feathered masking tape to paint the selection of the dog green, the feather would cause the two colors to fade together slowly over the distance of 40 pixels.

Dog selection with no feather filled with green.

Dog selection with a 20 pixel feather filled with Green.

Pixels and Channels

A pixel is the basic unit of information within a digital image. Continuous tone digital images (scanned photographs of real objects) are a two-dimensional array of pixels. If the image was 2,000 pixels wide by 1,600 pixels high and we were printing it at 200 pixels per inch, then the image would print at 10 inches wide by 8 inches high (2000/200 = 10, 1600/200 = 8).

If we are working with a black-and-white image, each one of these pixels contains one byte of information, which allows it to have 256 possible gray values. A black-and-white image has one channel in which each pixel is one byte in size. A *channel* is just a

The Channels palette for a grayscale image with the single black channel, Channel #1, which is the image.

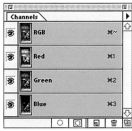

The Channels palette for an RGB image. Each of the red, green and blue channels is a grayscale image. You only see color when you view Channel #~, the RGB channel.

Load Selection from Channel.

Save Selection to Channel.

New Channel or Layer.

Throw Channel or Layer away.

term referring to a two-dimensional array of bytes. If we are working with a RGB color image, it has three channels (one for each of red, green, and blue). A CMYK image has four channels. You can see these channels by choosing Window/Show Channels. In an RGB file, Channel #1 is red, Channel #2 is green, and Channel #3 is blue. There is also an imaginary Channel #~ which allows you to see the red, green and blue channels at the same time. (This is how you see color.) The RGB channel, Channel #~, is an imaginary channel because it doesn't take up any additional space beyond that which the red, green, and blue channels take up.

SAVING SELECTIONS AS MASK CHANNELS

When you make a selection, you are making what is called a *mask*—the selection masks out the part of the image that you don't select. You can save a selection to a mask channel, which allows you to use it again later. This is especially useful for a complicated selection that you don't want to have to remake later. To do this, choose Select/Save Selection or just click on the Save Selection icon at the bottom of the Channels palette. The new mask channel you would create by doing the Save Selection would be named #2 if you were working in a grayscale image and #4 if you were working in an RGB image. Photoshop assumes Channel #1 is the image and Channels #2 and higher are mask channels when you are working with a grayscale image. In RGB, Photoshop assumes Channels #1, #2, and #3 are red, green, and blue, and that Channels #4 and higher are mask channels. You can rename a mask channel by double-clicking on the channel, entering the name you want, and then clicking on OK. If you Option-click on the Save Selection icon, the Channel Options dialog box opens as you make the mask channel and you can type in the new name right there.

HOW MASK CHANNELS WORK

A *mask channel* is just another channel like the others we've described. When you save a selection to a mask channel, the parts of the image that you selected show up as white in the mask channel and the non-selected parts (the masked parts) show up as black. When you have a blend between two partial selections, it shows up as gray in the mask channel. Feathered selection areas also show up as gray. A mask channel has 256 possible gray values, just like any other grayscale image.

EDITING MASK CHANNELS

You can actually edit a mask channel just like you would edit any grayscale image. Sometimes you may want to make a selection using one of the selection tools, save it to a mask channel, and then edit the selection within the mask channel. When you edit a selection, you use the selection tools. When you edit a selection saved as a mask channel, you use pixel editing tools, like

Image with dog selected.

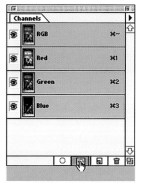

Saving this selection using the Save Selection icon.

The mask that gets saved for this selection.

The Channels palette after doing the Save selection and renaming Channel #4 DogMask.

Chapter 10: Selections, Masks and Channels

the Pencil, Paintbrush, and Gradient tools, from the Tool palette. White in a mask means totally selected and black means totally unselected. If you edit a white area to be gray, you make it less selected, or, partially selected. You can edit a black area and make part of it white; doing that adds the white part to the selected area. You may save a selection in a mask channel so you can edit it there, or you may just save it so you can use it again later.

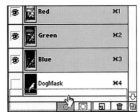
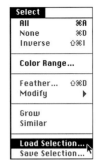

Load Selection the quick way; dragging the mask channel to the Load Selection icon at the bottom of the Channels palette. You can also hold the Command key down and click on the Mask channel you want to load.

Load Selection from the menu bar.

We do many things with mask channels in this book. Sometimes we use the terms *selection, mask,* and *mask channel* interchangeably since they all refer to an isolated part of the image. To do something to the image with a mask that is saved in a mask channel, you must first load it as a selection. Choose Select/Load Selection from the menu bar or click on the mask channel you want to load and drag it to the Load Selection icon at the bottom left of the Channels palette. You also can load a selection by Command-clicking on the channel you want to load. When a selection is loaded, you can see the marching ants.

Here are the options you have when you do a Load Selection. The Add, Subtract and Intersect options only show up if you have an existing selection at the time of the load.

Sometimes people get confused about the need to have both selections and mask channels. Remember, a selection actually masks out the non-selected areas of the currently active channel(s) and layer. After you create a selection or do a Load Selection, you can change the active channel(s) or layer within a document and the selection remains. It just always affects what you do to the active channel(s) or layer. A mask channel is just a selection saved for later. Unless the mask channel is currently loaded, it doesn't affect any other channel(s) or layers or anything that you do to them with the painting tools or filters. You can have up to 21 mask channels in an RGB Photoshop document plus the Red, Green, and Blue channels, for a total of 24 channels. You can load any of these mask channels as a selection at any time.

When you load a selection, you can combine that new selection with any existing selection present before the load. Command-clicking on a mask channel loads it as a new selection and throws out any existing selection. Command-Shift-clicking on a mask channel adds this new selection to any existing selection. Command-Option-clicking on a mask channel subtracts this from an existing selection and Command-Option-Shift-clicking on a mask channel intersects the new selection with the existing selection, giving you the parts that the two selections have in common. If you don't want to remember all these command options, they show up in the Load Selection dialog box, and you can access it by choosing Select/Load Selection or by Option-clicking on the Load Selection icon.

DELETING, MOVING, AND COPYING CHANNELS

You can remove a mask channel by clicking on that channel and then choosing Delete Channel from the Channels palette's pop-up menu, or by clicking on the channel and dragging it to the Trash icon at the bottom right of the Channels palette. You cannot, however, delete the Red, Green, or Blue channels this way.

You can copy any channel, including the Red, Green, and Blue channels, by clicking on the channel and dragging it to the New Channel icon at the bottom of the Channels palette. You also can make a copy of a channel by choosing Duplicate Channel from the Channel palette's pop-up menu.

Deleting a mask channel from an RGB image using the Channels palette's pop-up window.

Deleting a channel from a grayscale image the quick way by dragging to the Trash icon at the bottom right of the Channels palette.

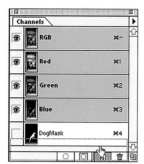

To copy a channel, drag it to the New Channel icon at the bottom of the Channels palette.

The copied channel appears at the bottom with its name being #5. If you use Duplicate Channel from the Channels palette menu, the new channel will be the same name with "copy" at the end.

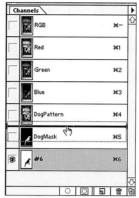

To move a channel, click on it and then drag it until the line is dark between the channels where you want to put it.

The moved channel appears in its new location.

You can move a channel from one location to another by clicking on the channel you want to move and then dragging it until the line becomes dark between the two channels where you want to put this channel. Let go of the mouse at that point and you have moved the channel. You cannot, however, change the location of the original Red, Green, and Blue channels.

USING THE CHANNELS PALETTE EYE ICONS

After you save a selection in a mask channel, you can then work with it in a different way than by just seeing the marching ants lines around the edge of the selection. Notice that the Channels palette has two columns. The leftmost column is the

Normal state for working in RGB, Channel ~, with Red, Green, and Blue Eye icons on and the DogMask off.

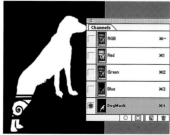

When working on a mask channel directly in black-and-white, you normally have its Eye icon on with its channel grayed. All the other channels have their Eye icons off and they are not grayed.

thin one that has the Eye icons in it. This column signifies the channels that you are currently seeing—the ones with the Eye icons on. The rightmost column is the one that has the name of the channel. Clicking in the rightmost column for a particular channel grays that channel, which signifies that you are working on it. That makes it the Active channel. Clicking in the rightmost column for Channel ~ (the RGB composite channel), grays the Red, Green, and Blue channels because Channel ~ represents all three of them. If you also have a mask channel defined, like the picture here with the dog mask, then there are different things you can do to work with that mask channel in relation to the other channels.

The Eye icons for the Red, Green, and Blue channels normally are turned on, and those channels are grayed when you are working with an RGB image. The normal state is displayed here in this first picture to the left.

If you click on the rightmost column of the DogMask channel, that channel becomes the active one. It shows up in black-and-white and if you do any editing with the painting tools, you do so in black-and-white in the DogMask channel. The Eye icons for the RGB channels turn off now. The second picture to the left shows this state.

If you want to edit the mask channel while also seeing the RGB image, do the following. After you make the mask the

Chapter 10: Selections, Masks and Channels

active channel by clicking in its rightmost column, you can then click on the Eye icon column of Channel ~, which turns on the Eye icons for RGB. You will see RGB, but these channels are not active. They are not grayed, which means that you are seeing them but are still working on the grayed DogMask channel. The parts of the mask that are black will show up with an overlay color, usually red. If you paint in black with the Paintbrush tool, you add to this black part of the mask. The paint shows up in the red overlay color. If you paint with white, you add to the selection, and subtract from the red overlay color. If you want to change the overlay color, double-click on the mask channel to bring up its Channel Options, click on the color swatch, and change its color in the Color Picker. Be sure to leave its opacity at lower than 100% so you can see the picture through the overlay.

If you want to, you can also view the DogMask while working on the RGB image. Click on the rightmost column of Channel ~, which activates the RGB channels so that when you paint with the Paintbrush, you modify the RGB image. Now if you click on the Eye icon column of the DogMask channel, you see this channel as an overlay while working in RGB.

You can also work on a mask while looking at the RGB image too. To get into this state, first click in the second column of the Dog-Mask channel to activate the mask and then click in the first column of Channel ~ to turn on the RGB Eye icons without activating the RGB channels. Here you will be editing the DogMask channel.

If you want to work on the RGB channels while seeing the mask, first click on the right column of Channel ~ to activate RGB, then click in the Eye icon column of the DogMask channel. Here you will be editing the RGB channels.

LAYERS, LAYER MASKS, AND ADJUSTMENT LAYERS

Terms and concepts for working with layers, adjustment layers, and layer masks, and using them for prototyping and effects variations.

"Night Cab Ride in Manhattan" an image with many layers. Here we see all the layers. This image, called LayersIntro, is included in the Layers&LayerMasks folder on the CD. You may want to open it and play while reading this section.

Think of each layer in a RGB Photoshop document as a separate RGB file. Each layer has its own separate Red, Green, and Blue channels. As you look at the layers in the Layers palette, imagine that the one at the bottom of the palette is a photographic print laying on the bottom of a pile of prints on your desk and that each layer above that in the Layers palette is another photographic print laying on top of that bottom one in the order you see them in the palette. You have a pile of photographic prints on your desk. Now imagine that you can look at the top of this pile of photographs and see through them, seeing all of them at the same time through to the bottom of the pile. It's even better than that because you can control how much of each photo you see, as a percentage of the whole, and you can control what parts of each photo you see. You can run a variety of effects, called Blend modes, on each of photo in the pile so the possible combinations of how you see them all together numbers in the thousands. You can change the order of the photos in the pile and also move them and distort them in relationship to each other. All these things and more is what layers in Photoshop allow you to do.

LAYERS AND CHANNELS

Layers are similar to channels in the ways you move them around, copy them, and delete them. To work with layers, you use the Layers palette, which you activate from Window/Show Layers or by using F10 with ArtistKeys. If you use layers and channels at the same time, which you usually do, you may want to separate the palettes so you can see them in different places on-screen at the same time. Just click on the Layers or Channels name tab at the top of that palette and drag it to a new position on-screen. You can then hide or bring up the Channels palette with Window/Show Channels or by pressing Shift-F10 with ArtistKeys.

Each layer is like a separate Photoshop file that you can superimpose on top of other Photoshop layers in the same document. Take a look at the NightCabRide image at the beginning of this chapter; we created it using many layers. Each layer has its own set of Red, Green, and Blue channels. When working with layers, you can view one layer at a time, several layers at a time, or all the layers at once.

A SIMPLE EXAMPLE

Consider the Paris Dog image we were working with in the last chapter. You can open a copy of this from the Layers&LayerMasks folder on your CD. Make sure your Channels and Layers palettes are visible, using Shift-F10 and F10 (if you have ArtistKeys loaded), or by going to Window/Show Channels and Show Layers. You start out with a simple image that has a single layer, called Dog. You can make a copy of this Layer by clicking on the Dog layer in the Layer palette and dragging it to the New Layer icon at the bottom of the Layers Palette. Holding down the Option key while doing this brings up the Duplicate Layer dialog box, where you can give this new layer a name. We will call it Dog Pointillize, since we're going to run the pointillize filter on it. Notice that the Layers palette now has a second layer above with the name we gave it. New layers come in above the current active layer and they then become the active layer.

Now choose Filter/Pixelate/Pointillize and run the Pointillize filter on this new layer with a value of 5. Since this layer is on top of the Dog layer, you can no longer see the Dog layer. The Dog Pointillize layer has its own set of RGB channels, so now the document is twice as big as it was when we started.

MAKING A LAYER MASK

Do a Load Selection from the DogMask channel in the Channels palette by Command-clicking on that channel. Now we have a selection of the dog. Option-click on the Layer Mask icon at the bottom left of the Layers palette to add a layer mask where the selection is removed from this layer. Notice that the layer mask appears to the right of the Dog Pointillize Layer icon now and is black where the dog is. Also, notice that it shows up in the Channels palette and is called Dog Pointillize Mask. Now the Dog Pointillize layer is removed in the area of the Dog and you see the original dog in the layer below. If you press Command-I at this point, to invert the mask, you will see the original background with the dog now pointillized.

When you first add a layer mask, it comes up in the mode in which you are editing the mask but seeing RGB. In this mode, the mask has a black line around it in the Layers palette and shows up as gray (is active) in the Channels palette. Option-clicking on this layer mask icon in the Layers palette at this point switches you to the mode in which you are editing and seeing the mask. The Eye icon is now on for the

Making a copy of the Dog layer by dragging it to the New Layer icon. You could also choose Duplicate Layer from the Layer Palette menu to accomplish the same result.

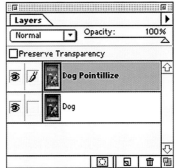

After the Dog Layer has been copied and named Dog Pointillize.

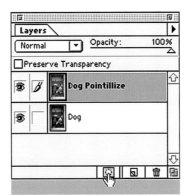

Adding a Layer Mask by Option-Clicking on the Layer Mask icon. Clicking on the Layer Mask icon will remove everything but the selection from this layer. Option-Clicking removes the selected area. If there is no selection, then Clicking on the Layer Mask icon selects the entire layer and Option-Clicking hides the entire layer.

After a Layer Mask is added, it shows up as an icon to the right of the Layer icon in the Layers Palette. It also shows up in the Channels Palette below the Blue channel. Since the eye icons are on for RGB in the Channels Palette but the Layer Mask is active, we can now edit the mask but we will see the changes in RGB.

When editing the layer, you see the Paint-brush icon to the right of the Eye icon and the Layer icon has the dark highlight.

When editing the layer mask, you see the Mask icon to the right of the Eye icon and the Layer Mask icon has the dark highlight.

mask and off for RGB in the Channels palette. Option-clicking again returns you to the original mode of editing the mask and seeing RGB.

To edit the layer itself and also see the layer, Option-click on the Layer icon in the Layers palette. For each layer in the Layers palette, the Layer icon is the one to the left and the Layer Mask icon is the one to the right. To the left of the Layer icon, in Photoshop 4, you see an icon that looks like a mask when you are editing the mask and like a paintbrush when you are editing the layer itself. The item you are editing also has a black highlight line around it.

ADDING AN ADJUSTMENT LAYER

Now Option-click back on the Layer icon for the Dog Pointillize layer (that is, the icon on the left, not the Layer Mask icon on the right). You should now see the Paintbrush icon between it and the Eye icon. Command-click on the New Layer icon at the bottom middle of the Layers palette to bring up the New Adjustment Layer dialog box. Set the Type to Curves to choose a Curves adjustment layer, click OK, and then pull the curve down and to the right to darken the entire composite (this works because this new adjustment layer is on top of all the others). An adjustment layer can be of Type Levels, Curves, Brightness/Contrast, Color Balance, Hue/Saturation, Selective Color, Invert, Threshold, or Posterize. Although an adjustment layer acts like any other layer, it does not make you pay the price of adding another set of RGB channels for the new layer. The color correction adjustment you make in the adjustment layer applies to all the layers below that adjustment layer. You can turn this correction on and off simply by turning the Eye icon on or off for that particular adjustment layer. If you double-click on the name of the adjustment layer, you can actually change the adjustment—in this case, the curve settings—as many times as you want without degrading the color in the file. If you would have had a selection when you created this new adjustment layer, its layer mask would have only darkened the selected area. Adjustment layers only have a Layer Mask icon; they don't have a Layer icon because there is actually no RGB data associated with adjustment layers. Click on this Curves Adjustment layer in the Layers palette and drag it down between the Dog Pointillize layer and the Dog layer until you see a black line form between these two layers. Release the mouse button at that point. This moves the adjustment layer down so that now it darkens only the Dog layer and not the Dog Pointillize layer.

The New Adjustment Layer dialog box allows you to choose the type of adjustment layer and also give this new layer a name.

You now see Curves Mask in the Channels palette below the Blue channel, because now the Curves layer is active. Click back on the Dog Pointillize layer to make it active and notice that the Dog Pointillize mask is now below the Blue channel in the Channels palette. Finally, click back on the Dog layer and notice that all these layer masks have been removed from the Channels palette. Only the layer mask for the active layer shows up in the Channels palette.

MORE ABOUT LAYERS USING NIGHTCABRIDE

Let's take a look at the NightCabRide image with its several different layers and see how this works. Open the LayersIntro file in the Introduction to Layers folder, and use that file to try out the different options that we discuss here. In the Layers palette for NightCabRide, you see that this image has six layers. Currently, we are looking at all of them since the Eye icons, in the left column of the Layers palette, are all on.

Imagine that all the layers are in a pile with the bottom layer, here called All Black, at the bottom of the pile. As you add layers on top of this, like Canon, Building, and Cab in this example, they are blended with the layers below them. The active layer, the one that is highlighted, HeadlightsPizza, is the layer that is modified by changing the settings for Opacity and Blend mode at the top of the Layers palette. You click in the right column of the Layers palette to make a layer active. The active layer will also be changed by anything you do with any other Photoshop tools, like Levels or Curves. If you do something to the active layer while all the other layers' Eye icons are on, you can see the changes as they are combined with the other layers, but the other layers themselves do not change.

The Channels palette shows you the channels and Eye icon state for the layer you are working on. What you see in the Channels palette depends on the layer you have activated and which Eye icons are on in that layer and other layers. If you just want to work on that one layer and see only that layer, you can click on the Eye icons of the other layers to turn them off. Another, quicker, way to turn them all off is to Option-click on the Eye icon of the layer you want to work on. Doing that also changes the RGB display in the Channels palette, so that you see just the Red, Green, and Blue channels of the one layer. To turn all the other layers back on again, just Option-click again on the same layer's Eye icon. Also, then, the RGB display in the Channels palette once again shows a composite of all the visible layers.

THE BACKGROUND LAYER

If you open any single layer image into Photoshop, like a TIFF file for example, and look at the Layers palette, you will notice that the image's layer is called *Background*. It is called *Background* in italics because the *Background* layer differs from a normal layer. The *Background* layer, when it has that name, must be the bottom layer and cannot have any transparent areas. If you make a selection in the *Background* layer and clear or delete that selection, the selected area fills with the background color (usually white). If you delete a selection in any other layer, that area fills with transparency (the checkerboard pattern). Transparency is a hole where you can look through a layer and see other layers below it. You cannot move other layers below the *Background* layer or move the *Background* layer above other layers. To convert a layer from *Background* layer into a normal layer, just double-click on it and give it a new name. It becomes a normal layer and you can move it above other layers, as well as create transparent areas in it. The *Background* layer determines the initial canvas size for your layered document. You want to make sure the canvas is large enough to encompass the parts you want to see in all your layers. Therefore, you may want to put your largest picture element,

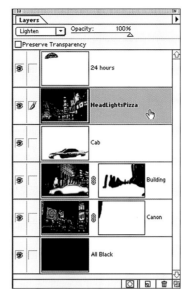

The Layers palette with the HeadLightsPizza layer active and all the Eye icons on. Here we are viewing the large icons. Choose Palette Options from the Layers Palette menu to set the size of your icons.

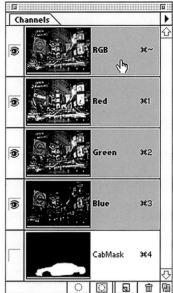

Since all the Eye icons are on, the Channels palette shows you a view of the Red, Green, and Blue channels of all layers as a composite image.

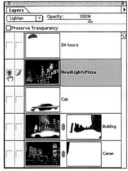

Option-click on the HeadLightsPizza layer's Eye icon and all the other layers are no longer visible.

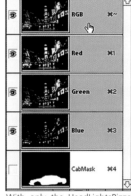

With only the HeadLightsPizza Eye icon on in the Layers palette, you see just that layer's Red, Green, and Blue channels in the Channels palette .

LayersIntro with just the HeadLightsPizza layer visible.

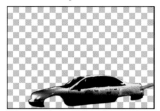

When you turn off the other eye icons and look at the Cab layer alone, the transparent area appears as a checkerboard.

Moving the cab and building with the Move tool.

The moved cab and building.

The Layers palette setup for moving the cab and building which are linked together. Notice that the cab opacity is set to 85%.

Lighten mode causes the headlights, and not their black background to show through the cab. Try Normal mode instead of LIghten mode here to see the difference.

often your main background, down as your first layer. If you add additional layers that are larger in horizontal or vertical pixel dimensions than your *Background* layer, you can see only as much of the image as fits on the *Background* layer on-screen. However, you can still move these other layers using the Move tool to expose parts left hanging outside the canvas area. In Photoshop 4, these parts that hang off the edge are permanently cropped only when you use the Cropping tool or the Image/Crop command. To expose these parts of the image, you can always increase the canvas size using Image/Canvas Size.

WORKING WITH ADDITIONAL LAYERS

When you add additional layers that are smaller than the *Background* layer, or if you copy a small item and do an Edit/Paste with it, the extra area around these smaller items shows up as transparent (a checkerboard pattern). When we look at just the Cab layer in this NightCabRide image, we see that it's entirely transparent aside from the cab itself. Through those transparent parts, when all the Eye icons are on, we will see the lights and buildings from the other three layers below the cab.

DRAG AND DROP, MOVING, AND LINKING

You create additional layers in Photoshop by copying something from another image and then choosing Edit/Paste. You can name these layers by double-clicking on them in the Layers palette. Using the Move tool, you can also click on a layer in the main document window, or the Layers palette in image "A," and drag and drop it on top of image "B's" main document window to create a new layer in image "B." In Photoshop 4, you can also drag and drop a whole set of layers if they're linked together. Having one layer in a perspective set active, you can link other layers to it by clicking on the Link column (the one to the right of the Eye icon) of the other layers you want to link to it. Layers that are linked can all be Moved and Transformed (scaled, rotated, and so on) together. This is a great new feature of Photoshop 4 especially for Web and multimedia designers.

You can move layers from side to side or up and down using the Move tool. Just click to activate the layer you want to move in the Layers palette, then select the Move tool from the Tool palette (V or the Command key), click and drag on the layer in the main document window, and drag it to its new location. If you have all the Eye icons on, you can see its relationship to the other layers change.

You can influence layers using the Opacity, and Blend modes. The Cab layer is partially transparent because its opacity is set to 85%. The reason that it looks like you are seeing headlights through the cab, however, is that the Blend mode on the HeadLightsPizza layer is set to Lighten.

MORE ABOUT LAYER MASKS

If you want part of a layer to be temporarily removed, or made invisible, you can add a layer mask to any layer. The parts of the layer mask that are black are transparent in that layer, which allows you to instantly prototype a layer and its composite with the other layers without seeing the masked-out part. If you later decide you want to restore that part of the image, just remove the layer mask by Shift-clicking on its icon to turn it off. When you activate a layer that

Chapter 11: Layers, Layer Masks, and Adjustment Layers

The Building layer without its layer mask. Only the hole where the car will sit is transparent.

The Building layer mask.

The Building layer with its layer mask removing the newly transparent areas from the final composite.

has a layer mask, that mask is also added to the channels in the Channels palette. It only appears in the Channels palette while you have that layer activated. If you want to edit the layer mask while still looking at the layer, just click on the layer mask's icon within the Layers palette. When you paint with black in the main document window, you add the black to the layer mask and remove those areas from view in the layer associated with the layer mask.

In Photoshop 4, you can create a layer mask by clicking on the New Layer Mask icon at the bottom left of the Layers palette. If you have a selection at the time of that click, the selected area will be the only thing that is white in the mask and therefore the only visible part of that layer. If you Option-click on the New Layer Mask icon, everything except the selected area will now be visible and the selected area will be made black in the layer mask.

If you want to edit the layer mask while looking at the mask itself, Option-click on the layer mask's icon within the Layers palette. The main document window will now just display the black-and-white mask and your Layers palette will have all the Eye icons dimmed out. The Channels palette now shows this layer mask channel as active with its Eye icon on. When you want to return to editing the layer itself, click or Option-click on the layer's icon within the Layers palette.

To edit the layer mask while still looking at the layer, just click on the layer mask's icon. You will see the Layer Mask icon to the right of the Layer icon. The Channels palette will display the mask as above, active, with its Eye icon off. The Eye icons are on for RGB, so you see those channels, yet you edit the mask since it is active.

To edit the layer mask and see just the mask in the Document window, Option-click on the layer mask's icon. You will see the Layer mask icon to the right of the Layer icon. The Channels palette will display the mask highlighted with the Eye icon on as above. The Eye icons are off for the RGB channels since you don't want to see them. Now Option-clicking on the layer mask's icon will toggle between just seeing the layer mask and seeing the RGB channels but you will always be editing the mask until you click or Option-click on the Layer icon again or click on RGB in the Channels palette.

MOVING, REMOVING, AND COPYING LAYERS

You can remove a layer by clicking on it, choosing Delete Layer from the Layer palette's pop-up menu, or clicking on the layer and dragging it to the Trash icon at the bottom right of the Layers palette.

You can make a copy of any layer by clicking on the layer and dragging it to the New Layer icon at the bottom middle of the Layers palette. You can also make a copy of the active layer by choosing Duplicate Layer from the Layers palette's pop-up menu. The copied layer will have the same name but with "copy" appended to its end.

You can move a layer from one location to another in the Layers palette by clicking on the layer you want to move and then dragging it until the line becomes

Deleting a layer the quick way by using the Trash icon at the bottom of the Layers palette. If the Layer is active, you can just click on the Trash icon and if you don't want the delete warning message to come up, just Option-click.

To copy a layer, drag it to the New Layer icon at the bottom of the Layers palette. Just clicking on this icon creates a new blank layer with a generic name or an Option-click allows you to name it while creating it.

To move a layer, click on it and drag it until the line is dark between the layers where you want to put it.

The moved layer appears in its new location now below the cab.

dark between the two layers where you want to put this layer. Let go of the mouse at that point, and the layer is moved. When you move a layer, it changes the composite relationship of that layer with the layers around it. Notice how the headlights no longer show through the cab after you move the HeadlightsPizza layer from above the cab to below the cab.

THE LAYER OPTIONS DIALOG BOX

If you double-click on a layer, you bring up the Layer Options dialog box, which enables you to name a layer, group it with other layers, or composite it using only a partial range of its 0..255 pixel values. This partial compositing feature is very powerful! The "Posterize, Bitmaps, and Patterns," "Blend Modes, Calculations, and Apply Image," and "Night Cab Ride in Manhattan" chapters explain Layer Options in great detail. All the layers features, as well as the creation of a more complex version of the NightCabRide image, are explained in "Night Cab Ride in Manhattan."

FLOATING SELECTIONS

When you have made any type of selection and it is highlighted on the screen with the dotted lines moving around it (those marching ants), you can now choose Command-option and then click and drag to float that selection. A floating selection is another copy of the pixels of the active layer in that selected area floating on top of the original layer below. A floating selection is like a temporary layer and it actually shows up in the Layers palette. In the Layers palette, you can change the opacity and blend mode of a floating selection. Before Photoshop had layers, it always had floating selections and they were more powerful. In older versions of Photoshop, all the things we do with layers today had to be done one at a time using a floating selection. You can only have one floating selection at a time and when you deselect it, by clicking outside it or choosing Select/None or by running a filter or any command on it, it becomes embedded in the layer it is floating above. At that point, you can no longer move it. A layer, on the other hand, is like a permanent floating selection and you can have many layers. Layers don't go away like floating selections do. You can always turn a floating selection into a full-fledged layer by double-clicking on it in the Layers palette. If you really want a layer from a selection though, just choose Command-J (Layer/New/Layer Via Copy) to create a new layer with a copy of the current selection. Floating selections have had most of their power removed in Photoshop 4. It seems like it would have been simpler if Adobe would have removed them completely. If you used floating selections a lot before, you should learn to do things with layers now!

CONTROL KEY CONTEXT MENUS

If you Control-click while working with layers, you can get some very useful context menus. When you are using the Move tool (or with Control-Command-click), you get a context menu showing all layers that have pixels at the current mouse location and also have their Eye icons on. You can then drag this menu to activate the layer you want to work on. If you are in a selection tool or a painting tool, you will get a different context menu. This is great power user stuff!

PHOTOGRAPHY

AND

OVERALL COLOR CORRECTION

DIGITAL IMAGING AND THE ZONE SYSTEM

Digital imaging as it relates to traditional
photography and the Zone System, and
how to create a high-quality original photograph.

Images in nature that you see with your eyes have the greatest beauty because they usually are illuminated by very wonderful light and have depth and texture that we can only simulate on a print or computer screen. The range of light, from the darkest black shadow to the brightest sparkling highlight, reflected from reality to our eyes is far greater than we can reproduce in any printed or screen image. Our eyes can adjust as we gaze into a shadow or squint to see a bright detail. When you look at a scene in nature, it has the best quality and the most detail. The T.V. set, which we watch so much, has the least amount of detail and sharpness. Go out and see the real world!

TRANSITIONS TO THE DIGITAL WORLD

There are many reasons to copy a scene from nature, a pretty face, or a product, and reproduce the image so it can be carried around and seen again. How to do this, and get the best quality, is the subject of this book. I give thanks to Ansel Adams, perhaps the most well-known nature photographer, and his great series of books: *The Camera*, *The Negative,* and *The Print,* for my introduction to an understanding of artistic photography. These titles by New York Graphic Society Books are must-reads for anyone who wants to understand how to take the best quality photographs. *Ansel Adams: An Autobiography* is also a wonderful book. Many of Adams' discussions are about black-and-white photography, but the concepts apply to color. The depth and joy of his philosophies are something all people who deal with images should have a feeling for.

Although he died in 1984, before digital imaging became easily available and popular, Ansel Adams was ahead of his time and says in his book *The Negative;*

> *"I eagerly await new concepts and processes. I believe that the electronic image will be the next major advance. Such systems will have their own inherent and inescapable structural characteristics, and the artist and functional practitioner will again strive to comprehend and control them."*

This chapter should help you to understand the nature of an original image and how to control and improve it in the digital world.

ACHIEVING YOUR VISUALIZATION

The Zone System, developed by Ansel Adams in 1940, gives photographers a way to measure an image in nature and then capture it on film so it can be reproduced with the photographer's intentions in mind. Adams uses the term "visualization" to explain a technique where photographers imagine what they want a photo to look like as a print before taking the photo. Once this image, the visualization, is in the photographer's mind, the photographer uses the Zone System to get the correct data on the film so that visualization can be achieved in the darkroom. Getting the right data on the film or into a digital camera is very important in the process of creating a digital image too. We use the Zone System to explain what the right data is, and then we discuss how to get that data onto film or into a digital camera. If you get the right data into a digital camera, you can transfer it directly into your computer. When you capture the image on film, you need to scan it correctly to make sure all the information gets into your computer.

CAPTURING THE DYNAMIC RANGE

When you look at an image in nature, or in a photography studio, you can use a photographic light meter to measure the range of brightness in the image. On a very sunny day, out in the bright sun, you may have a very large range of brightness between the brightest and darkest parts of your image area. We will call this range, from the brightest to the darkest part of an image, the *dynamic range* of that image. Each photographic film, and each digital camera, has its own dynamic range of values from brightest to darkest that the particular film or camera can capture, called its *exposure latitude*. Many photographic films and digital cameras cannot capture the full dynamic range of brightness present in the original scene, especially on a bright contrasty day. I'm sure you have all taken photographs where the prints don't show any details in the shadows or where a bright spot on a person's forehead is totally washed out. The objective of the Zone System is to measure, using a light meter, the brightness range in the original scene and then adjust your camera so the parts of that brightness range that you want to capture actually get onto the film or into the digital camera.

DIVIDING AN IMAGE INTO ZONES

The Zone System divides an image into 11 zones from the brightest to the darkest. Ansel Adams uses Roman numerals to denote the zones from 0 to X. These zones in the printed image reference how light or dark each area will be. Zone 0 is pure black where there is no detail showing whatsoever. In a photograph, a Zone 0 area would be solid black; in a halftone you would see no white dots in the solid black ink. Zone I is still a very dark black, but it is not pure black and has no real measurable detail. If you look at a Zone I halftone with the naked eye, it still looks black without detail, but if you were to use a loupe or other magnifier, you would see very small white dots in a sea of black ink.

On the other end of the scale, Zone X is solid white, so in a print this would be the color of the paper; in a halftone there would be no dots in a Zone X area. You would use Zone X to represent a specular highlight like the reflection of the sun on a chrome bumper. Zone IX is a very bright white without detail, but again you can see some very small halftone dots if you use a loupe. The range of image brightness areas that will have obvious detail in the printed image include Zone II through Zone VIII. Zone VIII will be very bright detail and Zone II will be very dark detail. In the middle of this area of print detail is Zone V. In a black-and-white print, Zone V would print as middle gray, halfway between pure black and pure white. In a color print, a Zone V area would print as normal color and brightness for that area if you were looking at it in normal lighting conditions with your eyes adjusted to it. When you set the exposure setting on your camera, areas in the image that have a brightness equal to that exposure setting are getting a Zone V exposure. We will explain this further in this chapter.

GETTING A GOOD EXPOSURE

Let's talk for a moment about how you take a picture with a camera. We will use black-and-white negative and color positive transparency as examples in this discussion. Normally, when you take a transparency picture with a camera, you measure the range of brightness in the original scene and set the exposure on your camera so as to reproduce the range of brightness on the film to look the same way it did in the original scene. When you use an automatic exposure camera, the camera does this for you. When you use a manual camera with a hand-held light meter, you need to do it manually. Even though many of you probably have automatic cameras as I do, let's describe the manual camera process so we all understand what needs to happen to take a good picture. The automatic cameras of today have computerized light meters that do all this for you, although you sometimes still need to do it manually to get exactly what you want. This discussion also applies to getting a good exposure with a digital camera.

MEASURING THE BRIGHTNESS

To get a good exposure, you need to measure the brightness range of different subjects within the photograph. Let's say you were taking a photograph of a Spanish home in Costa Rica. You want to set the exposure somewhere in the middle of the brightness range that occurs naturally in the setting. That middle position, wherever you set it, then becomes Zone V. A hand-held spot light meter allows you to point at any very small area in a scene and measure the amount of light reflected from that area. The light meter measures the brightness of light, the *luminance*, reflected from the metered part of the image. This is all you really need to measure whether you are taking a black-and-white or color photo.

In the Spanish home picture, the brightest areas are the little bit of sky at the top and the reflection of the sun in the right side of the window frame at the bottom. The darkest areas are the shadows in the bottom right corner. Measuring these with a light meter that allows spot readings might produce readings like exposure value 17 for the bright section of sky at the top and exposure value 7 for the dark shadow at the bottom. Each change in the exposure value settings on a professional light meter is equal to a difference of two in the amount of light measured.

In the building picture, if we have exposure value readings from 7 in the darkest area to 17 in the brightest area, there is a difference of 1024 times the brightness from the darkest amount of light to the brightest amount of light. This is because each jump in the exposure value represents twice as much light. Here's how we get 1024 times as much light: exposure value 7 = 1 (the lowest amount of light), EV 8 = 2

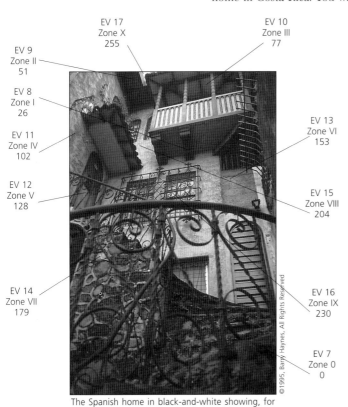

EV 17 Zone X 255
EV 10 Zone III 77
EV 9 Zone II 51
EV 8 Zone I 26
EV 13 Zone VI 153
EV 11 Zone IV 102
EV 12 Zone V 128
EV 15 Zone VIII 204
EV 14 Zone VII 179
EV 16 Zone IX 230
EV 7 Zone 0 0

The Spanish home in black-and-white showing, for each zone, the exposure value (EV) read by an exposure meter, the corresponding zones, and lastly the 0 to 255 digital value based on placing Zone V at exposure value 12 on the door.

Chapter 12: Digital Imaging and the Zone System

(twice as much light), EV9 = 4, EV10 = 8, EV11 = 16, EV12 = 32, EV 13 = 64, EV14 = 128, EV15 = 256, EV16 = 512, EV17 (the brightest reading) = 1024. This is 1024 times as much light from the darkest area to the brightest.

PLACING THE ZONE V EXPOSURE

After measuring the range of exposure values within a scene that you want to photograph, you usually set the camera's exposure to a value in the middle of that range. The value that you set your exposure to causes the areas that have that exposure value within the scene to show up as a middle gray value on the film and print in black-and-white or as a normal middle detail exposure in color. Where you set your exposure on the camera is called "where you are placing your Zone V exposure." Here we are placing our Zone V exposure at exposure value 12, the reading we got from the door. Usually you set your exposure to the area within the image that you want to look best or most normal. If a person were standing on the steps in this photo, you might set the exposure to a reading that you would take off the person's face.

When you decide where to set the exposure, you affect what happens to each of the zones within the image area, not just Zone V. If the Spanish home image were a transparency, it would reflect an exposure where you set Zone V based on the reading taken from the middle of the door. If the film is then processed correctly, the middle of the door in the transparency would look correct, as though you were looking straight at it with your eyes adjusted to it. When you set the exposure to the middle of the door, the areas that are lighter or darker around it, the zones above and below Zone V, become correspondingly lighter or darker on the film. The bright window, at exposure value 16, will then be placed at Zone IX and will show up as very bright and with almost no detail on the film. This is because it is 4 zones above, 16 times brighter, than where we set our exposure (at exposure value 12).

If you were to set the exposure on the camera to exposure value 16, the exposure value for the bright window, you would do to the camera and film what happens to your eye when you move up very close to an area in the bright part of a contrasty scene. The iris on your eye closes and you start to see a lot of detail in that bright

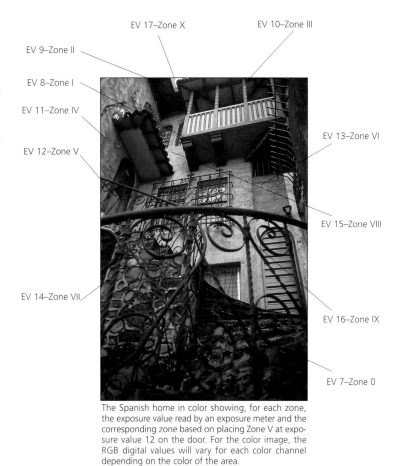

The Spanish home in color showing, for each zone, the exposure value read by an exposure meter and the corresponding zone based on placing Zone V at exposure value 12 on the door. For the color image, the RGB digital values will vary for each color channel depending on the color of the area.

area. It is no longer a white area with no detail, because the focus of your field of vision moves up and your eyes adjust to encompass just that area. If you set the exposure on your camera to exposure value 16, that bright window area in the picture would show up as a middle gray for black-and-white or a normal color in a transparency. By changing this exposure, you would then be placing Zone V at exposure value 16. Now the door would be at Zone I, 16 times darker, and everything darker than the door would be in Zone 0, totally black. This would give you details in the

Zones	0	I	II	III	IV	V	VI	VII	VIII	IX	X
Approximate Digital Values	0	26	51	77	102	128	153	179	204	230	255
% Black	100%	90%	80%	70%	60%	50%	40%	30%	20%	10%	0%

A stepwedge file of the 11 zones in the Zone System with the approximate corresponding digital values and percentage of black ink. The digital values shown here fall somewhere in the center of each zone. Where the actual zone values and digital values appear for each image depends on the type of output you choose. You will have more latitude of where the Zone I detail begins and Zone IX details end when you print at a higher resolution and line screen. If you are printing to newsprint, all of Zone I may print as 100% black and all of Zone IX as 100% white.

If you want to know more about the Zone System and how to take the best photographs, you should read Ansel Adams' book, The Negative. It contains very useful information. It also shows you some very good techniques for extending or shortening the exposure latitude of your film by under- or over-developing. Another great book on the Zone System is, The New Zone System Manual by White, Zakia, and Lorenz from Morgan Press, Inc.

highlights, but you would lose the details in the darker parts of the scene. By measuring the scene and noticing that the bottom of the stairs has exposure value 7 and the sky has exposure value 17, then setting the exposure on your camera in the middle at exposure value 12, you place Zone V there and thereby obtain the full range of these values on the film.

UTILIZING YOUR EXPOSURE LATITUDE

Different films have different exposure latitudes. The *exposure latitude* of a film is the number of different exposure values it can record at once. The Zone System covers a range of 11 exposure values, a brightness going from 1 to 1,024 times as bright. Most films cannot capture detail in so broad a range of lighting situations. This is a contrasty scene on a sunny day with the sun shining directly on it. Some films can capture detail over a range of 7 exposure values and some over a larger range. In Adams' description of his zones, detail is captured only from Zone II through Zone VIII or over a 7 zone range. Things in Zones 0, I, IX and X are pretty much void of detail and either black or white. Some films have a lesser exposure latitude and others a greater one. If you know the exposure latitude of your film or digital camera when taking a picture, you can determine which parts of the picture will have detail and which will be black or white by measuring the range of your image area and setting your exposure, your Zone V area, so the other zones, or brightness ranges, fall where you want them.

We could have gotten more details in the highlights in this picture by placing Zone V, our exposure setting, at exposure value 13 or 14 instead of 12, but then the shadow areas at exposure values 8 or 9, the areas underneath the roof and balcony overhangs, would have shown up as totally black. Some pictures will not be very contrasty, and you will know, by taking light measurements, that the exposure latitude of your film, or digital camera, can handle the total number of zones in the image. All you need to make sure of then is that you set the exposure in the middle of that range so all the areas of different exposure values fall within the latitude of the film or digital camera and you thus capture their detail.

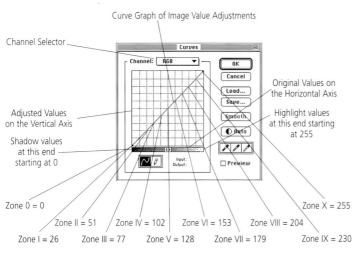

Channel Selector
Curve Graph of Image Value Adjustments
Original Values on the Horizontal Axis
Highlight values at this end starting at 255
Adjusted Values on the Vertical Axis
Shadow values at this end starting at 0
Zone 0 = 0
Zone I = 26
Zone II = 51
Zone III = 77
Zone IV = 102
Zone V = 128
Zone VI = 153
Zone VII = 179
Zone VIII = 204
Zone IX = 230
Zone X = 255

Using the Curves tool, if you want to modify the colors or brightness of the items in a certain zone or zone range of the image, this diagram points out the part of the curve you would modify to change those zones. Using the Eyedropper tool with Curves, you can measure any part of the image and the location of its values will show up on the curve as a small circle. This makes it very easy to adjust any range of values or colors using Curves.

The measurements and diagrams in this chapter don't accurately measure any particular film. They simply illustrate how the process works.

The Advantages of a Digital Image

Once you have captured all the information you need on the film, you want to move it into your computer by doing the best possible scan. If you have a digital camera, you don't need to scan; you can digitally transfer the image from the camera to the computer. Your objective is to make sure that your image retains all the zone detail you captured for you to play with. For more information on scanning and bringing images into the computer from Photo CD, see "Scanning, Resolution, Histograms, and Photo CD."

When you look at the histogram of a digital image using the Levels or Curves commands in Photoshop, you see all those values, all those zones, and you can move them around and adjust them with much more precision than you would have in the darkroom.

If you are not familiar with Levels and Curves, read "The Grand Canyon," "Kansas," "Grand Canyon Tweaks," "Kansas Tweaks," and "Color Correction, and Output," later in this book.

Looking at a scan of the Spanish home image in Levels, we can actually see how many values in the image fall within each zone. Notice that in this image that many values fall in Zones I, II, and III. That's because this image has a lot of dark areas in it. There are not many values in Zones IX and X since this image does not have many very bright areas. To move the values that are in Zone V toward Zone IV, making the image brighter, or toward Zone VI, making the image darker, you can use the Brightness/Contrast slider in Levels. To move the values in Zones I and II over to Zone 0, making the shadows darker, you can use the Input Shadow slider. In later chapters, we show you how to use these techniques with the Levels command to give you more control over the different brightness and color zones in your images. We will also show you how to use Curves to do pretty much anything you want with your image data.

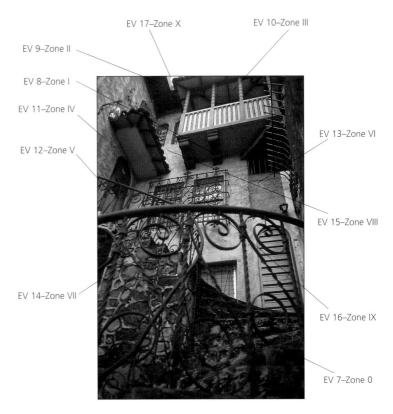

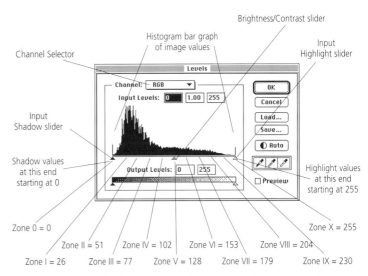

Here are the main controls of Levels and how the zones pointed out on the previous pages show up in the histogram of the Spanish home. The approximate digital value, in the 0 to 255 range, is also shown for each zone.

CALIBRATION

Here you learn how to use the tools that come with Photoshop (and the images on the Photoshop 4 Artistry *CD) to calibrate your monitor and output devices, and we discuss color management systems.*

AN OVERVIEW OF THE PROCESS

Many issues arise in attempting to get quality output to a digital printer, film recorder, or imagesetter. First among them are calibration issues. You must calibrate the output device and keep it calibrated. When your output device is not calibrated and consistent, any calibration and correction you do on your computer is less useful. Next, you need to send some known, good output to your output device, make a proof of that output, and compare that proof to the image that made the proof on your monitor. You adjust your monitor so the image on your monitor looks like your proof when you view both under your standard lighting conditions. We discuss calibration in this chapter.

Second, you have information issues. When you scan an image or have it scanned or put onto Photo CD, you need to know how to get the best scan. If you are not doing the scanning yourself, you need to know how to check the scans that others have done to make sure that the maximum amount of information is available. And, you need to understand how to make the most of the information that you have.We will cover this part of the process in "Scanning, Resolution, Histograms, and Photo CD."

Finally, you have color correction issues. Once you have the best possible scan from your input device, you need to color correct that scan. For the purposes of this discussion, we assume that your original scan is in RGB format (the format that most desktop scanners and Photo CDs use). Your first step in color correcting the scan is overall color correction, and after that, correcting specific areas that need special adjustments. At this point, you would apply any compositing or special effects to your corrected image or images. The last step in the process is to sharpen the image. If you're outputting to an RGB device, you are now done. If you are outputting to a CMYK device, you need to convert to CMYK and perhaps make final color adjustments in CMYK. These steps are covered in "Color Correction and Output."

If your scan was done at a high-end color house in CMYK, you may not need to color adjust it at all. High-end drum scanners often also sharpen the image. In that case, you would simply do any necessary compositing or effects and then output the CMYK file to your device. If you know that you are not adjusting the color or contrast of the file because it was done by the scanner operator, that the image on your screen look exactly like your output is not so important. That's crucial only when you are adjusting the color and contrast of the file.

100	98	95	90	80	75	70	60	50	40	30	25	20	10	5	2	0

A grayscale stepwedge file used in calibration.

CALIBRATING YOUR OUTPUT DEVICE

Trying to calibrate your monitor or perfect your process of doing color corrections doesn't do any good unless the output device you are sending to (imagesetter,
color printer, film recorder, or whatever) has been calibrated. A good way to test calibration is to send a group of neutral colors to your output device. I have created this
file, called the StepWedgeFile, for use as a test file for calibrating your output device.
The StepWedgeFile consists of wedges of neutral gray that have a known value.
There are two issues involved in calibrating your output device. The first issue is
whether the device will print the correct density. If you send a 50% density value
(numerically, 128) to the device, it should measure and look like 50% when it prints.
All densities should print as they are expected. The second issue is getting colors to
print correctly. If you get the output device to print these neutral gray values correctly, it's a good sign that it will also print colors correctly. You want the densities on
the gray wedges to be correct, and you also want each wedge to continue to look gray.

To calibrate an imagesetter, send a grayscale version of the StepWedgeFile to
the imagesetter and output it as one piece of film. Use a densitometer to measure
the densities of the swatches on the film. They should match (plus or minus 1%) the
densities that you sent from the file. Make sure the imagesetter is calibrated for density before you start worrying about color.

PRINT KNOWN COLOR OUTPUT TO MAKE A TEST PRINT

Once you know that your output device has been calibrated for density, you
should also check it for color. For CMYK output, you need a CMYK file that you
know contains good color separation values and images. For RGB output, you need
a known quality RGB original. On the following pages, we present examples of the
type of file you should create for your test. This file, called KnownOutputTest, contains known CMYK values at the top in the neutral grays and also various colors you
can use to test how known CMYK colors print on your output device.

The CMYK makeup of the colored swatch values we used here is printed at the
back of Chapter 6 in the Adobe Press book, *Imaging Essentials*. Create these
swatches in a CMYK file by selecting the area of each swatch and then going into the
Photoshop Color Picker and typing in the CMYK values that make up that swatch's
color. Use Edit/Fill to fill the selection with the color you just created. The
KnownOutputTest file also contains photographs that were separated using known
color separation techniques. We have a bigger version of the Ole No Moiré image
from Adobe; the Bryce Canyon and Santa Cruz images are mine; the flying books is
an Apple magazine cover shot by Marc Simon with effects by me; and the fourth
image is by one of my students, Will Croff. All these images and these separations
have been previously printed on a press with very good results.

For your test image, you should create grayscale bars and color bars like the
ones shown here (you can get the CMYK values from *Imaging Essentials* or by measuring my file) and then include several images that you know are good separations
of work typical of the type of image you normally separate. You can also include the
Ole No Moiré image, which you can get from the the KnownOutputTest file in the
Calibration and output folder on the CD. A big version of Olé No Moiré is also now
available on the Photoshop 4 CD in Other Goodies/Calibration/Olé No Moiré. After

Here is our KnownOutputTest CMYK file. This file
should use known CMYK values and separations.
Use it to make a test proof and to calibrate your
monitor to that proof.

you output and proof this file in the way you would normally work, you open the file that you used to create the proof and adjust your monitor so the image on-screen matches the proof as closely as possible. We will show you how to do that shortly. For calibrating an RGB output device, use similar images that you know have worked well when output to that type of device.

CHECK PHOTOSHOP SEPARATIONS ON THIS DEVICE.

To see if your Photoshop color separation preference settings are working well, we will create your Photoshop separation test. Before you do so, be sure to read the "Setting System and Photoshop Preferences" chapter and set up your Photoshop separation preferences correctly. If you already have Photoshop separation preferences that work well for you, just continue to use those. Create an 8.5 x 11 canvas in RGB mode, fill it with a neutral gray background, and save it as Photoshop Separation Test. Now convert the grayscale StepWedgeFile, in the Calibration and Output folder, to RGB and paste it into the Photoshop Separation Test file.

Next, find some RGB images that are typical of your normal work. Copy these images and paste them into your test file. (We have created a Photoshop Separation Test file from some of the images in this book. It is included in the Calibration & Output folder on the *Photoshop 4 Artistry* CD and also printed in this chapter.) Save the final RGB version of this file. Use *your* Photoshop Separation Test (you can try ours if you don't have one), to output all four of the cyan, magenta, yellow, and black pieces of film in the same way you do your normal production. If you normally use the Photoshop Mode menu to convert from RGB to CMYK, then do just that on the Photoshop Separation Test. If you use someone else's separation tables, do it that way. If you normally save your files as EPS/DCS from Photoshop and then put the file into Quark, do the same thing in your test. Save your final CMYK version of the file under a different name than the RGB version.

Print the Photoshop Separation Test to film on your normal imagesetter and make a laminated proof. The densities should look correct in the stepwedge on the proof and they should also look gray. If the stepwedge densities are not right, or if they have a cyan, magenta, or some combination of color casts, it's a sign that either the imagesetter isn't calibrated or something's not right about the way you make separations. You did not alter or color correct the stepwedge file using your monitor, so it should be gray. If it doesn't look gray or the densities are not correct, refer to the separation section and try to adjust your separation values to solve this problem. If the stepwedge looks good but your images have a color cast in the proof, the problem might be the calibration of your monitor. If this test prints with the correct densities and no color casts, you know you're set to calibrate the rest of your system.

CALIBRATING YOUR MONITOR

Now you are going to take your Known Output Test and your Photoshop Separation Test and use these files along with their proofs to calibrate the monitor. Consistent lighting in your office for color correcting images is a must. If you have an office with a large window right next to your screen, achieving consistent lighting on-screen is just about impossible. Ideally, you should have a color correct, 5000° Kelvin viewing box next to your monitor where you could place your proofs for consistent viewing. You want a room where the lighting on your monitor is always the same. You can then adjust the monitor, using the Gamma tool that comes with Photoshop or a hardware monitor calibrator, so the color and contrast of the image on-screen looks as close as possible to the proof.

SETTING THE BACKGROUND

First, make sure the background on your monitor is neutral gray. On the Mac, go to Control Panels on the Apple menu and locate the Desktop Pattern Desk Accessory. Click on the arrows on either end of the slider until you find a neutral gray, then click on the Set Desktop Pattern button to invoke the change. In Windows 95 and NT, click on the Start button, select Settings, Control Panel. Now click on the Display Icon then click on the Background tab and select None in the Pattern and Wallpaper drop-down menus. Select the Appearance tab and click on the Color button. Now choose one of the neutral grays from the pop-up swatches or click on the Other button to open the Color dialog box. This dialog box gives you more color swatch selections and also allows you to choose a gray value from the Color Picker or to enter a value, like 128, for RGB in the Red, Green and Blue settings. If you use the Color dialog box, you will have to press OK to apply the change from this dialog box, in either case, press OK from the Appearance tab to apply the changes.

SETTING THE GAMMA

First, locate Gamma in your Photoshop folder within the Goodies/Calibration folder and move it to the Control Panels folder within your System folder, so that the adjustments you make to your monitor will come up every time you reboot your system. PC users access the Gamma utility (called Calibrate in the PC version of Photoshop) by clicking on the Calibrate button in File/Color Settings/Monitor Setup. Now, you want to create your *basic gamma*. The basic gamma is a gamma close to the 1.8 and white point close to the 6500°K that you set in your monitor preferences. A monitor's gamma is similar to its amount of contrast. The color balance of the monitor affects the way various colors appear on the screen. Bring up the Gamma control panel (Calibrate for PC) against the standard gray background.

Before you set the gamma, be sure to set the brightness and contrast knobs on the monitor where you like them. After the monitor has been calibrated, you should make sure that nobody touches these knobs—any adjustment will throw your calibration out of whack. If there is more than one person using your computer, tape these knobs down and put a Do Not Disturb sign on them. Place the Gamma control panel in the middle of the screen and set Target Gamma to 1.8. (*PC users:* There is no Target Gamma setting on Calibrate, so skip this action.) Make sure that the Black Point, Balance, and White Point settings are all in the non-adjusted positions. If you move the Gamma Adjustment slider quickly and radically back and forth, you will notice that the two lines of vertical bars sometimes look similar and sometimes look quite different. Sit way back and squint, and then move the Gamma Adjustment slider until the two sets of gray bars look as similar as possible. That ought to give you a gamma of about 1.8. If your final output device will be an RGB film recorder or a video monitor for multimedia, you may find that you want to use the 2.2 radio button, which gives you a 2.2 gamma when you perform this procedure. If you do that, you will also need to change the Gamma value in Monitor Setup to 2.2. I usually just leave all my gamma settings at 1.8 all the time and that works well for me, even for creating images for the Web.

ADJUSTING THE WHITE POINT

Get some paper typical of the paper you normally print on, or use the background color of your normal proofing paper. Now click on the White Pt. adjustment and move the Red, Green, and Blue sliders to try to get the whites in the Gamma dialog box to look more like the whites on your print or proof paper. Remember, you are viewing that paper under your standard viewing light box or lighting conditions.

Use Desktop Patterns to make sure your background is neutral gray.

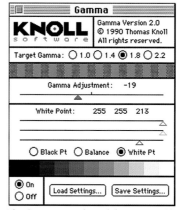

The Gamma control panel that comes with Photoshop can be used to calibrate your monitor.

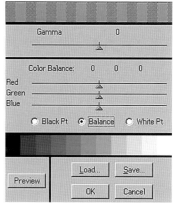

The Calibrate utility in Windows 95 and Windows NT is accessed from the bottom right corner of the Monitor Setup dialog box. You need to click on the Preview button to see the changes.

Put the images within Photoshop in Normal Screen mode so you can see them and Gamma at the same time.

You also (hopefully) have your standard lighting conditions set in the room to view your monitor. Moving the Blue slider to the left adds yellow to your whites. Moving the Red or Green slider to the left adds cyan or magenta, respectively. If you want to add the color of one of these sliders, say green, you need to move both of the other sliders (Red and the Blue in this case) the same amount to the left.

Don't get too obsessed with getting the whites on the monitor to exactly match the whites on your standard paper: It's extremely hard to do with most monitor and paper combinations. When you calibrate a monitor, you're trying to get the monitor to resemble your output as much as possible, but realize this: It will never look exactly the same and getting whites to look the same is probably hardest of all. If the whites on the monitor look a little blue, for example, just move the Blue slider a little to the left to take away some of that blue cast. Don't move these highlight sliders too far or you'll throw off the calibration.

SETTING THE COLOR BALANCE

Click on the Balance adjustment button in the middle and adjust the Red, Green, and Blue sliders left or right until the middle values in the grayscale in the bottom part of the Gamma tool look as close to gray as possible. If you have trouble judging gray, place a standard Kodak Color Separation Guide and Grayscale (Q13 and Q14) in your proof viewing box and compare the grays in the Gamma tool to those on the printed chart. You can also use a MacBeth Color Checker color rendition chart to make this comparison. Moving the Red, Green, or Blue slider to the right adds more of the respective color to the color balance of the middle values that appear on your monitor. Moving any of the sliders to the left adds the complementary color, such as magenta for the Green slider, to the monitor's balance.

SETTING THE BLACK POINT

Finally, click on the Black Pt. button to adjust the dark parts of Gamma's grayscale wedge. Moving the Blue slider to the right adds blue to the shadows. To add yellow to the shadows, move Red and Green equally to the right.

FINE-TUNING THE ADJUSTMENTS

After you adjust White Pt., Balance, and Black Pt., you may want to return to the Gamma slider and fine-tune it so that the two rows of gray bars are still the same. Now you have adjusted your monitor so the gamma, which is similar to the amount of contrast, is close to 1.8 and the color balance is close to neutral. (I preface these with "close to" because this is a subjective procedure.) Click on the Save Settings button and save these settings in the Calibration folder of your Photoshop folder and call it Basic Gamma 1.8. PC users need to include the .AGP suffix on the file name. When you are working with grayscale images, you may find this monitor setting a good one to use. We are going to make a different monitor setting that is calibrated to each different output device you work with. Whenever you start to calibrate to a new output device, first use Load Settings in Gamma to reload this Basic Gamma 1.8 setting. PC users need to click on the Preview button to see the Gamma change on the entire screen, and then click on OK in the Calibrate dialog box, and click on OK again in Monitor Setup to apply the changes. Mac users, can just leave Gamma turned on and make sure it is stored in the Controls Panels folder.

CALIBRATING YOUR MONITOR TO YOUR OUTPUT DEVICE

Bring up the digital files that created your Known Output Test and Photoshop Separation Test. You can use our Known Output Test and Photoshop Separation Test (both are in the Calibration folder on the *Photoshop 4 Artistry* CD) if you haven't made your own test files yet. These will get you in the ball park. You must calibrate your monitor to your own output device(s), however, for maximum accuracy.

Have these two CMYK digital files open and on-screen in Photoshop. You always want to do your final critical color corrections in Photoshop because Photoshop will alter the display of CMYK images to match your output device as closely as possible. Remember to set and tape down the monitor contrast and brightness knobs. Open Gamma and do a Load Settings on the Basic Gamma 1.8 settings you created in the preceding section. Now you have a starting point. Place the proofs of the two images in your color correct lightbox or in the standard location you use for viewing proofs. Make sure that the lighting on the screen and on the proofs is your standard lighting and that you can see the screen and proofs well. Put the images in Photoshop in Normal Screen mode so you can view them and the Gamma settings at the same time. You will adjust changes to Gamma to make the images on this screen look as close as possible to the images in the proofs. When you do this adjustment, you have to compromise. You won't be able to get the images on-screen to look exactly like your proofs. If you move the image to a different computer, you will need to calibrate its screen too, using these same steps. If your final output is to an RGB device, like a film recorder, your test file should be in RGB format on-screen when you calibrate your monitor, because that's the format where you did your final color correction and output.

When you do the color correction exercises in this book, you will find the directions most accurate if the book's images look on your screen much as they looked to us on our screens. For that to happen, you should use the following monitor calibration method to calibrate the Photoshop Separation Test file on your screen to the full page print of this file earlier in this chapter. The Photoshop Separation Test is in the Calibration & Output folder on the *Photoshop 4 Artistry* CD.

SETTING THE CONTRAST AND BRIGHTNESS

First, adjust the Gamma Adjustment slider so the contrast and brightness of the images on the screen look like your proofs. Don't worry about the gray stripes in the Gamma control panel this time; just get the screen image to match the proof. Pay particular attention to the shadow areas, such as the gray background behind the woman in the Ole No Moiré image. Also, look at the stepwedge file and try to get the different gray steps on the screen to look similar to the proof. Doing these things should bring your screen as close as possible to having the same overall brightness and contrast as in your proofs.

SETTING THE COLOR BALANCE

Click on the Balance adjustment and adjust the color balance of the midtones by moving the Red, Green, and Blue sliders to the right for more red, green, or blue and to the left for more cyan, magenta, or yellow. Getting your monitor as close as possible to your proofs does take some practice. Small adjustments in balance can make a bigger difference than you might think. Take it slow and keep an eye on your neutral colors and flesh tones. If you get the neutral colors—like the gray background and stepwedge file—to look correct, the other colors will come pretty close. You will find that getting exact matches on bright saturated colors is particularly difficult, especially bright reds and saturated blues. Don't throw your neutrals out of whack trying to get a bright color to look just right.

FINE-TUNING THE ADJUSTMENTS

After adjusting the balance, you may want to readjust the Gamma. Now tweak the White Pt. and Black Pt. adjustments to get your bright whites and dark shadows to match your proof as closely as possible. You may find getting bright whites to match impossible. Again, go back and tweak the gamma and balance. You may find that one picture in your proof set matches really well but another not as well. Calibrating phosphors on a monitor to reflected light from a print is difficult and you always have to compromise. Just come as close as you can within reason.

SAVING YOUR SETTINGS

At this point, choose the Save Settings button and save these settings under an appropriate name. Call it Photoshop Artistry Gamma if you are calibrating to the calibration photos printed in this book. Use a name that refers to the type of proofs that you use or that your service bureau uses. You need to create a different calibration setting for each type of output that you do and maybe, for each service bureau that you work with. If you output to color transparency film, you should put the transparency on a color correct light table located next to your monitor, and then, in Photoshop, calibrate the RGB digital file used to create the transparency to the actual transparency on the light table. You can get color correct viewing boxes that allow for both transparency and proof viewing—I recommend the GTI Soft-View D5000. It's the one I use and it's great.

CHECKING THE RESULTS

Now, use the button at the bottom left to turn off the Gamma tool. With Gamma off, you see the screen without any calibration. Hopefully, the screen is much closer to your proof when you have Gamma on. You can see that you are better off with the Gamma control panel settings than with no monitor calibration at all. Turn Gamma back on. You will get used to the differences between the way an image looks on-screen and the way it looks on a proof or transparency. Certain colors and brightness values never look exactly the same and you will learn how to pick up on these subtle differences. The purpose of calibrating your monitor is to get the screen colors as close as possible to the colors of the proof; it's noticeably better than no calibration at all.

To adjust your monitor using a hardware calibrator, use the directions that come with that calibrator. Using the gamma utility or a hardware calibrator, you can never quite get the image on-screen to look exactly like the proof, but you can come much closer than if you didn't calibrate. If you don't have a color correct lightbox next to your monitor, just make sure that you always view the proof in the same lighting conditions and that you can see it well with that light. Also, make sure that the light in the room that hits your monitor is always the same.

A CUSTOM SETTING FOR EACH TYPE OF OUTPUT

If you work with several different service bureaus to do different types of output, you may need to have a different monitor setting for each type of output at each service bureau. When I output 4x5 transparency film to Robyn Color in San Francisco, I use different monitor calibration settings than when I output to my Radius ProofPositive color printer. Whenever I am working on a job for Robyn Color, I load the Robyn Color Monitor settings; this way, I know the colors on my screen will be very similar to the colors on their final output on their RGB film recorder. You may want to have a different monitor calibration setting for printing grayscale images and maybe yet a different one for duotones, besides the ones you use for working with CMYK. Experiment, and see what works for you. To do the separations for this book, we asked the printer to use their Match Print proofing system to make proofs. We then calibrated our monitor to the KnownOutputTest and Photoshop Separation Test proofed with that system. The advantage of this system of calibration is that you can do it yourself with the tools that come with Photoshop, so you have complete control over it.

COLOR MANAGEMENT SYSTEMS: WHAT THEY DO

Color management systems take a standard image that you have corrected on your computer screen and remap that image based on the different color gamut of the particular output device it is being printed on. The color gamut of an output device is the set of colors and brightness ranges that the output device can print. Each different output device, such as a digital printer, CMYK proofing system, transparency writer, and so on, has its own specific gamut. If you take the same digital file and print it, unmodified, on a number of different output devices, each print will look different—from each other, and also probably different from the image on your screen.

The monitor calibration technique we just took you through in the last section shows you how to calibrate your monitor to make it look as much as possible like the output of one particular output device, but you will have to do this calibration routine separately for each output device you use. A color management system measures the difference between different types of output devices and creates a device profile for each device. When you send an image to a particular device, the color management system changes the image, on the fly, using that image's device profile, to try to make it print in a standard way on that device. If you print the same picture on many devices, the color management system does its best to make all those pictures look as close as possible to each other. I say "does its best" because you cannot always get the same colors on one device that you can on another. Each device has its own color gamut.

Some examples of color management systems are the Kodak KEPS, Agfa's Foto-Tune, and Apple's Color Sync systems. Apple's system is a generic one that allows many other third-party companies to contribute device profiles for their specific products. Color management systems are a step in the right direction toward standardizing color. The problem with them in the past has been that they haven't incorporated a good way to deal with the subtle differences between each instance of a particular device. I have, for example, a Radius/SuperMac ProofPositive dye sublimation printer. I love the photographic quality prints it gives me. If I took the digital file that produced a print on my ProofPositive printer and printed the same file on someone else's ProofPositive printer, even using a color management system, you would see subtle differences between the two prints. The other printer may have a different batch number on its ribbon, it may be slightly out of alignment, the temperature and humidity at the other printer's location might be different, and for

Color Management System

MONITOR

A separate device profile for each device converts the gamut of that device to some standard.

DEVICE PROFILE

SCANNER → DEVICE PROFILE →

COMPUTER

DIGITAL PRINTER

DEVICE PROFILE

DEVICE PROFILE

POSTSCRIPT IMAGESETTER FOR CMYK PRINTING

whatever reason there may be other subtle differences. Color management systems have not dealt with these matters in the past, but they are now starting to.

To solve these problems, the systems need to be able to measure the output from your particular device and create a custom device profile for it at any particular time. Some newer products emerging on the scene, such as the Colortron II color Spectrophotometer from Lightsource, are starting to help users take these measurements and incorporate them into newer versions of color management systems.

Color management systems can also characterize different types of scanners and film input types, different types of monitors, and other factors that affect color production along the way to final output. The "Why Is It So Difficult to Get Predictable Color?" chart here shows you the types of color systems and contortions that a color image can go through in the process of being transferred from a scene in nature to a photograph in a magazine, a transparency, or another final output format. Given the great many variations in what can happen to the colors, it's no wonder color calibration and correction often prove so difficult.

Color management systems can help you deal with the differences in the gamut and characteristics of different types of input and output devices, and they are improving all the time. Some color management system marketing implies that these systems can automatically scan, correct, and output images so that they print like originals. Color management systems can be adjusted to give you a higher degree of calibration and control between devices, but doing this correctly still requires a lot of careful measurement and control of every part of your color production system. Don't invest in a color management system unless you are willing to take the time and ensure the control.

To do art and advertising quality photographic output, photographers and artists always want to be able to tweak their images and possess as much control as possible over their results. We want prints that look better than the original based on our visualization and digital skills. We hope to help you understand the things you need to know to work with color in the real world and produce beautiful output.

Why Is It So Difficult to Get Predictible Color?

Steps in Process	Media	Applicable Color Theory	Form and Range
Nature START	Reflected Light	CIE Chromaticity	Analog ∞ range
Photo Original	Photo dyes and silver	Photo RGB (CMY)	Analog 3.0 – 1.7 optical density
Scan	Magnetic or optical data recording	Photo Separation RGB	Digital 24-bit
Digital Storage	Magnetic or optical data recording	CMYK RGB HSV LAB	Digital 24-bit
Display	Phosphor emission	Video RGB	Analog variable gamma
Output Master	Halftone film	CMYK	Digital halftone
Proof	Proof pigments	CMYK	Analog 2.0 optical density
Offset Print FINISH	Cyan Magenta Yellow and Black inks	CMYK	Analog 2.0 or less optical density

When you transfer an image from nature to film, scan it into the computer, output to proofs and film, and then finally print it on a press, the image goes through many changes along the way. Each change can affect the colors in the image in that particular media and how you see those colors. Managing all these changes and ending up with an image that looks like the original nature scene when you're done is difficult. This diagram shows you the steps in the process, the media used in each step, the color theory associated with that media, and the form and range of that color theory.

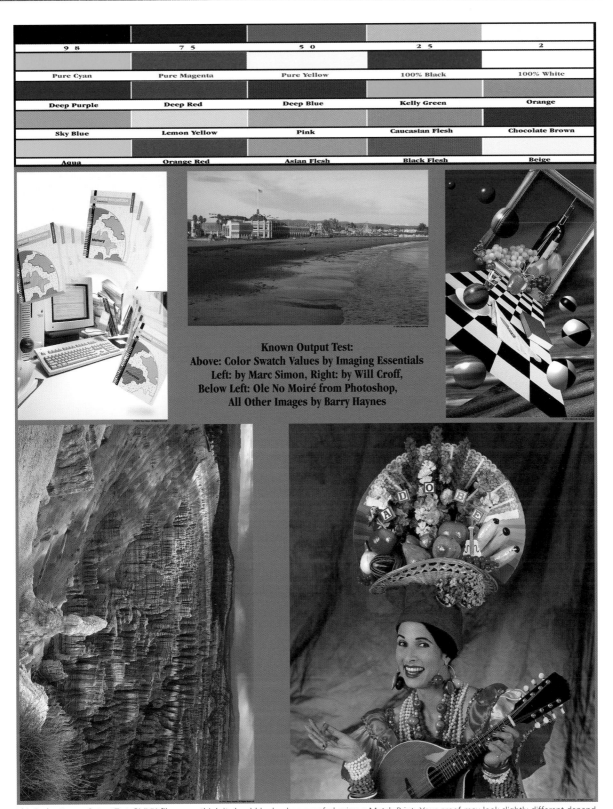

9 8	7 5	5 0	2 5	2
Pure Cyan	Pure Magenta	Pure Yellow	100% Black	100% White
Deep Purple	Deep Red	Deep Blue	Kelly Green	Orange
Sky Blue	Lemon Yellow	Pink	Caucasian Flesh	Chocolate Brown
Aqua	Orange Red	Asian Flesh	Black Flesh	Beige

Known Output Test:
Above: Color Swatch Values by Imaging Essentials
Left: by Marc Simon, Right: by Will Croff,
Below Left: Ole No Moiré from Photoshop,
All Other Images by Barry Haynes

This is the KnownOutputTest CMYK file as we think it should look when proofed using a Match Print. Your proof may look slightly different depending on the type of proofing system you use. If your proof of this test looks a lot different, you possibly have a problem with the calibration of your imagesetter.

| 100 | 98 | 95 | 90 | 80 | 75 | 70 | 60 | 50 | 40 | 30 | 25 | 20 | 10 | 5 | 2 | 0 |

This is our Photoshop Separation Test file converted to CMYK using our preferences settings as we think it should look when proofed with the a Match Print. Use Gamma and the techniques we demonstrate in this section to calibrate this file on your screen so it looks like this, then use Save Settings in Gamma to save this calibration. Use Load Settings in the Gamma tool to load these calibration settings when working on the color correction exercises in this book. That way, the book's images will look as close as possible on your screen to how they looked on the our screen when we wrote the exercises, making them better for comparing your results to ours.

SCANNING, RESOLUTION, HISTOGRAMS, AND PHOTO CD

Here you learn how to make a good scan at the right resolution and file size, how to use histograms to evaluate and improve scans, and how to make the best use of Photo CD scans.

WHAT ARE BYTES, BITS, AND DPI?

To learn how to make a good scan, you need to understand resolution and the issues involved in determining what size to make the scan. Since we're going to be talking about size in bytes, let's take a minute to talk about bytes, bits, and dpi. A *byte* (8 bits) is the most common unit of measurement of computer memory. All computer functionality is based on switches that can be turned on and off. A single switch is called a *bit*. When a bit is off, it has a value of 0. When a bit is on, it has a value of 1. With a single bit, you can count from 0 to 1. With two bits lined up next to each other, you can count from 0 to 3 because now there are four possibilities (00=0, 01=1, 10=2, and 11=3). Add a third bit, and you can count from 0 to 7 (000=0, 001=1, 010=2, 011=3, 100=4, 101=5, 110=6, and 111=7). When there are 8 bits, or a byte, you can count from 0 to 255, which is 256 possible values.

A grayscale digital image has one byte of information for each value scanned from the film. A value of 0 is the darkest possible value, black, and a value of 255 is the brightest possible value, white. Values in between are different levels of gray, the lower numbers being darker and the higher numbers being lighter. You can think of these values like you would think of individual pieces of grain within a piece of film: the more values you have per inch, the smaller the grain in the digital file. Also, the more of these values that you have per inch, the higher the resolution (alias dpi [dots per inch] or samples per inch) in your file. An RGB color digital image has three bytes of information (24 bits, one byte for each channel of red, green, or blue) for each value scanned from the film. And CMYK files have four bytes per pixel.

If you have an enlarger in the traditional darkroom, you can make a 20x24 print from a 35mm original. Its quality will not be as good as a 20x24 print on the same paper from a 4x5 original of the same type of film, because the 4x5 has more film grain with which to define the image. If you were printing on different types of paper, the paper's grain would affect the look of the final print. It's the amount of grain in the original film that makes the difference when you project that film on the same paper to make a traditional darkroom print.

When you make a print on a printing press, the line screen of the halftone is analogous to the grain in the photographic paper. When you make a print on a digital printer, the dpi (dots per inch) of the printer is analogous to the grain in the photographic paper. The dpi of a digital printer is the number of individual sensors, or ink jets, or laser spots, that the particular printer can put down per inch. Each digital printer has its own maximum possible dpi, based on its own specific physical limitations. The relationship between the dpi of a scan and the line screen or dpi of a digital printer is analogous to the relationship between the grain size of film in the enlarger and the grain size of the paper you are printing on in a traditional darkroom. A scan of 100 dpi will print on a digital printer that can output at 300 dpi but it won't look as good as a 300 dpi scan for the same printer. Similarly, a print on photographic paper from ASA 1600 (large grain) film won't look as good as a print on the same paper from ASA 25 (small grain) film.

HOW BIG SHOULD I MAKE A SCAN?

When you are having an image scanned, you should know the intended purpose of the scan well ahead of time.

The formula for calculating the optimal byte size for a scan of this 6x7 image is (6x300 dpi) x (7x300 dpi) x 3. This file would be 11,340,000 bytes in size. (The final factor represents the number of bytes for each pixel in the image; 3 is the number for an RGB color image.) For a CMYK scan, the factor is 4 instead of 3 because there are 4 bytes for each pixel in a CMYK image. If you do a black-and-white scan, you can remove this factor because they require only one byte per pixel. When scanning for publication, you generally should scan an extra ¼ inch for each dimension to give the stripper (electronic or manual) a little extra space for fine adjustment. Here's the general formula for the required byte size of final publication scans:

Scan Size = ((height of image + ¼") x (2 x line screen dpi)) x ((width of image + ¼") x (2 x line screen dpi)) x 3 (for RGB)

If you scan a file for output to a digital printer, such as the Radius/SuperMac ProofPositive or the Tektronix Phaser SDX, you need to do the scan at the same dpi as the resolution of the printer you plan to use. For output to the Radius/SuperMac ProofPositive, which has a resolution of 300 dpi, the formula and byte size would be (6x300 dpi) x (7x300 dpi) x 3 = 11,340,000 bytes. Most other dye sublimation digital printers (RasterOps, Radius/SuperMac, Fargo, Mitsubishi, GCC, et al.), and also the IRIS ink jet printer, have a printed dpi of 300. You should find out the resolution of the printer your service bureau is using and do your scans accordingly.

If you scan a file for output to a film recorder, such as the Kodak LVT (Light Valve Technology), or Cymbolic Sciences' Light Jet 2000, remember that they require a very high dpi. If you want the output to have the same quality as original film, the dpi can be around 1200 or more. To output a 4x5 RGB transparency at 1200 dpi would require a file size of (4x1200) x (5x1200) x 3, or 86,400,000 bytes. For film recorders, the dpi of the file needs to match the maximum dpi of the film recorder for optimal quality.

If you have trouble remembering formulas and don't want to bother with a calculator, there is an easy way to calculate the file size you will need: by using the New command in Photoshop. Choose File/New, then enter the width and height dimensions in inches for the largest size at which you expect you might want to print the image you are scanning. Based on the current discussion, set the resolution in pixels/inch to match what you will need for your line screen or printer resolution. Now set the mode to Grayscale, RGB, or CMYK, according to the type of scan. The image size that shows up at the top of the dialog box is the size in megabytes that you should make your scan. Now you can cancel from this dialog box; Photoshop has done the calculation for you.

If the image is to be published as a halftone on a printing press and you want the best quality, you need to scan it at a dpi (dots per inch or scan samples per inch) of twice the line screen of the publication. For example, if you are printing a 6-inch by 7-inch photograph in a 150-line screen publication, you should scan it at 300 dpi for the number of inches you're printing it at.

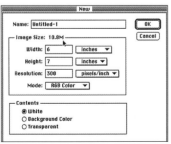

Use File/New to calculate the size of the scan you will need.

The formulas for file size that we present here are the ones you would use to obtain the best quality. Making even larger scans than these is unlikely to improve the quality but definitely will increase the time necessary to work with and output the files. Making smaller scans than these most likely reduces your quality but also decreases the time necessary to work with and output the files.

If you scan small files, usually measured in pixel dimensions, for Web sites or multimedia applications, you often can get better results if you scan a simple factor larger in each dimension. I recently did some Web images where the final spec for the GIF file size was 180 by 144 pixels. I scanned the files at 720 by 576 and did all my color corrections and masking at this larger, more detailed size. One of the final steps before creating the GIF files was to scale the corrected and sharpened files to 25% of the larger size. This 25% scale factor is a simple ratio that allows for very accurate scaling. See "Images for the Web and Multimedia" for the details of this process.

If you need some digital files to prototype a project, you don't need to start with the large scans we describe here. I find that RGB scans of about one megabyte usually provide plenty of screen detail for any prototyping I do. If you JPEG-compress these scans, you should be able to get 10 or so on a 1.4Mb disk. When you decide on the final dimensions for the images in your printed piece, you should do a final scan for the intended output device at those final dimensions. When you get a scan, archive the original digital file as it was scanned and use copies of it to do color corrections, color separations, and crops, so that you can go back to the original if you make a mistake and need to start over. Happy scanning!

EVALUATING HISTOGRAMS TO MAKE THE BEST SCAN FROM ANY SCANNER

Now that you know how big to make the scan, you need to know how to make a good scan and also how to do a good job of bringing an image into Photoshop from Photo CD. The key to these techniques is learning how to use the histogram in Levels to evaluate scans. This section presents a few histograms and talks about what they reveal about the images they are describing.

A *histogram* is a bar graph of the number of samples of each of the possible settings in the 0 to 255 range in the entire image. The diagram here shows you some of the useful information that a histogram can provide. When you have normal subject material, the

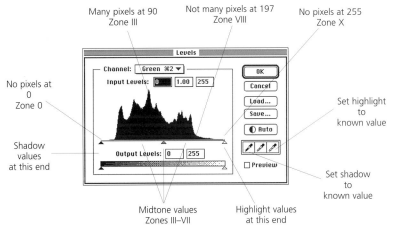

A histogram, like the one above, is the graph you get of an image when you look at it in Levels. For more information on levels and histograms, turn to "The Grand Canyon," where we furnish a detailed introduction to levels. Also refer to "Digital Imaging and the Zone System" to see how histograms relate to traditional photography and light.

best possible circumstance is to have an original image, transparency, or negative that has a good exposure of the subject matter and shows a full range of values from very dark to very bright but some detail in all areas. The previous chapter, "Digital Imaging and the Zone System," tells you how to create a high-quality exposure with a camera. If you have a high-quality image that contains values in all zones and has been scanned correctly, you see a histogram like the one shown to the right.

When you scan an image, you should aim to get a scan that has a full range of the values present in the original. For most common commercial uses of photography, you want a histogram that looks like the one shown here.

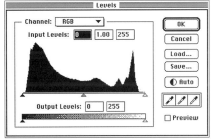

A histogram that has a full range of values.

SCANNING SHADOWS AND HIGHLIGHTS

You may not want the shadow values to go right down to 0 and you may not want the highlight values to go right up to 255, depending on the range of values in the original image and on the intended output device.

When you scan an image, there are several areas in which you need to be careful what values you obtain. There can be places within the scanned image that are totally black. These should occur only if the original has areas that are totally black (*black shadows*, Zone 0). Then there are the regular shadows, which are the darkest places in the image that still show texture or detail when printed; Zones I and II. On the other end of the spectrum are specular highlights, areas in the original that are totally white, such as the reflection of the sun in the chrome bumper of a car; Zone X. Next, there are regular highlights, the brightest areas of the image where you still want to see some texture or detail; Zones VIII and IX.

To some extent, we can call everything between the regular highlights and the regular shadow areas *midtones*. At the dark end of the midtones, are the *three-quartertones* (shadow areas where you can see a fair amount of detail) and at the bright end of the midtones, the *quartertones* (highlight areas where you should also be able to see a fair amount of detail).

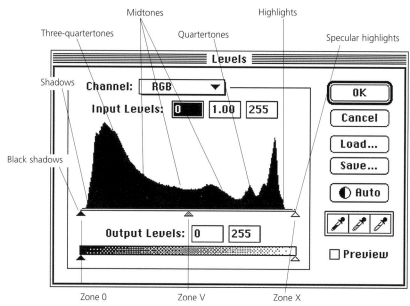

Here is a diagram showing what the different parts of a histogram refer to.

ADJUSTING THE SCANNER TO GET THE RIGHT VALUES

When you do a scan, the values that you want to obtain for the shadows and the highlights depend on the type of output device you are directing the final image toward. If you are not sure of the output device or if you might be using different output devices, the highlights (Zone IX) should have a value in the range of 245–250 and the shadows (Zone I) should have a value in the range of 5–10. With an original image that has a full range of colors in each of red, green, and blue, you need to adjust the scanner to get these types of highlight and shadow values. If you get the highlight and shadow values correct, the values of the quartertones, midtones, and three-quartertones usually fall between these endpoint shadow and highlight values. When you get this type of scan, the histogram starts out looking like the good histogram mentioned earlier. With this complete scan, you can always adjust the image in Photoshop to get different highlight, midtone, and shadow values, as well as different contrast, and you will know that you started with all the information from the scanner. I usually do my scans with the normal setting. Some scanners allow you to add a curve that adjust the image as you scan it. I generally don't use a preset curve in the scanner because I'd rather do the adjustment myself in Photoshop. When you have a scanner that scans more than 8 bits of info per color, for example 12, using a pre-set curve may help the scanner to decide which of the 12-bit range is used to reduce down to 8 bits per color. See if you get better results by applying the curve in the scanner versus doing it in Photoshop.

SCANNING STEP BY STEP

Whenever I scan in Photoshop, using any scanner, I always use the same simple technique. First I set up the default brightness, contrast, and color balance controls on the scanner. I remove any pre-set curves that would change the contrast of the scan from the scanner setting. I make sure that I set the scanner for the correct type of film. I then do a prescan, which shows me the image in the scanner's preview window. I crop the image to scan the area I want to scan. In the Nikon Scan dialog box at the bottom of this page, the prescan and crop are shown on the right. Next, I set the scanner to do about a 1Mb scan. I usually don't tell desktop scanners to sharpen the image, because I don't know how good their sharpening software is. If I get a good focused raw scan from the scanner, I know Photoshop sharpening can do a great job. The next step is to do the 1Mb scan at the default settings. I would only buy a scanner that had a Photoshop plug-in allowing it to scan directly into Photoshop. This saves a lot of time over scanning into another package, saving the file, and then having to reopen it in Photoshop.

Next, I evaluate the 1Mb scan for correctness by first cropping any extra information from around the edges of the scan and then using Levels in Photoshop to look at the image. You want to crop any black or white borders before you look at the histogram because they distort the accuracy of the histogram. At the end of this chapter, I show you some sample histograms and explain their problems and how to correct them by adjusting the scanner.

Histograms of different scanning problems and how to fix them.

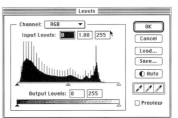

Highlights not bright enough, increase overall exposure on scanner.

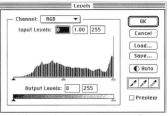

Highlights too bright, decrease overall exposure on scanner.

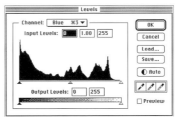

Blacks too dark in the Blue channel, lost shadow detail. Make sure original has detail in the shadows, and if it does, then change black setting in the scan for less black or for lighter shadows.

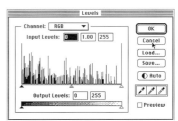

Original is posterized, or this is a bad, gappy scan.

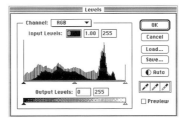

This type of look may indicate one channel was scanned badly. See the Red channel in the histogram to the right.

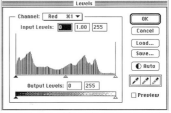

The Red channel from the histogram to the left. Need to lower exposure on red and also lighten black setting.

If the scanner allows you to make separate adjustments for each of the Red, Green, and Blue channels, look at the histogram from each channel and adjust the red, green, and blue scanner settings separately to get the best histogram in each color.

Scanner dialog box from a Nikon scanner. This is a good scanner interface because you can create the cropping box in the prescan window to the right, and set its dimensions and its dpi independent of each other. Nikon scanners also have good controls for brightness in each of the Red, Green, and Blue channels, as well as good controls for overall brightness and shadow settings.

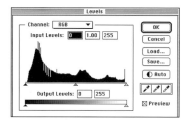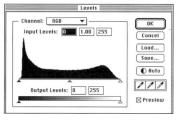
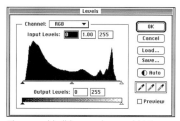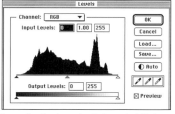

These could all be good normal histograms. Generally, the important characteristic in a good histogram of a typical photograph is to have values that go all the way from one end of the histogram to the other. This histogram would represent an image that has values from black, Zone 0, all the way to white, Zone X. The way the graph actually looks in between these two endpoint areas varies with the particular image. **For some images, such as soft fog on a mountain lake after sunset, or a subtle snow scene, there may not be bright highlights or dark shadows, and then you wouldn't have values that go all the way from one end of the histogram to the other.**

Keep on doing 1Mb scans and adjusting scanner settings until you get the best histogram you can. Once you get the levels to look correct on the small 1Mb scan, use the same scanner settings for exposure and color balance, and increase the size of the scan to give you the final number of megabytes that you will need. It is always best to get a good-looking histogram from the scanner before you make corrections to the histogram in Photoshop. If you aren't personally doing the scan, you at least now know how to evaluate the scans you get. When you cannot improve the scan using the scanner itself (you didn't do the scan, you don't have the scanner, or you already did the best that the scanner can do), the next step is to get the histogram correct using Photoshop's color correction utilities. I cover this process after the next section.

GETTING THE RIGHT HISTOGRAM

Time and again I am asked in classes, "What is a good histogram?" Let me ask a question in response. If you have three different photographers take a picture of a basket of apples, which would be the "good" photograph: the one that is dark, moody, and mysterious; the one that is light, delicate, and ethereal; or the one that is an accurate representation of a basket of apples in the sunshine? In actuality, any or all of the three may be excellent photographs. Judging a histogram is similar, in that many different histograms could be the "right" histogram for a given photograph, depending on the artist's interpretation of the subject.

COMPARING THE HISTOGRAM TO THE ORIGINAL

The histogram cannot be viewed separately from the original slide or photo. A good histogram of the original is one that accurately reflects the amount of information in the original. A good histogram of the final output accurately represents the artist's visualization. Never does the adage, "garbage in, garbage out" apply more fully than in digital imaging. If you have an original with no highlight detail, there is absolutely zero possibility that even a high-end scanner can give you something to work with. A good scan of a good original, however, gives you a full range of information that can be manipulated digitally, just as you would manipulate information traditionally in the darkroom.

If you start with a very low contrast original, your histogram will have a shortened value scale; that is, the representation of the pixel values will not stretch across all the values from 0 to 255. In general, as you color correct this scan, you force the values of the pixels in the scan to spread out along the luminosity axis all the way from deep shadows (between about 3 and 10) to bright highlights (around 245)—notice that we say "in general." If the effect that you wish to achieve is a very low contrast image, say, a photo that will appear ghosted back, you may need to do very little adjustment to the histogram. It all depends on what you are visualizing for the final output. Just as you use the Zone System to set where the values of the actual subject matter will fall on the film, in digital imaging you choose (by manipulating the histogram) where the values of the scan will fall in the final output. Therefore, you must view the histogram in the context of the original input and the desired output. You must ask yourself, "What is actually there?" and "What do I want the audience to see?"

MODIFYING WITH LEVELS AND CURVES

Once you get a good scan with a good histogram, you can modify it with Levels and Curves to get your visualization of that image for your final print. If you move the Levels Input Highlight slider to the left, you move your Zone VIII and IX values toward Zone X, brightening the highlights. If you move the Output Highlight slider to the left, you move your Zone X, IX, and VIII values toward Zone IX, VIII, and VII, respectively, dulling the highlights. Similarly, you can use the Shadow sliders to move the zone values around in the shadow parts of the histogram. If you move the Input Brightness/Contrast slider to the right, you move Zone V values toward Zone IV or III, making the midtones darker and more contrasty. If you move the slider to the left, you move Zone V values toward Zone VI or VII, making the image lighter and brighter.

The Curves tool allows you to make even finer adjustment to values in specific zones. Read "The Grand Canyon," "Kansas," and "Color Correcting Al" chapters to try out these techniques and see how digital imaging gives you more power to realize your vision. As Ansel Adams says in his book, *The Negative,* "Much of the creativity in photography lies in the infinite range of choices open to the photographer between attempting a nearly literal representation of the subject and freely interpreting it in highly subjective 'departures from reality.'" Many people think of Adams' prints as straight photos from nature. Actually, Adams did a lot of adjusting with his view camera and in the darkroom to create the visualization of the image that would bring forth his feelings and impressions from the original scene. I believe he would enjoy digital imaging.

WORKING WITH PHOTO CD IMAGES

The best way that I've found to open images that are on Photo CD discs is to use the Kodak Photo CD Acquire module. When you get an image scanned onto Photo CD, there are two possible formats: Regular and Pro Photo CD. Regular Photo CDs have five scans of different sizes of each image. The five sizes are 192x128, 384x256, 768x512, 1536x1024, and 3072x2048 pixels. For about $1 to $2 a photograph, you get all five sizes of scans of each photograph. The

Here are the five resolutions of regular Photo CD scans.

largest of these is an 18Mb file, which is useful for a 10"x6.8" separation at 300 dpi (that is, for a 150 line screen separation). With these 18Mb files, I have actually made some very high-quality 11x17 prints by using a Radius ProofPositive dye sublimation printer, resampling up the images, and sharpening them.

Kodak also offers Pro Photo CD scans. These scans have the same five resolutions as above, plus a sixth resolution that is 4096x6144, or up to 72Mb in size—big enough for 11x17 by 300 dpi without resampling up the scans. The Pro scans cost about $15 to $20 each and they seem to be very good as long as you give them a proper original exposure. I have been getting my Photo CD and Pro Photo CD scans done at Palmer Photographic and have been quite happy with the results. Palmer takes jobs from Federal Express and gives you 48-hour turnaround. To try them out, see the free coupon on at the end of the book.

If you have a difficult negative—one that is improperly exposed, too dark or too light—and you want to get the absolute most out of the scan, you may do better with a high-end drum scan. On the other hand, if the original is a good exposure with a full range of data, and you make sure that you tell the people doing the Photo CD scans the type of film you are sending them, you should be able to get very usable scans. As with any scan, however, the operator of the scanner and the quality control of the service bureau doing the scans is going to affect the results. If you are not happy with the results at your service bureau, try a different Photo CD scanning location.

The Photo CD scan puts your image onto a CD. A CD, be it an audio CD, multimedia CD, or whatever, can hold up to 650Mb of digital information. The Photo CD scans are compressed so that even if a file is 18Mb when you open it, it takes up only 4Mb to 6Mb of storage on the disc. That means you can get about 100 to 120 regular Photo CD scans on a single CD. The Pro format takes much more disk space; you can only get about 30 of them on a single CD.

BRINGING PHOTO CD INTO PHOTOSHOP

There are various options for bringing a Photo CD image into Photoshop. Depending on how you open the image, you should be able to get a better Photoshop histogram of it. When I first started to use Photo CD, I thought that the quality was not very good. The main problem seemed to be loss of highlight detail in bright clouds and other areas. I tend to take very contrasty photographs and require that the scan maintain the full range of contrast. I later learned how to use the Kodak Photo CD Acquire module to get a full range of data from the same CDs that had earlier given me problems.

USING THE KODAK ACQUIRE MODULE

The process of evaluating the histograms is the same as described earlier when talking about scanning. We just use a different tool, the Kodak Acquire module. When you first enter the Acquire module, you choose the particular scan that you want from the image glossary that comes with the CD. It shows you a tiny picture of each image along with the number that represents that image on the CD. Since a CD is a write-once device, the images are always stored by a number and you can't write a name on the CD.

In the picture on the next page, you see us selecting image number 38 from a Photo CD using Acquire version 2.3. The latest version is 3.0, which has a more advanced interface, but we are quite happy with the results we get from the version 2.3 and continue to use it. Once you select an image in 2.3, you get a little preview picture of it. If you click on the Edit Image button, you get a more detailed

You can obtain the Acquire module from Kodak by calling 800-242-2424, or download it for free by going to http://www.Kodak.com and choosing Digital Imaging and then Photo CD. Make sure that you get version 2.3 or 3.0 or later that can open both regular and Pro Photo CDs. For great Photo CD scans, call Palmer Photographic in California at 800-735-1950. We usually ship to them using Federal Express.

dialog box. The Edit Image dialog box lets you see a bigger version of the image that you can crop more easily. If you crop the image before you open it, opening becomes a much faster process because Photoshop then reads less data from the Photo CD. You can also choose the size (one of either 5 or 6 sizes) of the scan you want to open. However, the best aspect of the Kodak Acquire module is that it allows you to choose the gamma and color temperature that you want to use when opening the image. Version 3.0 also lets you choose the Source device, Destination device and Preview monitor but I haven't found the histograms better than the ones I get with gamma 1.4 and color temperature 5000°K in version 2.3.

With version 2.3, opening the 1Mb version at a gamma of 1.4 and color temperature of 5000°K seems to maintain the most information in the histogram, especially in the highlights on contrasty images. After making sure that any black borders have been cropped, I look at the histogram of this scan, measuring the highlight values and making sure detail has not been lost. This is not usually a problem when opening using gamma 1.4 but can be a problem at higher gammas. If the image is really dark, I may re-open it using gamma 1.8 or 2.2. I can usually get a good-looking histogram using this technique. After I decide on a setting to use, I use that same setting to open one of the bigger versions of the image (4Mb, 18Mb, or 72Mb) for the final usage. The end points of the histogram on the bigger file will be about the same as in the smaller test file, but histograms of bigger files are less likely to have gaps in them, which indicates that they have a full range of 256 shades of color for each channel.

The Edit Image dialog box allows you to sharpen the image as well as to adjust Saturation, Cyan/Red, Magenta/Green, Yellow/Blue, and Dark/Light balances as you open the image. I usually leave these controls alone and just try to get the best histogram by changing the gamma and color temperature settings. You can do the other adjustments more accurately in Photoshop after you get the best raw information from the Photo CD.

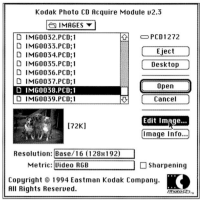

Choose Edit Image after picking the particular Photo CD image that you want to work on.

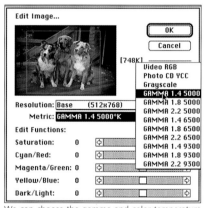

We can choose the gamma and color temperature of the Photo CD image upon opening. I usually use Gamma 1.4 and 5000°K which tends to give the most histogram information in Levels.

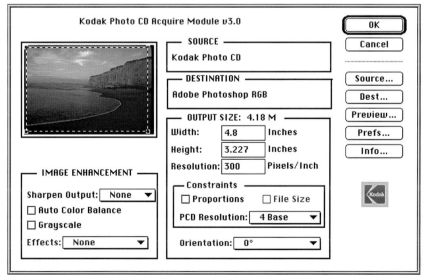

Here are the controls for version 3.0 of the Kodak Acquire module. It allows you to set up a lot of calibration parameters for both the source device, the destination device and the preview monitor. I have not used it as much as version 2.3 but my initial tests with it didn't convince me that I would get better histogram information than with opening using the gamma 1.4 and 5000 settings in version 2.3. I will continue to test it and post any new findings on our Web site at maxart.com.

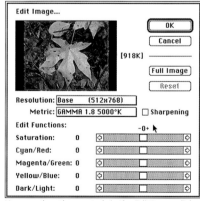

Here are the other controls in the Edit Image dialog box. You will have more control if you just get the raw data from the Photo CD and do these kinds of edits in Photoshop.

Poor Scans and Their Problem Histograms
(Different types of problems require different scanner adjustments)

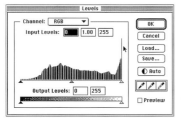

No highlight detail. Rescan with a lower exposure setting.

The image is too bright, obscuring the detail in the clouds and other highlights.

This scan has quite different ranges for each of the Red, Green, and Blue channels. Best to rescan and adjust each channel separately.

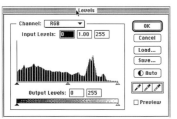

No shadow detail. Rescan and change the shadow setting on the scanner.

No matter what we do in Photoshop, we won't be able to bring out shadow detail because it was lost in the scan.

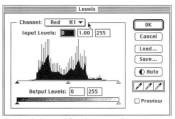

The Red channel for the scan above. Rescan with more exposure on red, and a different black value.

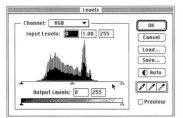

Not a broad enough range on the scan. We could correct this in Photoshop by bringing in the highlight and shadow sliders, but then we would end up with the gappy scan below. We are better off rescanning with more exposure and a different shadow setting.

The highlights and shadows are way too dull.

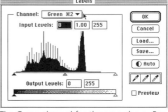

The Green channel for the scan above. Rescan with larger exposure for green; black is okay here.

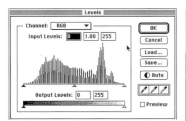

The histogram of the image above after fixing in Photoshop now has a bunch of gaps in it that represent lost tonal values. You will get more detail in the printed result by rescanning.

The corrected image with the gappy histogram still prints better than the uncorrected histogram.

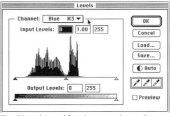

The Blue channel for the scan above. Rescan with a much larger exposure and possible black adjustment.

Corrected Photographs and Their Good Histograms

(Values in the middle of a histogram look different for each photo)

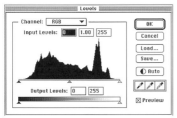

The correct scan and print for the sample image on the previous page. Lots of ¾ tones on the dark parts of the beach. The large number of ¼ tones are probably in the sky and the waves.

Santa Cruz sunset from the boardwalk.

Young Lakes.

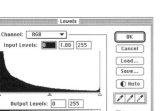

Lots of very dark areas and very bright areas, even totally black and white, are OK in this photo.

The Paris Cafe.

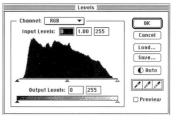

Lots of values everywhere across the full brightness range.

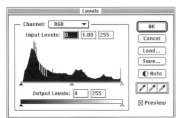

This histogram has lots of dark shadows in the trees and the fence. The spike at the far right is the white buildings.

The Burnley church.

Shells in Costa Rica.

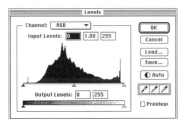

Notice the small spike for the dark shadow areas that are small but so important in the photograph.

Man on the beach at sunset.

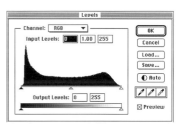

This histogram probably is so smooth because all the objects have a similar range of colors and subtle tones.

COLOR CORRECTION AND OUTPUT

*An overview of the color correction process, sharpening,
archiving, and outputting your file.*

COLOR CORRECTING YOUR SCAN OR PHOTO CD

Once you get the best possible histogram from the scanner or the Photo CD, you usually need to do some color correction work. The first step in color correction is to work some more on the histograms until you get them as close to perfect as you can given the data available. Before you start the color correction process, make sure that the Photoshop preferences are set up correctly. The parts of the preferences that affect color correction are

- Monitor Setup
- Printing Inks Setup
- Separation Setup
- Setting the Eyedropper
- The Highlight and Shadow settings in Levels and Curves

Using the "Setting System and Photoshop Preferences" chapter at the beginning of this book as a guide, make sure your preferences are set up as recommended. The recommended preferences settings are default settings for doing color separations for coated stock on a sheet fed press with about 20% dot gain. The settings would differ for newspaper and possibly for other presses. You should do color correction in a specific order. The next few pages offer an overview of the order and steps you should use in making color corrections. "The Grand Canyon" chapter, which is next, goes into much greater detail.

Before values   After values

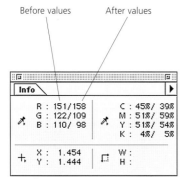

The Info palette shows you the original values, upon entering the tool, on the left. On the right, after the slash, it displays the values resulting from the tool's adjustments since you entered it this time.

THE STEPS FOR COLOR CORRECTING

The first step in color correcting is to bring up the Info palette and the Color palette by choosing Window/Show Info (F9) and Window/Show Color (Shift-F9), respectively. The Info palette shows you the RGB and CMYK values of the current location of the Eyedropper tool while in Curves, Levels, Hue/Saturation, or any color correction tool. It also shows you how your color correction is modifying these values by displaying before values on the left and after values on the right. When you move the cursor into the Levels or Curves dialog boxes, the values in the Info palette go away but you can use the Color palette to keep track of values at the last location you clicked with the Eyedropper. When you click down in a particular location, the values in that location show up in the Color palette. These values change only when you click in a new location or use Levels, Curves, or Hue/Saturation to make a

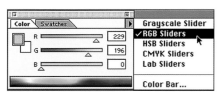

The Color palette shows values at the last place you clicked. You can see how the values at that location change when you make an adjustment using one of the color correction tools.

color adjustment that affects the location where you last clicked. It is useful to always have the Info palette showing and sometimes also the Color palette when you are making color corrections.

Before you start any color correcting, make a copy of the original scan and color correct the copy, so that you can return to that original if you make any mistakes while color correcting. The basic order for color correction when starting with an RGB scan is as follows:

1. Go into Levels.
2. Set the Highlight.
3. Set the Shadow.
4. Adjust the overall brightness and contrast of the image.

You do the first three steps in RGB mode using either Levels or Curves, although Levels is better because you see a histogram when you use it.

5. Go into the Red, Green, or Blue channel and remove color casts. being especially careful that neutral colors are neutral and don't have a cast.
6. Click on OK in Levels or Curves.
7. Go into Hue/Saturation and increase or decrease overall saturation. Make adjustments to the hue, saturation, and lightness of specific color areas.
8. Make color changes to isolated image areas using Selections or Layer Masks along with Levels, Curves and Hue/Saturation.
9. Sharpen the image.

At this point, you have a color corrected and sharpened RGB image. You can print this image directly to an RGB printer or output it to an RGB film recorder to make a transparency. You can use the RGB file for Web and multimedia projects, and as the final file if you use a third-party method to convert your images to CMYK on the fly from Photoshop or Quark. If you are going to convert the image to CMYK using Photoshop for separations, first save the final corrected RGB image, in case you need to go back to it later.

10. Convert to CMYK using the Mode menu.
11. Make minor color adjustments to specific color areas using Hue/Saturation, Curves, and Selective Color with or without selections.

Now I'm going to take you through these steps in more detail.

SETTING HIGHLIGHT

Go to Image/Adjust/Levels (Command-L). You work in Channel zero, the composite channel, to set the highlight and shadow. The *highlight* is the brightest point in the image where you still want to have texture. Everything brighter than the highlight prints totally white, with no dots. The RGB values here should read somewhere in the range of 240 to 250. Remember that after you set the highlight, everything brighter than the highlight location will print totally white. Setting the highlight also removes color casts from the whole highlight part of your image. You need to set the highlight at a place you want to be white in the end, as well as at a location you want to print as a neutral value. You want to pick a spot where the detail or texture is just fading but is not completely gone. This usually falls at the brighter end of Zone IX in the Zone System. Using the highlight Eyedropper, click down at the

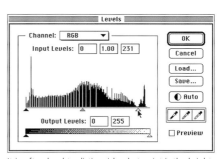

It is often hard to distinguish what point is the brightest on the computer screen. You can find the highlight by holding down the Option key while moving the RGB Highlight slider to the left. The first area to turn white on the screen is where you want to look for the highlight. Make sure you move the slider back to 255 once you see where the highlight is. This method only works if your computer supports video LUT Animation.

location where you want to set the highlight, and at the same time, watch how the Info palette shows the values (before and after in RGB and CMYK). When you click, the after values should change to the default preference white point values.

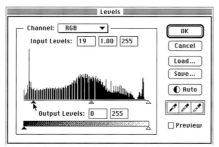

It is often hard to distinguish what point is the darkest on the computer screen. You can find the shadow by holding down the Option key while moving the RGB Shadow slider to the right. The first area to turn black on the screen is where you want to look for the shadow. Make sure you move the slider back to 0 once you see where the shadow is. Again, the Option key technique only works with Video LUT Animation.

SETTING SHADOW

Now pick the point where you want to set the shadow. The RGB values here should read about 5 to 10. It should be at a location you want to print with a neutral shadow value. This location would be at the darker end of Zone I in the Zone System. Everything darker than this point prints as totally black after you set the Shadow. If you want a lot of totally black places in your image, set the shadow at a location that isn't very dark, say 15, 15, 15. Everything darker than that location goes black. If you want a lot of shadow detail in your image, set the Shadow at a location that is as close as possible to 0, 0, 0 in RGB. These initial RGB highlight and shadow values vary somewhat from image to image. The purpose of setting the white and black is to normalize these values to neutral grays and also to set the endpoints of detail in the reproduction. Some images do not have a good point at which to set the highlight and shadow with the droppers. See the "Kansas" and "Bryce" chapters for examples of how to deal with this situation.

ADJUSTING THE OVERALL BRIGHTNESS AND CONTRAST

Use Channel RGB of Levels again for this step. Move the middle slider to the right to make the image darker and more contrasty. Move it to the left to make the image brighter and less contrasty. Move it around until the image has the level of brightness and contrast you want.

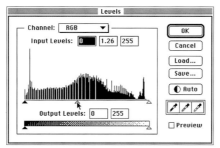

Adjust the overall brightness and contrast by moving the middle slider using Channel RGB.

ADJUSTING THE OVERALL COLOR CASTS

If the overall image seems too green, go to the Green channel in Levels and move the middle slider to the right. This will add magenta to the image and remove the green cast. If the image is too blue, go to the Blue channel and move the middle slider to the right to add yellow to the image. You just need to remember that the Red channel controls red and its complement, cyan; the Green channel, green and magenta; and the Blue channel, blue and yellow. The middle sliders of each channel are going to mostly affect the midtones as well as the quartertones and three-quartertones. The Highlight and Shadow sliders should have been adjusted correctly when you set the highlight and shadow at the beginning.

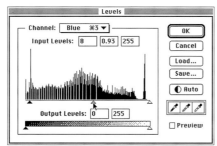

Now deal with color casts by adjusting the middle slider in the color channel that effects the color cast.

Sometimes you can get a color cast in the highlight or the shadow if the point at which you set the highlight was not a neutral location. Some images do not have neutral locations. In such cases, click the normal Eyedropper at a highlight or shadow location while in Levels and look at the values for that location in the Color palette. The values in the Color palette change only when you click down on the mouse. The Color palette remembers the last place you clicked. If the numbers are not neutral (for coated stock, the highlights should be around 244, 244, 244 and the shadows

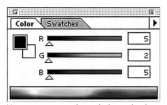

Here we can see the unbalanced values in the Color palette. The green value is less than red or blue.

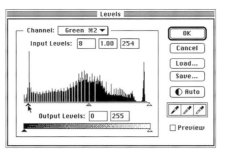

Make the change using the Shadow slider from the Green channel while looking at the values in the Color palette.

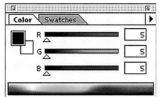

Now the Color palette shows the correction implemented to neutralize the shadow value in green.

should be around 5, 5, 5), use the Highlight or Shadow sliders for the color channel(s) that are out of adjustment to correct the numbers in the Color palette. Afterward, you may have to go back to readjust the midtone sliders to slightly adjust the midtone color cast again.

You should modify all these corrections in the Levels dialog box as one step. You don't want to say OK until you complete all these steps. If you say OK too many times in the color adjustment dialog boxes, you degrade the image. You don't want to go into Levels or Curves repeatedly. Do it all in one step if possible. After you finish the overall color correction in Levels, and only then, choose OK in the Levels dialog box. To have the ability to modify your changes over and over again, do them with adjustment layers instead of regular layers. For hands-on examples using these techniques, see "The Grand Canyon," "Kansas," and "Color Correcting Al."

Making Overall and Selected Changes to Hue, Saturation, and Lightness

You often want to increase the overall saturation using the Hue/Saturation tool from the Image menu (Image/Adjust/Hue/Saturation), especially if you had to brighten the image in Curves or Levels. To increase the overall saturation, move the Saturation slider to the right with the Master button selected. You can also selectively correct color if a certain color range in the image is off. For example, if the reds in the image were too orange, you could make them redder by first selecting the Red radio button, and then moving the Hue slider toward the M direction. This operation would add magenta to only the red areas of the image. This method differs from adding magenta using Levels or Curves because the latter method usually adds magenta to everything in the image.

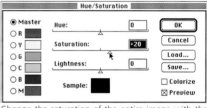

Change the saturation of the entire image with the Master button chosen.

When the Red radio button is selected, only the items in the image that are red have magenta added to them. If these items were unsaturated, you could add saturation to just the red items by moving the Saturation slider with Red selected. Similarly, you could add or subtract lightness in the reds. If your image contains different tones of red and you only want to adjust some of them, however, you should select those areas *before* you make the red adjustment.

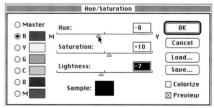

Change the hue, saturation and lightness of just the red colors in the image with the Red button chosen.

Making Color Changes to Isolated Areas Using Selections, Layer Masks, and Adjustment Layers Along with Levels, Curves, and Hue/Saturation

The color corrections I have discussed so far have been global color corrections to an entire image. If a particular area is the wrong color or too light or too dark, you may now want to make a selection of that area using Photoshop's selection tools, and then you may want to adjust the colors in that area using Levels, Curves, or Hue/Saturation. You can also use a layer mask to integrate that area from another layer or adjustment layer where the color has been changed.

Go through the "The Grand Canyon—Final Tweaks," "Kansas—Final Tweaks," "Bryce Stone Woman," and "Color Correcting Al" chapters for a complete description and some hands-on practice in using these techniques to change isolated areas.

SHARPENING THE IMAGE

As a final step, you often will want to use the Unsharp Mask filter or one of the other sharpening filters to sharpen the image. You will have to run some tests to determine the type and amount of sharpening that works best for your different categories of images. Because sharpening can take a lot of time, it is often useful to run tests on only a small area of an image. Select a small section that represents the entire image using the Rectangular Selection tool, and then make a copy of it. Next, choose File/New and create a new file. Since you just made a copy, the new file will be the size of the copied section. Choose OK in the New dialog box and then do an Edit/Paste followed by Select/None. To compare different parameters of the Unsharp Mask filter, you can repeat this or now use Image/Duplicate, until you have several small files that you can place next to each other on-screen.

Let me explain the three parameters of this filter.

AMOUNT: Controls the overall amount of sharpening. When you compare sharpening effects, zoom the image to at least 100% so you can see all the detail. Compare different copies of the same image area using different settings for Amount.

RADIUS: Photoshop sharpens an image by looking for edges in the photograph and enhancing those edges by darkening one side of the edge and lightening the other side. *Edges* are sharp color or contrast changes in an image. The Radius setting in the Unsharp Mask filter controls the width of pixels along an edge that are modified when you sharpen the image. Again, try running the filter with different settings, as well as comparing two copies of the same image side to side.

THRESHOLD: When you set the Threshold to 0, everything in the image becomes a candidate edge for getting sharpened. If you set the Threshold to 10, Photoshop finds and sharpens an edge only if there is a difference of at least 10 points (in the range from 0 to 255) in the pixel values along that edge. The larger value you give to the Threshold setting, the more contrasty an edge must be before it is sharpened and the more you are just sharpening the edges. When you find the correct Unsharp Mask values, use them to sharpen the entire file. See the "Kansas—Final Tweaks" chapter for a detailed hands-on example of using Unsharp Mask.

KEEPING YOUR MASTER FILE IN RGB FORMAT

If you are printing the file to an RGB digital printer, doing Web or multimedia work, or sending it to an RGB film recorder, you don't want to convert the file to CMYK format. You get the most quality and flexibility if you keep the largest required version of your master files in RGB format and then use copies of this master file to generate smaller images for your Web page and multimedia needs or to make specific CMYK separations for each different printing situation. Always save the final RGB version of the file before converting it to CMYK, and then save the CMYK version using a different name. This way you will have the color corrected RGB version to go back to if you are not happy with the way the separations work on your CMYK version. If you want to save the masks and layers you made while working on the image, you need to save this RGB file in Photoshop format. Every time

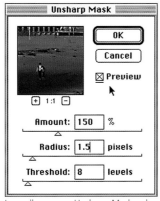

I usually use an Unsharp Mask value similar to this for sharpening 18 meg Photo CD scans.

you convert from RGB to CMYK or from CMYK to RGB, you lose information. Because of this, if you convert from RGB to CMYK and then back to RGB again, you will not have as good an RGB file as you started with.

The sensors on all scanners actually scan in RGB. The high-end drum scanners have a knowledgeable scanner operator and built-in software to do the conversion and give you CMYK files that are overall color corrected right from the scanner. You can often get just as good results using a good desktop scanner or even Photo CD if you use the techniques that I demonstrate in this book.

CONVERTING FROM RGB TO CMYK

After making sure that your preferences are set up correctly for Monitor Setup, Printing Inks Setup, and Separation Setup, go to the Image/Mode menu and choose CMYK Color to convert the image from RGB to CMYK. Now use File/Save As to save the file under a different name. If you don't correct the RGB before converting to CMYK, Photoshop creates the Black channel on your CMYK file incorrectly. Unless your scans are done directly into CMYK, you should do overall correction on the RGB file before converting to CMYK. Scans made by high-end scanners in CMYK should already have had overall color correction done for you by the trained scanner operator. If they don't, correct them in CMYK using a similar procedure as that described here for RGB.

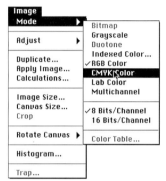

Converting from RGB to CMYK using the Image/Mode menu.

MAKING FINAL SUBTLE COLOR ADJUSTMENTS IN CMYK

When you are comparing the image on your screen to a proof made from CMYK film, you want to compare the CMYK version of the image on the screen to the proof. There are colors that will show up on an RGB monitor, and in an RGB image, that can't be printed with printing inks on a press. When Photoshop displays a CMYK image on the screen, it adjusts the colors to try to give you an accurate representation of how the colors will actually print on a press. It changes this adjustment based on the settings in Monitor Setup, Printing Inks Setup, and Separation Setup, so you need to be sure that the preferences values used to convert from RGB to CMYK are the same values that you use for displaying the CMYK image.

Because the CMYK image on-screen more closely matches the image on a press than the RGB image, you may need to do final subtle color corrections in CMYK mode. For some images, the CMYK version will look the same on the screen as the RGB version, depending on the colors in the image. Certain colors, for example, bright saturated red or deep blue, may get duller or change when you convert to CMYK. Also, the shadow areas may require a slight modification to be sure the correct balance is achieved in the neutral areas. To add contrast, you may want to run a curve or increase the black middletone. You can make these final color adjustments using Curves, Levels, or Selective Color.

SAVING THE CMYK IMAGE

Before you save the image, you should go into Image/Image Size and make sure that the Resolution and Print Size are set correctly for the box size into which the file will be placed in Quark or PageMaker. If you print directly from Photoshop, the file should be the size you want to print. Making these settings in Photoshop and then placing the images at 100% into Quark or PageMaker will give you the best quality output. You may also need to go into Page Setup in the File

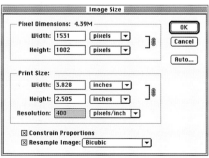

Make sure the image Width, Height, and Resolution are set correctly for your layout dimensions and line screen.

menu to adjust some of the settings. You should talk to the service bureau doing the output and ask them if you need to set Negative and Emulsion Down. Also, ask the service bureau how to set the Halftone Screens. Often, they will want you to not set either value in Photoshop because they will set them using Quark or the imagesetter. You really should coordinate with the service bureau concerning who's going to set what. Also ask the service bureau whether they want you to save the images as EPS/DCS, CMYK TIFF, or in some other format because this varies according to the type of output device that particular bureau uses.

If you save the image in EPS/DCS format for input into Quark, you will most likely use the settings in the dialog box here. You should check the Include Halftone Screen box only if you set up the screen angles and frequencies using the Screens dialog box (which you access from the Page Setup dialog box). If the screens are going to be set in Quark, leave the Include Halftone Screen check box unchecked. Good luck with your color. If you have any questions or comments about these techniques, please e-mail us at maxart.com or reach us via our contact information at the end of the book.

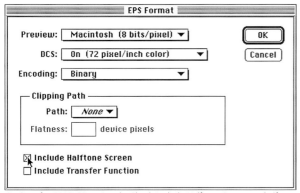

Settings for EPS/DCS to Quark. Check Include Halftone Screens only if you set the screens in Photoshop.

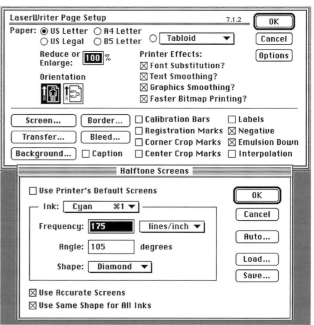

The Page Setup dialog box and its Halftone Screens dialog box. Check with your service bureau for how to set the screens and other settings here. They might want you to leave these unset in Photoshop if they're planning to set them in Quark.

HANDS-ON SESSION: The Grand Canyon

Introduction to Levels, using Levels and Hue/Saturation for overall color correction, introduction to Curves, using Curves to change specific color ranges.

When an image is originally scanned or brought in from Photo CD, the first thing you should do is check the overall color balance and saturation, and adjust them if necessary. When you scan with most desktop scanners or read images from Photo CD, you usually start out with an RGB image. At this point, you need to correct overall color and saturation before you convert to CMYK. Corrected RGB files convert to CMYK much better than a non-corrected RGB files. This session begins with an RGB image. If you normally begin work with CMYK images, see the note in Step 21.

In "Setting System and Photoshop Preferences," we showed you how to set the default highlight (C=5, M=3, Y=3, K=0, or R=244, G=244, B=244) and shadow (C=95, M=85, Y=83, K=95, or R=2, G=2, B=2) values for printing on a sheet-fed press to coated stock. These default values also work pretty well for output to most digital printers, film recorders, and for video. If you didn't already do so, go through "Setting System and Photoshop Preferences" before doing this exercise. If you don't set this setup information correctly, you may not get the expected results from using the techniques described in this chapter. If your output will be to a newspaper press or a film recorder, you may want to double-check with the technical specialist at your printer or service bureau to find out the recommended highlight and shadow settings for that particular device. Before you proceed, also read the chapters, "Calibration," "Scanning, Resolution, Histograms, and Photo CD," and "Color Correction, and Output." These chapters give you an overview of the entire reproduction process, show you how to calibrate your monitor, and give you a further understanding of histograms within the Levels tool.

INTRODUCTION TO LEVELS

Before you start actually color correcting the GrandCanyon image, let's take a tour of the Levels tool and

The initial uncorrected GrandCanyon image. Notice the green tint in the clouds and the overall flatness.

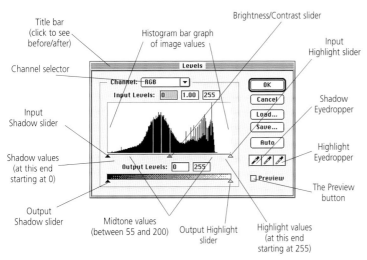

Title bar (click to see before/after)
Histogram bar graph of image values
Brightness/Contrast slider
Input Highlight slider
Channel selector
Shadow Eyedropper
Input Shadow slider
Highlight Eyedropper
Shadow values (at this end starting at 0)
The Preview button
Output Shadow slider
Midtone values (between 55 and 200)
Output Highlight slider
Highlight values (at this end starting at 255)

Study this diagram to learn the various controls of the Levels tool.

explain its different parts and functions. Levels contains two sets of controls, Input and Output, which can make the image lighter or darker as well as change its contrast. The Input controls on top include the histogram, the Input Levels numbers, and three sliders. The Input Shadow slider darkens shadows, the Input Highlight slider lightens highlights, and the Brightness/Contrast slider, in the middle, controls brightness, contrast, and color balance. The output controls on the bottom of this dialog box contain the Output Levels numbers, the Output Shadow slider for making shadows lighter, and the Output Highlight slider for making highlights darker or duller. The names "Input" and "Output" are chosen by comparing what happens with the Levels Highlight and Shadow sliders to what happens when you move the endpoints of a straight curve in Curves either along the horizontal (Input) axis or along the vertical (Output) axis of Curves. This may seem a bit obscure at this point, but maybe it will make more sense to you after you read this whole chapter, and then look again at the Curve diagrams and their captions at Step 23.

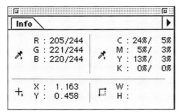

STEP 2: The Info palette with before values on the left of the slash and after values on the right.

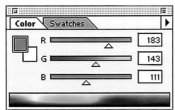

STEP 2: The Color palette. Hold the mouse button down and measure an image color area to change the values in this window.

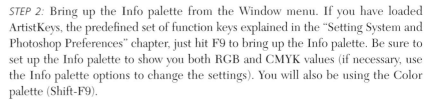

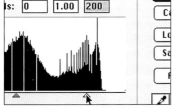

STEP 4: Move the Input Highlight slider to the left so the right Input Level reads about 200.

STEP 1: From the Grand Canyon folder on the CD, open the GrandCanyonPCDRaw file in Photoshop. Use the Marquee and then use Image/Crop to crop any white or black borders that you're not going to print. Use File/Save As GrandCanyon PS in Photoshop format on your hard disk; it is always good to save things in Photoshop format while you are working on them, since that also saves all your channels and layers.

STEP 2: Bring up the Info palette from the Window menu. If you have loaded ArtistKeys, the predefined set of function keys explained in the "Setting System and Photoshop Preferences" chapter, just hit F9 to bring up the Info palette. Be sure to set up the Info palette to show you both RGB and CMYK values (if necessary, use the Info palette options to change the settings). You will also be using the Color palette (Shift-F9).

STEP 3: Choose Image/Adjust/Levels and move the Levels dialog box out of the way as much as possible. You want to be able to see as much of the image as you can while color correcting it. Use the levels diagram at the beginning of this chapter as you review or learn the basic functions covered in Steps 4 through 9. Make sure the Preview button is turned off on a Mac; for Windows you probably want the Preview button on.

STEP 4: Move the Input Highlight slider to the left, and observe as you do so that the highlight areas in the clouds get brighter and that the Input Levels number on the right decreases from 255. Move the slider until the number reads about 200. Let go of the slider and move the cursor over an area of the image where the clouds have turned completely white. When you use any of the color correction tools, you automatically get the Eyedropper tool when you move the cursor over an area of the image. The Info palette shows you two sets of values for this white area. The values to the left of the slash are the original values at the Eyedropper location when you first entered Levels, and the values to the right of the slash show you what your levels changes have done to the digital values at the Eyedropper location. You can now see that moving the Input Highlight slider to the left makes the highlights brighter but also causes you to lose detail in the highlights if you move it too far. The original RGB numerical values that were in the range of 210 to 220 have now all changed to 255, which is pure white and prints with no color or detail—and you don't want that.

STEP 5: Move the Input Shadow slider to the right until the Input Levels number on the left goes from 0 to about 50, and the shadow areas of the image darken. Move the Eyedropper over a dark area and measure the changes in the Info palette. The RGB values originally in the range of 0 to 40 have all moved to 0 now; they have become totally black.

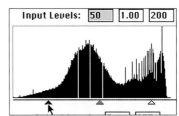

STEP 5: Move the Input Shadow slider to the right so the left Input Level reads about 50.

STEP 6: Move the cursor to the title bar at the top of the Levels dialog box. When you click on the title bar and hold the mouse button down, the image returns to the way it looked before you changed anything in Levels. When you release the mouse button, the image returns to the changed state with no highlight and shadow details. This quick preview feature is very useful for toggling quickly between before and after versions of an image to see if you really like the changes you have made. But it works only when the Levels Preview button is turned off. If the toggle isn't working for you, your video card may not support Video LUT Animation and, if so, you will need to work with the Preview button on all the time. See Video LUT Animation in the "Setting System and Photoshop Preferences" chapter for more information. Now, hold down on the Option key, and click on the Cancel button. The Cancel button changes to Reset, and clicking on it, restores the levels to their values when you entered Levels this time. All your changes are removed but you don't leave Levels. Calculating the Levels histogram can take a long time when you're working on large files, and this feature saves time. Notice that the values in the Info palette disappear when you move the cursor back into the Levels dialog box. Using the Color palette lets you remember values at a certain location and see how a change in Levels modifies those values.

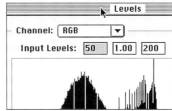

STEP 6: Click on the title bar and hold down the mouse to see before; let go to see after.

STEP 7: Use the Eyedropper tool to click on a midtone value in the GrandCanyon image; the orange/red rocks in the foreground will work. When you press down on the mouse button, the values in the Color palette change. Now move the cursor back into Levels; notice that these values don't go away, even when you're in the dialog box. Press down on the Input Brightness/Contrast slider and move it to the left; the image gets brighter and less contrasty

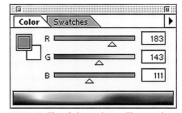

STEP 7: Use the Eyedropper tool to click on the red rocks. (In Levels, you are automatically in the Eyedropper.)

STEP 7: The Color palette. These values change as you move the Input Brightness/Contrast slider.

and the numbers in the Color palette get larger. Move the slider to the right, and the image gets darker and more contrasty and the numbers in the Color palette get smaller. Also, observe the middle number (the *gamma*) in the Input Levels numbers boxes, is changing. When you move the slider to the left, the gamma goes above 1.0, and when you move it to the right, the gamma goes below 1.0. If the Input Levels numbers read 0, 1.0, 255, you know you haven't changed the Input Levels.

STEP 8: Move the Output Highlight slider to the left until the Output Levels number on the right reaches 200. Then measure the brightest cloud values; notice that values originally in the 200 to 220 range have all dropped below 200. You changed

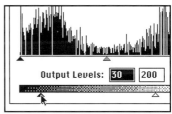

STEP 8: Moving the Output Highlight and Shadow sliders and looking at the Output Levels numbers.

the Output Levels number from 255 to 200, and the difference of 55, or close to it, has been subtracted from all these highlight values, darkening and dulling your highlights.

STEP 9: Move the Output Shadow slider to the right and notice how doing that makes the shadows lighter and duller. If you measure the changes with the Eyedropper and Info palette, you will notice that moving this slider increases the shadow's numerical values (which makes the shadows lighter).

SETTING THE HIGHLIGHT AND SHADOW VALUES

STEP 10: Steps 4 through 9 show you the basic functions of the different parts of the Levels tool. It is important to use those functions in the right order and to take careful measurements of your progress using the Info palette and Color palette. We will start out working with the Highlight and Shadow Eyedroppers to set the highlights and shadows on this image—a very important step in this process. All reproduction or printing processes, including sheet-fed presses, web presses, newspaper presses, digital printers, and film recorders, have certain endpoints to their reproduction process defined by the highlights and shadows. Many newspaper presses can't show detail for shadow values that are more than 85% to 90% black, and some newspapers are even worse. Sheet-fed presses, on the other hand, can sometimes show detail in areas with more than 95% black. In a digital file, these percentages are represented by numerical values ranging from 0 (100% black) to 255 (white, or 0% black).

When you color correct an image, you don't want that image to contain areas that the output medium you are using can't reproduce. Setting the highlight and shadow values correctly for your output device ensures that this won't happen. You also want the white parts of your image to print as white (not with a color cast of yellow, cyan, or magenta) and the black parts of your image to print as black (not dark gray with a green cast). You can ensure that they do by setting your highlights and shadows correctly. When you set the highlight, you are setting the brightest point in the image that is a neutral color, white, and that still has a dot pattern. The highlight would be the brightest part of Zone IX in the Zone System. Any point brighter than the highlight will print as totally empty paper with no dots. When you set the shadow, you are setting the darkest point in the image that is a neutral color, black, and that still has a dot pattern. The shadow would be the darkest part of Zone I in the Zone System. Any point darker than the shadow will print as totally black ink with no white holes to give detail.

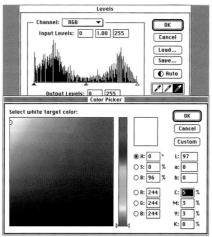

STEP 11: Make sure the highlight values are 5,3,3,0.

STEP 11: Photoshop allows you to decide where you want it to set the highlight. The highlight should be the brightest neutral point that still has detail. Double-click on the Highlight Eyedropper button and make sure that the CMYK values in the Color Picker are 5, 3, 3, 0 and the RGB values 244, 244, 244. These are the neutral values you would want your highlight to have for a sheet-fed press on coated paper. Due to the impurities in printing inks, you get a neutral color by having more cyan than magenta or yellow. Since this is a highlight, there is no black. Click on the OK button if you need to change any of the values.

STEP 12: Now double-click on the Shadow Eyedropper and make sure the shadow values are 95, 85, 83, 95 in CMYK and 2, 2, 2 in RGB. If both these shadow values are not correct, simply fixing the CMYK values should change the RGB values to 2, 2, 2. If not, you need to return to the chapter on "Setting System and Photoshop Preferences," and check the preferences for Monitor setup, Printing Inks setup, and Separation setup. Click on the OK button if you need to change any of the values.

SETTING THE HIGHLIGHT

STEP 13: Next, you use the Highlight Eyedropper to click on a highlight, which should be the brightest area of the clouds. You want the highlight to be a neutral white area—the last possible place where you can see a little texture. The RGB values in the Info palette should be in the 240 to 255 range, and the CMYK values in the 0 to 10 range. If you have specular highlights (the sun reflected off a chrome bumper, for example), these will not have detail and should have values of 255. You're looking for something just a hair less intense than that. Move the Levels dialog box out of the way so you can see the entire clouds area. To find the correct area for setting the highlight, hold down the Option key and move the Input Highlight slider to the left. The whole image area first turns black and then, as you move the slider to the left, white areas appear. Since this image has no specular highlights, the first white area that appears in the clouds is the point at which you should set the highlight. Remember where that location is in the window. Now move the Input Highlight slider back to 255 since you were only using it to locate the brightest point. Click on the Highlight Eyedropper in the Levels dialog box. Now move this Eyedropper up to that bright place in the clouds, and move it around in the area while looking at the RGB values in the Info palette for the highest set of numbers. When you find those numbers (I chose 205, 221, 220), click once and release the mouse button; don't move the mouse after you click. The right-hand numbers for RGB in the Info palette should now display 244, 244, 244 for that exact spot where you clicked. Now go to the Levels title bar and click on it. When the mouse button is down, you see the original image. When the mouse button is up, you see the image after the highlight change. Notice that this process of setting the highlight has removed the subtle green cast in the entire clouds area. The clouds should appear whiter when you are not clicked down on the title bar. (If your computer doesn't support Video LUT Animation, you will have to find the highlight point by measuring the areas that seem the brightest and setting the highlight where the largest numbers are. Then turn the Preview button on and off to see how the image looks before and after the change.) Setting the highlight actually moves the highlight sliders in each of the Red, Green, and Blue channels, which in turn moves the histogram in RGB all the way to the right. Press Command-Z once to undo and then Command-Z again to redo this change while watching the RGB histogram. See the differences?

SETTING THE SHADOW

STEP 14: Now we are going to use the Shadow Eyedropper to click on a shadow, which should be the darkest neutral area where you still want a little detail. The RGB values in the Info palette should be in the 1 to 10 range. The CMYK values in the Info palette will be in the 60% to 100% range. Move the Levels dialog box to the top so you can see the entire bottom half of the image. To find the correct area for setting the

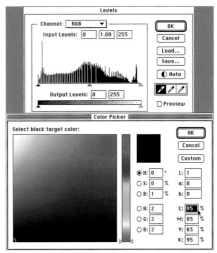

STEP 12: Make sure the shadow values are 95, 85, 83, 95.

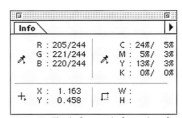

STEP 13: The before and after values for the highlight. Notice how the green color cast was removed and the default neutral 5, 3, 3, 0 values were inserted.

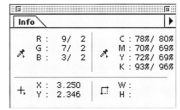

STEP 14: The before and after values for the shadow. Notice that the shadow CMYK values to the right are not the same as the 95, 85, 83, 95 default values you entered, but you should get exactly 2, 2, 2, or very close to it, in RGB.

shadow, hold the Option key down while moving the Input Shadow slider to the right. The whole image area first turns white, and then as you move the slider to the right, black areas appear. The first black area to appear, in the rocks to the lower right or in the tree, is the place where you should set the shadow. If you set the shadow at a location that has a value of about 1, 1, 1, you are setting up your image in such a way that almost no areas will be totally black when it prints. If you set your shadow at a location whose value is around 10, 10, 10, you are saying that you want everything darker than that totally black—and you will get lots of totally black areas. Now move the Input Shadow slider back to 0 since you were only using it to locate the darkest point. Click on the Shadow Eyedropper in the Levels dialog box. Now move this Eyedropper up to that darkest place, and then move it around in the area while watching the RGB values in the Info palette. You may want to zoom in to that particular area before you pick the darkest spot. Try clicking at a spot around 10, 10, 10 and see how dark this makes your shadows. I clicked at a spot around 9, 7, 3, one of the darkest spots under the rock, where I set the shadows for this image. When you find the right spot, click once and release the mouse button; don't move the mouse after the click. The right-hand numbers for RGB in the Info palette should now display 2, 2, 2 (or very close to it) for that exact spot where you clicked. Now go up to the Levels title bar and click on it. When the mouse button is down, you see the original image and when it's up, you see the image after the highlight and shadow changes. If you don't have video LUT Animation, you will have to find the shadow point by measuring the areas that appear darkest then clicking on the one with the lowest numbers, and you'll do the title bar compare by turning Preview on and off.

SETTING OVERALL BRIGHTNESS AND CONTRAST

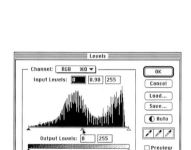

STEP 15: Move the Input Brightness/Contrast slider to the right to add depth and contrast to the image.

STEP 15: As you look at this image, you may notice that it's sort of flat. Move the Input Brightness/Contrast slider to the right until the middle Input Levels number reads about .90. Notice the increased depth and contrast. If you think back to our discussion of the Zone System, you could equate the initial location of the Brightness/Contrast slider with Zone V, the middle gray values. Moving the slider to the right moves Zone V up toward Zone VI or VII, depending on how far you move it. What was a Zone VI value now becomes a Zone V value; darker, and with more depth. This effect is similar to the one you would get by setting the original camera exposure at Zone VI or greater, except moving the Brightness/Contrast slider by a zone or two wouldn't change Zones I and IX as much. If you move the slider to the left, the image would look even flatter. Leave this slider at about .90, and a few steps from now I show you how to saturate your colors to add contrast and drama without sacrificing shadow detail.

CORRECTING FOR COLOR CASTS

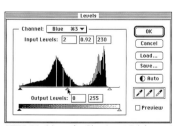

STEP 16: Move the Blue Input Brightness/Contrast slider to the right to add yellow to the image.

STEP 16: All adjustments so far have been done with the Levels Channel selector set to RGB (Channel ~). You can now use the Channel selector in Red (Channel 1), Green (Channel 2), and Blue (Channel 3) modes to control the color balance of the image and to correct for color casts. You can switch between channels by clicking on the pop-up menu and dragging up or down, or by using the key combinations Command-~ through Command-3. The Red channel controls red and its complement, cyan; the Green channel controls green and its complement, magenta; and the Blue channel controls blue and its complement, yellow. Try to commit this set of complementary colors to memory. To learn more about the complementary colors, refer to the RGB/CMYK table at the end of the "Color Correction Tools" chapter. This image has a slightly blue color balance, which makes it seem a little cold. Use the Channel selector or Command-3 to move to the Blue channel. Move the Input Brightness/Contrast slider far to the right until the middle Input Levels number reads about .5 and notice how yellow the image is. Now move the same slider far to the left to about 1.5 and notice how blue the image is. You can use this middle slider to control the color balance of the midtones. Move it back to the right until it reads about .92 and notice the difference in the color of the green grass and bushes in the foreground as well as the overall warmer tone of the image compared to when the slider was at the initial value of 1.0. You have added yellow to remove the blue cast in this image.

STEP 17: Press Command-2 to switch to the Green channel. As you move the middle slider to the left, you add green, and as you move it to the right, you add magenta. I moved it slightly to the right, to .92, which adds a little magenta to the whole image. If you press Command-1, you can use the middle slider to move between red and cyan. Again, I moved it slightly to the right, to .97, and added just a little cyan by removing just a little red. You may make these adjustments slightly differently depending on your preferences for color, and depending on your monitor. So long as you have calibrated your monitor to your output device, you should be able to obtain results that you like. If you made major cast changes to any particular channel, go back to RGB (Command-~) now and double-check your Brightness/Contrast adjustments. Before leaving Levels, click on the title bar to see how the image looked before you made any of the changes, and release the mouse to see the new improved image. You should be able to see the improvements on your monitor. When the Preview button is off, you can use Video LUT Animation on the video board to instantly simulate the changes you will see based on your levels adjustments. We have been doing these changes in Levels assuming the Preview button is off.

Many PC systems and compatibles, and a few Macs, don't support Video LUT Animation in their video boards. Video LUT Animation also does not work when you use an adjustment layer. If you don't have Video LUT Animation, just work with the Preview button on to see the changes as you make them, or turn it off to see the original image. You can't use the title bar as a before/after toggle without Video LUT Animation.

Also, on *all* machines, you may want to turn the Preview button on before leaving Levels and Curves just to check on the screen to be sure that the calculated changes, with the Preview button on, actually match the Video LUT Animation simulated changes. You also want to have the Preview button on if you are viewing a composite of several layers while making changes to only one of them. Click on the OK button to complete all the changes you have made in Levels. At this point, you should File/Save in case you want to revert to this version of the image, later. Go back into Levels and notice that the histogram, especially the Red channel, now has gaps in it because you stretched out the original set of tonal values. These gaps now represent missing tonal values in the 0..255 of possible values. Step 18 will fill in those tonal ranges again.

STEP 17: The GrandCanyon image after the Levels corrections.

STEP 19: Click on the Red radio button and notice how the red rocks change as you move the slider between -5 and +5.

If your initial scan was done in CMYK, it probably was scanned on a high-end scanner, and the scanner operator should have already done these overall color corrections. If you started with a CMYK scan, you should check out the image in CMYK mode to make sure it is has already been overall color corrected; do not convert it to RGB to do the corrections because you can lose information in the CMYK to RGB to CMYK conversion. If you are paying the extra cost to get CMYK scans and they are not already overall color correct, you should get the scans done elsewhere or just do them in RGB.

ENHANCING COLOR WITH HUE/SATURATION

STEP 18: In Step 15, when you moved the Brightness/Contrast slider to the right to increase contrast, you may have had the urge to go even further for a more dramatic effect. Going too far to the right would remove too much shadow detail, however. You can add contrast and drama without losing shadow detail by choosing Image/Adjust Hue/Saturation and moving the Saturation slider to the right to about +17%. The screen may take a few seconds to update, but you will notice all your colors become more saturated, which builds more contrast into the image. When you saturate all the colors, only the midtones change; the highlights and shadows remain the same. When using the Hue/Saturation tool, you want to have the Preview button on, since Photoshop can't calculate these more complex changes using the monitor on the fly the way it can in Levels and Curves. When using Levels and Curves to correct the entire image, you usually want to have the Preview button off unless you don't have Video LUT Animation.

STEP 19: Besides being able to use the Hue/Saturation tool to saturate and desaturate all the colors, which you do with the Master radio button selected, you can also use it to change particular color areas in the entire photo. Click on the radio button next to the red color swatch, and then move the Hue slider a little to the left, toward the M, to about –5, to add magenta to the red areas of the image. Notice all the red rocks become a richer, darker red color. Now move this slider in the other direction to +5, toward the Y. This takes away magenta and adds yellow to the red parts of the image. Now the rocks appear more of a brown color. When you use channel 2 or 3 to add magenta or yellow in Levels, you add magenta or yellow to everything in the image. When you use the Red button in Hue/Saturation, you change only things in the image that are already red.

STEP 20: Click on the Blue button; now you can change the hue of blue objects toward cyan (to the left) or magenta (to the right). Move the Hue slider between –10 and +10 and observe how the colors in the sky change. You might combine this change with the adding or subtracting of saturation from the blue colors in this image. Remember that changing the blue values not only changes blues in the sky but also any other blues in the image. Keep an eye on the entire image as you make these adjustments. I moved the blues –5 toward cyan and the cyans +5 toward blue to try to even out the sky. I also desaturated both blue and cyan by –5. Click on the OK button after you finish the Hue/Saturation changes. Since these changes, unlike those in Levels, don't occur instantly, comparing before and after versions might not be as easy. If you choose

STEP 21: The GrandCanyon image after the Levels and Hue/Saturation corrections.

Undo from the Edit menu and then immediately choose Redo from the Edit menu, you can quickly see the before and after versions of the Hue/Saturation changes. Get used to using Command-Z to toggle between the Undo and Redo versions. We will soon learn how to completely isolate a portion of the image using selections and layer masks for very fine color control of that area. Go back into Levels and notice that the gaps in the channels are now filled in by the added saturation.

STEP 21: Save this color corrected version of the GrandCanyon image in Photoshop format so that you can use it in future steps.

INTRODUCTION TO CURVES

This section shows you how to adjust specific color ranges using Curves. Before you start making further adjustments to the GrandCanyon image, take a moment to examine the Curves tool and its different parts and functions.

Curves is a graph of input and output values with the input values at the bottom of the graph on the horizontal axis and the output values to the left side of the graph on the vertical axis. When you use Curves, the input values are the original unadjusted values before you invoked Curves. The output values are the adjusted values and depend on the shape of the curve graph.

In Levels, the histogram is a picture of the actual data that makes up the particular image. In Curves, you see a graph of how this curve would modify any image, but you don't actually see the data that is part of the image. That is why I recommend using Levels first after you do a scan; you can see how the scan worked. Many of the controls in Curves are the same as those in Levels. Both tools provide an OK button, which you press when you want the changes to become permanent, and a Cancel button, which you press when you want to leave the tool without any changes taking effect. If you hold the Option key down and then press Reset, you stay in the tool, all changes are undone, and the curve goes back to the default straight curve. Both Levels and Curves also have Load and Save buttons that you can use to load or save settings to the disk.

If you particularly like a curve that corrected one image, you can click on Save to save it, go into Curves while working on another image and click on Load to run it on the other image. Curves, also like Levels has Highlight and Shadow Eyedropper tools to

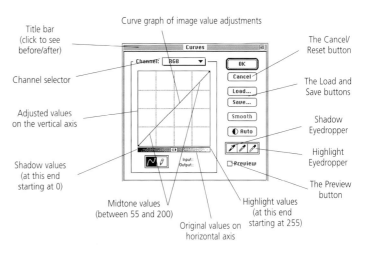

Study this diagram to learn the controls of the Curves tool.

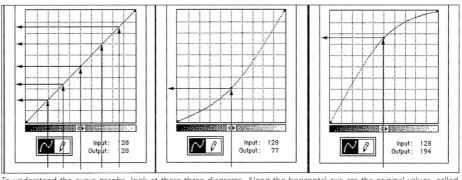

To understand the curve graphs, look at these three diagrams. Along the horizontal axis are the original values, called Input, with 0 (black) on the left side and 255 (white) on the right side. On the vertical axis of the curve, to the left-hand side, are the modified values, called Output, with 0 (black) on the bottom and 255 (white) at the top. Imagine that the original values are light rays that travel straight up from the bottom of the diagram. When they hit the curve graph, they make an immediate left and exit the diagram on the left side. When the curve is the straight default curve, the values go out the same as they come in, as you can see by the leftmost curve above. When the curve is dragged downward, like the middle curve, a value that comes in at 128 hits the curve sooner so it will go out at 77. Since lower values represent darker numbers, pulling the curve down makes the image darker. When the curve is dragged upward, as in the right-hand curve, the input value of 128 doesn't hit the curve until it gets to 194, and that is the brighter output value.

By default in Curves, the horizontal axis shows the shadows on the left. The grayscale on this axis is a hint at this, which is easy to remember since Levels does the same thing. Some curve diagrams show the shadows on the right. If you click on the arrow in the middle of the grayscale, you can flip this curve to put shadows on the right. Doing this turns everything else in the curve adjustment into a mirror image of what it was. Therefore, we recommend leaving shadows on the left. When you set the shadows on the right, the Input and Output values read as percentages between 0% and 100%. If you are more comfortable reading percentage values than the 0..255 values, you can make your Curves tool work this way. Just remember, though, that if you flip your curve orientation, the curves in this book will be opposite to yours.

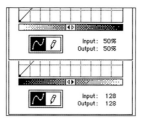

By clicking on the arrows in the middle, you can give the horizontal axis shadows on the left or the right. Leave shadows on the left for working with this book.

set the highlight and shadow the same way you do in Levels. In fact, Curves uses the same preference values for the highlight and shadow numbers as you set in Levels. These preferences are system-wide. The curve graph is just a picture of what happens to all the values from 0 to 255. To move the curve, you click on it and drag it to a new position. When you let go, Photoshop leaves a point along the curve graph, a point that causes the entire curve to move. To get rid of a point, you click on it and drag it outside of the Curves window. When you do this, the curve bounces back to where it would be without that point. Let's experiment a bit now with Curves before you make final adjustments to the GrandCanyon image.

STEP 22: Using the same image you saved at the end of Step 21, choose Image/Adjust/Curves (Command-M) and look at the Curves dialog box. If the curves graph area is divided into only four sections, both horizontally and vertically (the default), you can get a more precise grid. Move the cursor to the middle of the graph—Input and Output will both say 128—and Option-click on this center point. Now the Curves graph will have 10 sections in each direction. To get a bigger, more exact Curve window, click in the box at the top right of the title bar. Make sure the that Preview button is off; leave it on if you don't have Video LUT Animation.

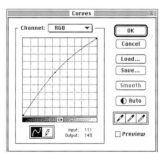

STEP 23: This curve makes the image lighter and brighter. To do this in Levels, you would move the Input Brightness/Contrast slider to the left.

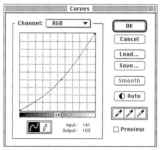

This curve makes the image darker. To do this in Levels, you would move the Input Brightness/Contrast slider to the right.

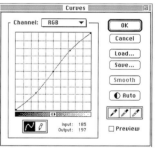

This S-curve makes the midtones more contrasty and the shadows and highlights less contrasty. Overall, the image is more contrasty. You can't do exactly the same in Levels.

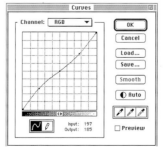

STEP 23: This backwards S-curve makes the midtones flatter and increases contrast in the highlights and shadows. You can't do exactly this in Levels.

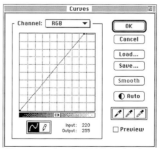

This curve makes the highlights brighter. This is similar to when you move the Input Highlight slider in Levels to the left.

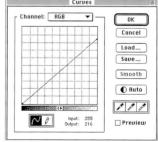

This curve makes the highlights duller. This is similar to when you move the Output Highlight slider in Levels to the left.

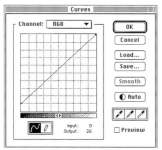

STEP 23: This curve makes the shadows brighter, like moving the Output Shadow slider in Levels to the right.

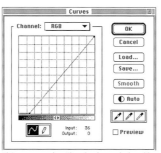

This curve makes the shadows darker, like moving the Input Shadow slider in Levels to the right.

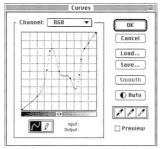

Try this curve to see a prehistoric Grand Canyon! You can't do this kind of adjustment in Levels.

STEP 23: Now click down in the middle of the curve and move the mouse up and down, left and right, and notice how the curve shape changes, and notice the corresponding changes to the image. Try out all the curves in the diagram above. Option-Cancel between each one to reset the curve to straight. Make sure you understand why each curve changes the image the way it does. Remember that each input value has to turn instantly to the left and become an output value as soon as it meets the curve. Trace some values for each of these examples, and I think you will understand how the curve graphs work. You need to understand these curve graphs because they come up all over the place in Photoshop (in Curves, Duotones, Separation Setup, and Transfer functions) as well as in many books and other applications dealing with color.

CHANGING COLOR RANGES WITH CURVES

STEP 24: Cancel all the different things you tried with Curves and go back to the image you ended up with at the end of Step 21. Choose File/Revert if you somehow destroyed the image while playing with Curves. Now you're going to use what I call the LockDownCurve to do fine adjustments to the greens in the valley of the Grand Canyon. Enter Curves (Command-M), and move the Curves dialog box so that it isn't covering the green field in the middle of the GrandCanyon image. Since we want to change the greens in the field, select the Green channel from the Channel selector. If you move the cur-

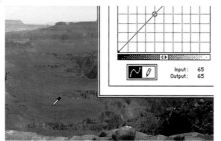

STEP 24: Click on the Eyedropper tool while over the green field and hold it down while moving around to measure the range of greens in the field. The circle appears to show you where these values are on the curve graph.

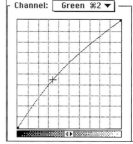

STEP 24: This type of curve adds green to the entire image.

sor out over the field, it changes to the Eyedropper tool, you are automatically in the Eyedropper whenever you use a color correction tool. If you click on the Eyedropper and hold the mouse button down as you move it around over the green field, a circle appears on the curve showing you where the values you are measuring occur along the curve. Visually remember where those values are in the curve as you move the mouse back within the Curves dialog box. Click on the curve in that location and move it diagonally, either up and to the left, for more green, or down and to the right, for more magenta. You want to brighten these greens in the field. Notice, however, that the rest of the curve also moves, causing you effectively to add green, or magenta, to the entire image. What you want to do is add green to just the greens that have the same green color range as this field.

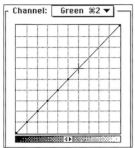

STEP 25: Creating a lock-down curve.

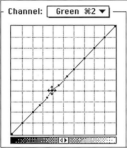

STEP 25: Modify greens in valley color range.

STEP 25: Option-Cancel to restore the curve to the default. You will now create what I call a *lock-down curve*. Click at each intersection of the vertical and horizontal lines in the green curve to leave a point that locks the curve at its present location. Make sure that the Input and Output numbers are equal before you click. Now you have a lock-down curve in the Green channel. Remeasure the green field to see where the measurements fall between the points on the lock-down curve. Clicking in the box at the top right of the title bar to get a bigger curve at this point might help. Move the points on either side of this range so that only this range is open and so that there are lock-down points at either end. Now click down in the middle of the range, and move the mouse again (up and left for more green, or down and right for more magenta). I added green for my example. Notice that the only greens that changed were the ones in this valley, and in other parts of the image, that had the same range of greens. To save time when doing lock-down curves, we have pre-saved a curve, called LockDownCurve, that has locked points on all four channels. When you want to tweak a particular color area, just enter Curves, load the LockDownCurve with the Load button, and then you can change whatever part of any channel you want without changing the rest of that color. There is a copy of the LockDownCurve in the Preferences folder on the CD, and in chapter folders as needed.

STEP 26: Save this image as GrandCanyonPart1. You work on it again in "The Grand Canyon—Final Tweaks," where you lighten the dark tree and rock areas, remove the scratch, and spot the image to make it ready for final reproduction.

STEP 26: The GrandCanyon image after using Curves to pop the greens in the valley.

Chapter 16: The Grand Canyon

HANDS-ON SESSION: Kansas

Overall color correction on a problem scan
without good white or black points.

In this example, you will do overall color correction but use some different techniques than in the Grand Canyon session because its histogram looks different. For the purposes of this example, we assume that you have done the Grand Canyon example.

SETTING HIGHLIGHTS WITH CHANNELS

STEP 1: Open the file KansasRawPhotoCD. This is a 4Mb Photo CD scan of a picture I took while driving through Kansas during a summer vacation when I was in college. Use the cropping tool or Marquee to crop the copyright notice from the bottom. Choose File/Save As and save this file as KansasLevels. Put the image in Full Screen mode by clicking on the middle icon at the bottom of the Tool palette. Bring up the Info palette (F9 with ArtistKeys) and the Color palette (Shift-F9 with ArtistKeys), and then choose Image/Adjust/Levels (Command-L) to enter Levels.

STEP 2: Look at the original RGB histogram pictured here and notice that the values don't go all the way to the right, highlight, side, which is why the picture looks dull. Press Command-1, then Command-2, and then Command-3 to look at the Red, Green, and Blue channels, respectively. I always do this when I

The initial Kansas Photo CD scan.

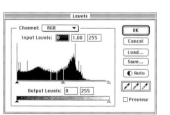

STEP 2: Original RGB histogram with lack of highlight values.

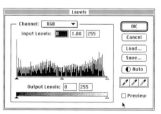

STEP 2: Final RGB histogram data is spread from 0 to 255.

first look at a scan to see if it has any potential problems. In this image, all the channels have dull highlights but each of them has highlight detail that ends at a different point on the histogram. Press Command-~ to go back to RGB, and then hold down the Option key while dragging the Input Highlight slider to the left. (Remember, the Option key technique only works if you have Video LUT Animation and the Preview button is off.) You would normally set the highlight at the first area to turn white. In this photo, there is no good, neutral place to set a highlight, which should be pure white after that setting. The "white" buildings aren't really that white and the brightest area is actually in the blue clouds somewhere. That's a sign that the Eyedropper may not be the best way to set the highlights in this image. Type

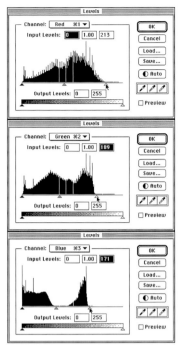

STEP 2: Move the Input Highlight sliders of the Red, Green, and Blue histograms to the left until they touch the beginning of the data. This moves all the data to the left of that point all the way to the right, spreading out the values in each histogram.

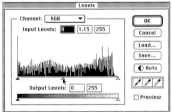

STEP 4: After setting highlight and shadow, set overall brightness and contrast. Move middle slider to left in RGB.

Command-1 again and move the Red Input Highlight slider to the left until it reaches the first real histogram data, at about 213. Do the same things for the Green (189) and Blue (171) channels, and then press Command-~ to return to RGB. Notice how much brighter the image looks now and also how much more complete the RGB histogram looks. We have set our highlight for this image.

STEP 3: Notice that the shadow values in the Blue channel suddenly drop off a cliff on the left side, unlike those in the Red and Green channels, which taper off like they should; this is a sign that the scanner did not get all the shadow detail in the Blue channel or that there was no more detail in the film. Since this is a Photo CD scan, we have to live with it or buy our own scanner. When this happens to you, look at the original transparency and see if there was actually detail in this area. If there was, you might be able to get better results by rescanning with a high-end drum scanner. However, in the real world, we often have to correct problem images and scans, so hold the Option key down (only if you have Video LUT Animation) and move the Input Shadow slider to the right to test for a shadow point. There are some good shadow locations on the right-hand side of the wheat in the front and also within the big green tree by the house. Click on the Shadow Eyedropper and measure these shadows until you find the darkest neutral spot (I found a few at 5, 5, 5) and click on that spot with the Shadow Eyedropper. The new value for that spot should be around 2, 2, 2 on the right side of the Info palette and your black shadows should look neutral. If they don't, click on a new neutral darkest spot until your shadows look and measure neutral. Now you have set your shadow.

BRIGHTNESS, CONTRAST, AND COLOR CAST

STEP 4: Move the Input Brightness/Contrast slider in RGB until the overall brightness of the image looks correct. I moved it to the left to bring out a little more shadow detail in the foreground wheat and in the dark trees around the house. You can't bring out more detail in an area that is totally black, so don't go too far on this shadow detail thing.

STEP 5: Since we moved the highlight sliders differently on each of the color channels, we need to go into each channel and correct for color casts, which is easiest to do if you try to fix the most annoying cast first, and then fine-tune the other colors and other casts that appear along the way. The wheat in the foreground seems to have a greenish cast. I often have a hard time with these greenish casts because they're sometimes both green and cyan. This one looks greener, so go to the Green channel (Command-2) and move the middle slider to the right to add magenta; that should improve the situation, make the wheat look more golden. Move the slider until the

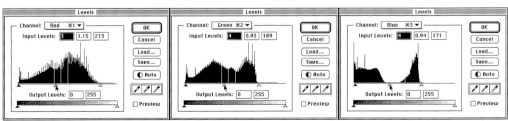

STEP 5: Here are the adjustments I made to the middle sliders of the Red, Green, and Blue channels to adjust for color casts in this image. Since the wheat is the major component here, getting that to look good was the main goal. Other parts of the image can be fine-tuned later.

wheat looks *too* magenta, then move it back until you start to see the green again, and then add just a little magenta. If the image still has a greenish tinge, it might be that there is a cyan problem too, so move to the Red channel (Command-1) and add a little red by moving the middle slider to the left. Finally, add a little yellow by moving the middle slider in the Blue channel a little to the right. At this point, before leaving Levels, you might want to click on the Preview button just to make sure that the video simulation of your corrections matches the calculated changes that you set when you click on Preview. They usually match really well on my system. When you're happy, click on OK and save. Now you have done the initial Levels adjustment on this difficult image.

STEP 5: Kansas, after all the Levels adjustments.

SATURATING COLORS

STEP 6: Having completed the initial overall histogram correction with Levels, you're ready to use the Hue/Saturation tool to saturate and enhance the colors that are most important to this image. Choose Image/Adjust/Hue/Saturation and make sure that the Preview button is on. When you use Levels or Curves on the whole image, you want to work with the Preview button off, because when you do, Photoshop gives you an instant preview using Video LUT Animation, a technique that instantly changes the internal adjustments on the monitor. The calculations performed on your image in Hue/Saturation are too complicated to preview with Video LUT Animation, though, so in it you need the Preview button on. Depending on the speed of your computer, you may need to wait after every change for the screen to update the image, which it does starting in the top left corner working down to the bottom right in rectangular increments. When you first start Hue/Saturation, the Master button is selected. Any master changes you make apply to all the colors at the same time. Move the Saturation slider to the right to about 15, making all colors more vivid.

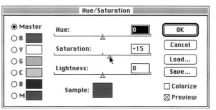

STEP 6: In Master, saturate all the colors by 15.

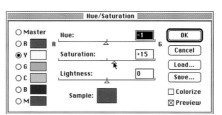

STEP 7: In Yellow, saturate the yellow colors by 15, and move yellows slightly toward red.

STEP 7: Since the wheat is mostly composed of yellow, this is an important color to tweak. Click on the Yellow radio button to restrict the changes you make to apply only to the yellow parts of the image. Move the Saturation slider to the right by 15

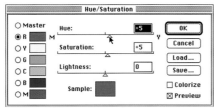

STEP 8: Red Hue/Saturation changes.

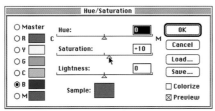

STEP 8: Blue Hue/Saturation changes.

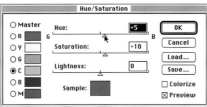

STEP 8: Cyan Hue/Saturation changes.

and move the Hue slider a little toward red; –1 will make the yellows a little warmer and more intense. The changes you make may be a little different depending on your personal taste and exactly how you have adjusted your version of this image so far. The last two steps are the other changes I made to the image.

STEP 8: Click on the Red radio button and move the reds toward yellow by 5, and saturate reds also by 5. Click on the Blue radio button and saturate the blues by 10 points, to make the sky blue deeper. Click on the Cyan radio button and move the cyans toward blue by 5, and saturate them by 10. The cyan changes also affect the sky.

STEP 9: In color correcting this image, we have made all the corrections we can make without creating selections. Save this image as KansasCorrected so you can return to it to do some final color tweaks in the chapter "Kansas—Final Tweaks," using selections along with Curves and Hue/Saturation.

STEP 9: Kansas, after Levels and Hue/Saturation adjustments.

HANDS-ON SESSION: Burnley Graveyard

How to work with duotones, how and why to adjust duotone curves, and how to save and calibrate your duotone output.

Duotones are used to print black-and-white photos on a press and get more tonal range. Black-and-white (B&W) digital images can have up to 256 tones in digital format, but you can't get those 256 tones on a printing press with just the single black ink. If you use two or more inks to print B&W images, part of the tonal range can be printed by the first ink and part of it by the second ink. Many of Ansel Adams' well-known B&W posters are actually duotones. Besides giving you a larger tonal range, duotones allow you to add rich and subtle color to your B&W images.

Typically, you use black ink for the dark shadows and a second color, maybe a brown or gray, for the midtones. You can add a third and even a fourth color to enhance the highlights or some other part of the tonal range. Many books are printed with two colors, black for the text and a second color, such as red or blue, for text

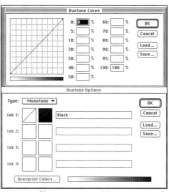

STEP 1: The BurnleyGraveyard image printed as black-and-white using only black ink.

section titles, underline, and other special colored areas. If this type of book has photographs, you can often make them more interesting by using duotones instead of just B&W.

CREATING A DUOTONE

STEP 1: Open and crop the BurnleyGraveyard image from the Burnley Graveyard folder on the CD. Choose Image/Mode/Duotone to start working with the Duotone Options. Start out with the Type set to Monotone and the curve for Ink 1 straight. If the curve is not already straight, click on the Curve box, the leftmost one, for Ink 1, and bring up the curve. Click and drag any extra points in the middle of the curve to outside the dialog box to remove them. The horizontal axis of the curve diagrams in Duotone Options has the highlights on the left and the shadows on the right, the opposite of the default for Levels and Curves. The numbers in the boxes represent percentage of black. Box 0, for the brightest highlight, should read 0, and box 100, for the darkest shadow, should read 100. All the other boxes should be blank in a straight curve. Click on OK in the Duotone Curve dialog box. The Ink box for Ink 1 should be black and Black should be its name. Change the Type to Duotone to activate Ink 2 with a straight curve. To pick the color of Ink 2, click in the Color box, the

STEP 1: Change type to Monotone mode and start with a straight curve.

133

STEP 1: The BurnleyGraveyard image created in Duotone mode as a duotone with black and PANTONE 10 C inks, both having straight curves, and later converted to CMYK for this final output.

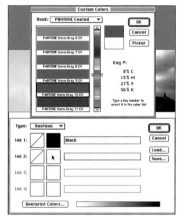

STEP 1: Picking the second color by clicking on the rightmost color square for Ink 2.

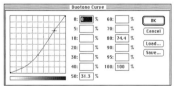

STEP 2: The black curve emphasizing the shadows.

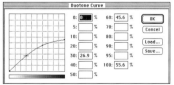

STEP 2: The midtone curve for Ink 2, lowering this color in the shadow areas.

rightmost one, for Ink 2, to bring up the Custom Colors picker, and then select a PANTONE, Focoltone, Toyo, Trumatch, or other color from one of the Custom Color Systems. Look in "Picking and Using Color" if you need help using the Custom Colors picker. If you were going to print your duotone on a two color book job or a job with a spot color, you would probably use one of these color systems. We selected PANTONE 10 C for Ink 2. You now have a black ink and a medium gray ink, both with straight curves. Click on OK on the Custom Colors palette and click on OK in the Duotone Options dialog box. When you leave the Duotone Options dialog box, Photoshop adjusts the image on-screen to give you a preview of what it should look like with the current inks and curves. Printing two inks, both with straight curves, is like printing the image in black and then printing the exact same image again with the second ink color. When printing with halftone screens, the second ink will be printed with a different screen angle to add some additional tonality over just using one ink. Printing the two inks using the same curve will cause the image to have too much density and thus seem very dark. Printing using the same curve is not taking advantage of the real possibilities for duotone improvements.

ADJUSTING YOUR DUOTONE CURVES

STEP 2: Go back into Image/Mode/Duotone and click on the Curve box, the leftmost box, for Ink 1. You want to adjust the black ink to make it prevalent in the shadows but less prevalent in the midtones and highlights. To do this, click on a point in the middle of the curve and drag that point downward to remove black from the midtones and highlights. Now click on the shadow end of the curve, to the middle right, and drag it up to add a little more black to this area of the image. See the illustration of the black curve here. Click on the OK button for black and then click on the Curve button for Ink 2, middle gray, so you can work on its curve. Because we want the dark areas of the image to be represented mostly by black, we need to remove the gray from the shadows. Click at the top right of the curve and drag it down to about 55. Now you need to put the gray back into the highlights and midtones, so click a couple of points in the middle of the curve to pull it up so it looks like the curve here. To see these changes, click OK on the Curve dialog box and then click OK on the Duotone dialog box; you have made the basic adjustments for your duotone curves. Now change each curve just a little bit, one curve at a time. Tweak these curves and after each change click on OK to leave the Duotone Options dialog box so you can see what that change did to your image. When you are happy with your duotone, save the image as BurnleyGraveyardDuo.

CREATING A TRITONE

STEP 3: To further enhance this image, you can add a third ink for the highlight areas. Before doing so, however, take time to make a copy of the two-ink version of the image so you can compare them on-screen. Choose Image/Duplicate and name this copy BurnleyGraveyardTri. Choose Image/Mode/Duotone, and select Tritone from the Type menu in Duotone Options so that a choice for Ink 3 will be added. Click on the Ink Color box and choose a lighter gray for the high-lights. (We chose PANTONE 422 CV.) Adjust the curve for this highlight color so that it has ink only in the brightest part of the image. Here is the curve we chose for the third ink. Notice how we moved the 0 position of the curve up to 6.3 instead of leaving it at 0. This strategy actually adds some density to the brightest parts of the image; that is, in the clouds and where the sun reflects off the gravestones, two areas that previously were pure white. Click on OK to see the results of adding this third color.

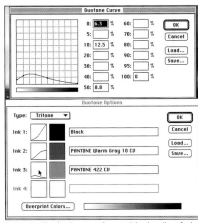

STEP 2: The BurnleyGraveyard image created in Duotone mode as a duotone with black for the shadows and PANTONE 10 C for the midtones and highlights, after adjusting the curves for those two colors, and later being converted to CMYK.

STEP 4: You may want to measure some values on the screen using the Eyedropper. When working with duo-tones, you want to set the Eyedropper to Actual Color, so that it will give you measurements of the ink density per-centage of each color. If you measure one of those high-light areas in the clouds, you can see that there is no density there from Inks 1 and 2, but that Ink 3 has 6% density in that area. If you measure a shadow area, the maximum density there will be from Ink 1, black. There will be some density from Ink 2 and there will be no density from Ink 3, because its curve specifies no ink in the shadow areas.

STEP 5: You have added a third color specifically for the highlights; therefore, you may want to go back to Ink 2 and remove some of the midtone ink from the high-light areas. Click on the Curve box for Ink 2, and lower its curve in the highlight areas by clicking a point there and dragging it downward. Here is the final curve we used for Ink 2 in the tritone. Our final tritone image appears on the next page.

STEP 6: Go back and try some different colors and different curves for this duotone or tritone. Try some blues, greens, purples, magentas, yellows—lots of wild things. Experiment with some radical inverted curves to discover the great range of effects you can achieve with the Duotone options.

STEP 3: Final tritone values with details of the highlight curve. Notice how this curve actually starts above 0 on the Y axis. This adds density in the very brightest areas.

Calibrating and Outputting Your Duotones

You may find that you need to calibrate your monitor differently for duotone output than for CMYK output. If duotones on your monitor aren't matching the final output, redo the monitor calibra-tion steps with Gamma for duotones, and make a duotone proof to create a separate Gamma setting for working with duotones. We rec-ommend that you leave your preferences set up the same as those for CMYK output in the chapter "Setting System and Photoshop Prefer-ences." When you output your duotones, you have several choices to make. If you actually print with PANTONE or some other custom spot color, you need to save the file as a duotone in EPS format. You can set your screen angles for the duotone in Photoshop using the File/Page Setup/Screen but-ton, or you can set your screen angles in Quark if you are placing your duotone into that page layout application. Talk to your service bureau about how and where to set your screens and what screen angles and frequencies to use; they may be different depending on the type of imagesetter your service bureau uses. Make sure the Short PANTONE Names option is chosen in File/Preferences/General. This option makes

STEP 4: Set the Info palette to Actual Color for duotones.

STEP 4: The Info palette measuring a shadow in Tritone mode.

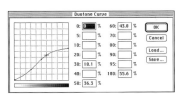

STEP 5: The midtone curve for the tritone with a small dip in the highlight area and a bigger dip in the shadows.

The dialog box and settings for saving the file as EPS Duotone. The dialog box and settings for saving the file as EPS/CMYK are the same except that there also is a DCS menu.

Converting a file from Duotone to CMYK format for output to process colors.

the PANTONE names chosen in Photoshop more compatible with those specified in Quark, Illustrator, and other layout applications. Make sure the name of each color is exactly the same (including upper- and lowercase letters) in your page layout application; otherwise, your duotone may be output as CMYK. To save from Photoshop as a duotone, leave the Mode menu set to Duotone, choose File/Save As, and then set the Format to EPS. In the EPS dialog box, set the Preview to Macintosh (8 bits/pixel) and the Encoding to Binary, and click on the Include Halftone Screen check box only if you have set your screens and frequencies in Photoshop.

If you want to convert the duotone to CMYK to output it with process colors, use the Image/Mode menu to convert the image to CMYK color. You will probably still save the file as an EPS, but there will be an additional option for DCS, which you should set to "On" (72 pixel/inch color) to get the 5 file format with a color preview. For more information on the options for saving CMYK files, see "Color Correction and Output."

You can also convert your duotones to RGB format if you want to composite them with other images for multimedia use, or for output to a film recorder or some other RGB device. To do the conversion to RGB, just select Image/Mode/RGB.

When you work on a duotone or tritone, the Channels palette just displays a single channel, your original black-and-white image. When you print the tritone, this same black-and-white channel prints three times, and each time the separate curve for the particular tritone color is used to modify it before it goes to the printer. If you want to see each of these three color tritone channels as they will look after the curves are applied, switch the Image/Mode menu to Multichannel. The Channels palette will now show you three channels: Channel 1 for black, Channel 2 for PANTONE 10, and Channel 3 for PANTONE 422. You can then click on each channel in the Channels palette to see how that channel will look on film on the press. If you wanted to edit each of these channels separately, you could do so now, but then you could not convert them back to Duotone mode. They would have to be output as three separate black-and-white files. Normally you would choose Edit/Undo to undo the mode change and put things back into Duotone mode.

The final BurnleyGraveyard image created in Duotone mode as a tritone with black for the shadows, PANTONE 10 C for the midtones, and PANTONE 422 CV for the highlights, and later converted to CMYK for this final output.

IMPROVING COLOR
AND MOOD

WITH

SELECTIONS, LAYERS, ADJUSTMENT
LAYERS, AND LAYER MASKS

HANDS-ON SESSION: The Car

Using the Magic Wand, the Lasso tool,
and Quick Mask mode to
select the red car and change its color.

STEP 1: The original perspective Acura ad with the red Acura.

Suppose the image for an ad has been created and the clients love it. They are ready to run the ad, when the art director and the boss enter insisting on a purple car. You try to explain to them that red really looks better because the background is mostly purple, but they insist on a purple car. You don't want to have to go out and reshoot the car—that never happens in the digital world—so, you just select the car and change its color.

SELECTING THE CAR

STEP 1: Open the RedAcura file from The Car folder. Double-click on the Magic Wand tool, set its tolerance to 75, and make sure Anti-aliased is on. The larger the tolerance, the more adjacent colors the Magic Wand selects. Having the Anti-aliased feature on makes edges of the selection easier with their surroundings. Click down on the bright red color just to the right of the Acura emblem above the bumper to select most of the bumper area. Now Shift-click on the reddest part of the hood, in the middle. Holding the Shift key down while making a selection adds that selection to what you have already been selected. Change the tolerance to about 45 and then continue to Shift-click on unselected red areas with the tolerance set to 45. If adding any new area makes the selection lines go outside the area of the car, choose Edit/Undo (Command-Z) to undo that last part of the selection. Your previous selections should still be there. After you select most of the red areas of the car without going beyond its boundaries, your selection should look like the one pictured here.

STEP 1: The Magic Wand tool with its tolerance set to 75 and Anti-aliased on.

STEP 2: Double-click on the Lasso tool, make sure its feather is set to zero, and make sure that Anti-aliased is also on for the Lasso. Again, hold down the Shift key first and then circle areas that you didn't select with the Wand. While adding to the selection with the Lasso tool, you should zoom in closely to the area you are working on. Make sure that the Shift key is down or you might accidentally move the selection instead of adding to it. When you hold down the Shift key, the cursor appears as either a cross-hair or the

STEP 1: This is about as much of the selection as you should try to get with the Magic Wand. Now use the Lasso tool.

Lasso, depending on how your preferences are set up. In either case, you will see a little plus to the bottom right of the cursor to tell you that you are adding. When the Shift key is not down, the cursor looks like a white pointing arrow with a selection box. Clicking and dragging at this point will move the selection. If you do this by accident, immediately choose Edit/Undo (Command-Z). Use Shift with the Lasso tool to circle all the areas not selected. When adding to the selection, first put the cursor on top of an area already selected, hold the Shift key down, and then press and hold down the mouse button while circling the areas you want to add. If you accidentally select something along a border that you don't want to select, move the cursor into an area nearby that isn't selected, hold the Option key down, press the mouse button down, and use the Lasso to circle the part of that border area you want to deselect. When you hold down the Option key, you see a minus to the right of the cursor signifying a subtract from the selection. When doing selections along a border with the Lasso tool, you have to trace the edge pixel by pixel. The Lasso tool has no intelligence to detect where color or brightness changes, so this is a hand-eye coordination exercise. Be sure to select everything that is part of the red car, even the reds that have a purple tone or are almost black. If they're part of the painted car, you should select them. Just like an auto body shop that is putting masking tape on the chrome and other areas for a paint job, you need to make sure that all areas to be painted are selected and all areas not to be painted are not selected. Pretend that the unselected areas have masking tape on them.

STEP 2: The Lasso tool and its options.

STEP 2: No Shift key down, so white arrow cursor moved selection. Choose Edit/Undo (Command-Z) immediately if this happens.

Once you have started a Lasso selection, addition, or subtraction, the mouse button is down and you are drawing with the button down. At this point, if you hold the Option key down, you can release the mouse button and draw straight line segments between mouse clicks. If you want to draw in freehand again, hold the mouse button down again while drawing. In any case, the Option key or the mouse button needs to remain down until you are done with this selection change because when you release the Option key and the mouse button at the same time, the two end points of the selection will join. The hand, eye, mouse coordination in this maneuver can be tricky! Let's go through the most difficult case, when you are subtracting from the existing selection. First press the Option key and hold until you click down on the mouse button. Starting with the Option key tells Photoshop you want to subtract. Next, you click down the mouse button and hold it down while drawing in freehand. Now you can release the Option key as long as you keep the mouse button down. If you want to draw straight line segments, press down the Option key again after its initial release. Now each time you mouse click, you are defining a corner point, and straight lines will be drawn between clicks. To draw in freehand again, press and hold down the mouse button while drawing. When you have looped around what you wanted to subtract, release the Option key and the mouse button, and the end points of this selection will be joined. Remember, this works for both adding to (Shift key starts) and subtracting from (Option key starts) a selection.

SAVING AND LOADING YOUR SELECTIONS

STEP 3: After you work on this for a while, you may get nervous fearing you could lose all your hard work with a random mouse click. Remember, if you click without holding down the Shift key, you make a new selection and will lose and the selection you have worked on so hard. If this happens by accident, choose Command-Z to Undo. Another way to protect against this happening is to save your selection into a mask channel. To do this, bring up the Channels palette, Window/Show Channels (Shift-F10 with ArtistKeys), and click on the Save Selection icon (second from the left) at

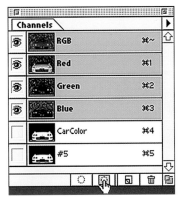

STEP 3: Click on the Save Selection icon to save your selection.

STEP 3: To load your selection again, click on the channel and drag it to the Load Selection icon at the bottom left or just Command-Click on the channel.

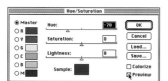

STEP 4: The sample swatch changes to purple when you move the Hue to –70. With the Preview button on, the selected area will change also.

STEP 5: Unless your selection was perfect, you may have a red border around the edge and you might notice other areas that are still red after you turn the car to purple. Zoom in using Command-Spacebar-click to see selection edges closely.

Quick Mask mode selector (Quick Mask Icon)

STEP 5: The Quick Mask mode selector is at the bottom right of the Tool palette. Here we see the color swatch in the Quick Mask Options dialog box. Note: As a shortcut, you can also use (Q) to toggle back and forth between the regular and Quick Mask modes.

the bottom of the palette. A new channel is created; it's white in the selection and black (or masked) everywhere else. If you want to save your selection a second time after you work on it some more, choose Select/Save Selection, and then choose Channel #5 and the Replace Channel option. This new selection overwrites the old saved selection. To retrieve your selection from the mask channel, choose Select/Load Selection of a New Selection and set the Channel pop-up to #5. A short-cut for doing Load Selection is to hold the Command key down and click on Channel #5 in the Channels palette. That selects the white parts in the channel. The mask channel CarColor is a completed selection that you can use to check the accuracy of your selection. Leave this mask channel on the palette until the end, and then compare your finished selection to it for an idea of what you need to improve, if anything. If you have questions about how channels or the Channels palette works, see the chapter "Selections, Masks, and Channels."

CHOOSING A NEW COLOR

STEP 4: When you think you have finished the selection process, choose Command-H with your selection loaded and active to hide the selection edges. This operation removes the marching ants and lets you see the edges of your selection as you change the color of the car. If your selection is not correct, problems usually show up along the selection edges. Now choose Image/Adjust/Hue/Saturation (Command-U) to bring up the Hue/Saturation dialog box. While you are in a color correction tool, the Eyedropper is automatically selected from the Tool palette. Click down with the Eyedropper on the red area of the car just above the Acura emblem. The Sample color swatch in the Hue/Saturation dialog box will show this red. To use the swatch as a preview, you need to first set it to your starting color, as we just did. Move the Hue slider, the top one, to the left until the number reads –70. Notice that the swatch changes from red to purple, indicating that making the change would make your reds purple. If the Preview button is selected, the car will also change to purple after a brief delay. When you are working on a large file, this delay can be long, so you might want to move the Hue slider back and forth with the Preview button off, and use your swatch to get the new color in the ballpark of what it should be. The swatch will change instantly. When the swatch seems correct, click on the Preview button to see your selection change color. If the Preview button isn't on yet, turn it on now.

WORKING WITH QUICK MASK SELECTION MODE

STEP 5: In the Hue/Saturation dialog box with the Preview button on, use the Space-bar to scroll around the edge of your selection, making sure all the red areas of the car have changed to purple. You may notice a red edge around the car and in other areas, such as on the Acura emblem, which indicates that your selection isn't perfect. If you find some red, hit the Cancel button in the Hue/Saturation dialog box to return the car to red. Now you're going to use Quick Mask mode along with the Paintbrush tool to clean up your selection. In the Tool palette, double-click on the Quick Mask mode icon at the bottom right to bring up your Quick Mask options. Click on the color swatch, and set it to a bright green. The default color for this swatch is red, which won't work here because we have a red car. The default for Quick Mask mode is that the masked area, the non-selected area, is covered by a colored semi-transparent layer. This is like seeing a rubylith in traditional masking. The selected area is not covered. When you're in Quick Mask mode, you use the painting tools to add or subtract from your selection by painting with a brush. This gives you finer pixel-for-pixel control than you can get with the selection tools.

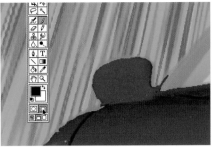

Type a D to set the default black and white colors. When the masked areas are overlayed, which is the default, painting subtracts from the selection and adds to the masked area. The default Quick Mask icon is gray on the outside. If you Option-click on the Quick Mask icon, it changes so the gray is on the inside and the selected areas are overlayed with green. When you paint in this mode, painting adds to the selection. Put yourself into this mode by Option-clicking on the Quick Mask icon until the circle in the middle of it is gray and the outside is white. Now the green overlay will be wherever your selection was.

STEP 5: In the default Quick Mask mode, the Quick Mask icon has gray on the outside, a white circle on the inside, and a semi-transparent green mask that overlays the non-selected areas. Painting with black here subtracts from the selection.

STEP 5: In the Selected Areas Quick Mask mode, the circle in the Quick Mask icon has gray on the inside. The green mask area overlays the selected areas. Painting with black here adds to the selection.

STEP 6: Using the Paintbrush tool, in Normal mode, with 100% opacity in the Paintbrush options, choose a 5-pixel brush, third from top left, in the Brushes palette (F12 with ArtistKeys). If you see a red border around the edge of your selection, paint this border area with the brush. You may need to pick a larger or smaller brush. You can use the left and right bracket keys to change your brush size without moving the cursor to the Brushes palette while painting. You can also double-click on any brush to change its size and attributes. If you are not sure how to pick brush sizes and options, see the earlier chapter, "The Tool Palette."

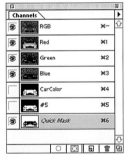

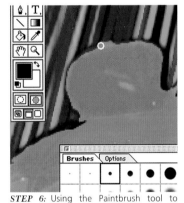

STEP 6: Notice that the Channels palette will get an extra channel called *Quick Mask* when you are working in Quick Mask mode. This goes away when you return to Normal Selection mode.

STEP 6: Using the Paintbrush tool to remove the red border from around the edge of the red car selection by adding to the selection.

Paint any red areas that still show up so they are overlayed in green. If you accidentally paint beyond the edge of the red area, you can Option-click on the Quick Mask icon and invert the overlay; then you're subtracting from the selection instead of adding to it. A faster way to erase mistakes is to type an X, which exchanges the foreground and background colors and allows you to paint with white. While you're in Quick Mask mode with selected areas overlayed, painting with black adds to the selection and painting with white subtracts from the selection.

When you have perfected your selection, the selection overlay should look like the diagram here. You shouldn't have a red border protruding around the overlay edge.

STEP 6: What the edge should look like with a perfected selection, before switching back to Normal Selection mode.

Be sure to check the Acura emblem and the red roof of the car. For an area where the red color fades into another color at the edge, you can use less than 100% Opacity on the Brush to blend the selection of the red into the other edge colors.

Working in Quick Mask mode can be confusing if you Load Selections or work with the selection tools at the same time. For now, use the PaintBrush and other painting tools to edit in Quick Mask mode.

STEP 7: What the Quick Mask icon should look like (gray on the outside with a white circle inside) after switching back to Normal Selection mode.

RETURNING TO NORMAL SELECTION

STEP 7: At this point, Option-click on the Quick Mask icon so that the masked areas are overlayed and the icon appears gray on the outside and white on the inside. Then click on the Regular Selection icon to get the marching ants back around your selection. If you leave the icon gray on the inside and white on the outside, when you save a selection after that your masks will be inverted. The selected part will be black instead of white. This may confuse you. Believe me, it has confused many of my students! Now use Select/Save Selection to update your selection in the Channels palette.

FEATHERING THE SELECTION

STEP 8: Choose Select/Feather and put a 1-pixel feather on the selection border before going into Hue/Saturation. This may blend away very fine reddish hues along some edges of the car.

MAKING THE CAR PURPLE

STEP 9: Now choose Command-H to hide the edges of your selection, go back to Image/Adjust/Hue/Saturation (Command-U), and move the Hue slider back to –70. Your purple car should now look great, and have no red edges. If it does, choose OK from the Hue/Saturation tool. If it still isn't perfect, choose Cancel in Hue/Saturation (or choose Edit/Undo if you already said OK), and go back to Quick Mask mode for more fine-tuning with the Paintbrush tool. When you're done, choose File/Save As to save your final purple car under a different name.

STEP 9: The final purple Acura.

HANDS-ON SESSION: The Grand Canyon—Final Tweaks

Using selections and adjustment layers to change shadow areas, and using the Rubber Stamp tool to remove spots and scratches.

In this session, you further improve the GrandCanyon image by using selections and adjustment layers to dodge and burn. You also remove the scratch, and spot the image.

USING SELECTIONS AND ADJUSTMENT LAYERS TO BURN AND DODGE

STEP 1: Open the final color corrected version of the GrandCanyon image which you create in the earlier "The Grand Canyon" chapter. Put the image in Full Screen mode by clicking on the middle icon at the bottom of the Tool palette. If the tree trunk, the big rock on the lower right side, the bushes on the lower left, or some other parts of the image are too dark or too light, you may want to change them like you would in a darkroom by holding something over the enlarger light source in the trouble area or by adding extra light to that area while making the print. In traditional darkroom terms, this called *dodging* or *burning*. I often burn and dodge using selections and adjustment layers instead of the dodge and burn tools, because they give me greater flexibility with different types of effects that are always undoable. Double-click on the *Background* layer and rename it Orig Image to change it from a *Background* layer into a normal layer. Double-click on the Magic Wand tool, or type W, and set its tolerance to about 8. Lowering the tolerance to 8 will make this tool select a smaller range of colors. Make sure the Anti-aliased option is turned on. When Anti-aliased is on, the edge of the selection is given something like a very slight feather to blend changes you might make to that selected area with the background. Making a selection with Anti-aliased on produces a result that differs from a feather. Usually, when you want to blend a selection with the areas around it, you want to have Anti-aliased on. If you don't have it on, the edge of the selection is very abrupt; you get no blend between the edge and the background. Now click down in the dark part of the tree trunk with the Magic Wand. It will select the tree trunk and it may select more than that. If you don't like what it selects, press Command-Z for Undo and try again. You may want to select other dark parts of the tree trunk by holding down the Shift key while clicking on those parts. Remember, Command-Z returns you to the last selection, so if you try to add a part and it messes up your entire selection, Command-Z is your friend. You can also choose Select/None to remove this selection, change the tolerance on the Magic Wand, and try again.

STEP 1: Tree shadow selection with anti-aliased on.

STEP 1: Tree shadow selection with anti-aliased off.

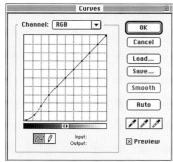

STEP 2: The Wand Curve adjustments we made to darken the tree trunk.

STEP 2: When you are happy with your selection, Command-click on the New Layer icon at the bottom of the Layers palette to add a new Curves adjustment layer (be sure to choose Curves from the Type menu). Name this Layer Wand Selection. The new layer will automatically be set up with its mask isolating the selected area. Click on the Load button in Curves to load the LockDownCurve from the essential files folder of this example. Use the Eyedropper to measure values in the tree trunk, remembering to click and drag on the trunk if you want the circle to show up in the Curve diagram. The values will be in the shadow parts of the curve, so click there and drag up and to the left to make the tree trunk lighter or down and the the right to make the trunk darker. Notice how the edges of the selection blend with both other parts of the trunk and the background. The Preview button needs to be on for you to see this. If you do too much lightening, the edges start to distort. When you're happy with the changes, click on the OK button. The great thing about using an adjustment layer is that you can always go back to Curves later and change it. The pixels in the image layer below are not permanently changed until you flatten the image or merge the adjustment layer with the one below. Now you can toggle back and forth by turning the Eye icon on and off for this layer. This allows you to quickly see this change before and then after. We are going to show you another way to make this selection in Step 3.

STEP 3: Another method for making a selection to dodge an image is to use the Elliptical Marquee tool to select a large area of the image around the entire tree with the center of this oval over the dark part of the tree bark. This dark part is the area that you really want to lighten. To do this, type an M, which gets you to the Rectangular Marquee, and then type another M, which will toggle to the Elliptical Marquee. If you continue to type M, you will toggle between the two Marquees. This is a good thing to remember since it is good to stay in one of these two tools whenever you are not using another tool in the Tool palette. It is difficult to accidentally damage your image with them and they are useful for other reasons. While in the Elliptical Marquee and holding the Option key down, click and drag an ellipse from the center of the dark tree trunk area. The Option key centers the selection where you first click down. After you make a selection, you can move the entire selection without moving the contents of the selection by clicking down inside the selection and dragging the selection marquee to wherever you want to place the selection. If you click and drag while holding down the Command key, you move the contents of the selected area and the background color or transparency fills the vacated area. You usually don't want that to happen, but if you do it by accident, remember good old Command-Z. If you Command-Option-click and then drag a selection, you create a copy of the selected area as a floating selection, and leave the original selected area unaffected. The command keys for moving and copying selections have changed between Photoshop 3 and Photoshop 4, so this exercise probably is easier for new Photoshop users, who aren't accustomed to the old keys.

STEP 3: An oval selection of the parts of the tree you want to change.

STEP 4: Now choose Select/Feather (Command-Shift-D) and set the feather to about 25 pixels. This smoothly blends over a large area the changes you are about to make in Curves. This technique is very similar to moving the dodging object up and down in the darkroom to make a soft edge when printing with an enlarger. Now Command-click on the New Layer icon again to make another Curves adjustment layer. Make sure you choose Curves from the Type menu. Name the new adjustment layer Oval Selection.

An oval selection with no feather.

The same selection with a 25-pixel feather.

A curve to lighten causes a spotlight effect with no feather.

The same curve causes a blended effect with the feather.

STEP 5: Now use the Eyedropper to measure values in the tree trunk; remember to click and drag on the trunk to get the measurement circle to show up in the Curves diagram. The values will be in the shadow parts of the curve, so click there and drag up and to the left to make the tree trunk lighter or down and to the right to make it darker. Since we didn't load the LockDownCurve this time, a movement in the shadow part of the curve will also affect the rest of the image that is not a shadow. Although the feather weights this selection toward the center, where the dark trunk is, the area surrounding the trunk also becomes lighter. The Preview button needs to be on for you to see the effect of this feather. If you click on a point in the middle of the curve, and drag it back toward its original location, you reduce the lightening effect in the lighter parts of the image around the trunk. I used a curve called OvalCurve (pictured here), which you can load from the GrandCanyonTweaks Extra Info Files folder. This curve has two points on the bottom left that darken the light tree shadows, but they also darken the area surrounding the tree a bit. The effect should be similar to what you would get if you dodged the entire area in the darkroom. When you arrive at your final curve, click on the OK button in the Curves dialog box.

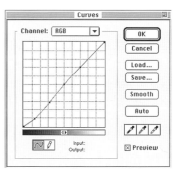

STEP 5: Curve adjustments to darken oval selection of tree area.

DECIDING ON THE VERSION YOU LIKE

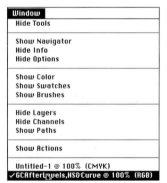

STEP 6: The Layers palette at the end of Step 5 with the Oval Selection and Orig Image layers turned on. To view the Wand Selection, Click to turn off the Oval Selection Eye icon and then turn on the Wand Selection. Notice the Yellow Tool Tip that tells you what the Eye icon does. You can turn off the Tool Tips by unchecking the Show Tool Tips check box in File/Preferences General.

STEP 6: Now you know two different selection techniques for using the Elliptical Marquee and Magic Wand for burning or dodging selected areas of an image. Now that you have created two adjustment layers, you can toggle between these two versions and decide which you like better. You can look at the original image by Option-clicking on the Eye icon of the Orig Image layer. This turns off viewing of the two adjustment layers you added. To view just the changes you made using the Wand Selection and Curve, click on the Eye icon for the Wand Selection layer. To view the changes you made using the Oval Selection and Curve, first click on the Eye icon for the Wand Selection to turn it off, and then click on the eye icon for the Oval Selection. You want only one of these on at a time, otherwise they act cumulatively on top of each other. Notice how the Wand Selection and Curve changes only values within the tree, whereas the Oval version darkens the tree and the surrounding area. You don't have to decide which of these you want until you save a flattened version of the image. I usually save my layered version in Photoshop format in case I want to change it later. To make a flattened version, I turn on the layers I want and then choose File/Save A Copy, enabling the Flatten option and then saving as a TIFF or EPS file under a different name. You also could apply both curves at the same time by having both Eye icons on when you save the flattened version.

SHARPENING AND SPOTTING THE IMAGE

STEP 7: After using selections on specific items and color areas, to do any necessary color fine-tuning you need to sharpen and spot the image. Make sure your general preferences for tools are set up as recommended in "Setting System and Photoshop Preferences." Specifically, be sure to set Painting Tools to Brush Size, and Other Tools to Precise. Click on the rightmost column of the Orig Image layer to activate it. The active layer, the one with the gray highlight, is the one that any changes will affect. Type Command-Option-0 to zoom your image in to 100%, and then choose Filter/Sharpen/Unsharp Mask and set the parameters to 150%, Radius of 1.5, and Threshold of 8. You can best see the effects of sharpening when zoomed in to at least 100%. We explain each of these settings in detail in "Kansas—Final Tweaks." Choose OK to sharpen your image.

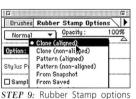

STEP 8: You can see the zoom ratio, 100%, in the Window menu.

STEP 8: Move the cursor to the sky in the upper right corner of the image, and do a Command-Spacebar-click to zoom in to that area; you will notice many dust spots. You should be zoomed in to 200% or 400%. In Full Screen mode, you can see the zoom ratio for your window in the Window menu. You can also see it in the bottom left of the Navigator palette. If you choose Command-Z, for Undo, and then Command-Z again, for Redo, you will notice that sharpening tends to enhance dust spots. Try to spot the image after sharpening it, so you don't miss any dust spots that sharpening adds.

STEP 9: Rubber Stamp options

STEP 9: The Rubber Stamp tool.

STEP 9: Double-click on the Rubber Stamp tool and set the options as shown here. Make sure that you are in Clone (aligned), Opacity is set to 100%, and Blend mode is set to Normal. You can most easily get these default options by choosing Reset Tool from the Options Palette menu.

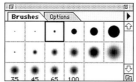

STEP 10: Now choose Window/Show Brushes (F12 in ArtistKeys) and choose the third brush from the top left, a 5-pixel brush. Refer to "The Tool Palette" if you need help understanding and setting the Brushes options.

STEP 11: You're going to use the Rubber Stamp tool to remove the spots in the sky and the scratch in the canyon. Move the cursor near a spot you need to cover. You should be about 1/4 inch from the spot and over a color and texture that you want to use to fill that spot. Hold down the Option key and click on the mouse. This tells the Rubber Stamp tool where to pick up image detail to use in removing the spot. (When the Option key is down, the cursor turns into a cross-hair with a circle in the middle.) Now, move the cursor to the spot you want to retouch and click on the spot without holding down the Option key. Without the Option key down, the cursor should appear as a clear white circle the size of the brush you're using. Image detail copies over the spot from where you Option-clicked. If it's a big spot, you may have to move the cursor a little with the mouse button down to completely erase the spot. When you hold the mouse button down, you will notice a circle where the cursor is and an x where the Rubber Stamp tool is picking up the pixels to copy. As you move the cursor with the mouse button down, the x and the cursor move together, showing you where the tool is copying from and to. That's why this mode of the Rubber Stamp tool is called *Clone (aligned).*

STEP 10: The Brushes palette and your brush.

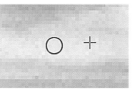

STEP 11: A spot to the left with the Option key down and cursor on the right. Option-click next to the spot to show Photoshop where to pick up color and detail.

STEP 11: Click on the spot without the Option key down. The cursor should look like this before you click and the spot should be removed when you click using the pixels from where you Option-clicked before.

STEP 11: The circle and the cross-hair that you see while cloning with the mouse button down. Photoshop picks up detail from the cross-hair and places it down at the cursor circle.

STEP 12: Use the technique described in Step 11 to remove all the other spots in the sky on this image. Don't forget that you can scroll by pressing down the Spacebar and clicking and dragging with the Hand tool. If you are trying to make sure that you remove all the spots in the image, you can go back into Normal Screen mode and start out in one corner, like the top right here. After spotting that top rightmost area, click in the gray area of the horizontal scroll bar to scroll the image one full screen at a time. Move across the image, screen by screen, removing the spots in each of these areas. When you get to the other side of the image, you can scroll down one full screen by clicking in the gray area of the vertical scroll bar. Now work your way back across to the other side. If you go through spotting your image in tiles in this manner, you are less likely to miss a spot.

REMOVING SCRATCHES

STEP 13: If you look in the rocky area to the right, just below the horizon, you can see a one-pixel wide white scratch, which we created to simulate the types of scratches you get when the film processor has dirt on it and puts a streak right across your favorite picture. You're going to remove that scratch, and you can use the same technique to easily remove film processor scratches. Before you remove this scratch, use

Another technique for removing dust is to use the Dust and Scratches filter. Select part of the sky with the Lasso, feather set to about 4, and then do Filter/Noise/Dust & Scratches. This technique seems to do a good job on clouds and soft areas, but it often blurs areas that are sharp, so you don't want to run it on the entire image. You should test it on a particular selection by comparing the image with and without the Preview button on in the filter to make sure it doesn't blur the image too much. You can also try different radius and threshold values in the filter. A Radius of 2 and a Threshold of 20 works well in this exercise.

STEP 14: First, Option-click below the left end of scratch.

STEP 14: Second, click on the left end of scratch, centered on - scratch, directly above where you Option-clicked before.

STEP 14: Third, Shift-click on the right end of the scratch, centered on the scratch.

Option-Spacebar-click to zoom out until the image is below 25% zoom ratio. In Full Screen mode, you can see the zoom ratio by clicking on the Window menu and looking at the name of this window (it will have a check mark next to it). Notice that at this small size, less than every fourth pixel in the image is displayed and the scratch is not visible. This is why when you spot or remove blemishes, you should always zoom in to at least 100%. Use Command-Spacebar-click or the Navigator palette to zoom back to 200%.

STEP 14: Move the cursor to about 1/8-inch below the left end of the scratch line. Hold down the Option key and click on the mouse to tell Photoshop to pick up image detail here. Now move the cursor directly upward and click on the left end of the scratch (no Option key this time) with the cursor centered vertically on the scratch. A piece of the image is cloned here from below the scratch where you Option-clicked. Release the mouse button, move the mouse to the right end of the scratch, and then Shift-click on the right end of the scratch. The scratch should fill in with image data from right below it, as though you had cloned from below by holding down the mouse and drawing on top of the scratch from left to right. You may have to practice this trick several times to get it correct. Choose File/Save As and save the image as GrandCanyonSpotted.

STEP 14: The Grand Canyon after lightening specific areas with Adjustment Layers. We sharpened this image with Unsharp Mask using settings of 150 Amount, 1.5 Radius and 8 Threshold then spotted the image using the Rubber Stamp Tool.

HANDS-ON SESSION: Kansas—Final Tweaks

Using selections with Curves, Hue/Saturation, and Unsharp Mask to finish color correcting a problem scan; learning about CMYK Preview; using Gamut Warning and Color Range to deal with out-of-gamut colors.

In this session, you use Curves and Hue/Saturation to add color adjustments to specified areas of the overall color correct image of Kansas. This session also demonstrates using the highly important Unsharp Mask filter, the Gamut Warning, and CMYK Preview.

IMPROVING SELECTED COLOR AREAS

STEP 1: Open your corrected file from the earlier "Kansas" session, or use our version, called KansasLev&HueSat. Double-click on the Magic Wand tool and make sure that the Tolerance is set to 32 and that Anti-aliased is on; these are the defaults. You are going to select parts of this image and improve their color balance and/or density. Before doing so, go to the Layers palette and make a copy of the Background layer by dragging it to the New Layer icon at the bottom of the Layers palette. Call this copy New Colors. Make your corrections here so you can revert back to the original layer if you need to. Start out with the green strip of grass that separates the field from the sky, and the two big trees next to the house. This whole area seems a bit magenta to me and the trees seem too dark. Click on the grass and then Shift-click to add to the selection until you have selected all the grass and the two big trees. Be sure to click only in the green areas; stay away from the almost black parts of the trees. You can also use Select/Grow to increase the selection adjacent to areas you have already selected. If you accidentally select something that you shouldn't, choose Edit/Undo (Command-Z) and try again. You can also use the Lasso tool with the Shift key to add to the selection or with the Option key to subtract from the selection. After you select the entire area, choose Select/Feather and enter 1 to create a one-pixel feather. This feather will blend the color changes you will make along the edge of the selection.

STEP 1: Create the selection of the grass and trees with the Magic Wand.

149

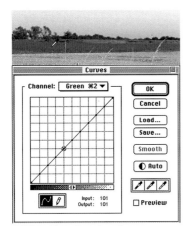

STEP 2: Measuring where the greens occur in the green grass.

STEP 2: Choose View/Hide Edges (Command-H) to hide the edges of the selection so that you can see whether the changes you make to the area blend properly with its surroundings. Choose Curves (Command-M) and load LockDownCurve from the Kansas Final Tweaks folder. Select the Green channel, and then click down on the Eyedropper in the area where the green grass seems magenta. Look at the circle on the curve, remembering which point in the curve to change, and then click on that point and move it up and to the left to add green to that part of the curve. Now measure the magenta in the darker parts of the big trees next to the house. Add green to that part of the curve, too. Switch to the RGB curve (Command-~) and measure the brightness of the dark trees. Don't measure the totally black places; they're too dark to have any detail worth saving. Measure the medium to darker parts of the trees and see how the circle moves around on the curve as you move the cursor around over these parts of the trees. Move the points in these areas up and to the left to make the trees lighter. Notice that making the trees lighter also makes the darker bushes in the selection lighter. Turn on the Preview button so you can see the changes you have made in the selection and how they blend with the unselected, unchanged areas. If the borders are not seamless, either you made a poor selection or your changes are too radical. If you have problems with the way the border looks, first back off on the amount of change you made, and if that doesn't work, cancel the Curves command and go back to edit your selection. You could also do this entire step using an adjustment layer, or use a layer mask to blend parts of the changed area back with the original. (To learn how to do this, see the "Color Correcting Al" or "Bryce Stone Woman" chapters.)

STEP 3: Use the Magic Wand again to select the red parts of the red barn, which is most of it except for the roof. For this job, you may get better results if you set the Tolerance to about 8, and then use the Shift key with the Magic Wand to keep adding to the selection. You can also use Shift or Option with the Lasso to add or delete from the selection. Again, choose a Select/Feather of one pixel to soften the edge of the selection. Use Command-H to hide selection edges, then choose Image/Adjust/Hue/Saturation and click on the Red radio button. You change only the things that are red in this selection. Move the Hue toward magenta by 10 points (−10) and increase the saturation by 10 points to make the red more vivid. Make sure that the Preview button is on so that you can see your changes. Click on the OK button and choose Select/None.

STEP 4: The gray roof on the barn has an excessively magenta tinge, and would look better darkened a bit. Since this color is not like any of the solid colors in Hue/Saturation, you will use the Curves tool on the roof. Select the roof with the Magic Wand and Lasso like you did the red parts of the building. Do Command-M to get to Curves, then load LockDownCurve again. Now click on the roof and measure around to see the roof's range of values on the RGB curve. Darken these parts of the curve by moving their lockdown points down and to the right. Now move to the Green curve and measure the parts of the roof that seem too magenta. Move them up and to the left to add green. If other parts of the roof seem too green, move them down and to the right to add magenta. The two-color areas should be in different parts of the curve. If you find it hard to get uniform color on the roof, you can add a color tint from one area to another by using the Rubber Stamp tool in Clone (aligned) mode at 50% opacity with the Blend mode set to Color. To see the differences in the changes you have been making, click on the Eye icon in the New Colors layer to turn it off and reveal the original colors underneath. You can always add a layer mask to the New Colors layer and paint with black in that layer mask to reveal the original colors in selected areas.

STEP 5: The white buildings in this image aren't very clean either. The building closest to the red barn is too dark and has a bluish cast. The other white buildings have various degrees of yellow tinge to them. Using similar techniques to what you used on the grass and barn, first select the dark building and use Curves to brighten it up. Then select all the yellow buildings and use either Curves or Hue/Saturation to clean them up. Save the image as KansasRGBBeforeGamut.

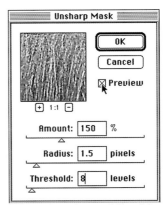

STEP 5: The Kansas image after specific color corrections using Selections.

THE UNSHARP MASK FILTER

STEP 6: Here you will use Filter/Sharpen/Unsharp Mask to sharpen your image for final output. After finishing color correcting, you usually want to use the Unsharp Mask filter. The Unsharp Mask filter has three different settings (Amount, Radius, and Threshold) that affect different parts of the sharpening process. You will have to run some tests to determine what value to use in each of these settings. It is often useful to compare tests on a small section of the image. Photoshop 4 does have a Preview button in the Unsharp Mask filter that allows you to see the filter of a selected area of the image, but it still doesn't allow you to compare one group of settings to another.

Select a section of the image that can represent the entire image, and whose sharpness is most important, and make a copy of it using Edit/Copy. (See the images on the next page to see what I selected from this photograph.) Now choose File/New (Command-N) to create a new file. Since you just made a copy, the new file will be the size of the copied section. Say OK to the New dialog box and then do Edit/Paste (Command-V) followed by Select/None (Command-D). Repeat this action several times, until you have five or six small files that you can place next to each other on the screen for comparison. Now run different tests on each file to see what the three parameters of Unsharp Mask each do.

AMOUNT: This setting controls the overall amount of sharpening. When you compare sharpening effects, you want to zoom in to the image, to at least 100% to see all the detail. Compare different copies of the same image area using different settings for Amount. You sharpen an image by looking for edges in the photograph and enhancing those edges by making one side of them darker and the other side of them lighter. Edges are sharp color or contrast changes in an image.

RADIUS: This setting controls the width of pixels along an edge that you modify when you sharpen the image. Again, try running the filter with different settings and comparing two copies of the same image side by side.

THRESHOLD: When you set Threshold to 0, everything in the image becomes a candidate for being an edge and getting sharpened. If you set the Threshold to, say 10, then an edge will only be found and sharpened if there is a difference of at least 10 points (in the range from 0 to 255) in the pixel values along that edge. The larger value you give to the Threshold setting, the more contrasty an edge needs to be before it is sharpened and the more you are doing just Sharpen Edges.

When you find the correct Unsharp Mask values, use those to sharpen the entire file. The settings I use most often for 18Mb Photo CD files are 150, 1.5, and 8. If the

STEP 6: The Unsharp Mask filter dialog box with its three settings.

Image with no sharpening.   Unsharp Mask 150, 1.0, 8.   Unsharp Mask 150, 1.5, 8.

Unsharp Mask 450, 1.5, 8.   Unsharp Mask 150, 4.5, 8.   Unsharp Mask 150, 1.5, 0.

Another technique for sharpening very saturated files is using Mode/Lab Color to convert the file to Lab Color mode and then sharpening the L channel. This method prevents your saturated colors from popping as much during the sharpening. You can then convert back to RGB.

original image is very grainy, I might increase Threshold, which lessens the sharpening of the grain. If the image is very fine grained, I might decrease Threshold, which allows me to sharpen the file a bit more without getting more than the normal grain appearance in the final image. Occasionally, I sharpen by 200% if I want to increase the size of an image and make it look sharp. You have to be careful not to over-sharpen. If your final output is a halftone, you can get away with more sharpening than you can for a transparency film recorder or even a digital print output, because the screen angles and dots in a halftone tend to lessen some sharpening artifacts. All artifacts show up if you output to a color transparency film recorder, however. We usually use the Unsharp Mask filter instead of the other Photoshop sharpening filters because Unsharp Mask provides much finer control over the many different types of images.

SPOTTING WITH THE RUBBER STAMP

STEP 7: After you sharpen any image, you should zoom in to at least 100% and then go through each section of the file, spotting them with the Rubber Stamp tool. Sharpening tends to enhance spots that may not have been obvious before, which is why you should leave spotting until after you do your sharpening. The procedure is the same as the spotting work demonstrated in "The Grand Canyon—Final Tweaks."

Save your final spotted file as KansasFinalRGB, and then read the following steps to convert to CMYK.

Note: In Extra Info files for this chapter, my version of this exercise contains the channel Sky Mask Threshold. That mask was created using Image/Adjust/Threshold with a copy of the Blue channel of my sharpened New Colors layer. My version also contains Sky Mask Contract 3, which I created using Select/Modify/Contract of 3 pixels from a loaded selection of Sky Mask Threshold. I used a selection of the contracted mask to spot my entire sky in one step, using Filter/Noise/Dust & Scratches with the settings Radius 2 and Threshold 20. Try this out using the Threshold techniques shown in "Versailles" and "Bruce Stone Woman."

OUT-OF-GAMUT COLORS

STEP 8: You can see many vivid colors on the computer screen in RGB that won't print in CMYK on a press. If you are working in RGB to send your final output to a film recorder and color transparency film, you can get more colors on film than you can on a press. If your final output is some Web or multimedia presentation, you can also get the colors there. You need to realize that each different type of computer monitor or digital color printer, or even press and paper combination, may have a different color gamut. The *gamut* of your output device is the range of colors it can actually print. For more information about these issues, see the chapter "Calibration." If you are going to print this file on a press in CMYK though, you may want to check your out-of-gamut colors and see if you need to correct them. Refer to "Setting System and Photoshop Preferences" and make sure that your CMYK preferences are set up correctly before you use any of the CMYK Preview or Gamut Warning commands. Choose Select/Color Range, and then choose Out-of-Gamut from the Select pop-up in the dialog box. Click on OK to see a selection of all the colors that you can see in RGB but which won't print exactly the same in CMYK. Choose View/Hide Edges (Command-H) to hide the edges of this selection.

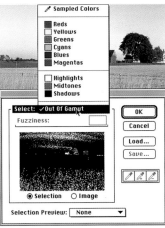

STEP 8: In Color Range, selecting out-of-gamut colors.

STEP 9: Some out-of-gamut colors, like red, often look quite different and usually muted when printed in CMYK. In many other colors, you may not notice the difference. Choose View/CMYK Preview for an estimate of what the image will look like when printed in CMYK. If you made the red barn really bright, you will notice it fades a bit. How many other changes did you see in the image? The sky may look a bit duller. Now choose View/Gamut Warning, and all these out-of-gamut colors will change to gray or whatever color you have set in Preferences as the gamut warning indicator. Remember that you have a selection, which you made using Color Range, of all the colors that are actually out-of-gamut. With Gamut Warning on, you can use this selection in conjunction with the Hue/Saturation command to fix much of the gamut problem. Colors often are out-of-gamut because they're too saturated. Choose Command-U for Hue/Saturation and move the Saturation slider to the left. Notice that the Gamut Warning areas get smaller the more you desaturate the selected out-of-gamut area. You may want to desaturate your out-of-gamut colors in several stages, or using the Sponge tool from the Tool palette, so you don't further desaturate colors that have already come back into gamut. To desaturate in stages, move the Saturation slider to the left, to, say, –10. Choose OK and then choose Select/None. Now go back to Color Range (see Step 8), and choose the new smaller set of out-of-gamut colors. Reduce the saturation on these also by –10. Continue this iterative process until you

STEP 9: The CMYK Preview and the Gamut Warning in the View menu can help compensate for differences between RGB and CMYK color gamuts.

have no more out-of-gamut colors, or until the out-of-gamut areas are so small they won't show.

STEP 10: Gamut Warning is a very useful tool for seeing colors that are going to be difficult to reproduce in CMYK. On the other hand, if you always desaturate all your colors so that no Gamut Warning areas show up, you may end up with duller colors on press than you would have gotten if you were a little less strict about desaturating all your RGB colors. I compared two conversions to CMYK of this image. The first had been pre-adjusted, via Steps 8 and 9, to remove out-of-gamut colors, and the second was of the same image without the out-of-gamut adjustments. The pre-adjusted image didn't change much at all when converted to CMYK, which is good. The image that I hadn't pre-adjusted for out-of-gamut colors did change and got a little duller, as with the red barn, but overall was a bit brighter and more vivid in CMYK than the pre-adjusted image was. So if you work in RGB and use bright colors, even out-of-gamut ones, you may get brighter color results by going ahead and converting these to CMYK. You know that some bright colors may get a bit duller, but you can deal with those dull or changed colors once you are in CMYK mode, instead of dulling them ahead of time by desaturating based on Gamut Warning and possibly desaturating them too much. Do some tests to see what works best for you!

CONVERTING TO CMYK

STEP 11: Now you have your final color corrected version of the RGB image. If your final output device is an RGB device, such as a film recorder or a video screen, your work is done. If you use a color management system or printer software that automatically converts your file from RGB to CMYK as you output it, you also are done. If your final output device is CMYK and you are going to do the conversion from RGB to CMYK in Photoshop, then you need to make sure all the preferences are set up correctly for CMYK conversion and for this particular printing project (review "Setting System and Photoshop Preferences"). Choose Mode/CMYK to convert the image to CMYK. Once in CMYK, Photoshop automatically adjusts the image display on the monitor to try to simulate your actual CMYK printed output. Consequently, some of the brighter colors may get duller or change slightly. You may want to do additional small color tweaks now that you are in CMYK, using the same tools you used in RGB. You can also use the Selective Color tool to tweak CMYK colors, as explained at the end of "Yellow Flowers" and "Color Matching Cars." For this particular image, we were happy with the CMYK version when it was converted from RGB, which is what we printed in this book. When you are happy with your CMYK image, save it as KansasFinalCMYK. See "Color Matching Cars" and "Yellow Flowers" for further discussion on final CMYK color tweaks.

STEP 11: The final RGB version of Kansas after all color corrections and using the Unsharp Mask filter.

HANDS-ON SESSION: Yellow Flowers

Using Color Range and Replace Color to change the colors of flowers and to enhance those colors; using Selective Color to improve the CMYK version.

In this session, you use the Color Range and Replace Color tools to select the flowers and change their color from yellow to orange. You then use the Selective Color command to enhance the color of the orange flowers.

ABOUT COLOR RANGE AND REPLACE COLOR

The first thing you do in this example is select all the flowers. There are two similar tools for making selections based on color in Photoshop 4. Select/Color Range allows you to specify a color using the Eyedropper tool, and then shows you a mask of all the areas in the current selection that contain that color. You can add to or subtract from that mask

Original version of the flowers picture.

using + or – Eyedroppers, so that when you leave Color Range, you have a selection that contains the final colors you specified. Another command that is similar to Color Range is Image/Adjust/Replace Color. It lets you make selections similarly and also change the colors of the selections at the same time, using controls that are like those in the Hue/Saturation command but not quite as powerful. You can load and save color sets between these two tools, so you need to understand the subtle but important differences between them.

The Color Range tool always returns a selection, which you can then use as you would any other selection, to modify the selected areas using other Photoshop tools. Because Color Range lets you make selections, it furnishes some very useful features for seeing exactly what you have selected. When you choose the Sampled Colors option from the Select pop-up menu in Color Range, you select colors by clicking on them with the Eyedropper (you do the same in Replace Color). You can add to the colors that you select by using the regular Eyedropper and Shift-clicking, and you

The Color Range tool lets you make selections based on these different color choices. When you use the Sampled Colors choice, you click on the colors you want to select within the image.

Preview set to Quick Mask

Preview set to None

At the top of this image, the Selection Preview is None and you see the image. At the bottom of the image you see the purple Quick Mask preview, which is very useful.

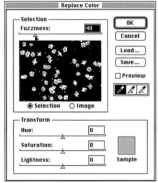

The Quick Mask icon

Click here to change the Quick Mask color.

Click on the Quick Mask icon to get the Quick Mask Options dialog box and then click on the color square and select a new color with the Color Picker.

The Replace Color dialog box with a mask showing the flowers selected.

can subtract from the selected colors by Option-clicking. Also, the + and − Eyedroppers always add to or always subtract from the selected areas. You see what colors are selected by looking at a black-and-white mask window in the dialog box. Here, white shows you the selected areas. To see the selected items in the most detail, choose the Quick Mask option in the Selection Preview pop-up and you will get a Quick Mask overlay on top of the unselected areas in the Actual Image window. If you choose the correct color for your Quick Mask (notice the purple in the diagram here), you can see when your selection is complete. You choose the color for your Quick Mask by double-clicking on the Quick Mask icon at the bottom of the Tool palette. (You need to do this before you enter Color Range.) See "The Car" for a discussion of Quick Mask mode. By the way, the other options in the Select pop-up allow you to select all the reds, yellows, greens, cyans, blues, magentas, highlights, midtones, shadows, or out-of-gamut colors in the part of the image that you selected before you entered Color Range. The out-of-gamut colors option can be very useful (see "Kansas—Final Tweaks"). Although Replace Color doesn't give you these other Select options, you can get them by using the Save button in Color Range to save selections made with these options, and you can use the Load button in Replace Color to load these selections.

The Replace Color tool also allows you to select colors with the Eyedropper in the same way as Color Range, but it has no Quick Mask Preview mode and no Select options. Replace Color doesn't provide as many options for selecting the colors or for seeing the selection as Color Range does, but once you make a selection in either one, you can click on the Save button to save the description of the selected colors. This feature allows you to select similar colors in other images or make the same color selection in the current image from Color Range or from Replace Color by going into either tool and using the Load button to load that color selection description. When you have the selection you want, the Replace Color tool allows you to change the color of the selected items by using the Hue, Saturation, and Lightness sliders at its bottom. The Preview box here shows you the color changes happening in the image on the screen. For changing color, Replace Color is even better than a selection preview, because you see whether the selection is correct as you actually change the colors you want. So, when you use Color Range, you are selecting a range of colors in an image and ending up with a selection. When you use Replace Color, you select a range of colors and replace those colors simultaneously. Now, let's try this out!

USING COLOR RANGE TO SELECT THE FLOWERS

STEP 1: Open the Flowers image in the YellowFlowers Example folder. Put Photoshop into Full Screen mode by clicking on the middle icon at the bottom of the Tools palette. Double-click on the Quick Mask icon, click on the colored square, and then set the color to medium blue or purple. Find a color that has no yellow in it so that any flower parts not selected show up easily. Make sure the Opacity is set to 50%. Say OK to these dialog boxes and click back on the regular Selection icon to the left of the Quick Mask icon. Now press the Tab key to remove all the tool windows from the screen. Choose Select/Color Range. Set the Fuzziness to 40. The Fuzziness, which works the same in Replace Color and Color

Range, is like the Tolerance on the Magic Wand; the higher the Fuzziness, the more similar colors are selected. Unlike using the Magic Wand, you can move the Fuzziness after you make a selection to change the range of selected colors. Set Select to Sampled Colors and set Selection Preview to None, for now. Use the Eyedropper to click on the yellow flowers and you will notice that wherever you see a flower, you should get some white showing up in the mask window. Hold the Shift key down and click on different areas of the flowers, adding more to the mask. If white areas or spots show up in the mask window where there are not any flowers, press Command-Z to undo that last Eyedropper click. When you think you have selected all the flowers and no areas that are not flowers, set the Selection Preview to Quick Mask.

STEP 2: In Quick Mask, you will notice a see-through purple layer covering everything not selected by the mask. That's the Quick Mask preview. If you notice that parts of the flowers are covered by purple, Shift-click on them to add them to the selected areas. If you select a really bright part of the flower or a really dark part of the flower, you may also notice the purple overlay coming off other areas of the image that are not flowers. If so, you have selected too much, and should press Command-Z.

STEP 3: When the purple mask covers nearly none of the flowers but still covers everything not a flower, you have done what you can do with Color Range to select the flowers. Click on the Save button and save this set of colors as ColorRangeToRC. If you click on OK now, you end up with a selection of the flowers. If you wanted to work on these selected items with one of the other color correction tools, such as Hue/Saturation or a filter, you could have used this procedure to get a selection of the flowers. We had you do the first step of this exercise in Color Range so that you could see the differences between it and Replace Color. You could have done the whole session in Replace Color.

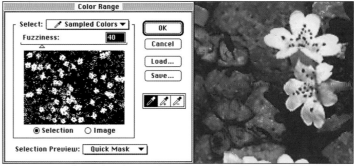

STEP 2: Part of the flower on the right is covered by purple. Shift-click on it to add it to the selection.

STEP 2: Here we have selected too much. You can see the mask coming off things that are not flowers, like the green leaves to the left of the flowers.

USING REPLACE COLOR TO SELECT AND CHANGE THE COLOR

STEP 4: You are now going to use Replace Color for the rest of the exercise. Choose Select/None, because you're actually going to improve on this selection using Replace Color. Double-click on the Eyedropper tool and set the Sample Size to Point Sample. Choose Image/Adjust/Replace Color, and click on the Load button. Select the ColorRangeToRC file you just saved from Color Range. This will give you the same selection you just had, but this time you only see the black-and-white mask in the dialog box. Shift-click on a yellow flower at a place that is a middle yellow color. This color should be a shade of yellow that best represents the flowers as a whole. Notice that the sample box at the bottom right of the dialog box now has the yellow color you clicked on in it. Getting the color into the sample box is why you Shift-clicked here. Shift-click adds a color to the color selection range instead of starting a new selection range. It does the same thing as the +Eyedropper. Now go down to the Hue slider and move it to the left to –20. The yellow sample is now orange. When you click on the Preview button, all the selected yellow flowers will turn orange. This is the one type of selection preview that you can't do in Color Range, and it is very useful. If most of the flowers look orange but have a little bright

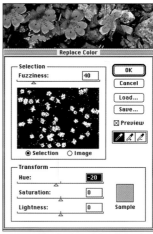

STEP 4: The Replace Color dialog box previewing yellow to orange.

The flowers, after changing them to orange.

yellow around their tips, you have 'em right about where you want 'em. If all the flowers are orange without a trace of yellow, you should look around the rest of the image and make sure you didn't change the color of anything else that had some yellow in it but wasn't totally yellow, such as the green leaves on the ground.

STEP 5: Now you need to change the yellow in the tips of the flowers to orange. Since the Eyedropper is now set to Point Sample, this will allow you to select minute color differences that are only one pixel in size. Now zoom in (Command-Spacebar-click) on any flowers that still have too much yellow around the tips of their petals. Hold down the Shift key, or use the +Eyedropper, as you carefully click on those yellow tip colors and add them to the color set. As you do this *with Preview on*, the tips of other flowers also turn orange. You can also increase the Fuzziness; you will notice that more little dots show up as selected in the mask. This may also improve the blending of any remaining yellow in the flower tips. Some of the brighter tips may actually just be highlights, so you don't need to change every last one. They just need to look natural as orange flowers. Some of the flower petals were actually burned and dried on the yellow flowers, so don't try to get them to turn orange also. If you do, you will make the Color Set too large. Click on the OK button in Replace Color when you are happy with your flowers. It may be faster to change the dried tips using the Rubber Stamp tool, cloning color from another flower or another part of the same flower. You still will want to do this in the Clone (aligned) setting using either the Normal or Color blend mode.

STEP 6: Use File/Save As to save the file as Flowers-Orange, and then open the original Flowers file and compare the two images. The flower colors and tones should look as natural in orange as they did in yellow. Bring back the Tool palette by pressing Tab and then double-click on the Eyedropper tool to set the Sample Size back to 3x3 average.

USING SELECTIVE COLOR

STEP 7: When you are happy with the RGB version of this image and have saved it (in Step 6), you should convert it to CMYK using Mode/CMYK. You may notice a slight dulling of the flowers when the image converts to CMYK, although this particular orange color converts to CMYK quite well. Once in CMYK, you can use the Selective Color command to make further subtle tweaks on colors. This command

STEP 7: After measuring the orange flowers, we notice in the Color palette that this orange color is made up of 97% yellow and 52% magenta. We then choose yellow as the color to change with the Colors pop-up.

changes a particular color based on the respective amounts of cyan, magenta, yellow, and black that comprise it. Bring up the Color palette using the Window menu (Shift-F9 with ArtistKeys). Use its Options menu to change it to CMYK Display mode. Now choose Image/Adjust/Selective Color to bring up the Selective Color tool. With this tool, you have to select the main color that you would like to change using the Colors pop-up menu at the top. The choices are Red, Yellow, Green, Cyan, Blue, Magenta, White, Neutral, and Black. If you want to change the orange flowers, you'll probably notice that orange is not one of these colors. Use the Eyedropper and click on an orange flower in a shade of orange typical of the orange color of all the flowers. Notice in the Color palette that this bright orange consists mainly of yellow and magenta. Since yellow is the main component of this orange color (it's 97% yellow, in fact), you should now choose Yellow from the Colors pop-up. Next, you change the percentages of the other colors that make up your yellows.

STEP 8: Notice that the orange color already is very close to completely saturated in yellow but that the magenta component is only 52% saturated. On the lefthand side of the Color palette, you see a swatch of the color where you last clicked. The Magenta bar in the Color palette shows that if you add magenta to this color, the flowers will look a deeper orange, and eventually reddish, in color. If you take away magenta, the flowers will become more yellowish. Move the Magenta slider in Selective Color to the right, to +20%. In our example, the Method radio button at the bottom of the dialog box is set to Absolute, which should mean that you're adding 20% magenta ink to the 52% magenta already in the yellows, resulting in 72%. If you were

STEP 8: The orange flowers after adding 20% magenta. Notice that the Magenta value actually changes from 52% to 61%.

STEP 8: The orange flowers after removing 25% magenta. If you click on a sample color after entering Selective Color, the Color palette shows you the actual new CMYK percentages as you make adjustments in Selective Color.

to set Method to Relative, you would add 20% of the 52% percentage of magenta already there, which should bring it up to about 62%. In reality, Absolute mode brings the 52% magenta up to 61%, and Relative mode brings it up to 57%. If you are trying to add a specific percentage, you should measure the results you actually get using the Color palette rather than assume the percentages in the Selective Color dialog box will be exact. Now subtract 25% magenta from these orange flowers to get the lighter, more yellowish orange you see in our third Selective Color illustration. These operations are examples of how you use the Selective Color tool to make subtle tweaks in specific color ranges. When you set Colors to Neutral, Selective Color is also very good at removing color casts in the neutral areas. Photoshop is good at identifying which colors should be composed of equal quantities of cyan, magenta, and yellow.

A More Flexible Way to Set This Up

For a more advanced way to set this up, click the Save button in Replace Color at the end of Step 5, and save the final Color Set as YellowFlowerSet. Now cancel out of Replace Color, choose Select/Color Range, load the YellowFlowerSet, and click on OK. You now have selected the parts of this image that you want to change. Now Command-click on the New Layer icon in the Layers palette to add a Hue/Satura-

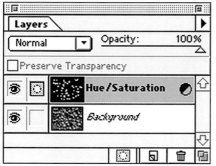

tion adjustment layer above the existing still yellow *Background* layer. Set the Type pop-up to Hue/Saturation, click on OK, and, when you go into the Hue/Saturation dialog box, set the Hue to –20. Your flowers will now change to orange and only the flowers will change because your selection will have been automatically put into the layer mask of this Hue/Satura-tion adjustment layer. With the adjustment layer active, you can now use Gaussian Blur and the painting tools to fine-tune the adjustment layer's built-in layer mask, and you can go back to the adjustment layer at any time to change the color of the flowers. I found that a Gaussian Blur of 1 on the adjustment layer layer mask improved the color change blend. This solution allows for an infinite number of changes without degrading the image. See the Yellow/Orange Layers file in the Extra Info folder for this chapter and try this out for yourself!

A MORE FLEXIBLE WAY: The Layers palette for this more flexible way to change the color of the flowers and leave your options much more open.

The orange flowers after final color correction choices have been made with Selective Color.

HANDS-ON SESSION: Buckminster Fuller

Making a fine black-and-white print the digital way: increasing contrast, brightening the white areas using electronic ferricyanide, and burning in the edges to emphasize the middle. Colorizing a B&W image.

(Original Concept by Bruce Ashley)

You start out with a scan of an original black-and-white negative of Buckminster Fuller, and in order to make it a fine print, you need to darken it and increase its contrast. You also want to brighten the white shirt and the candles a bit, and finally, add a little twinkle to Fuller's eyes, sharpen the center, and burn in the edges of the print.

The original Fuller scan.

BRIGHTENING THE IMAGE

STEP 1: Open the Fuller file from the Buckminster Fuller folder on the *Photoshop 4 Artistry* CD, and use File/Save As to save it as FullerFixed. Bring up the Info palette with Window/Show Info, (F9 with ArtistKeys). Choose Image/Adjust/Levels (Command-L). Move the Cursor around in the bright area of Mr. Fuller's collar, noting that the RGB values that show up in the Info palette are not very bright whites. If we move the Input Highlight slider to the left, this would brighten the collar, but it would also blow out any remaining detail in the wall by the bright lamp. Instead, we are going to make a bright version of this image and then use that to selectively lighten (Electronic Ferricyanide) the shirt, candles, and eyes. Adjust the Input Brightness/Contrast slider in Levels to the left to brighten the collar until the values in the collar that were 215 read about 235. The Info palette values to the left of the slash are the original values, and the values to the right of the slash show the adjustments you made using this iteration of Levels. Exit Levels by clicking on the OK button to make the change.

STEP 2: Choose Edit/Take Snapshot to make a Snapshot version of the file. Then choose Edit/Undo

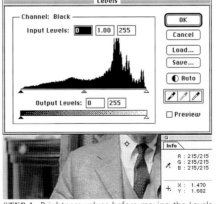

STEP 1: Brightness values before moving the Levels slider.

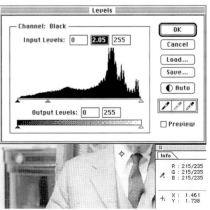

STEP 1: Brightness values after moving the Levels slider.

Levels to undo the Levels change that you just made. You can use the Take Snapshot command without changing the state of what will happen when you choose Undo. The Snapshot is a special copy buffer that now remembers the lighter version of the file.

STEP 3: Levels slider adjusted for greater contrast.

STEP 3: Choose New Adjustment Layer from the Layers Palette menu or Command-click on the New Layer icon to add a Levels adjustment layer. Make sure that the Type is set to Levels. Now move the Brightness/Contrast slider of Levels to the right to adjust this image for greater contrast. Make sure that large sections of the blackest blacks don't fall below 2 or 3 in the Info palette. It's okay to have a few small sections that go to 0, but you don't want them to be very large, because they will show up as pure black in the printout. Exit Levels using OK. The overall effect of giving the picture more contrast is pleasing, but the whites of Fuller's shirt are now muddy. Next, you adjust the whites using the following "Electronic Ferricyanide" technique. We did not adjust the highlight and shadow values within Levels in this image because they were correctly set by the original scan.

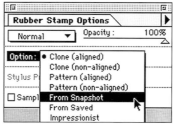

STEP 4: Choose From Snapshot as your Rubber Stamp option.

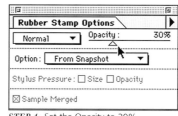

STEP 4: Set the Opacity to 30%.

STEP 4: Option-drag the *Background* layer to the New Layer icon at the bottom of the Layers palette. Call this new layer Working Image. You will make any actual changes on this layer, leaving the background image untouched. Double-click on the Rubber Stamp tool to get the Tool Options palette (or type S then Return), and then pull down the Option menu to From Snapshot. You can also continue to press the S key while Photoshop toggles through the options to get to From Snapshot. From Snapshot causes the Rubber Stamp tool to paint from the lighter Snapshot version of the image. In Rubber Stamp Options, set the opacity to 30% (your can do this by typing a 3).

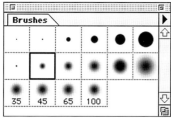

STEP 4: The Layers palette at the start of Step 4.

STEP 5: Choose Window/Show Brushes (F12 with ArtistKeys) and select a medium brush with a soft edge. You can use the left and right bracket keys to go to the next smaller or larger brush.

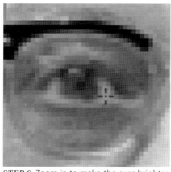

STEP 6: Use a small soft brush for the candles.

STEP 6: Zoom in to make the eyes brighter.

STEP 6: Because you are using the From Snapshot option, you just paint, you don't need to Option-click first as you do when cloning. Lighten the collar and sleeve by painting on it with the Rubber Stamp. Each time you paint over a section, it lightens it by using 30% of the lighter version in the Snapshot. If you want to remove the shadows on the white shirt next to his tie, several strokes there should turn them white. Now choose a very small brush, and click on the twinkles in Fuller's eyes to lighten them. Experiment with different size brushes; zoom in and out as you work. Command-Spacebar-click on the candles to zoom in to them, and continue to use the Rubber Stamp to clone from the Snapshot to lighten them. Use the left and right bracket keys to pick a brush the width of a candle. Click on one end of a candle, and then Shift-click on the other end, to draw a straight line the length of the candle. You may need to lower the opacity as you work on the candles to get more subtle shades of white. You may want to save your file now using File/Save (Command-S). Doing one Save flushes the Snapshot buffer, so don't do it until you finish lightening things.

SHARPENING THE CENTER AND BURNING THE EDGES

STEP 7: Option-click on the Marquee tool in the Tool palette or type the letter M until you have selected the oval-shaped icon. Select from the center by positioning the cursor on the tip of Fuller's nose, holding down the Option key before you click, and then clicking and dragging to isolate the oval area you want to sharpen and inversely burn in. If you've made the size and shape oval that you like, but it's not in exactly the position you want, click inside the selection border and drag to move the selection. Choose Select/Feather (Command-Shift-D) to set the feather to about 35 pixels, which creates a soft slow transition between the sharpened and non-sharpened areas and also between the burned and non-burned areas.

STEP 7: Make the oval selection on Fuller look something like this.

STEP 8: Go to Filter/Sharpen/Sharpen to emphasize the center of the portrait by making it a little sharper. Then use Select/Inverse to invert the selection, and select the outside of the image for burning. Choose Hide Edges (Command-H) from the View menu to make your upcoming Curves changes easier to see. Click on the Levels layer so that the next layer you add will be above Levels.

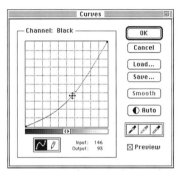

STEP 9: Command-click on the New Layer icon, this time setting the Type to Curves to add a Curves adjustment layer. Make sure that the Preview check box is on so that you can see how the changed area on the outside will blend with the unchanged area in the middle. Now adjust the Brightness/Contrast (move the center of the curve down) to darken the outside of the image. Move the curve up and down until you like the amount of darkness. Click on OK when you are happy. Notice that the feathered selection of the outside part of the image has been automatically saved as a layer mask in the Curves adjustment layer. The black part of this layer mask stops the Curves adjustment from happening in that center area.

STEP 9: Move the curve downward to darken the edges. Make sure the Curves dialog box is out of the way so you can see most of Fuller.

STEP 10: The advantage to this approach is that you now have a layered document where major steps in the process of refining this image can be looked at separately, and even changed or undone. If you turn off the Eye icon for the Curves layer, you remove the burn-in. If you want to change the amount of burn, just double-click on the word Curves and you can still change the Curve. You can turn the Levels adjustment layer on and off by using its Eye icon, and later you can change it too. If you click on the Working Image layer's Eye icon, you can see the original unsharpened, unwhitened image underneath in the *Background* layer. Try some of these things to quickly review your progress and changes on this image.

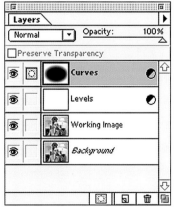

STEP 10: The Layers palette at the start of Step 10.

REMOVING THE BANDAGE

STEP 11: Option-drag the Working Image layer to the New Layer icon to make a backup copy called Working Image BU. Now click and drag this backup copy to below the Working Image layer, and then click on the Working Image layer to activate it. Next, double-click on the Rubber Stamp tool and set its Option back to Clone (aligned). Use the Rubber Stamp tool with different size brushes and with the Opacity set to 100% to remove the bandage on Fuller's glasses. Copy his skin at 100% opacity from different areas next to the bandage on top of the bandage. Don't copy the same piece of skin over and over again. You need to make sure the wrinkles on his forehead, for example, continue into the areas where the bandage was.

STEP 11: Final adjustments were made to burn in edges. We also used the Rubber Stamp tool to remove the bandage and fix his ear.

Put the cursor so you Option-click on the center of a wrinkle, then click to clone where you want the center of the wrinkle to be as the wrinkle now continues on top of the bandage. To adjust skin shading, you can now change the Opacity to 50% and clone lighter or darker skin areas over what you have already done to make sure that the subtle shading on the head looks right. After cloning out the bandage, you may need to use the Blur tool at a low opacity, perhaps 10%, to blend your changes together. As a final step after blurring a bit, I used the Lasso tool to select the area that was cloned and blurred, feathered the selection by 3, and then, used Filter/Noise/Add Noise to add about 3–5 of Gaussian Noise on top of the selected area. This will make the noise there match the rest of the image. You can always start over again on the bandage removal by using another copy of Working Image BU. When you are happy with the removal of the bandage, you can throw Working Image BU away.

COLORIZING MR. FULLER

STEP 12: Make sure your layers are in the final state you want for this image, then choose Image/Duplicate (F5) to make a duplicate copy of the image in Photoshop. Check the Merged Layers Only check box so the copy just has a single layer showing you the layers that currently have their Eye icons on. Choose Image/Mode/RGB to convert this image to RGB, which you need to do if you want to colorize it. Double-click on the Paintbrush tool and set its Blend mode to Color. This will change the hue and saturation but not the luminosity when you paint. The *luminosity* is the gray values that give the image detail and brightness. Use the Color Picker or the Picker palette to choose a color for his tie, and then paint that color over the tie at about 30% to 40% opacity. While painting, you can change the opacity simply by typing a number, such as 35 to get 35% opacity.

STEP 13: Now use the Lasso tool to select his jacket or vest. Make sure that the Lasso feather is set to zero. Pick a color for the selected item, and then choose Edit/Fill (Shift-Delete) to fill this area with the color you chose, making sure the mode is set to Color and the opacity is in the 30% to 50% range. You can use this technique to colorize most of the objects in the scene. Remember to try different feather values on the selection and different opacities of a color if needed.

STEP 14: If you want to be able to easily change the color of an object that has been selected with a rough Lasso selection, then Command-click on the New Layer icon to add a Hue/Saturation adjustment layer. Click on the Colorize option in Hue/Saturation, then move the sliders to get the color you want with your selected item. The Lasso selection was automatically converted to a layer mask for this layer, so you can now fine-tune the edges of the selection by painting with black where you want to remove the color and painting with white where you want to add the color. You can now go back into the Hue/Saturation adjustment layer to later change the color.

STEP 15: Another cool trick, for example, to add some wallpaper to the background, is to run a filter—try Pixelate—on the whole image. Then choose Edit/Take Snapshot followed by Edit/Undo of the filter, at which point the filter effect should be in the Snapshot, enabling you to paint it in where you want it using the Rubber Stamp tool with the From Snapshot option. Go ahead and paint in the wallpaper. To get a more even opacity on the wallpaper, you can also select an area, and then choose Fill in From Snapshot mode to fill that area with your pattern from a filter effect stored in the Snapshot. You could also run the filter on another layer that is a copy of the image and use a layer mask to have that filter effect appear wherever the layer mask is white. There are always at least three different ways to do anything in Photoshop. Have fun as you create your color version of Mr. Fuller!

STEP 15: Here is my colorized version of Mr. Fuller. Have fun creating yours, and try colorizing in as many ways as you can. That's how you find what works best for you!

HANDS-ON SESSION: Color Matching Cars

Measure and adjust the color of objects so differently colored items can be changed to match, and do subtle color tweaks after CMYK conversion to deal with faded CMYK hues.

The long shot is a red car, and you need to end up with two matching red CMYK images.

The closeup shot is a green car; you need to change its color to match the red car to the left.

Imagine that you want to create an advertisement using two photos of the Acura Integra. One of the photos is of a red Integra and the other of a green one. You need to convert the green car photo so that its color matches that of the red one. You also convert both cars to CMYK and do some final color matching there.

CHOOSING A MATCHING COLOR SPOT

STEP 1: Open the RedAcuraCM and GreenDetail files from the Color Matching Cars folder. Find a spot on the red car where the color appears to be an average intermediate color that could represent the color you want for the whole car. Both of these photos have highlight and shadow areas that you are going to want to match also. I've found that if you can locate a good midtone area in both images and get those midtone areas to match, the rest of the image will also match pretty well. I used the area on the front of the car to the right of the chrome Acura emblem just below the word "Acura," embossed in the red bumper. Because this spot exists and the lighting on it is similar in both photos, you can use this location on both cars to get the colors to match. We call this location the *color match spot*. Bring up the Color palette and set it to HSB mode. Put the Eyedropper over the color match spot and click to take a measurement. Hold the mouse button down and measure around a bit to make sure the spot you are using as this first measurement is an average

STEP 1: Here is the color match spot in the red car.

STEP 1: Here is the color match spot in the green car.

measurement for this area. Double-click on the Eyedropper to be sure it is set to measure a 3x3 average of pixels. When you click and measure, that measurement is remembered in the Color palette, even after you move the mouse. Write down the HSB values for that location.

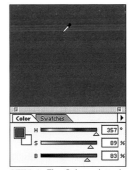

STEP 1: The Color palette in HSB mode. Write down the values you get.

STEP 2: Switch to the green car and find the same location right below the embossed Acura letters. Choose Image/Adjust/Hue/Saturation (Command-U) and use the Eyedropper to click and take an average measurement in this area. Taking this measurement after bringing up the Hue/Saturation tool fills the swatch color at the bottom of the dialog box with green from this color match spot. Turn off the Preview button for a moment and move the Hue slider so that the green swatch at the bottom middle of the dialog box matches, as closely as possible, that same area on the red car. You need to have the windows open on the screen so you can see both cars at the same time, and you might want to zoom in for now so that you see this part of both cars at the same time. Once the Hue/Saturation swatch matches fairly well, turn the Preview button back on, and the green car changes to red. Now move the Saturation and Lightness sliders back and forth until you get saturation and lightness values in the Color palette that match the numbers you wrote down for the color match spot on the red car. The Color palette continues to show you how the spot where you clicked in the green car has changed based on the Hue/Saturation slider movements. Don't worry about getting the hue numbers to match; they may not, because they are degree rotation values based on changes in the original hue. Getting the saturation and lightness values to match is the key. As you change one, the other also changes, so you must tweak both of them for a while until you get similar numbers to what you had in the red car. When you are happy with the adjustments, click on the OK button in Hue/Saturation.

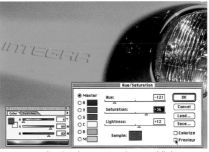

STEP 2: Adjusting hue, saturation, and lightness to get the Hue/Saturation green swatch to match the red in the red car.

STEP 3: Now convert the Color palette to RGB mode. Measure the color match spot again in the original red car and write down the Red, Green, and Blue values. They should be around 213 for Red, 23 for Green, and 31 for Blue. Switch to the green car, now converted to red, and then go into Levels. After you are in Levels, measure the color match spot in the green image and make sure that you can see the values in the Color palette. Go into the Red channel and move the Input Brightness/Contrast slider, the middle slider, until the Red value in the Color palette matches the Red value you wrote down for the original red car. Switch to the Green channel and do the same thing until the Green value matches on both. Finally, do the same thing for the Blue channel. Now the two cars should match fairly well.

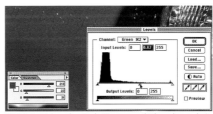

STEP 3: Using the Red, Green, and Blue channels in Levels to match the green car's RGB values to the red car's values.

CONVERTING TO CMYK MODE

STEP 4: Convert the Color palette to CMYK mode. Use Mode/CMYK to convert both cars to CMYK mode. The colors on-screen are now as close as possible to your printed colors. You may notice the intense red of these cars fade somewhat. Use the Selective Color tool to do final subtle tweaks of your red color in CMYK mode. Selective Color is a great tool for doing subtle adjustments to particular color areas

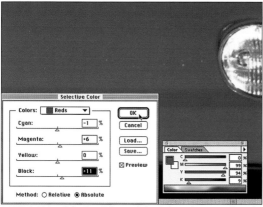

STEP 4: Using Selective Color and the Color palette to adjust the CMYK version of the red color at the color match spot. This will change the makeup of all the reds.

in CMYK. Switch to the original red car, the long shot, then go into Image/Adjust/Selective Color. Make sure that Colors is set to Reds, because you're going to be adjusting the red colors in the car. Set the Method to Absolute, so that you can make the color adjustments more quickly. Take another measurement at the color match spot on the car and notice in the Color palette that the color consists mostly of magenta and yellow. The colors of the sliders on the Color palette show you how the color at the color match spot will change if you add or subtract more cyan, magenta, yellow, or black ink. If the cyan value is greater than 0, subtract cyan using the Selective Color slider, until the cyan value reads 0 in the Color palette. This maneuver adds red to the car color. Add magenta until the magenta value in the Color palette is about 99 to make the car a deeper, richer color. Adjust the yellow until the yellow value in the Color palette reads about 94. To get a slightly darker, richer color, add some black until the black value in the Color palette reads about 9. You don't have to use the exact same numbers that we have, just adjust the cyan, magenta, yellow, and black percentages on the color match spot until you like the car's shade of red. Write down these final adjusted CMYK values from the Color palette.

STEP 5: Switch to the closeup shot and then again enter the Selective Color tool. Press down on the mouse button while taking a measurement of the color match spot in this image. Now adjust the cyan, magenta, yellow, and black inks, using the sliders in Selective Color, until the percentages match the final adjusted percentages you just wrote down from the other image. We used Cyan = 0, Magenta = 99, Yellow = 94, and Black = 9, but your values can be different. You just want the two red colors to match and both look the way you like them. This method is a good way to match the colors of objects that start out differently but have to end up the same.

The final green car after converting to red and CMYK adjustments.

The final long shot of the original red car after conversion and adjustment in CMYK.

HANDS-ON SESSION: Color Correcting Al

Color correcting this difficult exposure and scan, and using color channel swapping, adjustment layers, and intralayer blending to produce a print with natural, consistent, and pleasing tones overall.

One of my favorite pictures has always been this photo of my best buddy Al, taken on a desert trip we made together back around 1980. I always wanted to make a print of it, so when I got my ProofPositive printer, I had it and many other favorite pictures put onto Photo CD. When I brought in the photo, it was obviously oversaturated in the shadow area of the face. Because this is not a major area of the image, the first step to correct it is to do overall color correction to get the rest of the image to look right.

OVERALL COLOR CORRECTION

STEP 1: Open the OrigAl file from the Color Correcting Al folder on the CD. Crop any areas from around the edge of the image that are not going to be in the print. In this case, my copyright notice is the only thing you need to crop. Use F9 to bring up the Info palette and Shift-F9 to bring up the Color palette. Now go into Levels and use the steps outlined in "The Grand Canyon" and "Kansas" chapters to set the Highlight, Shadow, overall Brightness/Contrast, and finally the color cast. Here are the Levels settings I ended up with for Al. To set the highlight, I used the Highlight Eyedropper in Levels and set it to the white area on the tip of Al's right shoulder. For the shadow, I used the Shadow Eyedropper and set it to the shadow on the black tuft of hair below Al's ear and behind his neck. In case you later want to change these basic corrections, use the Save button in the Levels dialog box to save your Levels changes as AlBasicLevels, then Cancel from Levels. Command-click on the New Layer icon in the Layers palette to create a Levels adjustment layer that is grouped with the previous layer. Now, use the Load button to load AlBasicLevels and choose OK. This enables you to later change the levels without remodifying the file's pixel values. Doing the initial settings using Levels in the actual layer enables you to use Video LUT Animation to find the white and black points. Use File/Save As to save this

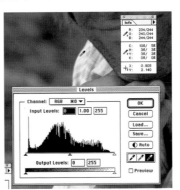

STEP 1: Setting the highlight by clicking with the Highlight Eyedropper on the whitest area of Al's shirt.

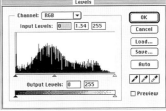

STEP 1: The overall corrected RGB histogram.

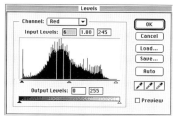

STEP 1: The overall red adjustments.

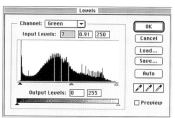

STEP 1: The overall green adjustments.

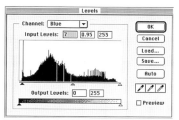

STEP 1: The overall blue adjustments.

as AlLevels. If your computer doesn't have Video LUT Animation, then just start out directly in the Levels adjustment layer.

STEP 2: Command-click on the New Layer icon to add a Hue/Saturation adjustment layer above the Levels adjustment layer. Below are the settings I made in Hue/Saturation. The goal was to saturate all the colors, as I normally would do, but then to not add more saturation to the face; in addition, I wanted to balance out the reds and yellows in Al's face. Try my settings and feel free to modify them to improve the image.

STEP 3: Al's RGB before using the Red channel to fix the saturated areas.

STEP 3: The Red channel we will use to fix the Green and Blue channels.

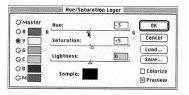

STEP 3: The unfixed Green channel is dark in all the saturated areas.

STEP 3: The Color Merged Fixed layer after fixing the Green and Blue channels.

FIXING THE OVERSATURATED AREAS

STEP 3: Use the Channels palette to look at the Red, then the Green, and then the Blue channels of the image to see if one of them has a noticeable pattern within the oversaturated area. You can see that the Green channel is very dark, magenta, in all the saturated areas. Option-click on the New Layer icon to add a new layer (call it Color Merged), and then hold down Option while choosing Merge Visible from the Layers palette menu. This maneuver merges the effects of the Levels and Hue-Saturation adjustment layers into the New Color Merged layer. You can now look at its channels and see which colors are causing the saturation problem. Option-drag the Color Merged layer to the New Layer icon and call this copy ColorMerged Fixed. Drag this layer to just below the ColorMerged layer and Option-click on the ColorMerged Fixed Eye icon to just work on it. Click on the Red channel in the Channels palette. Do Select/All and Copy, and then click on the Green channel and do a Paste. Lower the Opacity on the floating selection in the Layers palette until you have the lowest that is possible without disabling the Red channel's repair of the problem areas in the shadows. Click on the Blue channel which will drop the floating selection on the Green channel and make that permanent. Paste the Red channel on top of the Blue channel and do the same thing. You can turn on the Eye icon in the RGB channel to see the color balance as you make changes in the Opacity of the floating selection. You want the least Opacity that both repairs the dark areas and keeps a compatible color balance which will be somewhat fainter. Compare my Color Merged layer (with the layer mask off) to my Color Merged Fixed layer to see the relative color balance and lightness I used. My final version of this example is in the Extra Info Files folder of Color Correcting Al on the CD.

BLENDING THE TWO LAYERS

STEP 4: Click on RGB in the Channels palette to drop the floating selection, and also turn on the Eye icon for Color Merged. Now add a layer mask to the Color Merged layer, and use the Air Brush at 5% Pressure with soft brushes to paint black in the Color Merged layer mask. Doing so lets you slowly remove dark and oversaturated parts of the Color Merged layer to reveal the lighter fixed version of the Color Merged Fixed layer underneath. You want to have the Eye icons on for both Layers while doing this. Don't worry if the color balance of Color Merged Fixed isn't exactly right; just work on getting the saturation down in the damaged areas. When you are happy with the basic detail, click on the Color Merged Fixed layer to activate it then Command-click on the New Layer icon to add a Levels adjustment layer above it. Now you can change the color balance and contrast of this layer while watching how these changes affect the Color Merged layer's appearance. You should find that you can get Al's face to look much better. Now activate Color Merged, and add a new layer above it. Make sure that the Eye icons are on for Color Merged Fixed, the Levels adjustment layer above it, Color Merged, and the new layer, then choose Merge Visible with the Option key down to merge the three lower layers into this new layer. Name it Final Retouch and make it the active layer.

STEP 4: Al before retouch and sharpening.

THE WHITES OF HIS EYES

STEP 5: Now use the Lasso tool to select the white part of Al's left eye. Use Select/Feather to put a one-pixel feather on this selection. Go back into Hue/Saturation (Command-U) and try to brighten the white of Al's eye, and to make it more white. I added +10 to the lightness in Master mode, and then I moved the red hues toward yellow by +8 in Red mode, all of which made the eye stand out a little better and removed some of its red tint.

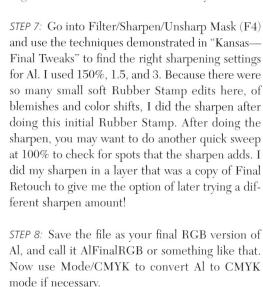

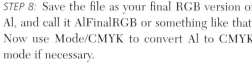

Step 8: The final Layers palette for this example.

CLEANING UP SOME BLEMISHES

STEP 6: Now use the Rubber Stamp tool with different size soft brushes and opacities to remove any blemishes and to tone out areas that are too magenta. If you set the opacity to 30–50% and then clone from an area next to the one you want to fix, it's easy to even out color areas that aren't quite right without losing the original detail in that area. You can also clone with the Blend mode set to Color to change the color of something without losing its original detail. Remember that you can change the opacity by typing a number on the numeric keypad between 0 and 9. Zero is for 100%, 9 for 90%, 8 for 80%, . . . 1 for 10%, or even 25 for 25%. You can also use the bracket keys, [and], to move to the next smaller or the next larger brush. Make sure that you have the preferences for Painting tools set to Brush Size, so that if the cursor is over your image, you can see the brush size relative to your image and zoom factor as you change the brush size with the bracket keys.

STEP 7: Go into Filter/Sharpen/Unsharp Mask (F4) and use the techniques demonstrated in "Kansas—Final Tweaks" to find the right sharpening settings for Al. I used 150%, 1.5, and 3. Because there were so many small soft Rubber Stamp edits here, of blemishes and color shifts, I did the sharpen after doing this initial Rubber Stamp. After doing the sharpen, you may want to do another quick sweep at 100% to check for spots that the sharpen adds. I did my sharpen in a layer that was a copy of Final Retouch to give me the option of later trying a different sharpen amount!

STEP 8: Save the file as your final RGB version of Al, and call it AlFinalRGB or something like that. Now use Mode/CMYK to convert Al to CMYK mode if necessary.

STEP 8: The final version of Al, after retouching and sharpening.

HANDS-ON SESSION: Bryce Stone Woman

*Advanced color correction using Threshold, layers,
and adjustment layers to combine red and
green versions of the same image to get the best color.*

The original Bryce Stone Woman scan is very dull; we will use some interesting techniques to greatly improve it.

This is one of my favorite photos of Bryce Canyon. The light rock formation in the front center, if you use your imagination a bit, could be a naked woman with long bushy hair sitting on the rock and admiring the view. Because the rocks are predominately red, it is hard to make the rocks look their best without making the green trees and shrubs look too dark and magenta. The solution is to use a layer mask to combine two versions of the image, one that optimizes the red parts and another that optimizes the green parts. We also use layer masks and adjustment layers so we can change things later if needed. We think you will like this technique!

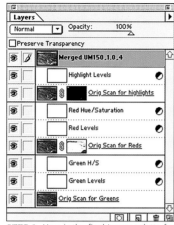

OVERALL COLOR CORRECTION WITH LEVELS

STEP 1: Open the BryceOrigScan image from the Bryce Stone Woman folder and crop (C) out any black or white borders. Double-click on the *Background* layer and rename it to Orig Scan for Greens. Option-drag it to the New Layer icon and name this second layer Orig Scan for Reds. Option-drag this to New Layer once more and call this one Orig Scan for Highlights. Drag this Orig Scan for Highlights layer to the bottom of the pile for now. I included the "Orig Scan for" at the beginning of each name to remind you that we are not modifying the pixels in the original scan until we merge the layers at the end. During this exercise, I will refer to these three layers as Reds, Greens, and Highlights. We are doing this entire project using adjustment layers so we can go back and tweak the color and contrast of each component as we please as well as change each component's mask as many times as we want too. Choose File/Save As and name this BryceLayers.

STEP 2: Click on the Reds layer to activate it; it should currently be the top layer. Now Command-click on the New Layer icon in the Layers palette and create an adjustment layer named Red Levels, of Type Levels, and check the Grouped with Previous Layer check box. This will make the color changes here apply only to the Reds layer directly below. Now take a look at the histograms. All of them are short for this image; that is, there is not a wide range of values from the brightest white to the darkest black. Looking at the Red, Green, and Blue histograms separately, each one is a little different. In this image, I tried to find a good white and black point for the Highlight and Shadow Eyedroppers, but was not very happy with the results. Instead, I went into each of the color channels and brought the end points in so they would cause a full spread of detail without losing any important information. I then went back to the RGB channel and adjusted the Overall Brightness and Contrast slider to the right, which adds contrast to make the red rocks to the right and the yellow highlights to the left look best. I moved the RGB Input Highlight slider to the left, to about 231, to brighten up the highlight areas and emphasize the places where the sun is shining on the rocks. Next, I went into each of the Red, Green, and Blue channels to adjust the color balance. The most important area to adjust for here is the red rocks, because it's the largest area. If you want to see exactly what I did here, you can load my final Levels settings for this Reds layer using the Load button in Levels. It's in the same folder as the Original Scan and is called RedLevels. You may notice that my settings blow out the highlight detail. Because we are using an adjustment layer, they are not lost in the original scan and we will bring that back later in the highlight layer. If you need more help with overall color correction, review "The Grand Canyon" and "Kansas." Click on OK to finalize your Levels.

When working in a Levels adjustment layer, Video LUT Animation is not available, so just work with the Preview button on. If you need Video LUT Animation, you can always do your adjustments in Levels in a real layer and then use the Save button to save your settings, and then Cancel at the end of your Levels session. After that, you could just create a Levels adjustment layer grouped to the actual layer and use the Load button to bring up these same settings.

STEP 3: Command-click again on the New Layer icon, but this time create an adjustment layer named RedH/S, of Type Hue/Saturation, and grouped with the previous layer. I increased the overall saturation in Master by about 25%. I moved the Reds toward Magenta and saturated them, and also saturated the Yellows. To change just the Reds or just the Yellows, click on the Red or Yellow radio buttons. You can check out my settings by using the Load button and loading RedH/S from the CD. Click on OK when you are happy with your Hue/Saturation changes.

USING LAYER MASKS TO BRING OUT COLOR

STEP 4: Click in the right-most column of the Greens layer to activate it, then Option-click on its Eye icon so only it is visible. Command-click on the New Layer icon to create a Levels adjustment layer named Green Levels that is Grouped with the Previous Layer. This time, adjust your histogram so that the green trees in the background to the left look best. Don't worry about the purple mountains that are way back there in the rain—concentrate on the green trees where you can see details. Because this is a fresh original scan layer, you will need to again start

STEP 3: The Bryce Stone Woman after the Reds have been adjusted.

out by bringing in the endpoints in each color channel and then going back to RGB and adjusting the overall Brightness/Contrast slider in the middle. You will probably want to make this layer a little less contrasty to bring out detail in the trees as well as in the bushes that are down between the rocks on the right side of the image. Go back into the Red, Green, and Blue channels again and use the middle slider to adjust the color balance of the midtones to make the green things look the best. Don't worry if the rocks don't look good here, we are just going to use the items that are green from this layer. You can check my settings if you want by choosing the Load button in Levels, but don't forget to save your own first. Click on OK when you are happy with your greens. You can always change them later!

STEP 5: Command-click on the New Layer icon again and make a Type Hue/Saturation adjustment layer, and name it GreenH/S. Use a similar Master saturation value as you used in the RedH/S layer. You may find that further adjustments here won't help the green items that much. Click on OK when you think the green foliage looks best.

MASKING WITH THRESHOLD

STEP 6: Click on the rightmost column of the Reds layer to activate it and then Option-click on its Eye icon twice to turn all the other layers back on. The Reds layer should currently be the top-most layer. Now click on the Red channel, then on the Green channel, and finally on the Blue channel in the Channels palette, looking for the one that has the most contrast between the green tree areas and the rest of the image. The Red channel will probably be the best choice. Now click back on RGB in the Channels palette to see color again. Click on the Layer Mask icon, which is the left-most one at the bottom of the Layers palette. This should create a layer mask for the Reds layer. Now choose Image/Apply Image and set the channel to Red and the blending to Normal. The Target should already be set to the Reds mask. When you choose OK, this should copy the Red channel of the Reds layer into the Reds layer mask. Wherever this mask is black, the Reds layer becomes transparent and you can see the Greens layer underneath, through the transparency. If

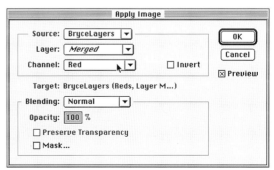

STEP 6: The correct settings for Image/Apply Image.

STEP 7: The blending of Reds and Greens layers by the Reds mask *before* the Gaussian Blur of one pixel.

STEP 7: The blending of Reds and Greens layers by the Reds Mask *after* the Gaussian Blur of one pixel.

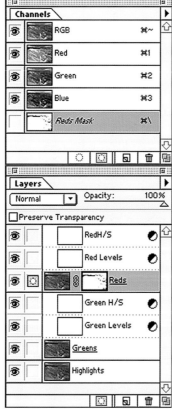

STEPS 7 AND 8: The Layers and Channels setups you need for painting in the Reds layer mask while seeing the composite of the Reds and Greens layers.

you look at your Channels palette now, the Reds mask should be active, but the Eye icons will be on for RGB, Red, Green, and Blue. This means you can work on the Reds mask while seeing the results in the RGB composite of the Reds and Greens layers controlled by the Reds mask.

STEP 7: Now choose Image/Adjust/Threshold (Shift-F7) to go into the Threshold command, which will make the mask either black or white depending on the location of the Threshold slider. You want to have the Preview button on as you move the slider so that you are selecting the green trees at the top left and the shrubs in the middle right from the Greens layer and most of the rest of the image from the Reds layer. Don't worry about the big green bush in the bottom right corner; we will adjust that by hand later. The edges between Red and Green will also look jaggy—we'll fix that too. The most important thing here is to get the horizon as close as possible where the green trees at the top left are separated from the darker purple background that is even further away. Also, you want the shrubs in the middle right to come from the Greens layer. When you think you have the closest Threshold mask, choose OK. Now you want to Gaussian Blur this mask to blend the edges better.

Choose Filter/Blur/Gaussian Blur and blur by one pixel with the Preview button on. You can see before and after in the image by turning the Preview button on and off. You can see before and after in the mask by clicking in the little preview window in the Filter dialog box. When you click down in the window, you see the mask before, and when you release, you see it after. Click down with the square icon on top of the Bryce image to choose the part of the mask that will show up in this window. Choose OK when it is clear to you how the blur is improving the mask.

STEP 8: Now you will have to hand edit the mask with the Paintbrush tool, so type a B, to get the brush, then D, for default colors, then 0, for 100% Opacity, and then you're ready to go. The foreground color will now be white, so with this you can paint where you want to see more of the Reds layer and not see the Greens layer. Type an X to exchange the colors and you will paint with black to see more of the Greens layer. I started out with a solid brush using white to remove any Greens layer stuff from the purple mountains in the far background of the image. Then I typed X to paint with black and bring in some of the highlights along the front of the row of trees at the top left. I then used a soft brush at 50% opacity (type a 5 and use the right bracket key,], to move to soft brushes) to paint more green into some of the stand-alone shrubs that are surrounded by red rock. For the big green bush at the bottom right, I used the largest soft brush (Shift-]) at

100% black and then changed (x) to white at 20% and backed off the greenness of this bush by painting over it again with white. I also lowered the greenness of some of the shrubs down in the rocks and in the background on the right side by painting over the mask there at 20% white. You might want to open my Bryce-Layers image in the Extra Info folder and compare my mask to yours. If you Option-click on the Reds layer mask, you will toggle between seeing the mask and seeing RGB, but in either case you will still be working on the mask.

STEP 8: The original Reds layer mask after using Threshold.

PUTTING BACK THE HIGHLIGHTS

STEP 9: Now drag the Highlights layer from the bottom of the Layers palette to the very top. Click on it to activate it. Option-click on the Layer Mask icon to create an all black layer mask so we don't see any of this layer. Type a D to get the default colors, or White and Black, then type 2 to use the Brush again at 20% opacity. Zoom in to the very top left corner of the image and paint over the clouds where all the detail was replaced by white. The detail will slowly come back from the Highlight layer as you paint several strokes with a soft brush. Zoom to the very bright rock to the left of the big bush at the bottom right and bring some detail back there, too. Now Command-click on the New Layer icon to add a Levels adjustment layer named Highlight Levels that is Grouped with Previous Layer. If you are using the initial Photoshop 4 release, a bug there will show you the wrong histogram for this grouped adjustment layer. Click on OK in Levels, then double-click on the rightmost column of this new Highlight Levels layer, and then you will go back into Levels seeing the correct histogram. Don't change the highlight or shadow settings here, but use the middle sliders in the Red, Green, and Blue channels to adjust the color balance of the highlight detail you just added to better match the rest of the image. Choose OK when you are finished here. Press Command-S to save your work.

STEP 8: The final Reds layer mask after applying Gaussian Blur of 1 and hand editing with the Paintbrush.

Because we have done all the color changes using adjustment layers, you can reenter any of these at any time, by double-clicking on their name, and change their settings. Now that you have everything set up, you might want to go back to the Red Levels layer and see if you like it better by adding a little more Magenta to the midtones, or taking some away for that matter. You can always use the Load and Save buttons in each color tool to load and save settings so you can go back to an earlier one if you like. You could actually make two different Red Levels layers and then compare them by turning off the Eye icon for one or the other so that you see one at a time. With this type of setup, the data in the original scan doesn't get changed until you flatten the image or merge layers together. If you always save your layered version and keep all your color shifts as adjustment layers, you can always tweak the results as many times as you want and then use File/Save A Copy to save different versions of the file for output to print or a film recorder for color transparency.

MERGING THE IMAGE INTO A SINGLE LAYER

STEP 10: Option-click on the New Layer icon one more time to create a new layer at the very top of the Layers palette, called Merged. Hold down the Option key while choosing Merge Visible from the Layers palette menu. This will merge everything you have done so far into this one layer but will leave all the other layers underneath. Choose Filter/Sharpen/Unsharp Mask to sharpen this image. Use the techniques described in "Kansas—Final Tweaks" to decide what settings are best for Unsharp Mask. I used 150, 1.0, and 4. Now use the Rubber Stamp tool to remove any spots, as we showed you in "The Grand Canyon—Final Tweaks" session. Choose Command-S to save this final RGB version of your layered document. To make a CMYK version, choose Image/Duplicate (F5) with the Merged Layers Only box checked. After making sure your Separation preferences are correctly set for this job, do an Image/Mode/CMYK to convert this image to CMYK. I found that this image did not change color much when converting to CMYK, so I did not tweak the CMYK version of the colors using Selective Color. If you do get a color shift after converting to CMYK, use Selective Color to adjust certain colors using the techniques explained in "Yellow Flowers" and "Color Matching Cars."

STEP 10: The final CMYK, sharpened Bryce Stone Woman.

COMPOSITING MULTIPLE IMAGES

WITH

LAYERS, ADJUSTMENT LAYERS, AND LAYER MASKS

HANDS-ON SESSION: Bob Goes to...

*Using the Pen tool for smooth curves and
Levels for hair to create a knock-out of Bob, and
then using layers to send Bob traveling!*

In this session, we explore various techniques for creating a knock-out of Bob. First we will use the Pen tool to trace the outline of Bob and remove his background. We will show you how you can use Threshold and Levels to automatically Knock out difficult hair and shapes that are hard for the Pen tool. After you separate Bob from his background, you'll use layers, layer masks, and Transform to send him to different locations.

You will find the selection and basic compositing techniques we show you here useful in many places. Since Bob has subtle curved edges and a somewhat soft distinction between him and the background, you can get a more exact selection if you use the Pen tool rather than the Lasso or Magic Wand. Before you do this example, you should be sure to read the "Navigating in Photoshop" chapter and set up your Actions palette using ArtistKeys. Also, read "Selections, Masks, and Channels" as well as "Layers, Layer Masks, and Adjustment Layers."

SETTING THINGS UP

STEP 1: Open the BigBob file in the Bob Goes To folder. Click on the middle icon at the bottom of the Tool palette to put yourself in Full Screen mode and use Command-0 to zoom BigBob so it fills the screen. Bring up the Channels palette (Shift-F10 with ArtistKeys) and then the Layers palette (F10). You can get these from the Window menu but using the function keys is faster. The keys F9..F12 and their Shift alternatives take care of most of the palettes. Put your Channels and Layers palettes along the side of the screen but make sure that you can see all of both of them at the same time. Notice that the Layers palette just has one layer, called *Background*. Double-click on the word *Background* and type in the name Bob, to change it from a *Background* layer into a normal layer. Now open the Vegas file from the same folder. Choose Select/All to select all of Vegas and then Edit/Copy to copy it. Then choose Window/BigBob to switch to the Bob file, and finally, choose Edit/Paste to paste Vegas as a new layer on top of the Bob layer. Notice that this new layer (called Layer 1) has been created in the Layers palette. Notice also that Layer 1 is black and white because you pasted on top of a black-and-white document. All the layers in a document have to be in the same color mode. Do Command-Z to undo the Paste, then choose Image/Mode/RGB to convert Bob to RGB. Red, Green, and Blue channels appear in the Channels palette, each a copy of the old black channel. Now do Edit/Paste again and the Vegas image will be in color. Double-click on its layer and name it Vegas and then choose OK. Imagine that Bob was a print laying on

STEP 1: The BigBob image as it appears when you first open it.

your desk and then you dropped the Vegas print on top of it. Think of each layer as a separate image, after all, it is—each layer has its own set of RGB channels. Review the "Layers, Layer Masks, and Adjustment Layers" chapter during this exercise if you need to refresh your understanding of layers.

STEP 2: You're going to want Bob standing in front of a background, so you want Bob to be the top layer. Click on the Vegas layer and drag it downward until you see a black line below the Bob layer. At this point, release the mouse to change the order of the layers. Bob is now on top and will completely hide Vegas for now. Press Command-Shift-S and save the file as Bob Goes To. You can now close the Vegas image, because you have created a layer for it in Bob Goes To. Choose Window/Show Paths (Shift-F11) to bring up the Paths palette. Click on the Pen tool in the Tool palette (P) and press Return to bring up the Pen tool's Options. Turn on the Rubber band option by clicking in it so you see an X in the box. Setting this option causes the Pen to show you how a line or curve will draw between two points.

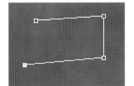

STEP 3: Clicking to enter corner points on a path.

CREATING A PATH FROM SCRATCH

STEP 3: If you already know how to use Paths, you can skip Steps 3 and 4. You can now use the Pen tool to learn how to create a new path. The Pen tool allows you to make selections, called *paths,* by clicking to create points between either straight or curved lines. If you click on a point and immediately release the mouse, you create a corner point. If you click on a point and drag before releasing the mouse, that point becomes a curve point. When you create or move a curve point, you get two lines coming out of the curve point; I call these *handlebars.* The handlebars control the shape of the curve. Try this out now! It's sort of like tracing, but more fun!

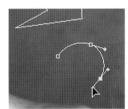

STEP 3: Clicking and dragging to enter curve points on a path. The handlebars should be tangent to the curve shape you are trying to draw.

Click anywhere on top of the Bob Image with the Pen tool and immediately release to create a corner point. Click four or five corner points to create a box. When you put the last corner point on top of the first, a little circle appears next to the arrow, indicating that you are closing the path. When you see the circle, click on top of the initial point again to close the path. If you're going to turn your path into a selection (as you are going to do here), you usually want the path to be closed. After closing the first box path, move the cursor down below that box, and in a new area, click and drag to create a curve point. Where you click is the location of the point, and dragging out the handlebar beyond the point affects the shape of the line segment between that point and the previous point. Draw an oval shape by clicking and dragging four curve points. Close the path by clicking again on the original point. You now have a box path made up of corner points and an oval path made up of curve points. If you look at the Paths palette, you can see them both there now in a new path called Work Path. Work Path is a temporary place where you can create a path without naming it. Actually, each of these two disjointed paths is a subpath of Work Path. Double-click on Work Path and rename it Play Path. After you name a path, any changes you make to it automatically save as part of that path.

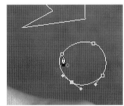

STEP 3: To close the curve, click on the first point a second time when you see the small circle next to the Pen icon.

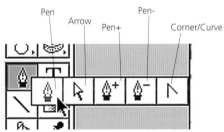

STEP 4: The different tools available from the pop-out menu for Pen in the Tool palette. NOTE: Adobe calls the Corner/Curve tool the Convert Direction Point tool. The Pen tool is for entering points initially. The Arrow tool allows you to edit points that have been entered. The Pen+ and Pen- tools are for adding and deleting points and the Corner/Curve tool is for changing points between corners and curves and for decoupling the handlebars.

STEP 4: Now select the Arrow tool in the Tool palette by clicking on the Pen tool's icon and scrolling to the right until you're on the Arrow and then releasing the mouse. See the diagram on this page; it gives the names of each tool. You can also scroll through the different Pen tools by continuing to type P until you get to the tool you want. Now

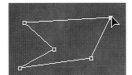

STEP 4: To move a corner point or a curve point, click on it and drag.

STEP 4: To adjust the shape of the curve, first click on the point whose handlebars affect the part of the curve you want to change. Second, click on the end of the handlebar and make it longer or shorter or change its angle. This changes the shape of the curve.

STEP 4: Changing the shape of a curve segment by dragging one end of a handlebar.

STEP 4: Moving a curve point to make the oval longer.

STEP 5: Start by clicking a corner point where Bob's arm meets the background. Now click and drag curve points as you follow Bob's shape upward and around.

use the Arrow tool to edit the path. First click on the box shape you made with the corner points. When you click on the box shape, its points become highlighted. To move one of these points, just click on it, drag, and then let go in the new location. This change saves automatically in your Play Path. Click on the oval subpath now and its points become highlighted. If you want to move one of these curve points to elongate the oval, just click and drag it like you would a corner point. To adjust the shape of the curve, first click on the point on one end of the curve segment that you want to change. This brings up the handlebars for that point. Now click on the end of the handlebar next to the segment you want to change, and make it longer or shorter, or change its angle to change the shape of the curve.

You can also add points with the Pen+ tool and delete points with the Pen– tool. To add a point, just click along the line segment where there currently isn't a point using the Pen+ tool. You can access the Pen+ tool from the Arrow tool by holding the Command and Option keys down while over a location that doesn't already have a point. The point you then add is a curve point. You can then change the shape of the curve by adjusting that point's handlebars. Command-Option with the Arrow over a location that already is a point to bring up the Pen– tool, and click to remove that point. If you're removing many points, you can just switch to the Pen– tool in the Tool palette.

If you want to change a curve point to a corner point, or vice-versa, click on it with the Corner/Curve tool (Adobe calls it the Convert Direction Point tool). To change a corner to a curve, you click and drag to define the length and angle of your handlebars. You also can use the Corner/Curve tool to decouple a curve point's handlebars. Clicking on either handlebar and moving slightly with this tool allows you to then use the Arrow tool to drag on each end of the handlebar to change its curve segment shape without changing the one on the opposite side of the handlebar's point. To recouple the handlebars together again, use another click of the Corner/Curve tool. You can also access the Corner/Curve tool from the Arrow tool by holding down the Control key and putting the cursor over a point. Using the Pen tool in Photoshop is a lot like using the Pen tool in Illustrator but there are some differences. If you are not familiar with the Pen tool or if you want to know all the little details, read the "About Paths" section in the Selecting chapter (Chapter 7) of the Adobe Photoshop 4.0 manual. We show you how to use Paths as you work on projects in this book. Click on the Play Path you just created and drag it to the trash at the bottom right of the Paths palette.

Making a Path Around Bob

STEP 5: Make sure you are currently using the Pen tool (type P until you get it, or click and drag on the Pen area in the Tool palette and then choose the Pen icon from the pop-out menu). Press Command-Spacebar-click to zoom into the bottom left of where Bob sits against his background. Click the Pen tool to make the first point in the lower left corner of Bob's body along the edge between Bob and the gray background. Now move the cursor up the curved shape of his arm and click and drag out a curve point for the second point. Release the mouse when the line segment between the first point and the second point match the edge of Bob against the background. You want the handlebars on curve points to always be tangent to the curved edge of Bob at the point's location. Now click and drag the Pen tool to create curve points around the edge of Bob and his background. Stay zoomed in close and use the spacebar to scroll when needed. If you make a mistake, you can Command-Z to remove the last point you entered. If you hold down the Command key while entering a path, you get the Arrow tool and you can go back and click on any other point you have entered so far and move it. Releasing the Command key puts you back in the Pen tool so you can enter more points. You can use the Tab key to get the palettes out of your way. Don't worry about making it perfect the first time since you can use the Arrow tool later to adjust the selection you're making here now.

STEP 6: Move your way up the left side of the Bob layer entering curve points all the way until you get to the hair. It is hard to do a good job of selecting hair using the Pen tool, so just rough out the basic shape of the hair as you go through that part of the selection. Selecting hair like this properly is one of the most common things people have trouble doing. We show you how to do this later in the session. When you get to the top left corner of Bob's edge, click there to make a corner point and then click again on the top right edge to make another corner point. Now trace down the right side of Bob, making mostly curve points until you click to make another corner at the bottom right edge. Now go back to the bottom left edge and click back on the original point when you see the small circle next to the Pen tool. This completes the path around Bob and you should now double-click on the Work Path name in the Paths palette and call it Bob Outline.

STEP 7: Use the Pen's pop-out in the Tool palette, or just type a P, to switch from the Pen tool to the Arrow tool. Click once on the outline of your path to bring the points back. If you were doing this for a comp, the path you have made so far probably would be fine. On the other hand, if you were going to use it for an ad or magazine cover, you would want to make the path as accurate as possible. For the most accuracy, zoom in close and now go back and scroll around the edge using the arrow key to move points and handlebars when the curve edge is off. You will want the edge of the curve to be just a hair inside the edge of Bob's surface because you don't usually want to have any pixels from Bob's old background showing on top of the new background. Remember to use the Command and Option keys to get the Pen+ and Pen–tools to add or delete points and the Control key to get the Corner/Curve tool. As you edit the path, it automatically updates to Bob Outline in the Paths palette.

TURNING PATHS BACK TO SELECTIONS AND MASKS

STEP 8: Once you are happy with the shape of your Bob Outline path, choose Make Selection from the Paths palette's pop-up menu. Make it a New Selection with the feather set to 0 and Anti-aliased on. When you choose OK, you will see the selection as well as your path still highlighted. To de-highlight your path, click in the empty area below the name Bob Outline in the Paths palette. The faster way to turn a path into a selection is to click on the path name in the Paths palette, and then drag to the Load Selection icon in the middle at the bottom of this palette. Your path turns into a selection using the options last set in the Make Selection dialog box, and it also becomes de-highlighted.

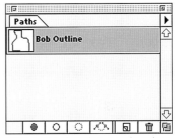

STEP 6: The Photoshop 4 Paths palette. The icons on the bottom, from left to right, fill a path with the current foreground color, stroke a path with current painting tool and brush, do a Load Selection from a path, turn a selection into a path, create a new or copied path, and throw a path into the trash. To use them, you click on the path you want and drag to the appropriate icon and then release when the icon highlights. Dragging to the New Path icon copies the path. To create a path from an existing selection, just click on the fourth icon from the left. Option-dragging or clicking on any icon brings up any option dialog box that the icon has.

STEP 8: Click in the empty space below your last path to dehighlight a path.

STEP 9: Click on the Add Layer Mask icon at the bottom left of the Layers palette to create a layer mask for the Bob layer with the selected parts of Bob showing but the background now removed. Remember that the black areas of a layer mask remove those parts of that masks layer. When you clicked on the Add Layer Mask icon, your selection turned into the layer mask with only the selected parts then visible.

STEP 10: Click on the Vegas layer to make it the active, highlighted, layer. Use Command-0 to make sure that you're zoomed in so you can see the entire image in the screen. Now press Command-T to get the Free Transform command. Click in the center of the Vegas Layer and drag it so its top left corner aligns with the top left of the document canvas. Next, hold down the Shift key while dragging the bottom right handle down and to the right, to scale the Vegas image. You can drag beyond the edge of the document canvas into the gray area to scale the image bigger than the canvas. Release the mouse button when you are happy with the scale. Press Enter (or Return) to finish the Transform or press the Escape key to cancel the Transform. Now that you have sent Bob on a trip to Las Vegas, let's try another location, too.

STEP 10: Using Free Transform to scale the Vegas image.

STEP 11: Use File/Open to open the Packard file in the "Posterize, Bitmaps, and Patterns" folder on the CD. Move the Packard window so you can see part of the Bob Goes To window below it. Type V to make sure that you are in the Move tool, and then click in the image area of the Packard image and drag until your cursor sits on top of the Bob Goes To image. The cursor should change to a hand at this point, and if you then release the mouse, you will drop a new Packard layer on top of the Vegas layer in the Bob Goes To file. Bob is now in Miami, where there are many photo shoots along the beach. Double-click on Layer 1 and rename it Packard, and then use Command-T (Free Transform) again to move and scale the Packard image so it is stretched across the screen. Press Enter to end the Free Transform session. Now you can see Bob in either Vegas or Miami by turning on the Eye icon for the layer you want to see as his background.

CLEANING UP BOB'S LAYER MASK

STEP 12: Click on the Bob layer and use the Move tool (V or Command) to move Bob until his hair on both sides is over the clear blue sky of the Miami scene. It should be pretty obvious that your Pen tool selection of his hair is not too natural. Bring up the Channels and Layers palettes and separate them so you can see both at the same time. Click on the left-most rectangular thumbnail in the Bob layer to activate the layer. This thumbnail, I call it the Layer thumbnail, should now have a black highlight around it in the Layers palette. The Channels palette should

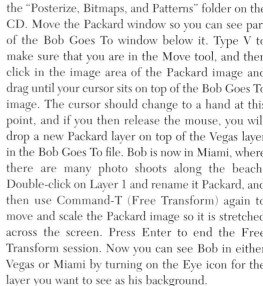

STEP 12: Painting Black in the layer mask removes that part of the layer. Here is what your Channels and Layers palettes should look like if you want to paint in the mask but view the RGB image.

show RGB as active with the RGB Eye icons on for channels ~–3. Type a B to go to the Paintbrush tool, and then type D to get the default colors, and finally, press the 0 number key to set the Brush Opacity to 100%. Try painting on Bob's face and you will see black paint on top of his image. Whatever you do now permanently affects Bob's layer. Use Command-Z to undo this painting. Now click on the Layer Mask thumbnail, which is the rightmost thumbnail in the Bob layer, and notice that it now highlights in black. The Channels palette now has a channel called Bob Mask activated, even though the Eye icons are on for the inactive Red, Green, and Blue channels. Type D again, followed by X, and then paint with black on top of Bob's face. You're now painting black into Bob's layer mask and you will notice the Packard layer through the area you paint with black. Use Command-Z again to remove your changes. Here you are changing the mask but seeing the changes happen to the composite of the RGB layers. The Channels palette shows you that you are seeing RGB but working on the layer mask. If you now Option-click on the Layer Mask icon, you will see the mask and can then work on the mask. Again, look at what is active and which Eye icons are on in the Channels palette. Option-click on the Layer Mask icon again to return to seeing RGB but working on the mask. You need to really be aware of whether you are working on the layer mask or the layer, as well as how the Layers and Channels palettes show you the current state.

STEP 13: Bring up the brushes palette, F12, and choose a mid-sized soft brush. Type a 5 to set the opacity to 50% and then paint with black where Bob's hair blends with the background to create a more subtle blend than you did with the Pen tool. Painting with black fades out and eventually removes parts of the hair and painting with white brings it back. Remember that you can use the left and right bracket keys to change brush size as you work. You sometimes want to paint with white at 100% along the hair edge to bring back all the hair and even some of the background. Then Xchange the colors and use black at 50% with different size brushes to slowly blend away the background and keep the hairs you need to make the composite look natural. After getting the hair correct, scroll around the entire edge of Bob and use a hard edge black brush at 100% to remove any light ghosts along the edge. Now do a File/Save.

USING LEVELS FOR BETTER, FASTER HAIR KNOCK-OUTS (OPTIONAL ADVANCED TECHNIQUE)

STEP 14: Doing a knock-out of hair using this method is one of the most difficult tasks and how to do it with less work and more accuracy is one of the most asked questions. You can use Threshold or Levels to create a mask that will sometimes do the knock-out for you. Here, we look at an alternative method to doing the hair knock-out and maybe even the entire knockout of Bob. Click and drag the Bob Mask channel in the Channels palette to the New Channel icon and make a copy of this channel called MaskByHand. Now click back on the Layer thumbnail for the Bob layer to reactivate the Red, Green, and Blue channels. Hold down the Shift key, and then click on the Bob Layer Mask thumbnail in the Layers palette to turn off this

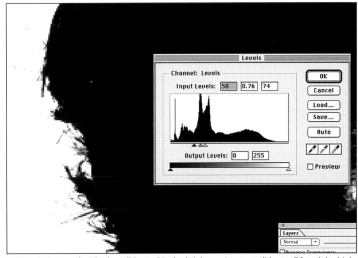

STEP 14: Setting the Shadow slider to 50, the brightness/contrast slider to .76 and the highlight slider to 74 creates a pretty good mask of the hair.

layer mask until you Shift-click again. Click and Option-drag the Red channel to the New Channel icon and call it Levels. Choose Image/Adjust/Levels to make some changes to this mask channel. Move the Input Shadow slider, the top left one, toward the right until it reads about 50. Move the Input Highlight slider, the top right one, toward the left until it reads about 74. Next, move the Brightness/Contrast slider, the one between the other two, until it reads about .76. You will see a pretty good mask of the hair. Now choose OK on Levels. You will use this mask only to replace the hair area of the existing Bob layer mask. Using Levels and moving the Highlight and Shadow sliders close together to create a mask of hair allows you to have some brightness variation from the pure black and white mask that you get when you use Threshold as you do in the next example, "Bob and the Kestrel." This variation can help blend the hair into the new background. I got the idea for this Levels technique from watching a demo Deke McClelland gave at the Photoshop conference in Orlando. In his technique, he used the High Pass filter first to isolate the edges and then followed that by Levels or Threshold. Check out some of his useful masking techniques in the *Macworld Photoshop Bible*.

STEP 15: First notice that the head in the existing Bob layer mask is white where the head in our new Levels mask is black. Choose Image/Adjust/Invert (Command-I) to invert our new mask. Now choose Select/All, and then choose Edit/Copy to copy the entire mask. Choose Select/None (Command-D) and then click on the Bob mask in the Channels palette to activate it. Turn on the Eye icon for the Bob mask and turn off the Eye icons for RGB, Red, Green, and Blue. Now you are just working on and seeing the Bob layer mask. Type L to get to the Lasso tool, and then select from the area of hair above Bob's ear to the top of his head. Now, choose Edit/Paste Into, which will use the new Levels mask to replace the Bob mask just in that selected area. To see the before and after results, click on the Eye icons to turn the RGB, Red, Green, and Blue channels back on. Just click on the Eye icons, not the right part of the channel. Now click on the Eye icon for the Bob mask channel to turn it off. You should still see a floating selection in the Layers palette. You are now seeing the composite with the new modified mask. Command-Z to see it again with the old mask, and then use Command-Z to toggle back and forth to decide which mask is

STEP 16: Here we used the final Versailles image from the "Versailles" example, along with Free Transform, to move and scale Bob until his eye lined up correctly with the sun. To create the composite effect, the Blend mode on his layer was set to Overlay and we modified his layer mask to remove him from where the palace of Versailles buildings start.

better. Choose Select/None if you like the new mask better; otherwise, Command-Z one more time to remove your floating selection and revert to the old mask. If you choose the new Levels version, you can now further improve it by doing more hand editing on it or by applying a very slight Gaussian Blur, about .5 pixels, in this new Levels area.

USING THE FINAL BOB MASK WITH FREE TRANSFORM TO SEND BOB TO DIFFERENT LOCATIONS

STEP 16: Now that you have a final mask of Bob, you can bring up different potential background layers and send Bob to many places. You can make a different Bob layer for each background by clicking and then dragging the Bob layer to the New Layer icon at the bottom of the Layers palette. Give each Bob layer an appropriate name, like Bob Vegas for the Vegas scene, Bob Miami for the Packard scene, and so on. Now use the Move tool to move this version of Bob to the appropriate place in this scene. If you need to scale a scene or the Bob for a scene, activate the layer you want to scale by clicking on it in the Layers palette and then type Command-T to bring up the Free Transform command. This will add handles to the corners and middles of a box that is drawn around the Layers contents. You can scale the layer by clicking and dragging one of the handles to make the image bigger or smaller. To scale proportionately, hold down the Shift key while scaling. To rotate the layer, move the cursor a little outside one of the corner handles; you should see the curved rotate icon. Click and drag at this point to rotate. You can move the layer while transforming it by clicking in the middle and dragging to the location you want to go to. Use the Command key while clicking and dragging a handle to distort the image, the Option key to scale evenly around a center point, and Command-Option-Shift to scale the image with perspective. The Escape key allows you to cancel Free Transform. To accept your transform, press Return or Enter. You may find that you need to do minor fine-tuning on Bob's layer mask to properly blend each different background.

STEP 16: In this version of Bob's travels, we used the Fill command in Color mode with 15% of the red from the Mint sign to colorize Bob, and then we moved him into place and made some minor adjustments to his layer mask using the Paintbrush so that his hair would blend best with the dark background.

SAVING CLIPPING PATHS FOR QUARK OR ILLUSTRATOR

When you finish editing the Bob Outline path at the end of Step 7, you could easily have used it to knock-out Bob as a clipping path in Quark or Illustrator. Importing with a clipping path into Quark or Illustrator would allow you to place Bob as an object with a transparent background. This way you could wrap text around him or you could place him on top of a background created in Quark or Illustrator.

STEP 16: Here we used Layer/Transform/Flip Horizontal on Bob's layer to make him face the other way, and then Free Transform (Command-T) to rotate, scale, move and skew Bob. Finally, we tinted him with a dark brown color using the Fill command with 15% Opacity in Color mode.

To save a path in this way, choose Clipping Path from the Paths Palette menu. Choose the path you want for your clipping path from the Path pop-up menu. In this case, you would choose Bob Outline. We recommend leaving the flatness value blank, which will use the printer's default setting. The flatness controls the accuracy of curved line segments created with PostScript. For more information on flatness, see the Photoshop manual and/or ask your service bureau for a recommended flatness setting for the type of output you are doing. Save this file in EPS format and when you open it into Quark, Illustrator, or other layout packages that support clipping paths, the background will be transparent in the application. Clipping path knock-outs don't allow for the subtle blending we have been doing here in Bob's hair using layer masks. Clipping path knock-outs cannot have a varied feather on their edges.

HANDS-ON SESSION: Bob and the Kestrel

*Using Threshold with hard- and
soft-edged masks and Paste Into
to combine images.*

(Original concept by Bruce Ashley)

The original Bob.

The original Kestrel.

This is a technique that would be difficult and tedious to do in the darkroom. Here, using digital imaging, it's easy. In this session, you create a complicated mask of the bicycle using Threshold and editing in a mask channel. You then add a gradient to the mask and use it to seamlessly place Bob behind the bicycle.

PREPARING THE KESTREL IMAGE

STEP 1: Use File/Open to open the OrigKestrel file in the Bob & Kestrel folder. Choose File/Save As (Command-Shift-S) and save it in Photoshop format to your hard drive with the name Bob&Kestrel. Open the OrigBob file from the same folder.

STEP 2: Crop the white and black borders from both of these files. Type C for crop, then draw a box around the images to exclude the borders. You can click and drag the handles on the edges of the box to change it after you draw it. Press Enter or Return to do the crop. Zoom in to 100% using Command-Option-0. Use Filter/Sharpen/ Sharpen Edges and then Filter/Sharpen/Sharpen to sharpen both images. You can use an action in the ArtistKeys Actions palette (F11) called SharpEdgesShp to run both these filters in the correct order by clicking on SharpEdgesShp or using the Play icon to play it. Whenever you sharpen something, you should be zoomed in to at least 100% so you can see all the details. We normally use Unsharp Mask for sharpening, as in the "Kansas—Final Tweaks" chapter, but SharpEdgesShp is a quick technique that works well with these small images, and also for comps.

STEP 3: Type the letter D, for the default colors. Use the Window menu to bring the Bob&Kestrel file to the top and then click in the middle icon at the bottom of the Tool palette to put it into Full Screen mode. Use Image/Canvas Size (F8) to make the image window the same width but 750 pixels high. Put the image in the lower center of the canvas by clicking on the middle square at the bottom. It will turn gray to indicate where the original image will be in the new canvas.

STEP 3: Set up the canvas size with the height of 750 pixels and the gray box at the bottom center to make room at the top of the file.

MASKING OUT THE BIKE

STEP 4: Go to Window/Show Channels (Shift-F10) and Option-drag Channel #1, the black channel, to the Channel Copy icon. Option-dragging brings up the Duplicate Channel dialog box, allowing you to enter a name. Name it Bike Mask by typing in the name and choosing OK. You will use this new channel to create a mask to separate the bicycle from Bob. Wherever Bob is to be in the final composite, the mask needs to be white (and it should be black where the bike will be). Check out the final image at the end of this chapter to see what we are trying to create here. Now imagine the mask you would need to create this composite.

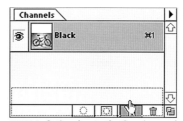

STEP 4: Option-drag to the Copy icon and make a copy of the Black channel to create a mask. Name it Bike Mask.

STEP 5: Using Image/Adjust/Threshold (Shift-F7), adjust the slider with the Preview button off (on if you don't have Video LUT Animation—most PCs don't) until you have created a good dropout of the bike frame. You don't want to etch too much from the edges around the bike frame and the seat. If gaps start to show on the frame edge, you have taken too much away. Don't worry about getting the tires completely; you can fix them later. Click on OK to finish your Threshold selection. Now click in the Black/White box in the Tool palette, or type D, to make sure the foreground is white and the background is black. Now type an X to make the foreground black and the background white. Each time you type an X, the foreground and background colors will Exchange.

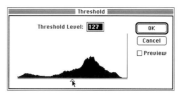

STEP 5: With the Preview button off, move the Threshold slider until you have the best mask for the bike. About 127 worked best for us.

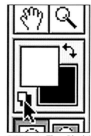

STEP 5: The Black/White box forces colors to white for the foreground and black for the background when you work on a mask channel.

STEP 6: Using the Lasso tool with feather set to zero, draw freehand around the areas of black that remain in the background on the mask, to select them, and then use the Delete key to set them to white. (You need to do this only above the center of the wheels.)

STEP 6: Selection to be deleted.

STEP 7: Go to Window/Show Brushes and pick the third brush from the top left. This should be a 5-pixel brush with the hardness set to 100%. Choose the Pencil tool (Y) and press Return to bring up its options. Choose Reset Tool from the Pencil Options palette's menu. Use the Pencil tool to add black to areas of the bike not yet filled in. You want the entire interior of the bike frame to be black so that when you combine the bike and Bob, Bob doesn't show through those areas. You only need to do this to areas above the height of the center of the wheel. Don't paint out beyond the edge of the original bicycle boundary. Without leaving the Pencil tool, you can switch between black, to fill in the bicycle, and white, to erase around the tires, by typing an X to exchange colors. You can speed up this painting process by using the shortcut of clicking on one end of a line and Shift-clicking on the other end to draw a black line with the Pencil tool. After you finish this step, you will have done a lot of work editing this mask, so do a Save (Command-S) to update your file on the disk in case you make a mistake in the following steps.

STEP 7: The mask with the bicycle filled in.

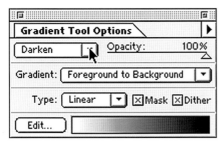

CREATING A GRADIENT MASK

STEP 9: Use the default Foreground to Background Gradient tool options but set the Blend mode to Darken.

STEP 8: Make a copy of the Bike Mask by Option-dragging the mask to the Copy icon at the bottom of the Channels palette. Name this Gradient Mask.

STEP 9: Type G for Gradient tool, then press Return to make sure its options are set as shown here. Notice that the Blend mode is set to Darken. You are going to use the Gradient tool to add a gradual blend from Bob at the top of the image to the bicycle at the bottom of the image. We are doing this in a copy of the Bike Mask so that if we make a mistake, we still have the original Bike Mask to try again. You use the Gradient tool by clicking in the place where you want 100% of the foreground color and dragging to where you want 100% of the background color. Everything between these two points will be a blend of the two colors. Everything outside these two points will be 100% foreground or 100% background. The Darken option will make the gradient change the Bike Mask only when the gradient makes the image darker than it was before.

STEP 10: To create the gradient, Shift-drag the gradient tool from starting just above the seat and ending ⅓ down the wheel.

STEP 10: Your final gradient mask should look like this.

STEP 10: Click on the Black/White icon at the bottom of the Tool palette, or type D, to set the foreground color to white and and the background color to black. With the Shift key down, click and then drag the Gradient tool from just above the seat downward to ⅓ down from the top of the back wheel. Release the mouse button before releasing the Shift key to be sure the Shift key is applied. The Shift key forces the gradient line to be vertical. You should now have the final mask shown here. When you do a Load Selection on this mask, the white area at the top will be fully selected with the black areas fully not selected. The gray blend becomes less and less selected the darker it gets.

STEP 11: Click on Channel #1, the Black channel, in the Channels palette. Now you should see the original Kestrel image. Load the Gradient Mask as a selection using Select/Load Selection or by Command-clicking on the Gradient Mask in the Channels palette. The bottom of the gradient selection (the marching ants line) shows up at the 50% gray point. All of the gradient is actually selected, although it is only selected to a very small amount as it turns to almost all black.

STEP 11: The appearance of the selection after doing a Load Selection.

PUTTING BOB IN THE PICTURE

STEP 12: Use the Window menu to switch to the OrigBob image. Choose Select/Select All (Command-A), followed by Edit/Copy to place Bob on the Clipboard.

STEP 13: Use Window again to return to the Bob&Kestrel window and do Edit/Paste Into, not just Paste, to paste Bob into the selection loaded from the Gradient Mask. Bob is now in a new layer called Layer 1. You will notice that there is also a layer mask on this layer that looks the same as your Gradient Mask. Where this layer mask is black, the Bob layer is made transparent, and you can see the Kestrel in the layer below. Turn off the Eye icon on the Kestrel layer, the bottom layer, to see how parts of Bob are now transparent. Turn this Eye icon back on to see the Kestrel again.

STEP 14: Make sure that Layer 1 is still active (highlighted in the Layers palette) then choose the Move tool from the Tool palette (type V or hold the Command key down). Click and drag to adjust the position of Bob. Make sure no gray transition line is visible at the bottom of Bob as he blends into the bicycle. You need to drag him down until the bottom of his image reaches the place where the Gradient Mask turns completely black. You can check that location in the mask channel by switching back to it using Command-3 or by clicking on the channel you want in the Channels palette. Do Command-1 to go back to the Black channel before moving Bob again. In the Move tool, you can use the arrow keys to move 1 pixel at a time and Shift-arrow to move 10.

STEP 15: When Bob is in the correct location, so that the transition between him and the Kestrel is completely transparent, then Crop (C) and save this as Bob&Kestrel in Photoshop format. Saving in Photoshop format with both layers will later allow you to reopen the file and move Bob again.

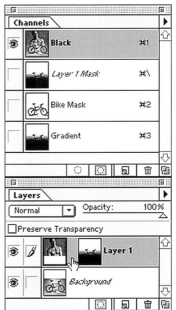

STEP 15: Here is the final appearance for the Layers and Channels palettes of this example. Notice, see the Hand icon, that the layer and layer mask are not linked in layers created by Paste Into. This means that when you move either, the other will not move with it, as is the case when you normally create a layer mask. Also notice that the Layer 1 mask shows up in the Channels palette when Layer 1 is the active layer.

The completed Bob&Kestrel image after cropping.

HANDS-ON SESSION: Versailles

Using two scans to get the full range of detail in a high contrast image; using layers, adjustment layers, and layer masks to color correct an image by combining the two scans, and how to apply filters selectively using layers.

This technique shows you how you can get more detail in a contrasty image by doing two scans, one for the highlights and another for the shadows, and then combining the two images using Layers. Multiple layers of the same image will be lined up with each other exactly. We use this procedure to our advantage in many of the techniques we present in this book, and especially to get better effects with filters in this chapter.

SCANNING THE IMAGE IN LAYERS

STEP 1: The original Photo CD Acquire using gamma 1.4 to get the most detail in the sky.

STEP 2: The original Photo CD Acquire using gamma 2.2 to get the most detail in buildings and foreground.

STEP 1: Open the Sky file in the Versailles folder. This file was originally opened using the Kodak Photo CD Acquire module with a gamma of 1.4 and color temperature 5000, which gave the most detail in the sky but made the foreground look too dark. We will call this version of the image Sky.

STEP 2: Open the Buildings file. This file was originally opened using the Kodak Photo CD Acquire module using gamma 2.2 and color temperature 5000, which gave the most detail in the buildings and foreground but made the sky too light. We will call this image Buildings. If you were going to use this technique with two different scans of the same image, you would need to make sure that both scans were pixel-for-pixel aligned. To do this, scan them at the same time and size without moving the original inside the scanner.

STEP 3: Make the Buildings image active, choose Select/Select All, and then choose Edit/Copy. Now switch to the Sky image and do an Edit/Paste. Double-click on this new layer and name it Buildings, then rename the sky layer, currently called *Background*, to Sky. We now have a two-layered document, with the Sky layer as the bottom layer and the Buildings layer as the top one. You also could have used the Move tool to drag the Buildings and then drop that image on the Sky file as a new layer. That's actually faster because it doesn't use the copy buffer, but in Photoshop 4, you need to remember to hold down the Shift key if you want drag-and-drop layers to be centered in their new location. You can now close the original Buildings image because it is now a layer in Sky. Use the Cropping tool to crop the black borders from around the image. Since you first made the Buildings image a layer on top of Sky, both images will be properly aligned and cropped exactly the same. Do

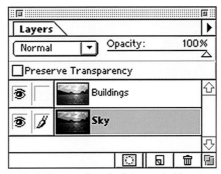

File/Save As and save the two-layered file in Photoshop format, and call it Versailles Layers.

MASKING THE SKY FROM THE BUILDINGS

STEP 4: You now need to make a mask that separates the sky from the rest of the image. Look at the different color channels by clicking in the right-most column in each of the Red, Green, and Blue channels in the Channels palette. Find the channel that has the most contrast between the tops of the buildings and the sky. In this case, it's the Blue channel from the Sky layer. The channels that show up in the Channels palette change depending on which layer is active and what layers are visible. Make sure that the Sky layer is active and the Buildings layer has its Eye icon turned off, as shown here in Step 4, and then choose the Blue channel in the Channels palette. Make two copies of this Blue channel using Duplicate Channel from the pop-up menu in the Channels palette, or by dragging the Blue channel to the New Channel icon at the bottom of the palette. Name the first copy Edges and the second copy Center. Now use Image/Adjust/Threshold (Shift-F7 with ArtistKeys) to make two masks using these copies of the Blue channel. You want these masks to separate the sky and the buildings. Zoom in to different areas along the edge of this boundary and notice how different values of Threshold do a better or worse job of accurately defining this boundary. You can click on the title bar of Threshold (make sure the Preview button is off) to toggle between the mask you're making and the original Blue channel. This makes it easier to accurately see the boundary. If your computer doesn't have Video LUT Animation, work with the Preview button on and turn it off when you need to see the original version.

I used a Threshold value of 74 in the Edges copy of the Blue channel to get the most detail between the buildings and the sky at the edges of the image. In the Center copy, I used the value of 107 to get the best detail between the buildings and the sky in the lighter middle portion. If you need more information on creating Threshold masks, see "Bob and the Kestrel."

STEP 5: Type D for the default colors. You will now combine these two masks to make your final Threshold mask. Choose Select/Select All and then Edit/Copy the Center mask. Choose Select/None, and then using the Lasso tool with a feather value of 0, first click on the Edges mask in the Channels palette and then select the center portion, where the Center mask gave better detail. Do an Edit/Paste Into to replace this portion of the Edges mask with that from the Center mask. Choose Select/None, Command-D, then rename this combined mask HardEdge. Now use the Lasso tool followed by Delete to fill any of the white reflections in the brick area in with black. The only thing you want selected in the end here is the sky area. You can throw out the Center Threshold mask by dragging it to the Trash icon in the Channels palette.

STEP 3: You now have both images inside a two-layered document with the Buildings layer on top and the Sky layer on the bottom.

STEP 4: Drag and drop the Blue channel from the Sky layer to the New Channel icon to make channels for your sky mask.

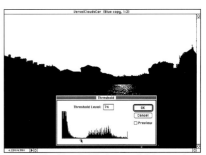

STEP 4: Use Threshold of around 74 to make a mask of the building/sky at the edges of the image.

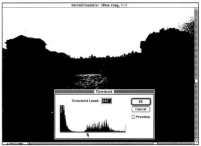

STEP 4: Use Threshold around 107 to make a mask of the building/sky at the middle of the image.

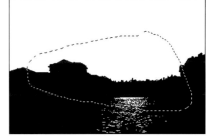

STEP 5: Select the center portion of the 74 mask, where the 107 mask gives better detail, using the Lasso tool with a feather value of 0.

MAKING A LAYER MASK

STEP 6: The Layers palette after adding the layer mask in Step 6. Notice that this mask is inverted from the one you made in Step 5.

STEP 6: Click on RGB in the Channels palette to go back to viewing color. Now click in the rightmost column of the Buildings layer in the Layers palette to activate that layer as well as to turn its Eye icon back on. Command-click the HardEdge mask in the Channels palette to load it as a selection. The sky should now be selected. Now Option-click on the New Layer mask icon, which is left-most at the bottom of the Layers palette, to create a layer mask in the Buildings layer that removes this selected area from view in the Buildings layer. You should now see the sky from the Sky layer and the buildings from the Buildings layer. Try turning the different layers off and on using the Eye icons so you can gain an understanding of the control you have over viewing the different parts of the image.

OVERALL COLOR CORRECTION

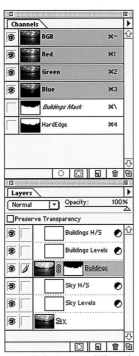

STEP 7: The Layers and Channels palettes after adding the adjustment layers to color correct the Buildings and the Sky layers.

STEP 7: Do a Command-Shift-S to save the image under a different name, and call it VersaillesColorCor. This will allow you to go back to the previous version if you make a mistake in doing the color corrections. Click on the Building Layer thumbnail, the left-most picture icon in the Buildings layer, and then do the overall color correction steps on the Buildings layer. Remember that you're concerned only with making the buildings look best from this layer because the Sky will come from the Sky layer. You are going to do these corrections using adjustment layers. Command-click on the New Layer icon in the Layers palette, and then set the Type to Levels and choose the Group with Previous Layer option to group this layer with the Buildings layer. Doing this creates a Levels adjustment layer that will change only the color of the Buildings layer. Using an adjustment layer will allow you to change these color settings again later.

In the initial Photoshop 4 release, there is a bug that causes a grouped Levels adjustment layer to display, the first time you enter it, the histogram of all the layers below it instead of just the histogram of the layer it is grouped with. The workaround for this bug is that when you first get into Levels, you click on OK to exit Levels. Then double-click on the name of this adjustment layer and it will re-enter Levels, this time showing you the correct histogram. This bug has been fixed in version 4.0.1 of Photoshop.

With Levels: set highlight, set shadow, set overall brightness/contrast, and then correct color cast. Now Command-click on the New Layer icon again to create a Hue/Saturation adjustment layer that is also grouped with the previous layer. In this Hue/Saturation layer, set overall saturation and adjust specific colors. See the "Grand Canyon" and "Kansas" chapters if you need a review of overall color correction. Now click on the Sky layer and do overall color correction on it by first adding a Grouped Levels adjustment layer and then a Grouped Hue/Saturation adjustment layer. When using these Levels adjustment layers, work with the Preview button on so you can see the relationship between the colors you adjust in the Sky layer and the ones you adjust in the Buildings layer. When you do this, focus on getting the part of each layer you will use in the final composite to look the best. The great thing about doing this with adjustment layers is that you can always go back and change the color adjustments later without further degrading the original images. You can also turn off the Eye icons for any of the adjustment layers and see what the images looked like before the color adjustments.

IMPROVING THE FOREGROUND

STEP 8: Now we will use an adjustment layer with a layer mask to improve certain areas in the foreground image. You may notice that the buildings and the brick courtyard on the left and right sides of the image have a green tinge to them, and that they are also a little dark. Use the Lasso tool with a 0-pixel feather to select these areas that are too dark and too green. Don't worry about the selection going up into the

STEP 8: The selection, before the Gaussian Blur of 25, used to fix the dark and green area in the Buildings layer.

sky; the sky will eventually come from a different layer. You will want the edge of this selection that is in the courtyard and on the buildings to have a large feather so that the color and darkness changes will blend over a larger area. Click on the Save Selection icon in the Channels palette to save this new selection, and then name it Green Fix. Click on Green Fix in the Channels palette and choose Select/None. Use Filter/Blur/Gaussian Blur, Shift-F4, to give this about a 25-pixel blur. Doing a Gaussian Blur of a channel, instead of just choosing Select/Feather, allows you to see the distance over which the blend will happen, and change the blur amount (similar to Feather amount) as needed. Now click on this channel and drag it to the Load Selection icon, which is left-most at the bottom of the Channels palette. Click on the top layer, which should be the Hue/Saturation layer for the Buildings. Now Command-click on the New Layer icon in the Layer palette to create an adjustment layer of type Curves. The selection you loaded will automatically save into the layer mask of this adjustment layer so that only the selected parts of the Buildings layer will be modified. Pressing down with the Eyedropper tool while in Curves will show you where in the Curve to make the adjustment for the darkness of the area as well as the green color balance. I used the curves pictured here to fix this part of the image. Click on OK in Curves when you are happy with your changes. Now you should zoom out so you can see the entire image and then toggle between having and not having this change by turning the Eye icon for this Curves layer on and off. If you made a good correction, you should see a significant improvement in the selected area of the image. If you are not happy, double-click on the Curve layer and change the curve. Do a Command-S to save the file and these new layers.

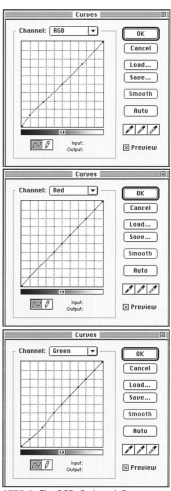

STEP 8: The RGB, Red, and Green curve changes to fix the dark and green areas in the Buildings layer. Yours may be different.

TWEAKING THE LAYER MASK

STEP 9: Now that you have your final color corrections done, you may notice some jagginess or tell-tale brightness variation along the edge between the sky and the buildings. Wherever the layer mask is black, you are seeing the sky from the underlying layer. Wherever the layer mask is white, you are viewing the Buildings layer. You may notice that the edge between the buildings and the sky is sort of jagged. That's because you made this mask using Threshold. Click on the Buildings layer mask in the Layers palette so that in the Channels palette Buildings Mask is active, highlighted, but the Eye icons are on for RGB, Red, Green, and Blue. Now go into Filter/Blur/Gaussian Blur to blur your mask by about .5 to .7 pixels. This will make the edge line up better. Type D to set the default colors, and then you can use the Paintbrush, B, to paint with white in the layer mask to see more from the Buildings layer. You can also type X to exchange the colors. Then you can paint with black to see more from the darker Sky layer. Use a small brush and fine-tune the mask along the edge to get even better blending between the two images. Remember that you can change the opacity of the Paintbrush by typing a number like 5 for 50% or 0 for 100%. Often a partial opacity mask adjustment is just what you need. You can use the left and right bracket keys to move to the next brush on the left or right in the Brushes palette. To draw straight line segments, click on one end of the line and then Shift-click on the other end. When you are finished here, do a Command-S to save the file.

MERGING THE LAYERS AND SMOOTHING THE BORDER

STEP 10: Click on the top layer in the Layers palette to activate it, then Option-click on the New Layer icon to create a new layer and name it Merged. Hold down the Option key while choosing Merge Visible from the Layers Palette menu. This will merge all the visible layers into this new top layer. You can now use the Gaussian

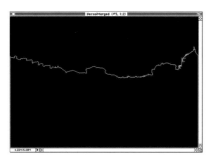

STEP 10: Use this mask to blur the edges of the border you have merged together.

Blur filter to reduce any remaining edge jagginess. Command-click on the Buildings layer mask to load a selection from it. Choose Select/Modify/Border and set the border to 4 pixels. This will make a selection of 4 pixels wide on either side of the border between the buildings and the sky, and also around the sides and bottom of the image. Now use the Lasso tool (L) with the Option key down to circle the sides and bottom of this selection and remove them, leaving only the selection along the border between the sky and buildings. Choose Select/Feather to feather this selection by 1 pixel. Now do Select/Hide Edges (Command-H) to hide this selection, and then do a Filter/Blur/ Gaussian Blur (Shift-F4) of .5 to blur the edge in the selected area. This should remove any remaining jagginess or color differences along the edge of the two images. Option-click on the Save Selection icon in the Channels palette to save this selection, and name it Border. You may want to use it again later.

SHARPENING AND SPOTTING

STEP 11: Now do Filter/Sharpen/Unsharp Mask (F4) of 150, 1.5, 4 to finalize this image. If the edge along the border becomes jaggy again, undo the sharpen and do a Load Selection of the channel you called Border. Choose Select/Inverse to select everything except for the border. Now redo the Unsharp mask and the border will be excluded from the sharpen. You might not want to sharpen the edge along the border because it might emphasize any imperfections generated from the merging of the two images. The Gaussian Blur and Unsharp Mask have to be done after the Merge Layers for their effects to be properly seen along the edge of the selection.

STEP 12: Zoom into the image at 100% or closer. Use the Rubber Stamp tool with a small brush to clone out any dust spots. It is best to do this after sharpening because sharpening can enhance dust spots that previously were not visible. Do Command-S to save this image along with all its layers and channels.

STEP 12: The Versailles image after removing the green tinge and lightening the edges and using the Rubber Stamp tool to remove any spots or blemishes. This version of the image was also sharpened using the Unsharp Mask filter with the 150, 1.5, 4 settings.

USING LAYERS TO APPLY FILTERS

By scanning, combining, color correcting, and sharpening, we've created a great straight photograph that we could use as our final image. If you would like to create a photo with a more surrealistic look, the following steps give you some ideas of how to use layers to enhance an image by applying filters with different opacities and blend modes.

STEP 13: Start with the final Versailles image from Step 12 of this chapter. Click on the Merged layer at the top and Option-drag it to the New Layer icon at the bottom of the Layers palette. Call this layer NoiseSky. Choose Filter/NoiseAdd Noise to create Gaussian noise with an amount of 25. This will add a grainy appearance to the image. Command-click on the Buildings layer mask in the Layers palette to load the mask as a selection, then Option-click on the Layer Mask icon to add a layer mask to the NoiseSky layer. The Option-click inverts the mask and removes the buildings from this layer. Now you see only the noise in the sky.

STEP 14: Option-drag the Merged layer to the New Layer icon in the Layers palette and call this layer UM500,10,0. We are going to apply the Unsharp Mask filter to this layer and use it as a special effect. Click on this new layer and drag it to the top of the Layers palette, then release when you see the black line above the NoiseSky layer.

STEP 15: Choose Filter/Sharpen/Unsharp Mask (F4) and set the parameters to 500 for the Amount, 10 for the Radius, and 0 for the Threshold. Click on OK to run the filter on this layer. This gives the photo a dramatic effect, but we may not want this effect to be completely applied.

STEP 15: The Layers and Channels palettes at the end of step 15. My final image uses this order of layers but has the opacity of the UM500,10,0 layer set to 25% and the Opacity of the NoiseSky layer set to 75% with its blend mode set to Overlay.

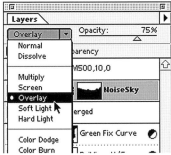

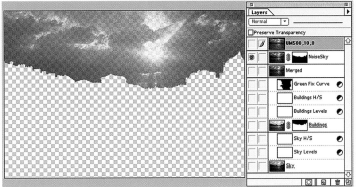

STEP 16: Now you have two copies of the final Merged layer with filters applied to them. You can now combine the Merged layer and these new filter layers to produce a variety of effects. What we want to do now is apply the mask/filter layers at different opacities and use different composite modes until we get the effect we want. The noise filter was a little bit too grainy, so I changed the NoiseSky Blend mode to Overlay and its opacity to 75%. Since I had applied this layer using a mask of only the sky area, these changes affect only the sky. To see these changes, you need to turn off the eye icon on the UM500,10,0 layer.

STEP 16: Change the mode on the NoiseSky layer to Overlay and set the opacity to 75%.

STEP 17: The Unsharp Mask filter of 500,10,0 produced a dramatic effect, but what I wanted to do was use this effect to slightly dramatize the image but still leave it in a more natural state. To do this, I activated the UM500,10,0 layer by clicking on it, and then set its opacity to 25%.

STEP 18: You can also turn on or off a particular layer completely by turning on or off its Eye icon. This allows you to see what the image looks like with or without that layer applied. It also allows you to look at just one layer. Try turning off or on particular layers and see how it affects your final image. Try changing the opacity of different layers and also changing the composite modes.

STEP 18: To look at the NoiseSky layer only, Option-click on its Eye icon. The bottom part of this layer is removed by its layer mask, and the sky is partially transparent because the Opacity is set to 75%.

STEP 19: Besides changing the opacity and composite mode of your layers, you can also change the order of the layers. By applying the filters in different orders, you can change the appearance of the final effect. To change the order of a layer, just click on the layer that you want to move and drag it up or down to its new location. When the line between two layers becomes black, then you can release the mouse to drop your layer between these two. Try all these things out and see which variation you like best.

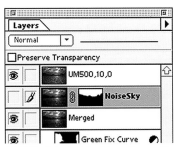

STEP 18: To look at the Merged layer with the Unsharp Mask layer applied at 25% on top, turn off the Eye icon for the NoiseSky layer.

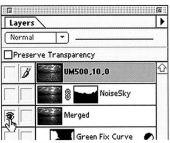

STEP 18: To look at the Merged layer only, Option-click on the Eye icon for that layer.

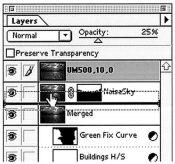

STEP 19: To move USM500 to between NoiseSky and Merged, click on USM500 and drag it downward. When you see the line between the other two layers turn black, let go.

The final version of this image along with the filter effects was produced by using three layers. The original Merged layer was the image from Step 12 of this example after we removed the green tinge and ran Unsharp Mask for basic sharpening. We then made a layer to add 75% of the noise filter to the sky using the Overlay Composite mode. The third and final layer adds 25% of the Unsharp Mask 500, 10, 0 to the entire image area. This makes the image more dramatic without taking away all the image detail that 100% of Unsharp Mask would have removed.

HANDS-ON SESSION: The Band

Create a composite of the band, Only Human, from non-matching original files using channels, layers, and graduated masks; color correct and adjust these images to match as closely as possible.

When you are compositing photographs together, you need to either color correct each of them separately before you composite them, or you can combine them first and then color correct the final image as one. The Layers feature in Photoshop 4 will allow us to combine the images first and still color correct each of them separately after compositing them. This will allow us to do the color corrections while we are looking at how the images are combining. To do this example, you will be using the Photoshop 4 Tool palette, the Channels and Layers palettes, the Info palette, and sometimes the Color palette. Refer to the chapter on navigating to learn the most efficient ways to use these windows. Refer to "Setting System and Photoshop Preferences" to see how to set up Command keys to open and close them. You will also be using the Levels and Curves tools, and should have already gone through the Grand Canyon chapter, which explains their basic functionality.

SETTING THINGS UP

STEP 1: Open the three files, Johnny, Chris, and Beth from the folder The Band. Place them in order with Johnny on the left, Chris in the middle, and Beth on the right. This is the order in which we will composite the photos together.

STEP 2: Click on Chris to make him the active window, and double-click on the Background Layer and rename it to Chris. By renaming Chris' background layer, we converted it into a normal layer. Adding Canvas to a normal layer will make the extra canvas transparent versus the canvas of the background color we would have gotten if we had left it as a background layer. Transparent canvas won't effect the histograms of Chris when color correcting, but canvas of the background color would. Now go to Image/Canvas Size (F8) to change the width of Chris to be three times the original width. We will be placing Johnny at Chris' left and Beth at Chris' right, so keep the gray area in the middle of the grid, which will add the extra white space evenly to either side of Chris. Just triple the value in the width field and click on OK. Now save this version of Chris in Photoshop format and call it TheBand.

BLENDING JOHNNY INTO CHRIS

STEP 3: Use the Move tool to drag and drop Johnny on top of Chris. Just click on the center of Johnny's image and drag the curser over the top of Chris' image, and then release the mouse button. This adds Johnny as a new layer on top of Chris. You could close the Johnny file now, if you are short on memory.

STEP 4: Double-click on the new layer in the Layers palette and call it Johnny. Use the Move tool (V, or press the Command key) to move Johnny over to the left of Chris. Click on the Add Layer Mask icon at the bottom of the Layers palette to add a layer mask to Johnny's layer. Click on the Black/White Default Colors icon, or type D to force the foreground color to white and the background color to black. D gives us white in the foreground (which means select this image) and black in the background (don't select this image) when working on a Mask channel. When working on an image layer, D gives us a black foreground and a white background. This difference was added to Photoshop 4, so old-time users have to make sure they know this change from older Photoshop versions where D always gave you a black foreground and a white background.

STEP 5: Double-click on the Gradient tool and choose Reset Tool from the Gradient Tool Options menu. This will reset all the default options in the Gradient tool. Use the tool while holding down the Shift key to create a blend from white to black starting just to the right of Johnny's face and dragging right to the right edge of the Johnny layer. The Shift key will constrain the blend to horizontal. You should let go of the tool when

STEP 3: Using the Move tool to drag and drop Johnny on top of Chris.

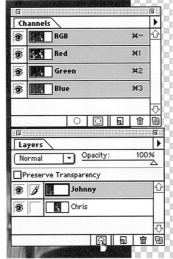

STEP 4: Adding a layer mask to Johnny's layer.

STEP 5: Creating the gradient that will blend Johnny into Chris.

STEP 5: What Johnny and Chris look like after the gradient is created and before Johnny is moved over.

STEP 6: What Johnny and Chris will look like after Johnny is moved over.

you reach the right edge of Johnny. Don't go beyond this right edge or this image will not fade completely out and you'll see a faint line. In the layer mask, you have defined the area where Johnny and Chris will blend together. Where the layer mask is black, Johnny's image is completely gone and where it is white, Johnny's image is completely there.

STEP 6: Use the Move tool (V or Command) and slowly drag Johnny to the right until the transparent area between Johnny and Chris disappears completely. If you find that you are having trouble making subtle movements with the mouse, you can use the arrow keys to move your selection one pixel at a time (Shift-arrow moves your selection 10 pixels at a time). We'll color correct Johnny after we add Beth to the image.

BLENDING BETH INTO CHRIS

STEP 7: Switch to the image of Beth and use the Move tool to drag and drop Beth on top of Chris. Move her completely to the right of Chris. Double-click on the new layer and call it Beth. Add a layer mask to her layer by using the left-most icon at the bottom of the Layers palette. Use the Gradient tool (G) and click to the left of her face and drag to the left edge (not beyond) with the Shift key down to blend out this part of her image. Use the Move tool (V or hold Command key down) to move her to the left until she blends in nicely with Chris. You can always change how Beth or Johnny blend with Chris by just using the Gradient tool again in their layer masks and then moving their layers as needed.

REMOVING PICTURE ELEMENTS

STEP 8: Press Command-0 to zoom out and see the entire Chris canvas. Type C to get the Cropping tool and then click and drag a rectangle around the edge of the three band members. Click and drag in the handles (the little squares around the edge) to fine-tune the cropping box, making sure all the white or transparent borders are removed. Now press Return (or Enter) to do the crop. You now have the three images blended together and cropped in their final size. Press Command-S at this point to save the file on top of the existing version of TheBand. Now you can revert to this version of the image if you are not happy with the following changes.

STEP 9: At this point, we have a problem with Beth's image, since the amplifier covers up Chris' arm and his cymbal. Click on the right-hand column of Beth's layer in the Layers palette to activate (highlight) Beth's layer. This allows you to work on Beth's layer without changing Johnny or Chris. If you click on the Eye icon of Beth's layer, it will turn off and you will see that Chris' layer is black underneath the spot where the amplifier is added beside Beth. If we could just remove the area of Beth's image where the amplifier is and see Chris' image in its place, that would solve our problem. To do this, we will use the existing layer mask. Click on the Eye icon of Beth again to make her layer visible. Her layer should also be the active layer, the one that is highlighted. Click on the layer mask to the right of Beth's layer thumbnail. Arrange things on your monitor so you can see the entire Layers palette and the entire Channels palette at the same time. Depending on the state of the Layers palette, it is important that you understand which channel(s) are actually being edited versus the channels that are only being viewed. Only the highlighted channels can be changed. You will notice that the Eye icons are on for Red, Green, and Blue, but the layer mask is active (highlighted). Painting now will affect the mask.

STEP 10: Anything that is black in the layer mask will make the corresponding part of Beth's layer not show. This is how the gradient removed her left side. Use the Paintbrush tool with 100% opacity and a large brush to paint over the amplifier with black as the foreground color. As you paint, the painted parts of Beth's layer will disappear and Chris' layer will show through from below. Paint over the amplifier and also over Chris' shirt and arm in the area where Beth's black background overlaps Chris. Now type a 5 to set the brush to 50% opacity, and then switch to a soft edge brush, and use this to blend in the two backgrounds above where the amplifier used to be. As you move further away from the amplifier, you may want to use only 30% opacity; to do this, type a 3. Blend the two images around the edges of the area you removed. If a transparent area starts to appear as you paint, you have reached the edge of the Chris layer's data. You will have to click on the Chris layer and clone (with the Rubber Stamp tool) some of the background area beyond the edge so it can replace Beth's background in the layer above. Now Option-click on the layer mask and you can view the mask without the layers. Notice how the black and gray areas in the mask cause the two layers to blend.

STEP 11: Option-click back on Beth's layer thumbnail if you want to edit the layer with the mask applied. Notice that all three RGB channels are now highlighted (active) in the Channels palette. This shows you that if you edit anything, these channels, in Beth's layer are the things that the editing will be change. You will still see all the channels and layers that have their Eye icons turned on.

COLOR CORRECTING THE IMAGE

STEP 12: Notice that the coloration on Johnny is much redder than that of Chris or Beth. He was standing under a red light when photographed. Since he is so different, we should color correct him to make him look closer to the others before proceeding with overall color correction. All these photos were taken without flash, using ASA 1600 film. Click on the right column of Johnny's layer, making it active (highlighted) and allowing us to edit this layer while still seeing the others. Click in the right-hand column in the Channels palette of each of the channels: Red (Command-1), Green (Command-2), and Blue (Command-3). You will notice that the Red channel of Johnny has lots of detail but the Green and Blue channels have very little detail, especially when compared to those channels of Beth and Chris. This is why Johnny looks so red and so flat. Since

STEP 10: The amplifier before it is removed by the layer mask.

STEP 10: The amplifier after it has been removed by the layer mask.

STEP 10: Option-click on the layer mask to see it by itself.

STEP 10: With Beth's layer mask activated, edits will change only the mask, which will add or subtract things to the appearance of Beth's layer without actually changing her layer. Since the Eye icons are selected on all the layers and all the channels, you will see everything while this is happening. Only the activated (highlighted) channel is actually changed.

STEP 11: With Beth's layer activated, edits will change the actual contents of Beth's layer; only the highlighted channels. Since the Eye icons are selected on all the layers and in all the channels, you will see everything while this is happening.

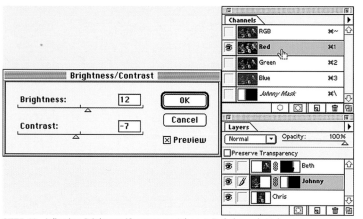

STEP 13: Adjusting Brightness/Contrast on Johnny's Red channel. Make sure your Layers and Channels palettes look like this.

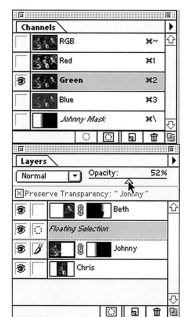

STEP 14: Change the opacity of the floating selection to about 52% or until Johnny looks similar to Beth and Chris in the Green channel.

Johnny doesn't have detail in the Green and Blue channels, we will first have to add some detail there to be able to color correct him in the normal way using Levels or Curves.

STEP 13: We are going to modify the individual channels of Johnny to make them look more like the channels of Chris and Beth. This will make his color in RGB a lot closer, and will add detail to the Green and Blue channels so we can color correct him further using the color correction tools. Click on the Johnny layer to make sure it is the active layer. Choose Red (Command-1) from the Channels palette. Use the Image/Adjust/Brightness/Contrast slider and move the contrast to the left to about –7 and the brightness to the right to about +12 to make the Red channel of Johnny have similar brightness and contrast to the Red channels of Chris and Beth. You want the Preview button in Brightness/Contrast on so you can see the changes to Johnny without any screen changes happening to Chris and Beth. Click on OK in the Brightness/Contrast tool. Type a D to get the default colors. Choose RGB, Command-~, from the Channels palette to select the Red, Green, and Blue channels of Johnny. Choose Select/All, Command-A, from the Select menu, followed by Edit/Stroke, and stroke the border with a 100% opacity, normal stroke of 4 pixels on the center of the selection. This will draw a black 4-pixel border around the entire image in Johnny's layer. Now choose the Red channel of Johnny again (Command-1) and do a Select/All followed by Edit/Copy to make a copy of the Red channel of Johnny. The black border needed to be drawn to remove transparency from the right two-thirds of the channel, so when we paste this channel on top of the Green channel, it goes down in exactly the same place. If we had not done this, the Copy would have only copied the left one-third of Johnny's Red channel (the non-transparent part) and then the paste on the Green channel, in the next step, would not line up correctly.

STEP 14: Switch the Channels palette to the Green channel (Command-2). Paste Johnny's Red channel on top of Johnny's Green channel. In the Layers palette, change the opacity of the floating selection (Johnny's pasted Red channel) to somewhere around 52%. Change the opacity until Johnny's Green channel looks like and blends well with Chris' and Beth's. Look at the tone and brightness of Johnny's face and also make sure the backgrounds look similar as they blend together.

STEP 15: Switch to the Blue channel (Command-3) and notice that the floating selection got dropped and made permanent. Now paste Johnny's Red channel (still in the Copy Buffer) on top of the Blue channel and adjust the opacity to make Johnny's blue look like the Blue channel of Chris and Beth. Set it to somewhere around 18.

STEP 16: Using the Channels palette again, switch back to the RGB channel (Command-~). This will drop the floating selection. Now Johnny should look much closer to Chris and Beth than when we started. Johnny is never going to look as good colorwise as Chris and Beth since we are making most of his color from the Red channel. Don't try to be a perfectionist here, just get them close and understand the process for future corrections on your own projects. Now use the Cropping tool (C) to crop the 4-pixel black border from around the image. Make a selection just inside this border and press Return to crop. Now that there is color information in each of Johnny's channels, you can use the other color correction tools to make him seem even closer in color to Chris and Beth. At this point, I used the Curves settings, which improved Johnny considerably.

I started the curve adjustments by entering Curves (Command-M), and then using the Load button to load the LockDownCurve. This curve allows you to measure specific areas in the image using the Eyedropper, then make a subtle adjustment to just that area. For more information on using Curves and the LockDownCurve, refer to "Grand Canyon—Final Tweaks" and "Kansas—Final Tweaks." The change made in the RGB curve was to darken the background of Johnny (measure the top left corner area) to make it match the other images better. The adjustment to the Red channel was to make Johnny's face (measure his face) a little redder. The adjustments to the Green and Blue channels were to remove a purple tone from the background behind Johnny (measure the top left corner area). The adjustments that you make may be different depending on exactly what you did to Johnny when working with the channels.

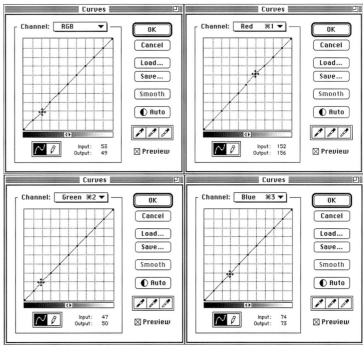

STEP 16: I used these curve settings, called JohnnyFixCurve, to adjust Johnny to make him look more like Beth and Chris. These settings are in the Extra Info Files folder for this chapter on the CD. Your changes may be different if you used different Brightness/Contrast and opacities on Johnny.

STEP 17: Once Johnny looks as close as possible to Beth and Chris, you now want to do overall color correction for the entire image. You have the choice here of merging the channels first so there is just one layer and then correcting the image as one unit, or correcting each image layer separately while looking at the merged image to make sure the corrections match. The second approach gives you more control and demonstrates an advantage of leaving the image in layers until the last possible minute. Do a File/Save As to save this version as TheBand.2.

TheBand after Step 16 and before final overall color correction.

OVERALL COLOR CORRECTION

STEP 18: Now we will do the standard overall color corrections to each of the three layers, matching them as we go. You will adjust the overall contrast and color balance of each of the layers using Levels, with the techniques discussed in the Grand Canyon chapter. Click on the Chris layer (right column) to make it the active layer. Choose Command-L for Levels and look at the histogram of Chris. Since Chris is in the middle, let's first set the white and black points. Use the Option key, as described in the Grand Canyon chapter, to decide where to set the white and black points. I set the white to the brightest place on his shirt using the Highlight Eyedropper and the black by moving the Input Shadow slider on each of the Red, Green, and Blue channels to the right until it reaches the histogram data for each color. I decided not to use the Shadow Eyedropper to set the black because the blacks in this image are not very consistent. By moving the Shadow Eyedroppers over to where the data starts in each color, you get a definite dark value. You then need to look at and measure the black values on the screen and adjust them so each of Chris, Beth, and Johnny have a visually matching black. I actually moved each of Chris' black values over 5 more points to the right. Once the overall white and black are set, adjust the Input Brightness/Contrast slider in RGB mode, and then go back to the individual channels to correct for color casts. Review the Grand Canyon and Kansas chapters if you have any questions on overall color correction.

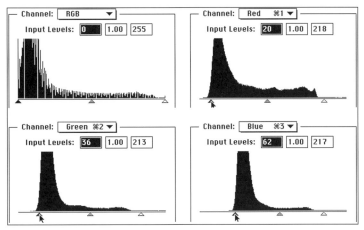

STEP 18: My final Levels color correction settings for Chris. Yours may be different.

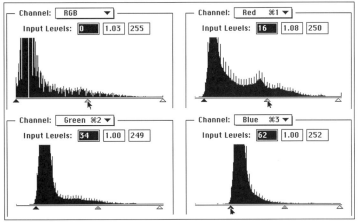

STEP 20: My final Levels color correction settings for Beth. Yours may be different.

STEP 19: Click on the Save button to save the Levels changes you want to make to Chris; call it ChrisFinalLevels. Now Cancel from Levels and Command-click on the New Layer icon, or choose New Adjustment Layer from the Layers Palette menu, to add a Levels adjustment layer to Chris' layer. Name it Chris Levels and set the type menu to Levels. Click the Group with Previous Layer option so that the adjustments you make here will affect only Chris' layer. Using adjustment layers here will allow us to go back and change the Levels adjustment on any of the three images as many times as needed without damaging the data of the image, because the changes are not actually made until the image is flattened. Click on the Load button to load the changes we just saved at the end of working on the Chris layer in Levels. Now click on OK. We made the changes in Levels first because adjustment layers don't allow you to use Video LUT Animation to instantly see before and after while evaluating subtle color changes to a layer. For more info on Video LUT Animation, see "The Grand Canyon."

STEP 20: Now click on Beth's layer to color correct it next. Command-click on the New Layer icon and add an adjustment layer of Type Levels that is grouped to the Beth layer and called BethLevels. The initial Photoshop 4 release had a bug where Grouped Levels adjustment layers showed the histogram of all previous layers on initial entry. The work around for this is to immediately click on OK in the adjustment layer, then double-click on its name to re-enter Levels. Now you will see the correct histogram. This has been fixed in version 4.0.1. Since we want to see the changes to Beth in relation to Chris, we will have to work with the Preview button on in Levels this time. I set the white point with the Highlight Eyedropper in RGB on Beth's forehead, but not at the absolute brightest spot there. You don't want her whole forehead washed out, but a little bright spot there looks good. Remember, you set the white point at the last place where you see detail, and everything brighter than that will be pure white with no dots. If you set it on the absolute brightest spot, there will be no specular high-light and that is not really what you want here. I set the black on Beth in the same way I did on Chris by moving the Input Shadow sliders for each color channel to the right until the data starts. I then adjusted the color balance on Beth to match Chris— his face, lighting, and background. Click on OK to finalize the Levels changes. Beth may be further improved by using Hue/Saturation to clean up the yellows in her hair. Some of the yellow hair looked green to me, but adding magenta in Levels messed up the rest of the image. I did this again by Command-clicking again on the New Layer icon to add a new Hue/Saturation adjustment layer Grouped to the Previous Layer(s) so only Beth was changed. Now just make the changes to Beth's Hue and Saturation in Yellow and click on OK.

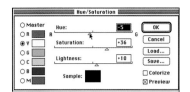

STEP 20: Final Hue/Saturation/Lightness changes for the yellows in Beth.

STEP 21: Now we need to adjust Johnny to make him look like Chris and Beth. As usual, Johnny will be the hardest image to adjust. Again, you want to switch the active layer you are working on to Johnny by clicking in the rightmost column in the Johnny layer. Now, again Command-click on the New Layer icon in the Layers palette to add a Levels adjustment layer Grouped with the Johnny layer. The only white point on Johnny is the reflection in his guitar, and this is pretty much a specular highlight. It is most important to make sure that the lighting on Johnny's face matches Chris and Beth as much as possible. To set the high-light, I moved the Input Highlight sliders for each of the Red, Green, and Blue channels over to the left until they were at about 225. This made Johnny's face look the best. I set the shadows on Johnny again by moving the Input Shadow sliders over to the right to where the data started and then a little bit more, moving each slider by the same increments. Then it's back to RGB to adjust the Brightness/Contrast slider in the middle and at the same time moving the Input Shadow slider (RGB) to the right to darken the shad-ows a bit more in all colors. Go back and forth between these two sliders so the shadows and the brightness/contrast looks like the best match with

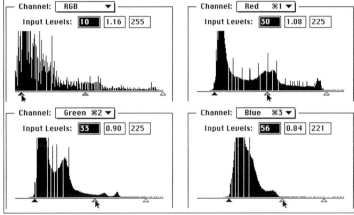

STEP 21: My final Levels color correction settings for Johnny, called JohnnyFinalLevels, in the Extra Info Files for this chapter on the CD. Notice how little data there is in the Blue chan-nel here. Your settings for Johnny will probably be different because each of us have already adjusted Johnny in a slightly different way.

Chris and Beth. Remember to leave the Preview button on. Now go back into the individual color channels and make any color cast adjustments and then press the OK button to finalize your Levels changes to Johnny.

STEP 22: Johnny's face is sort of flat compared to Beth and Chris, and his background doesn't match either. To fix this, click on the Johnny Levels layer and then Command-click on the New Layer icon to add a new Color Balance adjustment layer above Johnny levels and Grouped to Johnny Levels. Turn on Preserve Luminosity in Color Balance and then add lots of red and magenta to make a stronger version of the highlight color you will add to Johnny's face. Click on OK in Color Balance. Now choose Edit/Fill and fill the layer mask of this adjustment layer with black to remove this color change everywhere. Type a D to get the default colors of White for the foreground and Black for the background. Now airbrush with white at 5% Opacity with the Airbrush tool using a soft brush to add red highlights to Johnny's face. Wherever you paint with white in the mask, the Color Balance change will be applied. Just slowly add the reddish highlights to Johnny's face to better match that

---

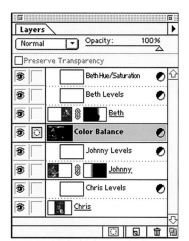

STEP 22: With this layer and adjustment layer setup, we can go back and change the color of each of the Band members as many times as we like. Since the changes are happening in an adjustment layer, the actual data in the digital file will not have permanent changes to it until we create a flattened version of the image.

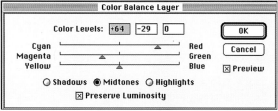

STEP 22: The settings I used for the Johnny Color Balance layer.

of Chris and Beth. In the end, I noticed a few greenish areas in the upper-middle background of Chris, and also on his shirt, so I Option-clicked on the line between the Johnny Levels layer and this new Color Balance layer to degroup this from Johnny Levels. I was then able to paint with white in the mask above Chris to remove these greenish tones also. To use this layer to alter anything in the Beth layers, I would have had to drag it above the Beth layers as well. I didn't do that, though, because I didn't need to add any red tones to the Beth layers.

MAKING FINAL ADJUSTMENTS

STEP 23: Now you have completed the compositing and color correction steps. Use File/Save As to save a version of this image and call it TheBandFinalLayers. You can use this version to show your clients the image, and you can also use the Move tool to move Johnny and Beth up and down and in closer to Chris if you want variations. If you want to move Beth and Johnny out farther away from Chris, drag Chris' layer to the New Layer icon at the bottom of the Layers palette. This will make a copy of Chris' layer right above the current one. Select the bottom version of Chris and fill it with Chris' background color. Now, if you move Johnny or Beth outward, instead of the transparent halo you got before, you just get more of Chris' background and it looks pretty natural.

STEP 24: Before sharpening and spotting this image, you need to choose Flatten Image from the Layers palette pop-up menu. This will merge everything back into a single document that you can save as a TIFF, EPS, or in some other format. Save it under a different name if you want to still be able to play with your layered

STEP 22: The final mask used for the Color Balance layer.

version. Now that you have just one layer, use Filter/Sharpen/Unsharp Mask to sharpen the image and then use the Rubber Stamp tool to remove any scratches or spots or imperfections in the image. There is a hairline scratch from the top to the bottom of the image just to the right of Johnny's face. Beth has a black hole in the corner of her lip and there are various dust spots and lines. These all need to be removed. For further information on sharpening and spotting, see "The Grand Canyon—Final Tweaks," and "Kansas—Final Tweaks."

STEP 25: Save the final version of the file. You can compare your different versions of this image to the ones of the same name that I created. They are in the Extra Info Files folder.

STEP 25: The final completed version of TheBand.

HANDS-ON SESSION: The McNamaras

Using adjustment layers and layer masks to color correct and composite the McNamaras family portrait where we need to move six smiling faces into the final image to create one where everyone is smiling.

I was an only child, so while growing up it was always more fun to go over to the McNamaras and play with their six kids. Now, as adults, we still get together a lot and I have had the joy of taking two of their five-year family portraits. Taking a family portrait of this many people, and especially this many kids along with their parents, is not the easiest task. I also wanted to use my 4x5 camera so there would be the maximum amount of detail in the image. All the kids are wiggling around, so it's hard to get them to smile at the camera, and then the parents often look down and give directions to their children at just that moment when all the children are actually looking at the camera. I knew this would be difficult to do with the 4x5, so I also brought along my trusty Canon F1 and shot two rolls of 35. With the 35mm stuff, I actually did get one picture where everyone was smiling and looking at the camera. That was the shot we used for the McNamara family. Still, though, I wanted to make a 4x5 version, because it would have so much more detail. Scans, with the Leaf 45 scanner, were made of enough of the 4x5 images that I had at least one smiling face of each person. Here we are going to composite all of them together to create the family portrait where everyone is smiling!

STEP 1: Make sure that the version of Photoshop you are going to use for this example is already running. From the Finder or File Manager, open the McNamaras folder and do Select All on all the files that end in JPG. The files for this example were JPEG-compressed. Choose File/Open from the Finder and all of them will open into Photoshop at once. If this doesn't work on your system, just open each of the files using the File/Open command in Photoshop. Choose the file McNamarasOrig from the Window menu and put it in Full Screen Mode by clicking on the middle icon at the bottom of the Tool palette. Type C to bring up the Cropping tool and crop out any black borders around the image. Choose File/Save As and save it as McNamarasPortrait.

The original McNamaras image before color correction or the addition of the smiling faces.

STEP 2: Choose Image/Adjust/Levels to start the overall correction for the main McNamaras image. We are going to do this in Levels, on the layer versus an adjustment layer, so we can use Video LUT Animation in the initial correction, then we will save the Levels settings, cancel from Levels, and load those settings into a Levels adjustment layer. Go through the basic levels adjustment, which you learned about in "The Grand Canyon" chapter. You may want to review that chapter if you are not sure what to do here. I used the Shadow and Highlight Eyedroppers to set the highlight on one of the white chairs and the shadow in the darkest leaves along the top of the photo. You can load my levels settings, called LevelsOne, from the CD if you want to check them out. When you are happy with the Overall Levels settings, click on the Save button in Levels and save these settings in a file called MyLevelsOne, then hit the Cancel button to exit Levels. Now Command-click on the New Layer icon to create an adjustment layer of Type Levels, and call it McLevels. Make sure you turn on the Group with Previous Layer option, then click on the Load button to load the LevelsOne setting you just saved. Now choose OK. We did this using an adjustment layer, so that we would have the option of changing it later after we get all the faces composited in. Now create another adjustment layer of type Hue Saturation, also Grouped with the Previous layer, and call it McHueSat. Do the Overall Saturation adjustments for the McNamaras family like we did in the Grand Canyon chapter. My adjustments are called HueSatMc, in case you would like to use the Load button in the Hue/Saturation dialog box to check them out. Choose OK in the Hue/Saturation dialog box when you are happy with the added saturation and tonal changes.

ADDING THE SMILING FACES

STEP 3: Type M to switch to the Move tool, then use the Window menu to switch one at a time to each of the smiling face images, and then drag and drop it with Move on top of the same person's face in your McNamarasPortrait image underneath. If you put the cursor on the nose in the smiling version, and then drag to the same person's nose in the McNamaras layer and release the mouse button at that point, you will have a good start on lining up the two heads. Go ahead and drag and drop each smiling person into their own layer, giving that layer the name for that person. The names of the smiling people's files are the actual names of that particular person. After dragging each person into their own layer, you can File/Close (Command-W) the file for that person. When you have moved all six people into their approximate position, go ahead and press Command-S to save the McNamarasPortrait with all their layers. Your Layers palette should now look like this one here.

STEP 4: Some of the smiling layers will overlap each other, but don't worry about that now, because we are going to work on each one of them separately to integrate it into the image in a custom way. Turn off the Eye icons for all the smiling face layers except for Jackey. You still want the Eye icons on for the McNamaras layer and its adjustment layers. Click on the Jackey layer to make it active, then type a 5 to set its opacity to 50%. You can now see 50% of the Jackey layer and 50% of the original image of Jackey underneath. Use the Move tool (V) to move the Jackey layer around a bit until you figure out which 50% comes from this layer. The face in the Jackey layer is a bit bigger than the original face underneath. Use the Move tool to line up the glasses and lips on each layer as best you can. Now choose Layer/Free Transform (Command-T) and use the Free Transform command to scale this Jackey layer exactly and move it into the exact position above the original head below. Remember to hold down the

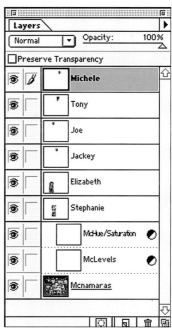

STEP 3: The Layers palette after moving all the smiling faces into the work file.

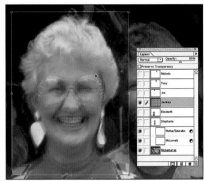

STEP 4: Here you see the two Jackeys before they are lined up. Pick an absolute position in the center of the image area, like her glasses corner here, put the cursor on that position, and then drag the cursor to the same position in the other layer to move the Jackey layer and line them up. You can use the arrow keys to scroll by one pixel and fine-tune the positioning. After you adjust the position, you may have to rescale a bit, readjust a bit, and so on, until you get it right.

STEP 5: Make a Lasso selection (feather 2) of the inner area of Jackey's face then click on the Layer Mask icon to create a layer mask only showing that part of the Jackey layer.

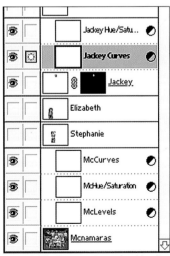

STEP 5: The Layers palette after blending Jackey's better smile into her previous head.

STEP 4: Here is how the two Jackeys look after they are lined up.

Shift key while clicking and dragging in one of the corner handles to make your scaling be proportional. To move the layer while in Free Transform, just click and drag in the middle of the box that defines the current image or use the arrow keys for fine adjustment. Press Return to end the Free Transform.

STEP 5: Type L to bring up the Lasso tool, then press Return to bring up its Options palette. Now type a 2, then press Return again to set the feather at 2. Now make a selection around the inside of Jackey's face. This is the part of her face we are going to use from the Jackey layer. Now click on the Layer Mask icon (the left-most one at the bottom of the Layers palette). You may notice a color difference between the skin and hair on the Jackey layer and the skin and hair in the original image. To fix this, add a Levels or Curves adjustment layer above the Jackey layer and grouped with the Jackey layer. I added Curves and Hue/Saturation adjustment layers above the Jackey layer and used them to match the color and contrast of Jackey's face and hair. I also added a Curves adjustment layer above the McNamaras layer, and I used it to add a little contrast to the McNamaras layer to better match Jackey. We may have to modify all of these as we add other smiling faces to the composite. After you get the colors to match fairly well, type a B to switch to the Paintbrush tool and then click on the Layer Mask for the Jackey layer. Type a 0 to get 100% opacity, then use a soft brush to paint in the layer mask to blend the two faces together even more. Paint with black to include more of the original Jackey face and with white to include more of the face from the Jackey layer. Sometimes you might want to paint with 50% opacity to blend the two images together. I also used the Rubber Stamp tool to clone away a little of Jackey's hair at the top of her head in the McNamaras layer.

STEP 6: The original Jackey actually had a pretty good smile, but I like the one from the Jackey layer better, you can now choose the one you like best by just turning the Eye icon on and off for the Jackey layer. The original image of Joe was definitely not smiling very much. Turn on the Eye icon for the Joe layer and you'll see that the new Joe definitely has a better smile. Now go through the sequence of adjustments you did for Jackey in Steps 4 and 5, but this time do them for Joe and the Joe layer. You'll find that the area of each person's face that you have to change is different. Pull up the McNamarasLayers file from the Extra Info Folder in the McNamaras example on the CD. This is my version of the final image. You can look at each of my layer masks and my adjustment layers to see what I did. Press Command-S to save your McNamarasPortrait file.

STEP 7: Let's do Tony next, and since he's actually standing behind Jackey, click on the Tony layer in the Layers palette and drag it down underneath the Jackie layer. Now do Steps 4 and 5 for the Tony layer. Don't worry about any overlap between Tony and Jackey; that will go away once you create the layer mask for the Tony layer.

To get Tony's head to look right in the composite, I ended up adding first a Levels, then a Hue-Saturation, and finally, a Curves adjustment layer above Tony and grouped with Tony's layer. To the right of Tony is Michele, so turn on the Eye icon for her layer and do her after Tony. To get her to look right, I had to include her neck as well as her head. For the color correction on her, I just used a Levels adjustment layer. In a similar way as you did Tony and Michele, now you should turn on the Eye icon for the Stephanie layer and blend in the slightly better expression for Stephanie. Do Steps 4 and 5 for her. I just had to add a Levels adjustment layer to get her facial color to match the original. Now might be a good time to save the file (Command-S).

STEP 7: Before Joe, Jackey, Tony and Michele's heads are replaced by smiling versions.

ADDING THE SMILING ELIZABETH

STEP 8: The last person who needs a better smile is Elizabeth. Since her feet were in sort of a strange position in the original and she was sitting in the front, I decided to replace her entire body. The best way I found to line up the two images of Elizabeth was to make the chair she is sitting in line up

STEP 7: After the smiling heads are installed.

between the two shots. Since there is quite a bit of movement between the two images of her, my initial Lasso selection included more than just the new Elizabeth. It also included the old Elizabeth. We will need to get rid of all of her from the original photo, so we might as well start out by seeing how the locations where she was in the original photo look if used from the new photo in those areas. After making your Lasso selection, click on the Layer Mask icon to add a layer mask that includes only the selected area, then set the opacity on the Elizabeth layer back to 100%. Now you need to use the Paintbrush tool in the layer mask, painting in either black, to remove the Elizabeth layer, or in white, to add parts of the Elizabeth layer. Do this until you get the two layers to merge the best that you can.

STEP 9: You will find there are some fringe areas that won't work from either the Elizabeth layer or the original McNamara layer. You will have to use the Rubber Stamp tool (S) to clone some of what you need in those areas. Before you do this though, go ahead and add a Grouped Levels adjustment layer and get the color of the Elizabeth layer to match the original photo. A good place to compare is the white chair that Stephanie is sitting on behind and to the right of Elizabeth. Part of the armrest for this chair will come from the original image and part of it will come from the Elizabeth layer. Get those whites to match and you will have the color pretty close. I also added a Hue/Saturation adjustment layer above Levels and Grouped with Elizabeth to saturate her colors a bit. Now that the colors match pretty well, use the Rubber Stamp tool to clone the areas that won't work from either layer. For me, this was the top right edge of the lower left corner of Stephanie's dress, which came from the Elizabeth layer, and little sections of the pants on the boy to the left of Elizabeth. Remember, the Rubber Stamp tool lets you clone from one layer onto another. Just have the first layer active when you Option-click to define where you are cloning from, and then activate the layer you are

STEP 8: The initial Lasso selection for the Elizabeth layer with Opacity at 50%.

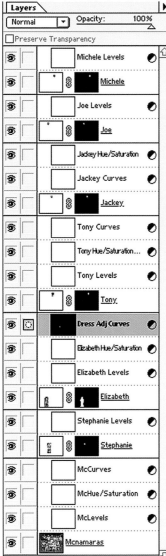

Michele Levels

Michele

Joe Levels

Joe

Jackey Hue/Saturation

Jackey Curves

Jackey

Tony Curves

Tony Hue/Saturation...

Tony Levels

Tony

Dress Adj Curves

Elizabeth Hue/Saturation

Elizabeth Levels

Elizabeth

Stephanie Levels

Stephanie

McCurves

McHue/Saturation

McLevels

Mcnamaras

STEP 10: The final Layers palette after working on the new image of Elizabeth.

cloning to before you begin to paint in the clone. To get the part of Stephanie's dress that I used from the Elizabeth layer to match, I Lassoed that part of the dress and then added a Curves adjustment layer (again, Grouped with the Elizabeth layer), and used it to match the two dresses. Since I had the dress area selected when I Command-clicked on the New Layer icon to create the adjustment layer, this automatically created a layer mask that allowed the Curves adjustments only in that dress area.

STEP 10: You now have all your smiling faces added and you have color corrected and masked them to match as best you can. Now it is time look at the image as a whole and further tweak the color or contrast of any head that doesn't seem quite right. A particular person may seem slightly off color or have a different brightness or contrast than the rest. You might also decide to adjust the contrast or color balance of the entire McNamara layer. Since you did all your color adjustments using adjustment layers, you can double-click on the name of any of them and change the adjustment as many times as you like without degrading the original pixels in any of the layers. The final color changes to the pixels will not be made until you flatten the image; even better, use File/Save A Copy to create a flattened version. When I zoomed out and looked at the image, I ended up changing the Joe and Jackey heads a little to make them fit in better with the rest of the faces. I used Joe's Levels adjustment layer to make his face a little darker and warmer, and I used Jackey's Curves adjustment layer to make her face a little warmer. My final version, called McNamarasLayers, is on the CD in the Extra Info Folder for this version. If you're having a problem with anything, pull up my version and see how I did it. Press Command-S to save your file when you finish it. Before printing this, I did Image/Duplicate to create a merged version, and then Unsharp Mask to sharpen it—and of course I converted it to CMYK.

The final McNamaras image after color correction and the addition of all the smiling faces. This was sharpened with Unsharp mask at 150 percent, Radius of 1.5, and Threshold of 3.

HANDS-ON SESSION: Night Cab Ride in Manhattan

*Learn the many feature variations of Layers
as we show you the creation of the
image, Night Cab Ride in Manhattan.*

In this example, we are going to be compositing many different images using the Layers features of Photoshop 4. All the images used in this example were taken by Barry during one cab ride from uptown Manhattan down Broadway to the Lower East Side. The film was Kodak Lumiere X and the scans are all Photo CD scans done at Palmer Photographic in Sacramento, California. The image of the cab and the New York Convention Center started as a 1024x1536-pixel, Photo CD scan, and all the other images started as 512x768-pixel Photo CD scans. Some of these were resampled up to 1024x1536 pixels, which is the final canvas size for this image. Barry wanted most of the neon signs to have sort of a soft effect, so resampling the smaller files up achieved this.

In this example, we will create this final version of Night Cab Ride in Manhattan with its many layers.

Since this is a long chapter and not really about color correcting, many of the files have been color corrected ahead of time. If you are not sure how to do some of the steps mentioned here, you should refer to "Layers, Adjustment Layers, and Layer Masks," which shows you the basic concepts and functions for working with layers.

CREATING YOUR BASE IMAGE

STEP 1: Open the Canon file in the Night Cab Ride folder, which is a picture of Times Square where the Canon sign is the most prevalent. This file is already 1536x1024 pixels, which is the final canvas size. Choose F10, assuming you have ArtistKeys keys installed, to bring up the Layers palette. Double-click on the Background layer and rename it Canon. Option-click on the New Layer icon in the middle at the bottom of the Layers palette and name the new layer All Black. Type a D to force the foreground color to black and the background color to white. Choose Select/All (Command-A) to select all of the All Black layer and then Option-Delete to fill it with black. Choose Select/None (Command-D) and then click on this new layer and move

The final Layers palette for this image with the Eye icons for the accepted layers on.

215

it to the bottom of the Layer palette below the Canon layer. In this example, we will add various layers of neon using the Lighter and Screen Blend modes, and we'll remove parts of some layers, so if we have pure black as the bottom layer, we can be sure to create a pitch black night effect. Choose File/Save As and save this as Night-CabRide. Click in the middle icon at the bottom of the Tool palette to put this window into Full Screen mode.

ADDING THE CAB

STEP 2: Open the Cab&Building file and bring up the Channels palette (Shift-F10 with ArtistKeys). You are going to copy just the cab from this file and make it a separate layer. Command-click on the CabMask channel in the Channels palette to load the selection that was previously made of just the cab. If you are using the JPEG-compressed versions of the images, you will need to open the CabMask file, then switch back to the Cab&Building window and choose Select/Load Selection to get the selection from the separate mask file. Once the cab selection is loaded, choose Edit/Copy and then switch windows back to NightCabRide. Make sure the Canon layer is the active one (the highlighted one) by clicking on the rightmost column in the Layers palette. Choose Edit/Paste and name the new layer Cab. Paste is one way to create a new layer. Type V to select the Move tool (or just hold the Command key down) and move the cab down to the bottom of the screen.

STEP 2: Make sure the Canon layer is activated by clicking on the rightmost column in the Layers palette.

TIMESSQUARE IN SCREEN MODE

STEP 3: Open the TimesSquare file and position it so you can see its window and the window for NightCabRide at the same time. Shift-click with the Move tool on the Background layer in the Layers palette of TimesSquare and drag it until you can drop it on top of the document window for NightCabRide. Let go of the mouse button when you see the hand icon and you will copy TimesSquare as a new layer in NightCabRide. In Photoshop 4, you need to hold down the Shift key when doing drag and drop layer additions to force those added layers to be centered when they are placed in the new document. Photoshop 3 would automatically center if both files were the same pixel dimension. This is no longer true for Photoshop 4. You can add a new layer doing drag and drop from one window to another either by dragging from the Layers palette, as we did here, or by dragging from the document window of the source window. Double-click on this new layer, which was called Layer 1, and rename it TimesSquare. Now change its Blend mode to Screen. The Screen mode gives the appearance of projecting this new layer, if it were a transparency, up on a screen using one slide projector with the composite of the previous layers underneath also projected on the same screen using another projector. This allows the bright parts of TimesSquare to show through the previous layers, but the dark parts don't really affect the previous layers. Notice that the headlights in the TimesSquare layer now show through the cab in the Cab layer. To get a better understanding of the Blend modes, read "Blend Modes, Calculations, and Apply Image."

STEP 3: Dragging the TimesSquare layer from its Layer palette to a new layer within Night-CabRide. You can drop it when you see the Hand icon.

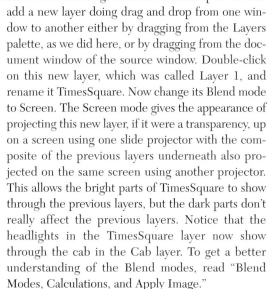

While TimesSquare is still the active layer, use the Move tool to move it a little to the left, so that the signs from the two Times Square shots line up nicely. Click on the Cab layer to activate it and then set its opacity to about 85%. This will allow more of the TimesSquare layer and also a little of the Canon layer to show through the cab. Use the Move tool to reposition the cab so the headlights shine through the cab in a pleasing location. Save this on top of the previous NightCabRide using File/Save (Command-S).

STEP 3: Changing the Blend mode of the TimesSquare layer to Screen.

STEP 3: Setting the Opacity of the Cab layer to 85%.

WORKING WITH THE BUILDING LAYER

STEP 4: At this point, you can close the TimesSquare file, but you are going to use the Cab&Building file again to create another layer. Click on the TimesSquare layer to activate it, then go back to the Cab&Building file and choose Select/None (Command-D). Now Shift-click on its document window and drag it on top of the NightCabRide window, and then drop it to create yet another layer. Double-click on the new layer and name it Building. We are going to scale part of this layer and use the New York Convention Cen-

This is how NightCabRide should look after Step 3.

ter building from that, and we are also going to use the Cab in this layer to provide a ghost image behind the existing cab. Notice that the Building layer is now on top and because its mode is Normal and its opacity is 100%, we can't see the other layers below it. If you click on its Eye icon, you will turn off viewing of this layer and again see the other layers below it. Notice that there is a lot of black sky in the lower layers above the

STEP 4: The two cabs right after adding the Building layer and turning off TimesSquare and Canon.

STEP 4: After moving the Building layer to line up the two cabs. Notice the cursor location on top of the building cab's door handle. I moved it there and waited for the screen display to catch up.

neon signs. We are going to use this building to fill some of that black sky. Put the Building layer in Screen mode and then turn off the eye icons for the TimesSquare and Canon Layers. Now you should see the relationship between the two cabs. Use the Move tool (V or hold down Command key) to move the Building layer so the cab in it is a little behind and above the cab in the Cab layer. This is easier to do now, because Photoshop 4 updates the composite on the fly. The quickest way to do it though, is to put the cursor in a location, like the door handle on the Building cab, and then imagine where that location would be in the composite after moving this cab to the correct place. Just click down and drag the cursor to that new loca-tion, then wait for the screen to catch up and release when you are sure the location is correct. Now choose the Rectangular Marquee (M) and make a selection the

STEP 4: The Layers palette after scaling the building showing the floating selection above the Building layer and the Eye icons off for Times-Square and Canon. When we choose Select/None, the float-ing selection will become part of the Building layer.

STEP 4: Select this part of the Building layer to scale upwards.

entire width of the NightCabRide window with the bottom of the selection just above the top of the Building cab and the top of the selection at the top of the building in the Building layer. Choose Layer/Transform/Scale and click on the top right handle then drag it to the top right of the window. Press Return or Enter to end the scale,

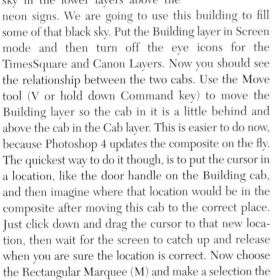

STEPS 4: Building layer after it is stretched to the top of the screen.

STEP 4: The image at the end of Step 4 with all the eye icons now on.

STEP 5: The Building layer by itself with its layer mask applied.

STEP 5: The Building layer mask by itself.

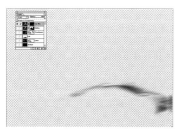

STEP 6: The Car Blur layer by itself with its layer mask applied.

and notice that there is now a Floating Selection at the top of the Layers palette. A *Floating Selection* is sort of like a temporary layer that is floating on top of the Building layer. Photoshop 4 has almost eliminated floating selections and greatly reduced their power. Choose Select/None (Command-D) to drop the floating selection and make it part of the Building layer. Now turn the Eye icons back on for the TimesSquare and Canon layers.

LAYER MASKS FOR CLEANUP

STEP 5: When you turn all the Eye icons back on, you may notice that the image becomes cluttered with too many things. Lower the Opacity on the Building layer to 70%. This tones down the building in the background but still leaves too much clutter. There are actually two parts of the image we are dealing with here. We want to use the building to fill the dark part of the sky and we want to use the second cab image here to make a blurred trail behind the Cab layer. Since we have two concepts here, let's put each in a separate layer. Click on the Layer icon in the Building layer (the leftmost thumbnail) and Option-drag it down to the New Layer icon at the bottom of the Layers palette, and name it Car Blur. Turn off the eye icon for this new layer for now. Click on the Building layer to make it active and then click on the Layer Mask icon, leftmost at the bottom of the Layers palette, to make a layer mask for this layer. Type a B to switch to the Paintbrush tool and then type 0 to set the opacity of the brush to 100%. Now type a D to set the default colors of white in the foreground and black in the background, and then press Shift-] to go to the largest soft brush in the bottom right of the Brushes palette. We will want to paint with black in the mask to remove the parts of the Building layer we don't want so type X to exchange the colors. Once you learn these shortcuts, you can switch to the Brush tool without bringing up the Tool palette and then quickly do the D, X, 0, Shift-] to get to your biggest brush and paint at 100% black. Now you want to paint with black in the layer mask to remove the parts of the Building layer that you don't want to see. If you make a mistake or change your mind, just type an X and paint with white to bring things back. Here is my Building layer after large parts of it are removed by its mask. Remember that you can always turn a layer mask completely off by Shift-clicking on its thumbnail to the right of the Layer thumbnail. This will allow you to see the entire layer again. Another Shift-click will turn the mask back on again. When you are happy with the effects of the Building layer, press Command-S to save your file.

STEP 6: Now turn the Eye icon off for the Building layer and turn the Eye icon back on for the Car Blur layer. Make sure that the Car Blur layer is active. You will only want to use the cab image from this layer, so type an L to get the Lasso tool, and then press Return to bring up its Options palette. You will automatically be in the feather box, so type a 3 and then Return to set its feather to 3, then make a selection around the entire cab, leaving some room around the outside, bottom, and back of the cab. This is the part of this image, that you want to keep. Now click on the Layer Mask icon, which is leftmost at the bottom of the Layers palette. A layer mask will be created with only the cab area of this image, your selected area, left visible. This will also get rid of the selection, because it has transferred it into the layer mask. Now type B for Paintbrush again and paint with black to remove more of this layer. All I really wanted from this layer was a ghost image of the cab a little on top and behind the original cab. I painted most of the area in the middle of the cab black and also removed the area below and in front of the cab.

Now we are going to use some filters to give this ghost image a blur effect. Click on the Layer thumbnail in the Car Blur layer so that we are working on the layer, not the layer mask. Choose Filter/Stylize/Wind and set the Method to Wind and the Direction to From the Right. This gives us part of our motion blur effect. Now choose Filter/Noise/Add Noise and add 40 of Gaussian Noise. Finally, we are going to blur this noise. Choose Filter/Blur/Motion Blur and do a Motion Blur with the Angle set to 6 and the Distance set to 40. You may want to increase or decrease the amount until you get the effect you want. Now you can go back to the layer mask and use the Paint-Brush again to fine-tune the parts of this blur you really want to see.

As a final step in creating this motion effect with the cab, Click on the Cab layer and use the Lasso with a 4–6 pixel feather to select the front edge and the back edge of the cab, and then use Motion Blur on them to blend them in with the Car Blur layer and enhance this motion effect.

STEP 7: Here is the composite image with all the new layer masks applied. Notice the current Layers palette.

STEP 7: Now add layer masks to the Times Square and Canon layers and paint with black in these masks to remove neon areas that seem too busy in the composite image. The images displayed here show each layer by itself with the parts I removed being transparent. To add a layer mask to any layer, first click in the rightmost column in the Layers palette for that layer to activate it, and then click on the Layer Mask icon, which is the leftmost icon at the bottom of the Layers palette. This adds the layer mask and puts you in the mode where you can see the layer but work on the layer mask.

When working on layers and layer masks, it is important to be aware of the layer you are actually working on, the active, highlighted, layer, and to know whether you're working on the layer or the layer mask. Option-clicking on the Layer Mask thumbnail, the rightmost thumbnail, toggles between seeing the layer mask while working on the layer mask, and seeing the layer while working on the layer mask. To work on the layer itself, click back on the Layer thumbnail, the leftmost thumbnail. When working on a layer mask, the Layer Mask thumbnail in the Layers palette is highlighted by a black line around it and the icon to the right of the Eye icon for that layer will be the Mask icon. When working on the layer, the Layer thumbnail in the Layers palette will have the black outline highlight, and the icon

STEP 7: The Times Square layer by itself with its layer mask applied.

STEP 7: The Canon layer by itself with its layer mask applied.

STEP 7: The way the Layers and Channels palettes look when working on the TimesSquare layer and seeing the layer (actually the composite of all the layers).

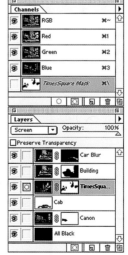

STEP 7: The way the Layers and Channels palettes look when working on the TimesSquare layer mask and seeing the layer (actually the composite of all the layers).

STEP 7: The way the Layers and Channels palettes look when working on the TimesSquare layer mask and seeing the layer mask.

to the right of the Eye icon is a PaintBrush icon. If you Option-click on the Eye icon of any layer, you will see just this layer by itself. Option-clicking a second time turns all the other layers back on, too.

ADDING SOME NEON

STEP 8: Use the Lasso to select Open 24 Hours only.

STEP 8: The final modification and location of this Open 24 Hours addition.

STEP 8: Now that we have completed the major background parts of this image, we will be adding small sections of neon to certain areas. These additions will be done so they can be easily removed and put back to show variations of this image to an art director, boss, or whoever you need to please. Click on the Car Blur layer to make it Active. Open the file called 24 Hours. Use the Lasso tool (L) with a zero pixel feather to select just the Open 24 Hours sign from this file. The closer you make the selection, the better. Edit/Copy this, switch back to NightCabRide, and do Edit/Paste. Name the new layer 24 Hours and set its Blend mode to Lighten. This will make the neon part of the sign show up without the black area around the sign changing the rest of your composite, since your composite is already black or some value lighter than black. If the Car Blur layer was active before you did the Paste, then 24 Hours is in the right place since new layers are created on top of the current active layer. Otherwise, click on the 24 Hours layer in the Layers palette and drag it on top of the Car Blur layer.

Use the Move tool (V or Command) to move this new sign to the top left black sky area. Make sure 24 Hours is the active layer in the Layers palette. Use Layer/Transform/Scale and then Shift-click in a corner icon and drag to scale proportionately; you want to make the sign quite a bit bigger to fill in more of the black area in the top left sky. Since this layer was made by selecting the sign and then doing Copy and Paste, the sign is surrounded by transparency, so you don't have to select it with a selection tool when scaling it or modifying it. The transparency in its layer is an automatic selection of the sign, the non-transparent area. Use Image/Adjust/Levels and move the Input Shadow slider, the top left slider, to the right to darken the background of the sign until it is totally black (0, 0, 0 for RGB values). Use the Rubber Stamp tool (S) in Clone non-aligned mode to remove any non-black areas around the neon text and to clean up any of the letters that have white ends. Clone non-aligned mode allows you to Option-click on a spot, like a solid bright yellow, to repair the yellow letters, then every time you click on a letter you will always start cloning from that same bright yellow spot. I wanted the sign to be a little blurry, so I did a Filter/Blur/Motion Blur of about 10 pixels with the angle set to 8 degrees. When you are happy with the size, blur, and location of the text, save the NightCabRide file again.

STEP 9: Lower left corner before adding San Leone Pizza.

STEP 9: Lower left corner after adding San Leone Pizza.

STEP 9: Now we will add San Leone Pizza to the lower left corner of this image. Open the Topless&Pizza file and select the San Leone Pizza shop with the Lasso tool. Choose Select/Feather to feather your selection by about 5 pixels. Arrange your window so you can see the NightCabRide window underneath the Topless&Pizza window. Using the Move tool (V), click in the center of your selection and then drag and drop this selection on top of the NightCabRide window. Like you did with an entire layer earlier, you can also drag and drop a selection to create a new layer. Name this new layer Pizza and set its mode to Lighten so that only its bright neon shows on top of darker places on the previous layer. Use the Move tool to move this into place in the lower left corner of the image.

STEP 10: Use the same sequence of steps to select the Exotic Show Girls Topless sign from the same Topless&Pizza file and to add that as the Topless layer on top of the Pizza layer. When you get this sign in place and set the Blend mode to Lighten, you can use Image/Adjust/Levels to darken the black background a bit, and then use Layer/Transform/Rotate to rotate the sign so it is tilting down slightly. You should also do a Gaussian Blur of about .7 pixels on this layer to make this sign stand out a little less. Do all of these steps with the Topless layer active.

STEP 10: *Before* adding the Topless sign.

STEP 10: *After* adding, rotating, and blurring the Topless sign.

STEP 11: Open the file XXX and select the neon sign and theater front, as shown here. Feather the selection by 8 pixels and then drag and drop it with the Move tool so it is on top of the Toplesslayer in the NightCabRide window; name this one XXX and set its mode to Lighten. Move this sign over to the lower right of the image, as shown here. This sign blends in better if you set the opacity to 80% and do a Gaussian Blur of .5 pixels on this layer. Remember, you can turn each of these layers on and off for the art director, or yourself, just by using the Eye icon for its layer. When creating this image, I did this so I wouldn't have to decide until the end which parts I wanted in the final image.

STEP 11: The selection, feathered by 8 pixels, for the XXX image.

STEP 12: Click on the Car Blur layer in the Layers palette and drag it down to just above the Cab layer. This should not change the appearance of the cab and its blur. We are going to try merging the cab and its blur into one layer. When you are trying this type of thing, you can always make a copy of each layer first and try the change, and then if you are happy with it, just throw the copies away. If you are not happy with the change, you can throw it away and return to the copies. Notice that the Blend mode on the Cab layer is Normal and the Blend mode on the Car Blur layer is Screen. When you merge layers together into one layer, there is only the possibility for one Blend mode and one Opacity setting. The Merge Layer commands tend to set the Blend mode and Opacity on the Merged layer to some combination of what you had before. You need to keep this in mind when merging. I actually changed the Blend mode on the Cab layer to Screen and found that this enhanced the speeding cab effect, so you might want to try it, too. Now click on the Car Blur layer to activate it, and then choose Merge Down from the Layers Palette menu. This will merge the Car Blur layer with the Cab layer below it. When you are finished, the mode on the new merged layer should be set to Screen and the Opacity set to 100%. A trick that works well for enhancing brightness when using Screen, is to create a second layer on top of the first. Drag your new merged layer down to the New Layer icon in the Layers palette to make a copy of it on top of the first. Both of these are identical with their modes set to Screen. This should brighten up the Cab a lot and enhance the effect of it speeding by in front of all the other neon and lights behind it. Click on the top of these two cab layers and choose Merge Down (Command-E) again to merge them together. You will notice

STEP 11: The final location for XXX.

STEP 11: The Layers palette after completing Step 11.

that the extra brightness stays there. Double-click on this final Cab layer and call it Cab & Blur. Merging layers is a good way to simplify your document and make working with it faster. Just remember that once the layers are merged and you have saved over the previous version of the file, there is often no easy way to unmerge them. Press Command-S to save this version of NightCabRide.

PLAYING WITH THE CAB LAYER

Let's say right now you are happy with this image but you know that your boss, art director, or whoever passes judgment on your artistic taste is (as always) going to want to modify your image in some way. Once they do this, they are happy. You have learned by now if you put something in the image that is a little bit tacky, something glaring you really want this person to remove, 80% of the time this item can get removed and your art critic's ego issues about having some influence on the project will be satisfied. People at high-end color houses have actually told me they do things like this to deal with that type of customer who always has to change something. Anyhow, this process will show you some neat possibilities for using the Clipping Group features of Layers.

STEP 13: The New Layer setup for the RedCab layer.

STEP 13: The Cab & Blur and Red layers are a clipping group. Notice how the line between them is dotted and the bottom Cab & Blur layer is underlined since it defines the clipping mask for the group.

STEP 13: With the RedCab layer's Eye icon on, the cab looks red.

STEP 13: Activate the Cab & Blur layer, then Option-click on the New Layer icon at the bottom left of the Layers palette. The New Layer dialog box will come up, and in this dialog box you need to name this layer Red, set the Blend mode to color, and click on the Group with Previous Layer check box. The new layer should come in right above the Cab layer. You will notice that the line between the two layers is dotted instead of solid and Cab & Blur is now underlined. This means that the Red layer will have the same transparent areas, and the same clipping mask, as the Cab & Blur layer. Leave this Red layer as the active layer. With the Eyedropper tool, click on the Coke sign to select the bright red from that sign as the foreground color. Choose Edit/Fill (Shift-Delete) to bring up the Fill dialog box, and then use the foreground color to fill at 100% Normal. This should fill this layer with 100% of the Coke red color. After waiting a minute for the screen to refresh, you will notice that the cab is now painted with a red tint. Since the Blend mode was set to Color when we created this layer, only the hue and saturation of the cab was changed; the details of the cab remain the same. If you turn off the Eye icon for the Red layer, the cab will return to its normal yellow. Let's play with the cab color some more!

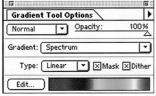

STEP 14: These are the options you want for the Gradient Rainbow.

STEP 14: Click and Option-drag the Red layer to the New Layer icon again and call this new layer Rainbow with the mode also set to Color and the Group with Previous Layer checked. Turn off the Eye icon for Red and make sure Rainbow is the active layer. Double-click on the Gradient tool and set the Type to Linear, Gradient to Spectrum, Blend mode to Normal, and leave the Mask and Dither options on. Now create a gradient by clicking on the front of the cab and dragging to the back of the cab. Wait for the screen to refresh and your cab will now be a rainbow color. Since the Rainbow layer is above, the cab will still be this color, even if the eye icon for the Red layer is also on. When you turn the Red layer's Eye icon off, it just makes it faster for Photoshop to redraw because it doesn't have to do the calculations for the Red layer. Option-click on the line between the Rainbow layer and the Red layer.

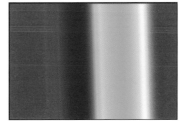

This removes the grouping between the Rainbow layer and the Cab & Blur layer. Notice that the Rainbow layer now colorizes all the layers below it. Now drag the Rainbow layer up to the top of the Layers palette and notice that it colorizes the entire image with its rainbow. If you change its Blend mode to Normal then you will see the Rainbow layer for what it really is. Now drag it back to above the Red layer, set its mode back to Color and regroup it with the Red layer by Option-clicking on the line between the two layers.

STEP 14: The RainbowCab layer when viewed by itself in Normal mode.

STEP 14: With the RainbowCab layer's Eye icon on, the cab is a rainbow color.

DECIDING ON THE FINAL VERSION

Now it is time to play with your creation. You may have an art director or some clients you want to show several variations of the project. This example represents that situation. Let's go through some of these variations, how to show them and what they look like. With the Cab & Blur layer and the other layers in its clipping group, you have a lot of options.

STEP 15: To show the client the basic final image, turn on all the Eye icons except in the Red and Rainbow layers. Now click on the Red layer to show the client a red version. Click on the Rainbow Eye icon to show them that version. Any car color can be shown by just filling the Red layer with a different color and making sure the Rainbow layer's Eye icon is off. If the client likes the Rainbow look, you can Option-click on the line that separates the Red layer from the Rainbow layer to remove the Rainbow layer from the clipping group. You can move the Rainbow layer up and down to selectively add Rainbow color to all the layers below it. If you Option-click on the line between the Rainbow layer and any other layer to make a Clipping Group, you add rainbow color to the non-transparent area of the layer below. If your client is concerned about some of the more risqué aspects of New York nightlife, you can click on the Eye icons for the Topless and XXX layers

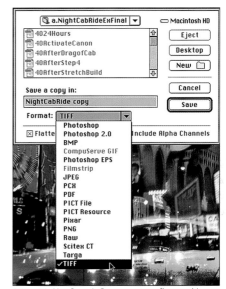

STEP 15: Use Save A Copy to save a flattened image in a different file format to print a proof or import into Quark, Illustrator, or some other layout application.

to remove these from the image. To print a proof of any of these NightCabRide versions, or to save them in a different format for placement into Illustrator or Quark, just choose File/Save A Copy (Command-Option-S) with the Eye icons, Blend modes and Opacities of that particular version set the way they need to be. You usually want to have Flatten Image and Don't Include Alpha Channels checked in Save A Copy since these extra copies don't need to have all the layers and channels. Always save your main development image in Photoshop format with all the layers and options intact. Have fun!

STEP 16: Once you, or you and your client, decide that you're going to use certain layers in the final image, you can merge those layers together into one. Turn the Eye icons on for the layers that you want to merge. Make sure one of the layers whose Eye icon is on is the active layer, by clicking on it. The other

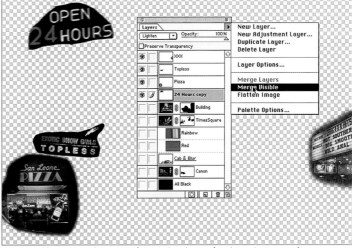

STEP 16: The Layers palette setup for merging the top four layers into one. After you merge the layers together, they will all be in the same 24 Hours layer. In this case, you would then want to set the Blend mode back to Lighten in that new merged layer or the composite would have been changed by the merge.

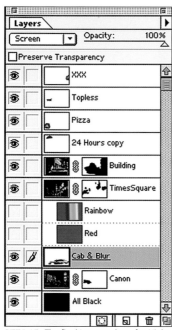

STEP 17: The final Layers palette for Night-CabRide with the layers I used in the final image turned on.

layers will be merged into the bottom layer whose Eye icon is on. Now choose Merge Visible from the Layers Palette menu. Here we are merging the top four layers that were just adding particular items to the image. If all those items are accepted as part of the final image, and you won't want to change this later, there is sometimes no need to keep them as separate layers. When you merge layers together, remember that the final merged layer will only be allowed one opacity, Blend mode, and set of Layer options. The Layer options, mode, and opacity of each layer that was set when you merged will be applied at the time of the merge to the set of layers that were merged. The Blend mode and opacity of the merged layer is then changed to best reflect the group, or sometimes just to Normal and 100%, respectively, and all its Layer options are set to the default. This can cause a different effect when the Eye icons for the other non-merged layers are turned back on. Be careful when you do this. Here, we need to make sure the Blend mode for the new layer is set back to Lighten or the merge changes the image dramatically.

STEP 17: When you are sure you will never need the layers again, you can select, by turning the Eye icons on, the layers you want in the final image. Choose Flatten Image from the Layers Palette menu. If you did not select all the layers, you will be asked "Discard Hidden Layers?" and if you choose OK, those layers will be thrown out. After flattening the image, it looks like a single layer image with just a *Background* layer. I always keep my multilayered version and instead of using Flatten Image, I use Save A Copy when I need to print a version with some of the layers on and some of them off. To do this, just turn the Eye icons on for the layers you want in this particular version and then choose File/Save A Copy. This command allows you to save a flattened copy of the image under a different name without removing the layers from your original image. That way, you can keep your options open.

STEP 17: The final NightCabRide image.

CALCULATIONS, PATTERNS,

FILTERS, AND EFFECTS

BLEND MODES, CALCULATIONS, AND APPLY IMAGE

How each of the Blend modes work; the subtleties of using modes in Calculations, Apply Image, Layers, Fill and the painting tools; when and how to use Calculations versus Apply Image versus Layers.

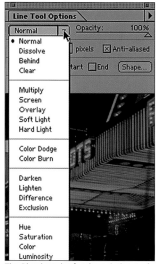

The Blend modes for the painting tools.

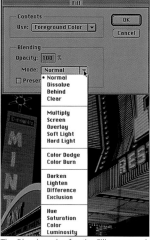

The Blend modes for the Fill command.

The Blend modes are used to determine how two groups of image information combine. The two groups of image information could be of various types within Photoshop. The first type could be a photographic image and the second a solid color that is painted or filled on top of the first image. You could do this using one of the painting tools or the Fill command. If you created a layer that was a solid color, then you could also combine this layer with a photographic image on a second layer by using a Blend mode in the Layers palette. In the Layers palette, you can determine which Blend mode to use to combine two photographic images in the same layered Photoshop 4 document. You can use the Apply Image command with different Blend modes to combine two-color photographic images that are in separate documents and have the exact same pixel dimensions. Finally, you can use the Calculations command with Blend modes to combine two images of the same size when you want a black-and-white mask channel as a result. The Blend modes appear in the painting tools, the Fill tool, the Layers palette, the Apply Image command, and the Calculations command. Not all of the Blend mode options are

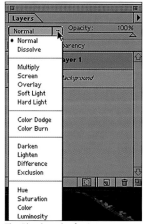

The Blend modes for Layers.

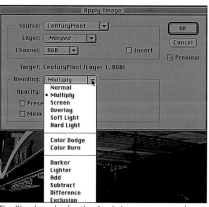

The Blend modes for the Apply Image command.

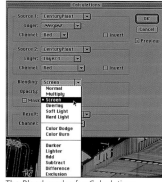

The Blend modes for Calculations.

offered in each of these areas. As we explain each Blend mode, you'll see why some of them make more sense in one or another area. All of these options also offer you a way to use a mask as you combine the two groups of image information. The mask will affect the parts of the two groups that are combined.

THE TOOLS FOR BLENDING

First, we discuss the different tools and methods for blending and when it makes the most sense to use each of them. Later, we discuss each of the Blend modes and its unique applications within each of the different blending tools. You can find many of the images we use in this chapter in the Blend Modes Cals & Apl Im folder on the CD. Although this is not a step-by-step hands-on session, we encourage you to play and explore these techniques with the images. By playing on your own, you learn new things, and you can have a lot of fun, too.

THE FILL COMMAND

The Edit/Fill command (Shift-Delete) is used to fill a selection, or the entire image if there is no selection, with something like the foreground or background color, or from the pattern, snapshot, or last saved file. The Blend mode and Opacity in the Fill tool just determines how this filling image will combine with what was there before. Normal, at 100% opacity, completely covers what was there before with the new color or image. An opacity of 50% will give half what was there before and half the new filled image or color. We usually use Fill to completely cover a selection or the entire image with a solid color or a tint. We also use Fill a lot to revert to the previously saved version of a file within a selected area. When you use Fill, you need to pick a source, opacity, and blend mode before you do the operation, and then you have to undo it if you want to change it. If you need to prototype the opacity or mode of your Fill, use the layer techniques we show you in the book, since it is quicker to make variations in the Layers palette. Only use Fill when you are sure of the look that you want. We used Fill to get the highlight effects in the pop-up dialog box on the previous page. Since we wanted them all to look the same, we just used the Rectangular Marquee to select the Blend Mode pop-up menu, used Select/Inverse to invert that selection, and then used Fill with 40% black in Normal mode to get the effect.

THE PAINTING TOOLS

You use a painting tool when you want to apply an effect by hand and softly blend it in and out, like you would do with an airbrush or paintbrush. These tools in Photoshop have a lot more power, however, due to the magic of digital imaging and the blending modes. Go through "The Tool Palette" to learn about the subtleties of each painting tool. With the Blend Mode options in the painting tools, you don't just lay down paint, or even a previous version of the image. Instead, you can control how this paint or image combines with what is already there.

COMBINING IMAGES USING LAYERS

Layers and adjustment layers are the most powerful ways to combine two or more images while keeping the most options open for further variations and many versions of your composite. Sometimes we use layers even when we are dealing with a pattern or solid color. The reason is that with layers, you can always go back and change something, move something, change the opacity or blend mode without having to totally redo your image. You can try an effect and be able to turn it on and off at will. Layers gives you the most sophisticated control of the blending modes as well

Here's how we created the highlighted pop-ups on the previous page with Fill.

The Night Cab Ride image produced using many layers.

as many other capabilities at the same time. If you don't understand layers, and if you haven't read "Layers, Layer Masks, and Adjustment Layers," you should read it now before you continue. When you use layers, your files may get much bigger, because many layers add at least the original size of the file in that layer to your document size. Adjustment layers allow you to do color changes with a new layer without adding all the extra file size. Layered documents have to be saved in Photoshop format to maintain the flexible layer information. Still, layers are WAY COOL!

COMBINING IMAGES, LAYERS, AND CHANNELS USING APPLY IMAGE

The basic function of Apply Image is to copy one image, layer, or channel, called the Source image, and use it to replace another image, layer, or channel, the Target image, of exactly the same pixel resolution. To combine two items with Apply Image, they must be exactly the same width and height in pixels. The two images are combined using a blending mode and opacity that are chosen from the Apply Image dialog box. You can optionally choose a mask, which will combine the images only where the mask is white. Apply Image is useful when copying a channel or layer from one place to another, especially when you want to put it on top of an existing channel or layer and combine the two with a Blend mode.

Before you enter Apply Image, you should choose the target image, layer, or channel. This will be modified when you leave Apply Image by choosing OK, so you may want to first make a copy of that target item.

If the Preview button is on, you can see the results of the operation in the target window. In choosing the source, you can pick any open document, layer, or channel, as long as it's the same exact pixel dimensions as the target. Like the source, the mask can be any open document, layer, or channel that is the same pixel dimensions as the target. The Preserve Transparency options will stop the Apply Image command from changing any transparent areas within a layer. Both the source and the mask have an Invert check box which you can check to turn that selection to its negative.

The Las Vegas Night image.

The Century Plant image.

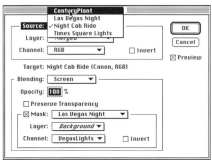

The Vegas Lights mask.

Here we see most of the possible options of Apply Image. Before we entered Image/Apply Image, we made Night Cab Ride the active document in Photoshop. Canon was the active layer within that document. This active item is always selected as the Target of Apply Image, so you will be changing that document, channel, or layer. The Source pop-up window shows you only documents that are the same pixel size and dimensions as the target document. Here, we chose the Century Plant as the Source. The Blending pop-up is where you choose the Blend mode. There is an optional mask, selected here, which causes the blending to happen only within the areas of the mask that are white. If the Preview button is on, you see the results of the Apply Image in the Target window. This lets you try different options and see what they do.

The results of the Apply Image settings shown in the previous illustration. The Century Plant image is brought into the Night Cab Ride composite where the Las Vegas Night mask was white. In that area, it is blended with the Canon layer using the Screen Blending mode.

In this chapter, we use three images that we have cropped to be exactly the same pixel size. They are the Las Vegas Night image, the Century Plant image, and a modified Night Cab Ride image. The Las Vegas Night image has a mask, called VegasLights, that is white where the neon lights are. There are no particular masks in the Century Plant image. Here are some other examples of using Apply Image, using the same three images, so you can get an idea what the command does. If you want to get a result that is more than one channel deep, you need to use Apply Image instead of Calculations. The effects you can create with Apply Image can also be achieved by using layers, by first copying the different components into a layer document. Layers gives you more flexibility because the different layers don't have to start out being the exact same size and you can move them around side-to-side as well as above-and-below in relationship to each other. Effects within layers can also be done and undone in multiple combinations using the Eye icons.

You should use Apply Image mostly in cases where you already know the spatial relationship between the objects being combined, and you have to do the operation quickly for some production purpose. Motion picture and multimedia work (where you are compositing many frames of two sequences together that have been pre-shot in registration, to be lined up exactly), is a good example of how you would use Apply Image. This process could be automated over hundreds of frames by using actions, or by using some other application automation software.

Here we see a more simple application of Apply Image. The source, target, and resulting images are shown here. The Screen Blending mode is analogous to taking transparencies of the two images and projecting them onto the same screen from two different slide projectors. The light areas of the images are emphasized. Setting the opacity to 85% made the Las Vegas Lights a little less bright in the composite image below.

The Times Square Canon image.

The Las Vegas Night image.

Actually, if you hold down the Option key while selecting Apply Image, you get an extra Result pop-up menu at the bottom of the dialog box, which allows you to direct the result of Apply Image to: the Current Target, a New Document, a New Layer, a New Channel, or a Selection. If you choose either New Layer, New Channel, or Selection, these end up in the target image.

COMBINING CHANNELS USING CALCULATIONS

The main purpose of the Calculations command is to use the Blend modes to combine images, layers, or channels and end up with a single black-and-white channel as the result. When you need a color result, use Apply Image; when you need a channel result, use Calculations. Calculations provides for two source files, Source 1 and Source 2, and a Result file. When you enter Calculations, all three of these files are set to the active window within Photoshop. You can use the pop-up menus to change any of these files to any other open file that has the same pixel dimensions. The source files are the two that will be combined using the blending mode that you choose. The Layer pop-up on each of these files is available for layered documents and allows you to choose the merged layer, which is the composite of all

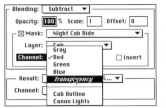

With the Channel pop-up you can select any channel including Transparency and layer masks.

The Headland sign, we want to make a mask of just the glow without the sign.

We have a soft-edge mask of the glow, including part of the sign. We put this into Source 2.

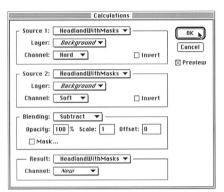

We have a hard-edge mask of just the sign. We put this into Source 1.

Here is the resulting mask where we subtracted the hard-edge mask from the soft-edge mask.

Here are the Calculations settings to produce the mask of the glow on the next page. When doing a Subtract, the item that you want to subtract should be in Source 1. The item you are subtracting from should be in Source 2. In this case, the result was a New channel. Depending on the choice we make for the Result file and Channel, the result could replace any existing channel in any file of the same pixel dimensions, or, by choosing Selection, it could be loaded as a selection.

layers that currently have their eye icons on or any other layer in the document.

The Channel pop-up allows you to choose any channel in the chosen file or layer. To access a layer mask channel, you need to first choose the layer that owns that layer mask. You can also choose the Transparency channel, which is a mask of any transparent areas in the chosen layer. This interface allows you to blend any two documents, layers, or channels that are open by using the blending modes, and to then put the result into any channel that is open. These open items must have the same pixel dimensions as the active window. The blending interface also allows an optional mask, which will force the blending to happen only in the areas that are white in the mask. Both source items and the mask have an Invert check box to optionally invert any of them before doing the composite. You will learn more about Apply Image and Calculations as you go through each of the Blend modes next. If you hold down the Option key when selecting Calculations, a smaller version of the dialog box will come up.

UNDERSTANDING EACH BLEND MODE

Let's start out with the Blend modes listed in the Edit/Fill command, which would have the same effect as the Blend modes used by the painting tools if you were painting with the same color, pattern, or image that you were filling with. When you use the Fill command, you fill a selected area. You can fill with the foreground or background colors as well as from the Snapshot, from the last saved file and from a pattern. All these options are available to paint from by using different flavors of the painting tools. The Rubber Stamp tool gives you the most options. When you paint, you select your "fill area" as you paint instead of from a selection.

In either case, the modes work the same. Some of these modes also apply to layers and to the Calculations and Apply Image commands.

NORMAL

When painting or filling in Normal mode, you are filling the selected or painted area with the foreground or background color or from the snapshot, pattern, or saved file. Normal mode for a top layer in the Layers palette means that the top layer will be opaque at 100% opacity. You will not see any of the layers below through this layer. You use Normal mode in Calculations or Apply Image to copy the source layer or channel to the target, or destination layer or channel without any blending. This totally replaces the the target, or destination, with the source.

DISSOLVE

Depending on the opacity of the dissolve, this mode appears to take the opacity as a percentage of the pixels from the blend color and place them on top of the base color. The base color is the color or image that was there before the dissolve. The blend color is the color or image that is being dissolved on top of the base color or image. Try this with two layers, setting the mode between them to Dissolve. If you set the opacity to 100%, you get all of the top layer and don't see the bottom layer. The same thing happens if you use a fill of 100% or paint at 100% in Dissolve mode. When you set the opacity to 50% and look at the pixels up close, you will see that there are about 50% pixels from the top layer and 50% from the bottom. If you set the opacity to 10%, only 10% of the pixels are from the top layer or color.

With Dissolve, the pixels seem to be entirely from one image or the other; there don't seem to be any blended pixels. On first impression, the dissolve appears to be random. If you do a 50% dissolve between two layers and then zoom to 100%, you should notice a pattern in the dissolve. It looks like Photoshop creates or uses some fixed dissolve pattern over and over again across the screen. You probably wouldn't see it if you were painting with a soft brush over a smaller area. Still, this pattern doesn't look good over the entire screen between two layers.

If you want to achieve this type of look between two images but without an obvious repeating pattern, create a layer mask on the top layer filled with solid white. Now, go into the Add Noise filter and add Gaussian noise to the layer mask. Where the noise is black, the bottom layer will show through and you will get an effect similar to Dissolve but this time without the annoying pattern. The more noise you add, the more you will see of the bottom layer. Also, in this case, some of the pixels are actually blends between the layers. Dissolve is not an option with Apply Image or Calculations, but you can get a similar effect here by using a Gaussian noise mask as you combine images, layers, and channels.

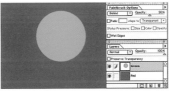

The green circle is in the top layer with red in the bottom layer. Now both layer's Eye icons are on.

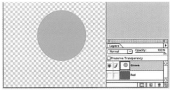

Here is just the circle with the Red layer turned off. The transparent area shows up as a checkered pattern.

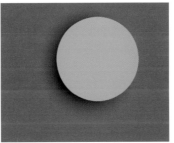

We have painted black into this transparent area using Behind mode with a large soft brush.

Here we see the shadow without the background color. When painting in Behind mode, we didn't have to worry about painting on top of the green. It is automatically masked out since it is not transparent.

BEHIND

This Blend mode is used to paint into the transparent part of a layer. It is available only from Fill and the painting tools and only if the layer has a transparent area. It is not available if the Preserve Transparency check box is checked for that layer. Behind allows you to paint a shadow or color behind an object (like a circle) in the layer, using a painting tool or the Fill command. The actual image in the layer won't be affected, because Behind only paints into the transparent area. Painting in Behind mode is like painting on the back of the acetate. Here we see a shadow that was added to a circle using the Paintbrush tool in Behind mode with a large soft brush.

CLEAR

The Clear mode is available only when in a layered document from the Fill command, the Paint Bucket tool, and the Line tool. It will fill the selected area, the line in the case of the Line tool, with transparency. This is the little checkerboard pattern that means you can see the layers below through the transparent areas. Clear

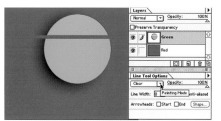

Here we used the Line tool to create the red line going across the circle by drawing the line in Clear mode.

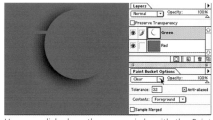

Here we clicked on the green circle with the Paint Bucket in Clear mode leaving only the shadow with this nice effect.

is also available as a menu item from the Edit menu, although Edit/Clear behaves a little differently depending on whether you are in a layered document. When in a layered document, Edit/Clear fills the selected area with transparency. When in a normal document, without layers, Edit/Clear fills the selected area with the background color.

This brings up an interesting thing about Photoshop and how it deals with layers and the special layer called the *Background* layer. When you open a TIFF file or some other file that doesn't contain layers into Photoshop and then go into the Layers palette, you will notice that these files contain a single layer called *Background*. This isn't really a layer in the true sense of the word, because it can't have any transparent areas. If you make a selection in a Background layer of an image and then choose Edit/Clear, the selected area will be filled with the background color. You will notice that Clear does not show up as an available option for a Background layer within Fill or the Line and Paint Bucket tools. If you double-click on this special Background layer within the Layers palette and rename it something else, it will turn into a real layer. Now, Edit/Clear will fill a selection with transparency and Clear is available in the Line and Paint Bucket tools. Until you rename the Background layer and make it a real layer, you can't interchange its order in the Layers palette with other layers.

MULTIPLY

Multiply is a very useful Blend mode that is available within all the Blend Mode pop-ups. When you multiply two images together, it is analogous to what you would see if both the images were transparencies and you sandwiched them together and placed them on a light table or projected them onto a screen. Anything that was black in either image would be black in the resulting composite image. Anything that was white or clear in either image would let you see through it to what was in the other image in that area. When you multiply two images together, the 0..255 values of the corresponding pixels in each image are actually multiplied together using the following formula:

A Multiply of the Century Plant and Las Vegas Night images, from the 2nd page of this chapter, emphasizes the darker areas of each image.

(Source 1) x (Source 2) / 255 = destination

Just like doing a multiply in mathematics, the order of the Source 1 and Source 2 images doesn't matter. Dividing by 255 at the end forces all the values to be in the 0..255 range. You can see that when either Source value is 0, black, you are going to get 0 as the result. When either Source value is 255, white, you are going to get the other Source value as the result, because 255/255 = 1, so you end up multiplying the other Source value by 1.

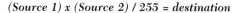

Chapter 33: Blend Modes, Calculations, and Apply Image

The original Glow mask we want to drop a gradient into.

Doing a Load Selection on the glow, left, and dropping the gradient into the selected area, produces the halo around the glow at the back of the arrow.

Unwanted Halo Effect

Create the gradient in a separate mask channel and use Calculations to Multiply for the effect at right.

A Calculations Multiply of the Gradient and Glow mask channels drops the gradient into the glow area without a halo.

A powerful use for Multiply is to seamlessly add a gradient to an existing selection. Let's say we wanted to use the Glow mask to create a glow that was bright at the front of the arrow and fading toward the back. To do this, we would want to drop a gradient into this mask. If you do a Load Selection on the mask and then create the gradient within that selection, you will get a light halo around the edge of the gradient toward the back of the arrow. This is caused by the loaded selection. To avoid getting this halo, just create the gradient in a separate channel and then multiply the two channels together, giving you a better fade.

SCREEN

Screen is sort of the opposite of Multiply, in that when you do a Screen between two images, anything that is white in either of the images will be white in the resulting image. Anything that is black in either image will show the other image in that black area. Screen, like Multiply, is also available in all the different Blend mode pop-ups. When you Screen two images together, it is analogous to what you would see if both the images were projected from two different slide projectors onto the same screen. The formula for Screen is:

$255 - ((255 - Source\ 1) \times (255 - Source\ 2) / 255) = destination$

You can simulate the Screen command using the Multiply command if you first invert both of the Source images and then multiply them together, and finally, invert the result of that multiply. That is exactly what this formula for Screen does: (255 - Source1) does an Invert of Source 1. With the Screen formula then: the Invert of Source 1 is multiplied by the Invert of Source 2 and then is divided by 255. That part of the formula does the multiply of the two inverted images. Finally, subtracting that result from 255 at the end does the Invert of the result of that multiply, giving you a Screen. The important thing to remember between Screen and Multiply is that a Screen of two images will emphasize the lighter areas and a Multiply will emphasize the darker areas.

A screen of the Century Plant and Las Vegas Night images emphasizes the lighter areas of each image.

SOFT LIGHT

In Soft Light mode, the original image is blended with the blend color, pattern, or image by making the original image either lighter or darker depending on the blend image. If the blend image is lighter than 50% gray, then the original image is lightened in a subtle way. Even where the blend image is pure white, the resulting image will just be lighter than before, not pure white. If the blend image is darker

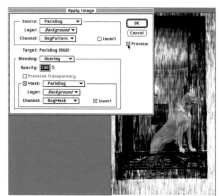

Apply Image was originally used to prototype the Paris Dog examples. The mask used to isolate the dog is seen here but we Invert it to actually get the effect in the background.

The original ParisDog image.

The original Dog pattern.

The Dog mask before inverting.

To actually produce the five final images, I set up a two layer document and then used File/Save A Copy to save each flattened version after changing only the mode between each save. That was just a better production choice.

The examples shown here use Apply Image and layers to combine my ParisDog image with a pattern that I created in Photoshop and a mask that stops the dog itself from being affected by the pattern. I initially tried this out using Apply Image. The original ParisDog image, the grayscale DogPattern, and the DogMask were all in the same file. Before entering Apply Image, I selected the RGB background of ParisDog; this made that the target. For the source, I selected the DogPattern, which applies the pattern on top of the ParisDog. I set the mode to Overlay and then decided that I didn't want the pattern on the dog. Choosing the Mask option allowed me to pick the Dog mask, and the Invert check box was turned on because the mask was actually white in the dog area. Turning on Invert made the mask white in the background and the white area of the mask is where the image is

Chapter 33: Blend Modes, Calculations, and Apply Image

applied. With the Preview button on, I tried all the different blend modes and could see that I wanted to use this as an example. At this point, I was going to have to produce five versions of this image, one for each blend mode. When you use Apply Image, it actually changes the Target image, so to do five versions with Apply Image, I would have had to make five copies of the ParisDog, one for each blend mode.

A more efficient way to do this, after prototyping the effect with Apply Image, was then to create the five versions from a layered document. The bottom layer was the ParisDog image. I added a layer above this for the DogPattern, and to that layer I added a layer mask for the inverted Dog-Mask channel. Now to produce the five different versions, all I had to do was change the blend mode in the Layers palette, once for each version, and then choose File/Save A Copy for each version to make a flattened TIFF copy with all channels and layers removed. For more information on using layer masks, see "The APDA Magazine Cover" or "Night Cab Ride in Manhattan."

Again, Photoshop layers are a great prototyping and production tool! When I took this photo on a residential alley in Paris, the dog was in this pose as I walked by. I pointed and focused my camera and then the dog went back inside just as I was about to shoot. I stood there for a bit with the camera ready, and, sure enough, the dog returned and posed for me. It has always been one of my favorite shots.

Overlay: This is contrasty but it still preserves some of the tone and detail from the original.

Multiply: Notice how dark the shadows are compared to Overlay.

Screen: Notice how bright the highlights are compared to Overlay.

Soft Light: This preserves the most tone and detail from the original.

Hard Light: The highlight and shadow values and the lightness values come pretty much directly from the pattern.

than 50% gray, then the original image is darkened in a subtle way. Even where the blend image is pure black, the resulting image will just be darker than before, not pure black. The tonal values and details of the original are fairly preserved, just subtly modified by the blend image. If you add a 50% gray layer above an original image and set the Blend mode to Soft Light, you can then use a soft brush and paint or airbrush with white or black to dodge or burn the image by lightening or darkening this gray layer. Use less than 100% opacity on your brush to get more subtle effects. This is better than using the dodging or burning tool because it's infinitely adjustable since you're not actually changing the original image. When you get an effect you like, just merge the layers to get a new final image. You can easily get a 50% gray layer by clicking the New Layer icon in the Layers palette, choosing Edit/Fill, and filling at 100% with Use: 50% Gray and Mode: Normal.

HARD LIGHT

In Hard Light mode, the original image is blended with the blend color, pattern, or image by making the original image either lighter or darker depending on the blend image. If the blend image is lighter than 50% gray, the original image is lightened and this lightening is a contrasty effect. If the blend image is pure white, the resulting image will be pure white. If the blend image is darker than 50% gray, then the original image is darkened and this darkening is a contrasty effect. If the blend image is pure black, the resulting image will be pure black. In Hard Light mode, the resulting image seems to take its lightness value from the blend color, pattern, or image. Since the tonal values of the original are not very preserved, the adjustment is a radical one. If you add a 50% gray layer above an original image and set the Blend mode to Hard Light, you can then use a soft brush and paint with white or black to dodge or burn the image by lightening or darkening this gray layer. This will be a radical, contrasty dodge and burn. Use less than 100% opacity on your brush or you will get pure white or black. Remember that this effect is infinitely adjustable because you are not actually changing the original image. When you get an effect you like, just merge the layers to get a new final image. See the "Soft Light" section for how to get a 50% gray layer above the image.

The shoes and the glasses have each been placed here separately.

You have one mask for the shoes.

Another mask for the glasses.

These Calculations settings using Lighter will create the new mask below to the left.

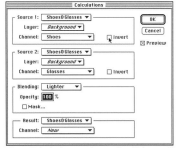

This mask of both shoes and glasses was created with Calculations using Lighter.

To create this background mask with a single calculation, invert both the source masks and use Darker instead of Lighter.

OVERLAY

Overlay does a combination of Multiply and Screen modes. The dark areas of an original image are multiplied and the light areas are screened. The highlights and shadows are somewhat preserved, since dark areas of the image will not be as dark as if you were doing a Multiply and light areas will not be as bright as if you were doing a Screen. The tonal values and details of the original are preserved to some extent, but this is a more contrasty transition than Soft Light just not as radical as Hard Light.

DARKEN AND LIGHTEN

The Darken and Lighten Blend modes are pretty easy to understand. In the Darken mode, each of the corresponding pixels from the original image and the blend color, pattern, or image are compared, and the darker of the two is chosen for the result. In the case of Lighten, the lighter of the two pixels is chosen for the result. Within Apply Image and Calculations, these modes are called Lighter and Darker. These Blend modes are most useful in combining masks to create new masks. An example of this, shown here, would be the situation in which you have pasted two objects into a composite scene and for each object you have a mask. When you Paste in Photoshop 4, you always have a mask of the object, which is the transparency of the object's layer. You have a mask of each separate object, and now you need one mask that contains both objects at the same time.

Using Calculations to do a Lighter between the two masks will create the mask of both the objects. You can then use the inverse of this mask to give you a mask of the background. To do this in one step, select the Invert check boxes on both the Source channels in Calculations. Since both Source masks have now been inverted, you would have to use Darker to combine the two masks and get the final inverted mask with the white background.

DIFFERENCE AND EXCLUSION

Difference is one of the most useful blending modes. Difference compares two images and gives you a mask that is black where each of the two images are exactly the same and is non-black and closer to white the more the images are different from each other. The formula for Difference is

| Source 1 - Source 2 | = Destination

Difference is similar to Subtract but the results are never inverted; they are always positive because the two vertical bars stand for absolute value and therefore make the result positive. With a little photographic planning, you can use Difference to automatically separate an image from its background. Pick a background that is quite different in color and brightness from the objects to be shot. First, place the objects, adjust your lighting, and shoot them. Without moving the tripod or changing the lighting, shoot the background without the objects. If these two photographs are scanned in register, doing a Difference between them can often automatically give you a mask of just the objects. The two objects in the example here were shot on a tripod using a Kodak DCS electronic camera. When using an electronic camera, scanning the images in register is no problem because they are sent directly from the camera to the computer. In this case, we had the computer in the studio, so we could try Difference and then adjust the lighting and exposure to make sure we'd get an automatic knock-out. Actually, to create the final mask of the objects, we brought the Difference mask into Levels

The objects as originally shot with the Kodak DCS system.

The background shot with the same lighting and camera position.

Difference between the Green channels of the background and the object shots. The Red channels also work well. Try each channel and see which does the best job.

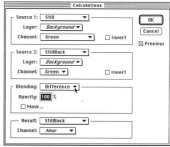

These Calculations settings using Difference will create the mask to the left.

Above mask after some quick edits and a brightness adjustment with Levels. Sometimes using Calculations to Screen a mask with itself will bring out the bright values even more. After that, Levels can by used to redarken the shadows, adjust the shadow midtones, and further brighten the highlights that represent the objects you are knocking out.

New background placed behind the objects using an inverted version of the mask to the left.

The Positive Version of the Image.

The Negative Version of the Image.

Exclusion of the top Black to White Layer with the Positive image in the Layer below.

Layer setup for Exclusion above.

Layer setup for Difference below.

Difference of the Top Black blending to White layer with the Positive image in the layer below.

and increased its brightness slightly. Then we did some quick editing of the masks of the actual objects. Still, this process was faster using Difference than if we had done the knock-out by hand. Using Difference to do knock-outs works even better for objects that have no shadows or where the shadow is not needed in the knock-out.

A digital camera hooked up to a computer is starting to become a reality for more and more photographers today, especially those who do a lot of repetitive catalog work. Also, consider the motion picture industry or multimedia applications where artists or technicians might have to knock out hundreds or even thousands of frames to composite two sequences together. With Difference and a little computer controlled camera work, this situation could also be automated. Say you're shooting some guys on horses riding across a field that you will later want to superimpose on another scene. Have a computer remember all the frame-by-frame motion of the camera while shooting the scene. Now immediately, while the lighting hasn't changed, use the computer to move the camera back to the original position at the beginning of the scene. With computer control, reshoot all those frames without the horses to just get the backgrounds. Now using Difference, and maybe QuickKeys, to automate hundreds of frames, you can quickly create a knock-out of all those frames.

Exclusion is a new Blend mode in Photoshop 4. It is similar to Difference but not as intense. An Exclusion with black will do nothing to the image, as will a Difference with black. An Exclusion with white will invert the image completely, as will a Difference with white. An Exclusion with 50% gray leaves you with 50% gray, whereas a difference with 50% gray still changes the image to make it appear partially negative. A Difference from black blending toward white is a slow transition from a positive image to a negative image with no gray section in the middle. As you Exclude an image with black blending toward white, the portion from black to 50% gray is actually a transition from the positive image toward 50% gray. From 50% gray, the image turns more negative as we Exclude toward white where the image is totally negative.

ADD AND SUBTRACT

Add and Subtract are available only in Apply Image and Calculations. Add takes the corresponding pixels of the original and the blend image and adds them together using the following formula:

Add = (Source 2 + Source 1) / Scale) + Offset = Destination

Subtract takes the corresponding pixels of the original and the blend image and subtracts them using this formula:

Subtract = (Source 2 - Source 1) / Scale) + Offset = Destination

Scale and Offset are additional parameters that you use with these blending modes in Apply Image or Calculations. The normal values for Scale and Offset for both Add and Subtract are 1 and 0. The order of the Source 1 and Source 2 parameters doesn't matter with Add, but it definitely does with Subtract. The Source 1 parameter is always subtracted from the Source 2 parameter, and the result has to be in the 0..255 range. When Source 1 is white, 255, which represents a selection, the result of the Subtract will always be black. The effect of the Subtract is then to remove the selected areas of the Source 1 mask from the selected areas of the Source 2 mask. This is a very useful function. Of the two, Subtract is the Blend mode I use more often, and I usually do Subtracts between masks. See the example of Subtract with Calculations on the Headland sign earlier in this chapter.

When doing either an Add or a Subtract, the Offset value will make the resulting mask lighter if the offset is positive, and darker if the offset is negative. The offset is a number, in the 0..255 range, that will be added to the result of each corresponding pixel's calculations. If we do an Add of two images and set the scale to 2, we are getting an average of the two. This would give us the same result having one image in a layer on top of the other with the top image having a Normal Blend mode and 50% opacity. With the Add command, you have the additional control of using the Offset parameter to make the resulting image either lighter or darker.

The Las Vegas Night image.

HUE, SATURATION, COLOR, AND LUMINOSITY

These blending modes will affect the original image by using either the hue, saturation, color, or luminosity of the blend color, pattern, or image as the hue, saturation, color, or luminosity of the original image. In these examples, combining the two sides of the desert (the original desert Century Plant and Las Vegas), you can see how the Century Plant scene is modified by the hue, saturation, color, and luminosity of the Las Vegas Night scene. The Las Vegas scene has very intense hues that are also very saturated so it is easy to see what happens with these two images. We placed the Las Vegas scene as a layer on top of the Century Plant layer and just changed the layer Blend mode of the Las Vegas layer to get the different effects. In Hue mode, you see the hues from the Las Vegas scene, but the saturation and the intensity of those hues, and all the details, come from the Century Plant scene. In Saturation mode, the highly saturated values from the bright neon lights intensify the

The Century Plant image.

more subtle hues and details from the Century Plant scene. Color mode combines the hue and saturation from Las Vegas with the details, or luminosity, of Century Plant. When you put the Las Vegas scene in Luminosity mode, then you are seeing all the details from that Las Vegas scene but the more subtle hue and saturation values from the Century Plant. In the Las Vegas scene, there are large black areas. These have no hue or saturation values, which is why they show up as gray when in Hue, Saturation, or Color modes.

A more interesting way to combine these two images is to double-click on the Las Vegas layer to bring up the Layer Options. Moving the left, Shadow, slider to the right in the This Layer part of Layer Options, removes the black part of the Las Vegas scene from

The Las Vegas Hue with the Century Plant saturation and luminosity.

The Las Vegas Saturation with the Century Plant hue and luminosity.

The Las Vegas Color (hue and saturation), with the Century Plant luminosity.

The Las Vegas Luminosity with the Century Plant hue and saturation.

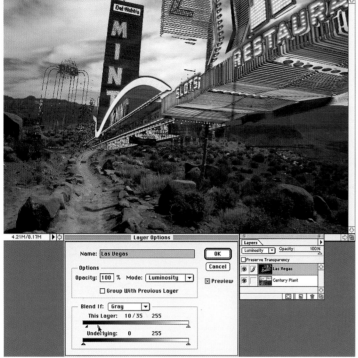

Here we see the results of using Layer Options in Luminosity mode to completely remove the black values in the 0–10 range and to blend out the black values in the 11–35 range from the composite of Las Vegas and the Century Plant. We double-clicked on the Las Vegas layer to get the Layer Options dialog box.

the composite. In the final example of this image, we have used the Move tool to move the Las Vegas layer up a little bit. Now Las Vegas is at the end of the trail in the desert. We then double-clicked on the Las Vegas layer to bring up its Layer Options. We are in Luminosity mode, but the colors of the Century Plant image show through in the black areas of Las Vegas because we have moved the Shadow sliders of This Layer over to the right.

First, we moved the Shadow slider to the right to 10. That removed all the digital values from 0 to 10 from the composite, allowing the Century Plant to show through. This produces jaggy edges on the transition between Las Vegas and the Century Plant backgrounds. By holding down the Option key and sliding the rightmost part of the Shadow slider further to the right, the Shadow slider has now split. We moved the rightmost part of this slider to 35. The meaning of this is that the black values in Las Vegas from 0 to 10 are completely removed and the values from 11 to 35 are blended out making a softer edge between these two images. The Luminosity values in Las Vegas from 36 to 255 are still retained within this composite. For more information on this very powerful Layer Options dialog box, see "Layers, Layer Masks, and Adjustment Layer" and "Posterize, Bitmaps, and Patterns."

COLOR DODGE AND COLOR BURN

Color Dodge brightens the original image as the blending color goes further toward white. A Color Dodge with black does nothing, then as the blending color gets lighter, the original image picks up brightness and color more and more from the blending color. Color Burn is similar but opposite. A Color Burn with white does nothing, then as the blending color gets darker, the original image picks up darkness and color more and more from the blending color.

Have fun with all the Photoshop blending modes!

The Positive version of the Image.

The Black to White layer by itself.

The Spectrum layer by itself.

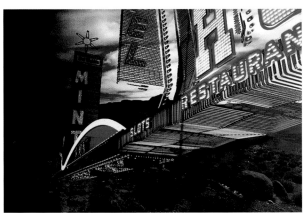

Color Burn of the Top Black blending to White Layer with the Positive image in the layer below.

Color Dodge of the Top Black blending to White Layer with the Positive image in the layer below.

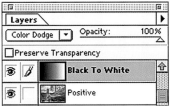

Layer setup for Black to White Color Burn and Dodge above.

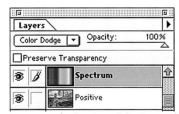

Layer setup for Spectrum Color Burn and Dodge below.

Color Burn of the Top Spectrum Layer with the Positive image in the layer below.

Color Dodge of the Top Spectrum Layer with the Positive image in the layer below.

HANDS-ON SESSION: Bike Ride in the Sky!

Combining two color images using two gradient masks and Multiply to create a high-flying bicyclist; using Blend modes versus Illustrator text treatments to create cool text effects.

The original bicycle.

Some interesting clouds!

I was playing in Photoshop one day and created one of my favorite images using two gradients to blend a cyclist into the clouds. Multiplying this image with its negative made it even more interesting. Here we use this image to play with some text effects.

COMBINING THE IMAGES WITH GRADATIONS

STEP 1: Open the Clouds and BikeRider files in the Bike Ride in the Sky folder. Click on the BikeRider file to make it active. Choose Window/Show Channels (Shift F10) and Window/Show Layers (F10) if the Channels and Layers palettes are not currently visible. Click on the New Channel icon to the left of the Trash icon at the bottom of the Channels palette to create a new channel.

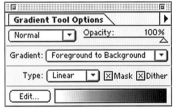

STEP 2: Gradient Tool Options.

STEP 2: New channel with gradient blend.

STEP 2: Double-click on the Gradient Blend tool (or type G and then Return) and set the options as shown in the illustration for this step. Type D to make sure the foreground color is white and the background color is black. Click at the top of the channel and hold down the Shift key as you drag downward to blend from white at the top edge of the channel to black at the bottom. The Shift key forces the line you draw to stay vertical. Make sure you start your blend exactly at the top edge of the file and finish exactly at the bottom; otherwise, the top won't be pure white and the bottom pure black. If you increase the window size to slightly larger than the file itself, finding the edges will be easier.

STEP 3: Drag the channel to the Load Selection icon at the bottom left of the Channels palette, or just Command-click on Channel #4 to load this selection. Now click on the RGB channel (Command-~) and choose Edit/Copy to copy the RGB channels of this file.

Now go to the Clouds file and choose Edit/Paste and you will notice that the bike rider fades out toward the bottom, since we did the Copy with the gradient selection loaded. We want a more dramatic fade-out with the wheels disappearing into the clouds, so choose Command-Z to get rid of the bike rider for the moment.

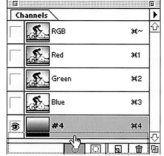

STEP 4: In the Clouds file, make a new channel and do a Gradient blend in this channel, just as you did in Step 2 with the bike rider. Command-click on this channel to load it as a selection. Click on RGB in the Channels palette to view the Clouds again.

STEP 3: Command-click the channel or drag to the Load Selection icon to load the selection.

STEP 5: You still have the bike rider in the copy buffer from the earlier copy, but instead of just pasting the file this time, choose Edit/Paste Into. The already faded bike rider is being pasted into a selection of the Clouds file that also causes fading toward the bottom. Because of this, fewer and fewer of the pixels in the lower portion of the Clouds file are affected by the Paste Into command. By doing the Load Selection on the bike rider before copying him, you are applying a mask that fades the bike rider towards the bottom. Doing the Paste Into applies a second mask to the image and fades it further at the bottom. When you copy with a selection loaded and then Paste Into another selection, you are using two masks to affect the resulting composite. If you turn off the Eye icon for the *Background* layer, you will see the bike rider as faded by both masks. Now hold down the Shift key and click on the Layer 1 Layer Mask to turn it off. This is the bike rider you copied from the other file. The Layer 1 Layer Mask was created because you did a Paste Into. This is the mask you had loaded as a selection when you did the Paste Into. Shift-click on the Layer Mask again to turn it back on, then turn the *Background* layer's Eye icon back on.

STEP 6: Use the Move tool (V or Command) to move the bike rider into a position that you like. Now use the Cropping tool (C) to crop the composite to your liking, and then choose Flatten Image from the Layers palette's menu to combine everything back to a single channel. Save this file in Photoshop format using the name NewBiker.

STEP 6: Move the bike rider and then crop the image and save as NewBiker.

USING MULTIPLY FOR A MORE INTERESTING EFFECT

STEP 7: Click on the *Background* layer and Option-drag it to the New Layer icon at the bottom of the Layers palette; name the new layer Inverse. The Inverse layer is now active (highlighted). Go to Image/Adjust/Invert (Command-I) to make a negative of the image. Change the Blend mode of the Inverse layer from Normal to Multiply. This does a Multiply of the pixels in this layer with the corresponding ones in the underlying layers. I have noticed that a Multiply of an image with its negative can often create interesting effects. We will be using Levels to look at this multiply composite and make it more interesting, but first we must merge these two layers or we will be running Levels on the Inverse layer alone. Choose Merge Down from the Layers palette menu. Now we can work on the composite as a single layer.

STEP 8: Go to Image/Adjust/Levels in the RGB channel and move the sliders to create more vivid color and contrast. Move the Input Highlight slider, the top right slider, to the left until you reach the beginning of the histogram information, then

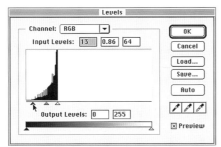

STEP 8: Adjusting levels makes this picture more interesting.

adjust the Brightness/Contrast slider to the right until you have an effect that you like. You may want to move the Input Shadow slider, the top left slider, a bit to the right also to darken the blacks. Click on OK in Levels.

STEP 9: Type L to switch to the Lasso tool, then press Return to bring up its Options palette. Now you can type a 5, then press Return again to pre-set the Lasso feather to 5 pixels. Lasso a portion of the clouds near one of what remains of the men holding up the bicycle. Now do Command-Option-click and drag to drag a copy of this selected area over on top of the man to cover what remains of him. Command-Option-dragging a selection creates a floating selection, a copy of the selected area, which you can move around by clicking and dragging inside its boundaries. Use Command-H to hide the edges of your floating selection; this makes it easier to see how it blends. When you are happy with its location, Choose Select/None (Command-D) to make it a permanent part of the current layer. If you hit the Delete key when working on a floating selection, it will go away. You could also double-click on it in the Layers palette to make it a permanent layer. You may have to take portions of several clouds to make the image look smooth. You can use the Rubber Stamp tool to clone portions of the clouds, the Smudge tool to soften the effect, or the Blur tool to smooth transitions at this point also. When you have removed all traces of the men, press Command-S to resave this file as NewBiker.

TEXT EFFECT ONE

This first type of text technique was originally learned from Kai Krause's helpful tips on channel operations that have been posted on America Online for the last few years. Check out the keyword Photoshop on America Online for all of Kai's interesting techniques and lots of useful Photoshop info from all over. The steps we are using here are somewhat different from Kai's channel operations, and they are made easier to understand by doing them using layers.

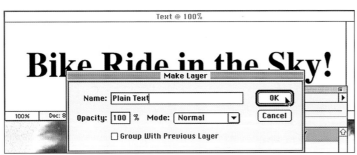

STEP 1: Rename the *Background* layer Plain Text.

STEP 1: Use File/New to make a new Mode/Grayscale document called Text that is 600 pixels wide by 150 pixels high with a Resolution of 72 dpi. Set the Contents to White, then click on OK. Click on the default colors box or type D to make sure the foreground color is black. Click down with the Text tool (T) to bring up the Text dialog box and type "Bike Ride in the Sky!" in Times Bold 60 pt., or a similar heavy bold font, with Anti-aliased on. Use the Move tool to position the type in the center of the white background, and then choose Merge Down from the Layers palette menu. Double-click on the *Background* layer and name it Plain Text. Make a copy of this layer by Option-dragging it to the New Layer icon at the bottom of the Layers palette and name it Blur & Offset.

STEP 2: Make the Blend mode for the Blur & Offset layer Darken. This chooses the darker parts of the two layers. Do a Filter/Blur/Gaussian Blur (Shift-F4) of 5 pixels and then a Filter/Other/Offset of 6 pixels to the right and 4 pixels down. Make sure Repeat Edge Pixels is chosen in the Offset filter. If you wanted black text with a gray drop shadow, you could stop now. We'll go further.

STEP 2: The Blur & Offset layer set to Darken mode.

STEP 3: Part 1, Equalize the Multiply layer .

STEP 3: Part 2, After the Equalize, Gaussian Blur 5 pixels and Invert with the mode set to Normal.

STEP 3: Option-drag the Blur & Offset layer to the New Layer icon and name the copy Multiply. Set its Blend mode to Normal for now. Choose Image/Adjust/Equalize, to spread the blur even further in this Multiply layer, then Gaussian blur this layer by 5 pixels to soften this spread, and finally, choose Image/Adjust/Invert. We invert this blur at the end because we will eventually want to colorize it as a glow, and for that purpose we need a light gray blur area. We also want the area surrounding the glow to be black so we can later remove it. Now, set the Blend mode for this layer to Multiply. Remember that Multiply will emphasize the dark areas of either image.

STEP 3: Part 3, Finally, the above image after changing its mode to Multiply. That multiplies this layer with the Step 2 results in the lower layers.

STEP 4: The result of a difference between Step 3 Part 2 and Step 3 Part 3. When you do a Difference, areas that are the same become black and areas that are far apart become white to gray depending on how far apart their corresponding pixels are.

STEP 4: Make a copy of this Multiply layer by again Option-dragging it to the New Layer icon. Name this one Difference. This actually copies Step 3: Part 2 (see illustration). Now change the Blend mode and this latest layer to Difference. Choose File/Save to save this layered version and then use Image/Duplicate (F5) with Merged Layers Only on to create a single layer version of this image called SkyText.

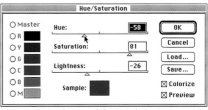

STEP 5: Final text after Hue/Saturation.

STEP 5: Now you are working on the single layer Sky Text file. Go to Image/Mode/RGB to change the mode to RGB. You need to do this to add color to the text. Now choose Image/Adjust/Hue/Saturation (Command-U). Click on both the Colorize and the Preview boxes and drag the Hue slider to the left until you get a nice purple, or some other color you like better. You may also want to lower the Saturation and the Lightness values to get a deeper, darker color. Choose OK when you are happy with the color. Now drag and drop a copy of this layer onto your NewBiker image. Use the Move tool to move the text to a location you like. Double-click on this new layer and name it SkyText. You will now be in the Layer Options dialog box. Drag the left-most This Layer slider to the right slightly until most of the black background is removed. Hold down the Option key and drag just the right side of that slider triangle further to the right until you get a shadow effect that you like. For more information on Layer options, see "Layers, Layer Masks, and Adjustments Layers" and "Posterize, Bitmaps, and Patterns." File/Save again as NewBiker.

STEP 5: Move the Hue slider to colorize text.

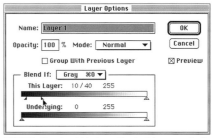

STEP 5: Blend out black on the text layer gradually with Layer Options.

The final Text One effect.

TEXT EFFECT TWO: PHOTOSHOP AND ILLUSTRATOR

Now we will be switching between Photoshop and Illustrator. We will be using both programs for several reasons: first, we want to set our type on a path; second, we want our type to print at a very high resolution to avoid looking jagged; third, Illustrator will allow us to easily kern and resize our type; fourth, we'd like the ability to make further corrections to the underlying Photoshop file without disturbing the text. So fasten your seatbelts!

STEP 1: In the NewBiker image, double-click on the *Background* layer and rename it to Biker, and then rename the Layer 1 layer to Text Effect One. We are going to add some text above the bike rider's back and it would be nice to have some more space between the top of the bike rider and the top of the file. Click on the Biker layer then choose Image/Canvas Size and set the height to 1.4 inches. Click in the bottom center to put the gray Anchor there. This will force the new canvas to all come in at the top of the image. Choose OK on Canvas Size, then use the Marquee to make a selection the entire width of the image from just above the biker's head to where the transparent area of the new canvas starts. Choose Layer/New/Layer Via Copy (Command-J) to create a new layer using this selected area. Now use Layer/Transform/Scale and click in the top middle handle, and then drag to the top of the window to scale this part of the clouds to fill the transparent area. Press Return to end the Scale, then choose Layer/Merge Down (Command-E) to merge this back into the Biker layer. Press Command-S to Save.

STEP 2: Open the Paths palette by going to Window/Show Paths (Shift-F11 with ArtistKeys). Click on the Pen tool (P) in the Tool palette. If you haven't used the Pen tool before, it might take several tries to get used to the feel of the tool, but keep at it. If you need to, go back to "Bob Goes To..." or "The Tool Palette" and review the Pen tool sections there. The Pen tool is a very powerful feature of Photoshop and once you get used to using it, you'll wonder how you ever worked without it. You are now going to build a path on which you will set type. You want the path to curve over the back of the bicyclist, so click the Pen tool underneath the bicycle seat to set the first point on the path and drag a handle from this point at about a 45° angle toward

STEP 2: The first click and drag.   **STEP 2:** The second click and drag.

the upper left corner of the file. Then, let go of the mouse button and click and drag a point somewhere near the biker's shoulder or above his head. Drag this point almost directly horizontal and to the right. You'll see the actual path grow and curve as you manipulate this handle. Now, click on the Pen icon in the Tool palette and drag to switch to the Arrow tool. Use this to modify the curve until you get a curve that matches the biker's back and is offset from his shape several pixels. Double-click on Path in the Paths palette and rename this path Text Path. Click in the white space below Text Path in the Paths palette to deselect that path.

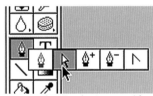

STEP 2: Choosing the Arrow tool from the Pen tool options in the Tool palette.

STEP 3: Choose Select/All to get the outline of your entire file and click on the SelectionToPath icon at the bottom of the Paths palette to make a new working path with this selection. Double-click on this new Work Path and name it Border. An alternative method is to Select/All and then make a path using the Make Work Path option in the Paths palette menu with the tolerance set to 1.5.

STEP 4: Once you have named this second path, you should do File/Save to save this NewBiker image again. Now, choose File/Export/Paths to Illustrator, choose All Paths from the Write pop-up item, and click on Save to save a new file called New-Biker.ai. This will give you the default name, which is the name of the current file with the extension .ai. If you have enough memory to run Illustrator at the same time you have Photoshop open, start Illustrator now. If not, you'll have to quit Photoshop to work in Illustrator and return to Photoshop to do your effects later. If you have no experience using Illustrator, try not to get frustrated with this part of the exercise. Illustrator, like Photoshop, is a large and wonderful program with lots of power and opportunities to make mistakes.

STEP 3: Converting the Select/All into a path.

STEP 5: From Illustrator, open the file you just exported, NewBiker.ai. When the file opens, you will probably see only four sets of crop marks and the outline of the page size that you have set in your document layout option. Don't worry about how things look for now. Just go to View/Artwork and you should see a rectangle the size of your Photoshop file and the path that you drew for the type.

STEP 6: Use the Magnify tool, Command-Spacebar-click as in Photoshop, to zoom in on the path for the type. Click on the Type tool in the Illustrator Tool palette and you

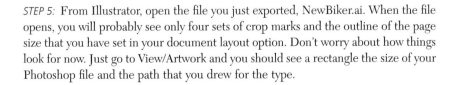

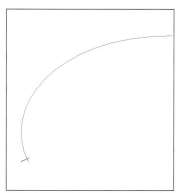

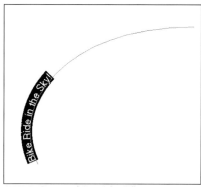

STEP 6: Click on the path with the Text tool.

STEP 7: Command A to Select/All.

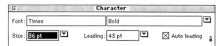

STEP 7: The Character dialog box in Illustrator. Your type sizes may be different depending on the font and resolution of your file.

STEP 7: Text kerned and resized.

will notice that the horizontal baseline under the tool becomes wavy as you put the Type tool on top of the Text Path. This is the Path Type tool. Click down on the path near the bottom left point and you get a flashing insertion point. Type "Bike Ride in the Sky!"

STEP 7: Then, with the Text tool still selected, press Command-A (Select All), and then Command-T, to bring up the Character dialog box. Change the type face to Times Bold at a point size where all the type fits and looks good (or go wild, choose Futura or some nice fat face). If you know how to use Illustrator, kern and resize the type to your heart's content. When you are happy with the type, use File/Save As to save the file with the same name in Illustrator 6.0 or 7.0 format or the most modern Illustrator format you have. Just overwrite the existing file when it asks you about that.

STEP 8: Back in Photoshop, reopen NewBiker if you had to leave Photoshop to bring up Illustrator. Click on the Text One layer to make it the active layer. Now go to File/Place and choose the Illustrator file New-Biker.ai. You will get a bounding rectangle with an X over it to show the size of the EPS file. In this case, it should be exactly the same size as the Photoshop file because of the Border path we created. Use Return to rasterize this text and that will create a new layer called NewBiker.ai. Rename it to Illustrator Text.

STEP 9: This Illustrator Text layer is back in Photoshop, so you can use Photoshop to create a shadow from it. If you are printing this file with an imagesetter, the actual text should be output from Illustrator to get the smoothest edges. If this is a multimedia or Web project and the final image will be low-res screen pixels anyhow, then you might as well make your text from Photoshop. In any case, you needed Illustrator to wrap the text around the path. Option-drag this Illustrator Text layer to the New Layer icon and call the new layer Shadow. Choose Edit/Fill (Shift-Delete) and fill this with black, making sure the fill options 100%, Normal, and Preserve Transparency are on. Now drag this Shadow layer below the Illustrator Text layer, and then use the Move tool to offset the shadow depending on the direction of your desired light source. Finally, do Gaussian Blur of about 2 to complete the shadow effect. You can also change the Opacity of the shadow from the Layers palette. Now click back on the Illustrator Text layer and change its color by picking the color you want and then using Edit/Fill again to fill this text with the new color. This allows you to see the effect with the colored text and shadow in Photoshop. If you were creating the entire image in Photoshop, you could use File/Save A Copy to save a flattened version with the layers you want for that usage. If you are printing the text from Illustrator, we need to go back there to complete the project.

STEP 10: Your goal now is to create an image you can import into Illustrator with the shadow for the text created in Photoshop. Turn off the Eye icons in the Illustrator Text and Text Effect One layers since we don't want them in the final Illustrator file.

The actual text will be created and output from Illustrator because it can then be output at Imagesetter resolution. Choose File/Save A Copy named New-Biker.eps in Photoshop EPS format with Flatten Image and Don't Include Alpha Channels on. In the EPS dialog box, make a Mac 8-bit preview (TIFF for Windows) and save in Binary with no clipping paths. Close Photoshop if you must to reopen Illustrator.

STEP 10: Layer palette setup and image as we save it in EPS format to be placed in Illustrator.

STEP 11: Go back to Illustrator and choose File/Place to place NewBiker.eps. In Illustrator 6.0, if you choose the Parse option that will now come up, you will get a more accurate preview. When you save, though, the image will become part of the final Illustrator document and it will be larger. If you don't parse NewBiker.eps, the preview won't look as good and you will have to remember to include New-Biker.eps in the folder when you go to print your document from Illustrator. After placing NewBiker.eps, if you are still in Artwork mode, you will see a bounding rectangle with an X across it. Use the Selection tool, the top left tool in Illustrator's Tool palette, and the arrow keys to position this rectangle exactly above the existing rectangle. For accuracy, you may want to zoom in considerably using Command-Spacebar-click. When the file is in position, send it behind the type by using Arrange/Send to Back. Then, use View/Preview to switch to Preview mode. You can use the Selection tool to click on the type baseline and change the color with the Paint Style dialog box at this point. Just click on the color you want. Use Window/Show Paint Style to bring up this dialog box. Just use File/Save to resave this final file as NewBiker.ai. This can now be printed to an imagesetter from Illustrator to get much finer edges on your text with PostScript text output. If you do further revisions to the Photoshop file, or have other versions of the file that you would like to try, you can click on the Photoshop image in Illustrator, and choose File/Place Art. If you placed your EPS file rather than parsing it, Illustrator will ask you if you want to replace the artwork that you have selected. If you say Replace to this prompt, your new artwork will pop into place automatically.

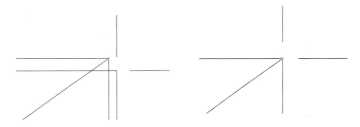

STEP 11: Your file may initially place out of alignment, like this.

STEP 11: Use the Selection tool and arrow keys to line up the file.

STEP 11: The final Text Effect Two as printed from an Illustrator EPS file placed in Quark.

HANDS-ON SESSION: Posterize, Bitmaps, and Patterns

Create interesting texture effects using Posterize, bitmaps, and patterns along with layers and Blend modes.

STEP 1: The original photo of the Packard.

There are many ways to create and integrate patterning into Photoshop images. Here we use bitmaps, filters, and various Layer options to add texture effects to images.

STEP 1: Type the letter D to get the default colors. Open the Packard image in the Posterize Bitmaps & Patterns folder and bring up the Layers palette (F10 with ArtistKeys). Double-click on the *Background* layer and rename it Packard. Choose File/Save As and save this as PackardLayers. Choose Image/Duplicate (F5) and name the duplicate copy PackardStreaks. You will use PackardStreaks later. Using the Window menu, go back to PackardLayers and do another Image/Duplicate, naming this one Packard/Mezzo. Use Image/Mode/Grayscale to change the mode on the duplicate copy to Grayscale and say OK to Discard Color Information. Choose Flatten if asked about flattening the image. Choose Select All (Command-A) then Edit/Copy and finally File/New (Command-N) to get a grayscale file the same size as the other Packard files. Before clicking on the OK button in the New dialog box, name the file MezzoTint and make sure that the White radio button is selected to fill this copy with white. Choose Filter/Noise/Add Noise and add 100 Gaussian noise. This is sort of a mezzotint pattern. Press Command-A again to select all of the grayscale pattern. Now choose Edit/Define Pattern to make this the pattern Photoshop is now using. You should now have four windows on your screen. The original color Packard, now called PackardLayers, the color PackardStreaks, the grayscale PackardMezzo and the MezzoTint pattern.

DIFFUSION DITHER BITMAPS AND MEZZOTINT PATTERNS

STEP 2: Return to the PackardMezzo window and choose Select/None (Command-D). Now choose Image/Mode/Bitmap and you will get a dialog box with a lot of options. Choose Diffusion Dither and say OK. Also say OK to the Flatten Image question if asked. The image will be zoomed to 100% because diffusion dithers don't look right unless the image is seen at 100% or closer. A diffusion dither bitmap is an image made up of only black and white dots; there are no grays. The Bitmap mode contains one bit of information for each pixel; it is either on or off, black or white. These images are very compact, which is useful for the Web and multimedia. A regular grayscale image contains 8 bits per pixel, so each pixel can have 256 different gray values. Diffusion dithers are very universal, because you can display them on any computer monitor and print them on any printer that can print black dots. Now choose Command-Z to undo the diffusion dither, choose Mode/Bitmap again and this time pick the Custom Pattern option. This will make a bitmap that uses the MezzoTint pattern you created and saved as the default pattern. Choose Select All, go to Edit/Copy, and then use the Window menu to switch to your color Packard image and do an Edit/Paste. Name this layer MezzoPattern.

STEP 3: With the MezzoPattern layer active and both Eye icons on, change the opacity to 40%. Now you can see the original Packard layer with MezzoPattern on top of it. The colors on the Packard will be muted since you are in Normal mode. Change the Blend mode in the Layers palette to Multiply to make the black dots more black. It will also bring out better color saturation in the non-black areas, and you will see better colors from the original Packard. Choose File/Save to update your file.

STEP 3: The Layers window should now look like this.

STEP 3: A section of the image with the 40% mezzotint pattern applied using Multiply mode.

A SUBTLE POSTERIZE EFFECT

STEP 4: Click on the Packard layer to make it the active layer, and then Option-drag it to the New Layer icon at the bottom of the Layers palette. Name it Posterize and choose OK. Option-click on its Eye icon to turn off the other layers for now. Choose Image/Adjust/Posterize and set the Levels to 6. This reduces each color channel in the Posterize layer to only six levels of gray, and gives this layer a posterized look. Now click on the Eye icon in the Packard layer to make that layer visible, but leave the Posterize layer active (highlighted). Move the Opacity slider to 40%, which will show 60% of the original Packard layer from below. This will give you a subtle posterize effect while still maintaining most of the original image from below. To quickly see the image with and without this effect, click the Eye icon to turn the Posterize layer on and off. Now turn on the Eye icon of the MezzoPattern layer to see all three layers together.

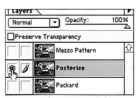

STEP 4: After Option-clicking on the Posterize Eye Icon, the other layers are not visible.

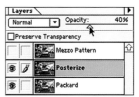

STEP 4: Seeing Posterize and Packard at the same time with Posterize being active at 40%.

STREAKED PATTERNS

STEP 5: Now we will create another pattern and add some more layers to give you other options with this image. When we add the next layer, we want it to be added above the MezzoPattern layer, so click on the MezzoPattern layer to make it the active layer. Switch windows back to the MezzoTint file and zoom out so you can see the whole file on-screen. Use the Rectangular Marquee tool (M) to make a long skinny selection on the left edge of the file the full height of the file. This rectangle should be about ¼ inch wide. Now use Layer/Transform/Scale and grab the middle right handle and drag it across the screen to the right side of the window. This stretches out the dots within this ¼ inch selection and gives you a streaking pattern. Press Enter or Return to finish the scale process. Command-Option-0 to zoom to 100%. Now choose Filter/Stylize/Emboss and emboss this pattern by 4 pixels, 150% at 135 degrees. Notice how the pattern changes depending on the Angle of rotation and the other Emboss parameters. Choose OK from Emboss. Choose Select/All (Command-A) and then Edit/Define Pattern to make this the current Photoshop pattern. Choose

File/Save As and name this pattern MezzoStreaks. Use the Window menu to switch to PackardStreaks that you made in Step 1. Use Image/Mode/Grayscale to convert it to grayscale and then use Image/Mode/Bitmap to convert that to another bitmap again using the Custom Pattern option. You will now get a streaked version of the Packard. Use File/Save As to save this as PackardStreaks.

STEP 6: Choose Select/All and and then Edit/Copy in the PackardStreaks document, and then switch to PackardLayers and do a Edit/Paste. This will make a new layer in the PackardLayers document above the MezzoPatternlayer. Double-click on this new layer and name it StreakPattern. When you double-click on a layer, the Layer Options dialog box opens. After typing in the new name, move this dialog box out of the way so you can see the PackardLayers document as well as this dialog box. From the Layer Options dialog box, we can change the Opacity and Composite modes. There are two sets of slider bars that are very cool—This Layer, which allows you to remove some of the pixels in the 0..255 range from the active layer, and Underlying, which allows you to specify the pixels from the underlying layers that will definitely be in the composite. Move the right-most highlight slider on This Layer until it says 247. This means that all the pixels from 248 through 255, the white pixels, will be removed from this layer in the composite. Now you see black streaks added to the composite image as the colors and pattern from below show through the white areas. Now change the opacity to 50%, and the black steaks turn to gray. Click on the OK button, and then do a Save (Command-S).

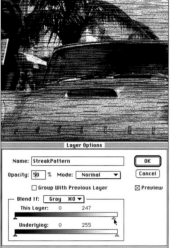

STEP 6: Using the This Layer slider to remove the whites from the pattern.

BLURRING BITMAPS TO ADD GRAY VALUES

STEP 7: Click on the StreakPattern layer and Option-drag it to the New Layer icon at the bottom left of the Layers palette. Name this new layer, which should be above the StreakPattern layer, StreakPatBlur. Set its opacity back to 100% and move the right-most This Layer slider back to 255. Say OK. Turn off the Eye icons on the StreakPattern and MezzoPattern layers and then click on the StreakPatBlur layer to make it active. Choose Command-L to look at this Layer in Levels and you will notice that only pure white and pure black values exist. Cancel from Levels. Use Filter/Blur/Gaussian Blur (Shift-F4) of 1 pixel to blur this new layer. Look at it in Levels again and you will notice that Gaussian Blur added many intermittent gray values. Now double-click on it to bring up the Layer Options dialog box again.

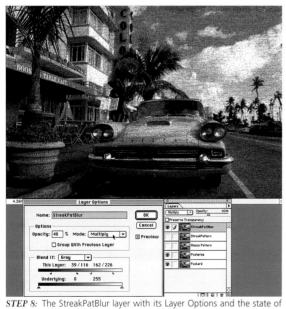

STEP 8: The StreakPatBlur layer with its Layer Options and the state of the Layers palette.

STEP 8: Now we can use the This Layer slider bar to do a lot of different types of effects. Zoom in to 100% (Command-Option-0) so you can see in detail what is happening. Move the left Shadow slider on This Layer to the right until it reads about 39. This removes the dark shadow values from 0 to 38. Now move the rightmost highlight slider to the left until it reads about 226. This removes the bright highlight values from 227 to 255. Notice that this modified pattern contains jaggy edges where the whites and blacks have been removed. While holding down the Option key, click on the right side of the left shadow slider and slide it to the right, which will split the slider in two. Drag the right side of the left slider until it reaches 116. Option-click on the left half of the rightmost slider and drag it until it reads 162. The numbers on the This Layer slider should now read, from left to right: 39, 116, 162, and 226. The meaning of this is that the shadow values from 0 to 38 are completely removed. The values from 39 to 116 are blended out slowly, which removes the jaggy edges. The values from 117 to 161 are completely opaque. The values from 162 to 226 are blended out, and the values from 227 to 255 are completely removed. Try changing the Blend mode between Normal, Multiply, Screen, Lighten, Darken, and Difference until you get the one you like best. You can also re-adjust the Opacity for each different Blend mode you try. Click on the OK button in the Layer Options dialog box when you are happy with this layer's effect. Do Command-S to save this version of the document.

STEP 9: You can obtain another interesting effect by doing the following. Have the Packard Layer at 100% Normal, Posterize at 50% Normal, and turn off the Eye icons for MezzoPattern and StreakPattern. Now set StreakPatBlur to 40% and Multiply with the Layer Options, as in the Step 8 illustration. Option-click on the New Layer icon and name the new layer Emboss. Make sure the new layer is above StreakPat-Blur. With the Emboss layer active, choose Option-Merge Visible from the Layers Palette menu to move all that you can now see into this Emboss layer. Now choose Filter/Stylize/Emboss and use the same settings you did in Step 5. Choose OK on the Emboss Filter, then change the Blend mode of the Emboss layer to SoftLight. If you now turn off the StreakPatBlur layer, you will notice that the pattern is embossed into the original colors without changing those colors much at all. The Emboss layer has a lot of neutral gray in it and the SoftLight Blend mode ignores neutral gray. Try the Overlay and Hardlight modes which also ignore neutral gray. You can change the opacity on the Emboss layer to lessen any of these effects. See "Blend Modes, Calculations, and Apply Image" to understand how these Blend modes actually work.

Here is the Layers palette setup for the image below.

TIME TO PLAY WITH LAYERS AND OPTIONS

STEP 10: Now you have several layers and effects that you can adjust until you get the final image you want. Remember that you can turn off any layer by clicking on its Eye icon. Play with Opacity, Mode, the This Layer slider, and the Underlying slider in the Layer Options dialog box for each layer until you get the final combined effect you like. Remember, the Underlying slider bar in the Layer Options dialog box forces pixels of lower layers into the composite. In the StreakPatBlur layer, if you move the rightmost Underlying slider to the left until it gets to 128, then all the values in the final composite from 128 to 255 will come from the lower layers, not from the StreakPatBlur layer. Play with these features until you understand them. When you are happy with a particular effect, you can use File/Save A Copy to save a flattened version of the file using only the layers that are currently visible. This way, you can save many variations of this multi-layered document.

My favorite layer combination has the Packard Layer at 100% Normal, the Posterize layer at 50% Normal, the MezzoPattern, StreakPattern, and StreakPatBlur layers off, and the StreakPatBlur Emboss layer at 100% SoftLIght.

HANDS-ON SESSION: Filters and Effects

*A tour of some of the more versatile Photoshop filters
as well as many useful layer and blending techniques
for getting the most out of all the filters.*

The best way to learn the simple filters is to just play with each of them. Try out all of the filters and all their features and compare different settings on the same image. Understand the range of possible things you can do with each filter. This is something that is fun and easy for you to do yourself and there are lots of other Photoshop books, including the Photoshop manual, that have charts of each filter and what it looks like during one particular iteration. Photoshop 4 comes with a set of over 75 filters, and with them and the rest of Photoshop you can do millions of different effects. There are hundreds of other third-party filters on the market, and some of them are really unique but a lot of them just give you a slightly easier way to do something that could already be done with the standard Photoshop filters by combining them with the other features of Photoshop.

In the rest of *Photoshop 4 Artistry,* we show you how to use the workhorse retouching filters in a lot of real world examples. Here in this chapter, we are going to concentrate on how to use layers and masks to combine filters in interesting ways. We are also going to talk about some of the more complicated filters and how to understand and make the best use of them. We also give an overview of the new Photoshop 4 filters toward the end of this chapter without going through each and every filter and and each of their options. You need to play with all the filters and options because the possibilities for effects and combinations are in the millions and using the techniques we show you here you can discover your own entirely new effects.

GETTING BOB READY

STEP 1: Open the file BobVegas from the Filters and Effects folder. Use the Cropping tool (C) to crop out the white stripe and copyright notice at the bottom. Click on the Bob layer in the Layers palette to make it the active layer. Click on Bob's layer mask, called Bob Mask, in the Channels palette and drag it to the Copy icon at the bottom of the Channels palette. Name this copy Bob Orig Mask. We can use this Bob Orig Mask in different ways to run different effects on either Bob, the background, or some combination.

STEP 2: Use the Eyedropper (I) to select a bright red, green, or yellow from the Las Vegas background as the foreground color. Click on the Bob layer, not the layer mask, then choose Edit/Fill (Shift-Delete) and fill the entire Bob layer, in Color mode, with 20% to 30% of this color. This should give him an interesting glow.

STEP 1: Open the file BobVegas from the Filters and Effects chapter.

STEP 2: Adding a red glow.

STEP 3: Click on the Bob Orig Mask in the Channels palette and make another copy of it, and call it Bob Blur Mask. Choose Filter/Blur/Gaussian Blur (Shift-F4) and put a 25-pixel blur on this mask channel.

STEP 4: Make a copy of Bob's layer by dragging it to the New Layer icon at the bottom of the Layers palette. Name the copy Bob Edges. Shift-click on the Bob Edges layer mask icon to turn it off for now. Run Filter/Stylize/Find Edges on this layer, and then press Command-I to invert it. Now go into Levels and manipulate the results of this filter to emphasize the main edges. First, move the Input Highlight (top right) and Brightness/Contrast (middle) sliders to the left to brighten the main edges and bring out more edges. Now move the Input Shadow (top left) slider to the right to darken the shadows and drop out the unneeded edges. Play with this for a while and then choose OK when the edges look right to you. Now Shift-click on the Bob Edges layer mask again to turn it back on and you will see the Vegas scene again. Turn off the Eye icon for the Bob layer for now and see the Bob Edges version on top of the Las Vegas.

STEP 5: To blend Bob Edges and Vegas together a bit, click on the Bob Edges layer mask and choose Image/Apply Image. Set the Source channel to the Bob Blur Mask channel, which will blend Bob Edges with the Las Vegas scene and make the top layer slightly transparent around the edges. You can always use Apply Image to copy any mask into a layer mask to change the appearance of the edges. Since we saved the Bob Orig Mask and Bob Blur Mask channels at the beginning, we can modify any other layer mask and still know we have these original versions to go back to later if we choose.

STEP 6: Now change the Blend mode on the Bob Edges layer to Difference, and see Las Vegas through the middle of Bob. Turn on the Eye icon for the Bob layer and at least Bob is no longer see-through. Now his skin looks sort of hard baked. Do a File/Save As here, then try out some of the other Blend modes for both the Bob and Bob Edges layers. Do File/Revert to continue with the exercise.

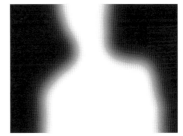

STEP 3: The Bob Blur Mask channel.

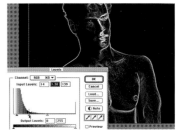

STEP 4: Using Levels to emphasize the main edges of the Find Edges filter.

STEP 6: Bob Edges in Difference mode, with Bob partying in Las Vegas.

STEP 5: Bob Edges blended with Vegas.

MOTION BLUR

STEP 7: Option-click on the Vegas Eye icon to turn off the Eye icons for all the other layers. Option-drag the Vegas layer to the New Layer icon at the bottom of the Layers palette and name the copy Vegas Motion Blur. Use Filter/Noise/Add Noise to add 35 of Gaussian noise. Adding noise before a Motion Blur enhances the motion effect. Now use Filter/Blur/Motion Blur of 40 at 23° to blur the Las Vegas street in the direction of motion down the block. Change the Blend mode on this layer to Luminosity and you will get an interesting effect between the blurred Las Vegas and the original Las Vegas. Again, press Command-S to save, then play with the other Blend modes on the Vegas Motion Blur layer. Multiply makes this look like a dangerous street to walk on, Screen turns it into party time, Overlay is sort of halfway between these two, and try Difference and Exclusion for a strange trip. Each Blend mode here gives the street a different mood. That's the great thing about combining filters

STEP 6: Your layers and channels should look like this after Step 6.

STEP 7: The new background with the motion blur effect.

with layers; there are thousands of different effects and you have to play with it to get the one that's right this time. Go back to Luminosity when you are done playing.

RADIAL BLUR

STEP 8: 20% Radial Blur, Spin Draft mode on Bob's left eye, then inverted.

STEP 8: With other layers on, set mode to Hard Light and set the Bob layer to 50%.

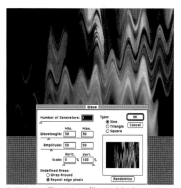

STEP 10: The Wave filter with the options simplified. The wavelength of a sine wave goes from one high point to the next. The amplitude is from the top to the bottom of a wave. It is a bit easier to see what the wave looks like because we are just doing it in the vertical direction.

STEP 9: What the Layers palette should look like after Step 9.

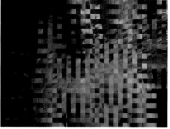

STEP 10: The new Merged layer after Square wave with the Blend mode set to Normal.

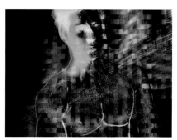

STEP 10: Changing the Blend mode to Overlay and turning on the other layers brings in an interesting effect.

STEP 8: Make of copy of the Bob layer and call it Bob Radial Blur. Drag it to be the topmost layer then Option-click on its Eye icon to turn off the other layers for now and Shift-click on its layer mask to turn it off, too. Use Filter/Blur/Radial Blur and click and drag in the Blur Center box to set the center of the blur to Bob's left eye. This may take you a couple of times to get right. Use Spin of 20 in Draft mode. The other quality modes will take longer, but don't forget that they are there when you need the absolute best quality radial blur. Use Command-I to invert this image to complete the first part of this step. Now Option-click on the Eye icon of this layer to turn the other layers back on. Set the mode of this layer to Hard Light, then set the opacity of the Bob layer to 50%, and you get the second effect of this step. Try some more effects yourself by playing with all the layers.

STEP 9: Choose Command-S to save your creation so far. Turn off the Eye icons of the top two layers and set the opacity of the Bob layer back to 70%. Option-click on the New Layer icon and name the new layer Merged Layer. Drag it up to the top of all the other layers. Hold down the Option key while choosing Merge Visible from the Layers Palette menu. This will stick a merged copy of the currently visible layers into this new top layer without actually merging the other layers into one. Whenever you get a certain look that you want to save, you can always do Option-Merge Visible to create this look in a single layer.

THE WAVE FILTER

STEP 10: Now choose Filter/Distort/Wave and look at the many options in this dialog box. The first step in understanding what the Wave filter can do for you is to simplify the options. Set the Number of Generators to 1, the Type to Sine, both Wavelengths to 30 and both Amplitudes to 50. For now, set the Scale to 100% in the Vertical dimension and 0% in the Horizontal dimension. The wavelength is the distance from the top of one wave to the top of the next. The amplitude is the distance from the top of a wave to the bottom. Getting one simple sine wave across the screen makes it easier to see what this filter actually does. Choose OK to accept the filter parameters if you want to see this in more detail. If you do this, press Command-Z to undo it—then Command-Option-F to run the filter again, but change the options. Now change the Type to Triangle waves and you can see that they look like the stitch of a zig-zag sewing machine. Try the Square wave Type, my favorite. It makes the image look like it went through a shredder and then was put back together again with the width of the shreds set by the wavelength and the separation of the two sets of shreds set by the amplitude. Play around with these parameters but keep it simple until you understand what each one does. They can be combined in interesting ways to create all sorts of wave shapes.

Go back into the Wave filter and set the shape to Square. Set the number of generators to 1, all wavelength and amplitude values to 50, and then set 100% Vertical and 50% Horizontal. Repeat Edge Pixels should also be turned on. This is a cool effect just by itself, but now try the different Blend modes and also different opacities to get lots of other neat effects. The one I liked best is shown here with all the layer's Eye icons turned back on and the Blend mode set to Overlay and Opacity set to 100%.

Now you should experiment with the Bob and Vegas images on your own. Create a new Bob layer by copying one of the existing Bob layers. Try out each of the filters with each of its parameters on a separate layer then combine them using the Blend modes and opacities of these layers. You can turn any layer on or off by using its Eye icon. You can move any layer to the left or right, or up or down, by using the Move tool. Do this to have two or three Bobs standing next to each other. Play and be creative. I am amazed at all the different types of effects the thousands of students who have worked with these two images over the years have come up with!

LINE DRAWING

STEP 11: Now let's open a different image and try some other types of filters and effects. Open the file called ParisDog from the Filters and Effects folder. Notice that it already contains a mask of the dog and a pattern that we created in Photoshop. See "Poster-ize, Bitmaps, and Patterns" for some ideas about how to create patterns like this in Photoshop. First, we will show you how to turn this image into a line drawing. Double-click on the *Background* layer and rename it Orig Dog. Make a copy of this layer by dragging it to the New Layer icon in the Layers palette. Name the copy Dog Edges. Use Filter/Stylize/Find Edges on the Dog Edges layer to find the edges of this image and use Image/Map/Invert (Command-I) to invert those edges. Use Command-L for Levels and move the Input Highlight and Brightness/ Contrast sliders to the left and the Input Shadow slider to the right to emphasize the main edges. You can also use the Load button to load the LevelsIsolateEdges preset levels settings from the Extra Info folder. Click on the OK button in Levels.

STEP 11: The original Paris Dog image.

STEP 11: The Dog Edges layer after Find Edges, Invert, and Levels.

STEP 12: Choose Duplicate Layer from the Layers palette pop-up with a New destination to make a copy of this layer in a separate file. Use Image/Mode/Grayscale to

STEP 12: The Dog Edges B&W layer by itself after being Inverted.

STEP 12: Dog Edges B&W combined using Lighter with the Orig Image channel.

STEP 13: The Dog Edges B&W Fat layer combined using Lighter with the Orig Image channel.

turn the copy into black-and-white. You need to do this in a separate file or else all the layers will be turned into black-and-white. You will now have white lines against a black background. Use the Move tool (V) to click on this grayscale file and then Shift-drag it and drop it back on the Paris Dog file. You need the Shift key down in Photoshop 4 to center the new layer when you drag and drop. Now you should have a new black-and-white layer on the top, so name it Dog Edges B&W. You should now have Orig Dog as the bottom layer, then Dog Edges, and finally, Dog Edges B&W on top. Turn off the Eye icon for Dog Edges and set the mode for Dog Edges B&W to Darken. Darken mode will give you a black background with colored lines where the white edges were. To get an even better effect, use Command-I to invert Dog Edges B&W, and then change the mode to Lighten. This will give you a white background with colored lines. I like this effect a little better. If you look at this layer by itself, you will see that it is just a black-and-white line drawing.

STEP 13: Now make another copy of the Dog Edges B&W layer, call it Dog Edges B&W Fat, and make sure that it is now the top layer. Turn the Eye icon off for Dog Edges B&W. You should now have the Eye icons on for Dog Edges B&W Fat (the active layer), and for Orig Dog. Run Filter/Other/Minimum of 1 on Dog Edges B&W Fat. This will make the edges here a minimum of 1 pixel wide and will give a chalk-drawing type effect. Try 2-4 pixels wide and notice the painterly effect this gives the image. I ended up using 3 pixels. The mode should still be set to Lighten, so you will see more color detail with these thicker lines.

STEP 14: Turn on the Dog Edges layer again and see how its different Blend modes affect the composite. Most of the effects created with this layer at 100% opacity are too radical to be very interesting. Try lowering the opacity of the Dog Edges layer and you will notice the effects getting more subtle and interesting. The one I like best is setting the Blend mode of this Dog Edges layer to Difference and the opacity to 20%. To see the effect any particular layer is having on the final composite, just turn the Eye icon for the layer on and off.

STEP 15: Let's say you like this effect but you really want to see the dog as it was in the Orig Dog layer and only have the effect apply to the image around the dog. To do this, with Dog Edges as the Active layer, you need to Command-click on the DogMaskRail mask in the Channels palette to load it as a selection. Now Option-click on the Layer Mask icon in the Layers palette to add a layer mask that will keep everything visible in this layer except the selected area. Now click on the Dog Edges B&W Fat layer to activate it, reload the DogMaskRail selection, and then Option-click on the Layer Mask icon again to create the same layer mask for this layer. Now the Dog is removed from the two effects layers so you see the original dog coming through from the Orig Dog layer at the bottom.

STEP 16: Let's assume that we want to selectively burn and dodge the dog a bit to add some contrast and definition. We want to do this in such a way that we can change it or undo it later. Option-click on the New Layer icon and name this layer 50% Gray. The new layer should be at the top of all the other layers. Choose Shift-Delete to Fill this layer with 50% Gray using the 50% Gray option in the Fill dialog box. Now your whole window will turn gray until you change the Blend mode on this layer to Soft Light. In Soft Light mode, 50% gray does nothing to the layers underneath, but if you paint with darker than 50% gray, the image underneath will be darkened and painting with lighter than 50% gray will lighten the image. Now type A to get the Airbrush and set its pressure to 5%. Type a D to get the default colors of black and white and then, using a soft brush, paint with black where you want to darken the dog and white where you want to brighten the dog. Since you are using the Airbrush, you can hold down the mouse button and paint to get more darkness or lightness. The great thing about burning and dodging this way is that you can undo the entire effect by just turning this layer on or off. You can also lessen the effect by changing the opacity of this gray layer. Now try changing the Blend mode to Overlay or Hard Light and notice that these also do nothing at 50% Gray. In Softlight mode, the effects are more subtle and you won't actually get full black or full white in your underlying image, even if you paint them in the gray layer. Overlay and Hardlight are more radical in their effects using the same gray layer, but you can always lower the opacity of the layer to lessen these effects. I often use this technique with Softlight mode to add highlights or burn or dodge. It's great when working with a client because you can show them different effects by just turning on one or the other 50% Gray layer and you can always undo any part of any gray layer by just refilling that part with 50% gray again.

LIGHTING EFFECTS

STEP 17: Click on the Dog Edges B&W layer, go into the Channels palette, and make a copy of its Red channel using the New Channel icon at the bottom of the Channels palette. Name this copy Lines Thin. We are going to use this as a pattern in the

STEP 15: The Dog Edges layer turned on again with Difference and Opacity of 20%. Here the dog is revealed as is from the Orig Dog layer.

STEP 16: The same image to the left after dodging and burning with the 50% Gray layer in Softlight mode.

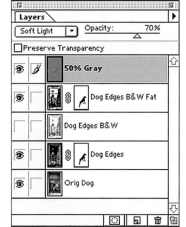

STEP 16: The Paris Dog layers as they should look at the end of step 16.

STEP 17: The Lighting Effects filter with texture created by the Lines Thin pattern.

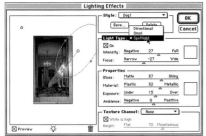

STEP 17: The different light types in the Lighting Effects filter.

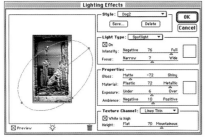

STEP 17: The Spotlight.

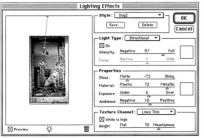

STEP 17: The Directional light and Texture Channel set to Lines Thin.

STEP 18: The setup for the Texture Channel and Dog Pattern.

Lighting Effects filter. In the Layers palette, make another copy of the Orig Dog layer right on top of that layer and call it Dog Pattern. Option-click on its Eye icon to turn off all the other layers for now.

Choose Filter/Render/Lighting Effects and notice the many options in this filter that allow you to add lighting with different types of lights to your image. The Photoshop 4 manual has a good description of this filter, which you should read if you want to understand all of its features. We are going to try some of them here. Set the light type to Default and click on the white circle over the dog preview in the dialog box. This is the original light. Drag it and place it on the dog's shoulder. Click on the other end of the line that is leading out of the white spot and move it around so it ends up above and to the right of the dog's head. This is a spotlight pointing at the dog and coming from above and to the right of the dog. Set its intensity and width as shown here. You change the width by clicking on the sides of the oval and then dragging to make the oval wider or thinner.

Now add a new light by clicking on the Lightbulb icon at the bottom of the dialog box and dragging a new light to the desired location in the preview window. Set its light type to Directional and place it at the top left of the image near where the chandelier meets the ceiling. Drag the line coming out of the spot far above and a little to the right. This creates a light coming from above at a subtle angle. Set its parameters as shown in the dialog box. Click on OK to see the effects of these lights in more detail. Choose Command-Z to undo these effects. Type Command-Option-F to bring up the Lighting Effects filter again and change its options. Go down to the Texture Channel pop-up and select the Lines Thin channel you created at the beginning of this step. Set the parameters as in the illustration here. Now choose OK from the Lighting Effects filter and you will see a texture formed around the line edges.

STEP 18: Choose Command-Z to undo the previous incantation of Lighting Effects and Command-Option-F to go back into the filter. Change the Texture Channel to Dog Pattern and set the parameters as shown. Click on the OK button. Now turn on

STEP 18: The Lighting Effects filter with texture created by the Dog Pattern pattern.

STEP 18: The Dog Pattern Lighting Effects combined with Orig Dog using Soft Light mode at 70% Opacity.

the Eye icon for the Orig Dog layer underneath. With Dog Pattern as the active layer, set the mode to Soft Light and the opacity to 70% to see the final effect pictured on the previous page. You should try some of the textures on the Photoshop 4 CD-ROM with the Lighting Effects filter.

DISPLACEMENT MAPS

STEP 19: Now let's play with displacement maps. Click on the New Channel icon in the Channels palette to create a new channel. Type D to get the default colors, then use the Gradient tool to do a linear gradient clicking down first with white at the top and dragging down to black at the bottom. Use Command-M to enter Curves, click on the Load button, and load the Displace Curve from the folder for this exercise. This will create a displacement map that is black in the center and white at the top and bottom. Using this as a displacement map will cause any value that is less than 128 to displace in a negative direction and any value that is greater than 128 to displace in a positive direction. Use the Duplicate Channel Channels pop-up to copy this channel to a separate, new destination file and save it in Photoshop format. Name this new file Left/Right Flop. Any Photoshop file can be a displacement map. Make the Orig Dog layer alone active, or make a copy of it, then choose Filter/Distort/Displace and set the parameters to displace as shown here. Make sure Stretch to fit and Repeat Edge pixels are turned on. When asked for a displacement map, open the file you just saved, Left/Right Flop. Notice that the pixels in the image whose corresponding pixels were less than 128, in the displacement map, moved to the right, and those that were more than 128 moved to the left. Use Command-Z to undo this. Now, try Displace again, but this time use –20 as the horizontal value. That causes the image to flop in the opposite direction.

STEP 20: Again, use Command-Z to undo the last Displace. Now use the Rectangular Marquee to select the rightmost small chain hanging down to the bottom left of the window. Also select a little of the gray around the chain. Edit/Copy this, do

STEP 18: The final Paris Dog layers and channels after Step 18.

STEP 19: The settings for Displace.

STEP 19: The Left/Right Flop displacement map created with a gradient and curves.

STEP 19: The dog after being displaced by 20 horizontally.

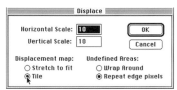

STEP 20: The Displace settings for the Chain Displacement map.

STEP 20: The dog after being displaced by the Chain Displacement map.

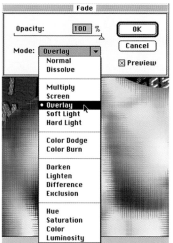

Here are the options of the Filter/Fade command which you can run right after using a filter. For the most flexibility, run the filter in a layer instead.

Command-N and OK for a new file, and then paste this section of chain in the new file. Save this as ChainMap in Photoshop format. Now choose Filter/Distort/Displace again, but this time, change the settings to 10 in each of the horizontal and vertical directions and turn on the Tile setting. This will cause the same displacement map to be repeated over and over again until the image is covered. Choose the ChainMap for your displacement map and you will get the image shown here. Try some other patterns for a displacement map. When there are two or more channels in the displacement map, the first channel is used to displace in the horizontal direction and the second channel is used to displace in the vertical direction. Displace is a very powerful and fun filter that can be used for a lot of great effects. You just need to create the displacement map that is appropriate for your needs!

THE NEW FADE COMMAND

When you run a filter in Photoshop 4, you have the new option of using Filter/Fade after running the filter to change the effect of the filter before it is made permanent. Using Fade is sort of like running a filter on the image in a separate layer above the image. If you do that, you can always go back and change the Opacity or Blend mode of that layer to blend the filter with the original image underneath. Doing this with layers is a great approach and we use it a lot earlier in this chapter. The Filter/Fade command is like running the filter in this other layer, but if you don't adjust it before you do something else, it gets merged with the layer below. The feature says: "Let's give them one more chance to tweak this filter, then we'll make the effect permanent on the layer that was active when you ran the filter."

To use Filter/Fade, just select it after running a filter and you will get the Fade dialog box shown here. You can switch the Blend mode or Opacity, but there is no Layer Options or Layer Mask. Adobe pretty much disabled floating selections in Photoshop 4, which is good, but it might have been better to completely remove them. Then they added the Fade command as sort of a lesser god. So, after you run a filter, you can choose Filter/Fade to change the effect through Opacity or Blend mode. You can then Undo and Redo the Fade, but when you do anything else that changes the Undo buffer, the ability to further change the Fade goes away.

If you really want flexibility, just make a copy of the layer you were going to run the filter on, put that copy on top of the layer and then run the filter on the copy. Since this is a separate layer, you have all the capabilities of Fade, plus you have

Layer Options, plus you can change it or undo it at any time just by changing the Eye icon, Opacity, Blend mode, or Layer Options. Maybe people will use Fade when making quick comps or if they don't have the memory to save the layer. I haven't used it much so far.

THE NEW (SORT OF) 4.0 FILTERS

In Photoshop 4, Adobe added a bunch of filters to Photoshop but they were not really new to the world. The Aldus Gallery Effects filters were tuned up and added to Photoshop. I guess this is a side effect of Adobe purchasing Aldus a few years ago. It is great to have these new filters, but I have the feeling that, when looked at by themselves, they are not as powerful as the standard set of filters that came with Photoshop 3. Adding them is certainly a plus for Photoshop 4, though.

These filters do seem to fall into several groups, as far as basic layout and functionality, and a particular group doesn't always go into the same submenu. There are the three option filters. All of them have the same size dialog box and they all have three options. The options have different names depending on the filter, but some of the names and functionality are shared among several of them. Another group is the Texture filters. They have a Texture section, at the bottom of their dialog boxes, that allows for an adjustment in the scale of the texture pattern, the intensity of the texture pattern, called Relief, and the direction of lighting on the texture. You can then choose the texture pattern from a small list of choices in an included pop-up menu or you can load a texture from a Photoshop file. The Photoshop 4 CD comes with a bunch of textures you can load from the Textures for Lighting Effects folder in the Other Goodies folder. These are not automatically installed with Photoshop, but you will find them on the same CD as the Installer. These textures work well with this set of filters as well as with lighting effects.

If you are browsing the Filter sub-menus, the filters in the Noise, Pixelate, Sharpen, Render, and Video menus are the same. The Artistic, Brush Strokes, Sketch, Digimarc, and Texturize menus have all new filters. Smart Blur has been added to the Blur menu; Diffuse Glow, Glass, and Ocean Ripple have been added to the Distort menu; and Glowing Edges was added to Stylize.

The Digimarc filters allow you to embed a watermark into your image for copyright protection. To get your own watermark, you need to register with the Digimarc people. I have not tried this myself, but recommend that you test the survival of their watermarks through the different types of JPEG compression, printing, and other digital contortions you will be doing before you assume it is a bulletproof solution to your particular copyright problems. I am hoping that it is a

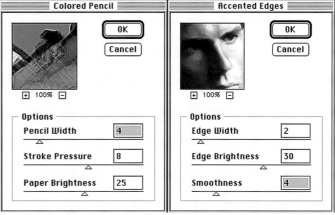

Some examples of the three-function filters. The top option is called Pencil Width in the Colored Pencil filter, but a somewhat similar option in the Accented Edges filter is called Edge Width. We have Edge Brightness in one, then Paper Brightness in another. Smoothness and Stroke Pressure seem to actually be different options. If you use filters a lot, you should play with each of these and decide which ones are worthwhile for you.

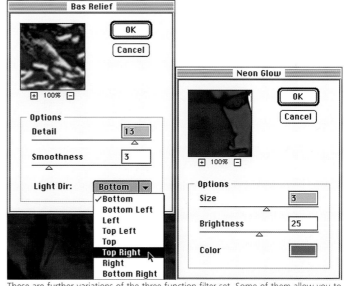

These are further variations of the three-function filter set. Some of them allow you to pick a lighting direction and Neon Glow allows you to pick the color of the glow. Some of the other filters in this new set just use the foreground color as the filter's color. Notice that Smoothness and Brightness appear here as in some of the other new filters.

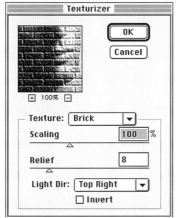

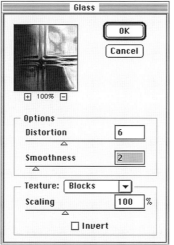

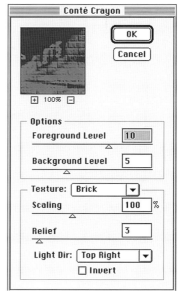

This is the basic variation of the Texture filter group I just mentioned. Here you can pick one of several built-in textures, or you can load a texture from a file. This also allows you to choose the lighting direction and even invert the lighting. Scaling scales the texture pattern and Relief controls how much the texture creates a 3D appearance.

This has some of the Texturizer options and a different set of other options. This filter is fun to play with. Increasing the Distortion makes the glass further distort the image underneath. The Smoothness controls the blending of the edges.

This has the same options as Texturizer but here they have added Foreground Level and Background Level.

great solution and, later in 1997, will be testing it myself. Check our Web site at Maxart.com for the test results and new information as it comes along. There is more information about Digimarc in the Photoshop 4 manuals.

As we mentioned at the beginning of this chapter, the best way to learn about the filters is to play with them and combine them using layers and the Blend modes. Have fun!

NEXT PAGE

Effects done by students in Barry Haynes' custom advanced courses where the students bring in their own projects and images. The image on the top left is by Susan Holland, the top right by Will Croff, the bottom left by Marita Gootee, and the bottom right by Jeffrey Myers.

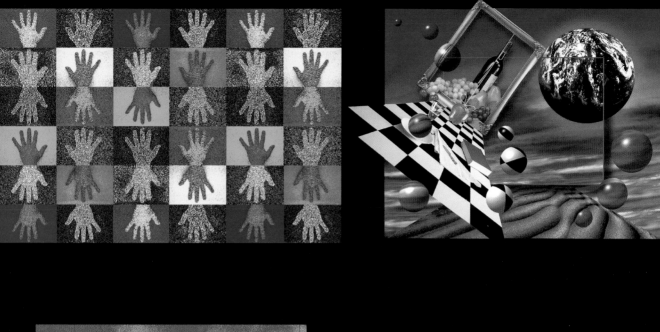

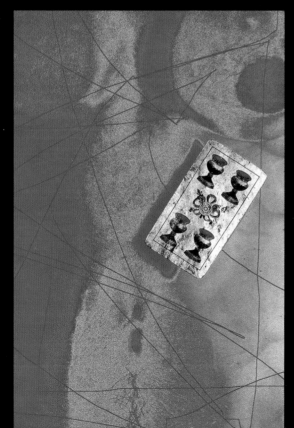

HANDS-ON SESSION: The *APDA* Magazine Cover

*Create an image from components for a specified canvas size,
a magazine cover; work with drop shadows, knock-outs,
motion effects, the Pen tool, and layers for high-quality output.*
(This magazine cover was produced for the Apple Programmers and Developers Association.)

This example describes the production of a published magazine cover for the February 1993 issue of the Apple Programmers and Developers Association magazine, *APDA: Tools for Developers.* This magazine is a catalog of tools and information for Macintosh software developers. This cover was designed to introduce some new QuickTime multimedia tools for writing software for the Macintosh and Windows. Dan Auvil, from Crane Auvil & Associates in San Francisco, came up with the concept for the cover, which he sketched to scale on an 8.5x11 sheet of paper. Dan then hired Marc Simon, also in San Francisco, to shoot the original photographs—the two computers and the multimedia objects that would be flying into the computer screen. The objects were shot together like this so the lighting and shadows on each object would look correct in relationship to each other when they were composited in the computer.

Marc had recently taken a Photoshop class from Barry, so he hired Barry to do the compositing on the Macintosh. Like many photographers today, Marc was considering purchasing a computer to add to his bag of darkroom tools. Since this project, Marc has purchased his own Macintosh and is now among those leading-edge photographers who do great studio work and also digital imaging. While working on this project, Barry and Marc had to look at Dan's hand-drawn sketch and produce the concept to scale with Marc's images on the computer screen. We will go through the steps here.

PRODUCING THINGS TO SPEC

One of the things we want to learn in this example is how to produce things to scale to a spec. Since the final magazine cover has already been produced, we will use that as a target to emulate instead of working from the hand-drawn sketch. The files in this example are in CMYK format because they were scanned from a high-end scanner, where the operators guaranteed that the color of the scan would match the transparency. Because we started

The final February 1993 *APDA* magazine cover image, as delivered to the advertising agency, Crane Auvil & Associates. They added text titles and logos using QuarkXPress to produce the final cover. This is the image you will produce in this example.

The original photograph of the computers by Marc Simon Photography. We refer to this as Computers in the example.

The original photograph of the multimedia objects by Marc Simon Photography. We refer to this as Objects in the example.

with high-end CMYK scans, we just had to do the compositing and effects; we didn't have to worry about color correcting.

SETTING UP THE CANVAS

STEP 1: Open the files ComputersOrigScan, PartsOrigScan, and FinalAPDA from the APDA Magazine Cover folder on the CD. What we want to do in this example is create the FinalAPDA image from the other two files. For the original magazine cover, all the files were 300 dpi; we have reduced them to 150 dpi and JPEG-compressed them here so they are not quite so big to work with.

STEP 2: The final cut magazine cover is 8.4 inches wide by 10.8 inches high. We want to produce something a little bigger, because the cover is a full bleed and there needs to be some leeway around the edges. We will make the final canvas size 9 by 11.4 inches, keeping in mind that it will be cropped to 8.4x10.8 when printed. When working on full bleed images for magazines, it is important that you get the specs from all the magazines ahead of time for the bleed size, trim size, and the live area size. The bleed size includes the amount of extra image that needs to hang off the edge, so that when the page is cut, there is always enough image to bleed off the edge. The trim size is the size of the actual product after the edges are cut off, and is smaller than the bleed size. The live area size is the rectangle in the trim size area where you place text and important information that you want to be sure makes it onto the page. This is smaller than the trim size, because magazines will not guarantee exactly where the trim will happen. They will guarantee that nothing inside the live area will get trimmed off. You put important things inside this live area box. We will use guides so we can see these areas as we work. Switch to the file ComputersOrigScan and choose Image/Canvas Size. Set the height to 11.4 inches and put the gray box in the bottom center so the new height will be added above. Leave the width as is and choose OK. Now type C to get the Cropping tool and then press Return to bring up its options. Set the options to Fixed Target Size with the width at 9 inches and the height at 11.4 inches. Leave the Resolution blank; we don't want the crop to resample the file. If we were actually printing this, the resolution would be 300 dpi, but we are going to leave it at 150 dpi. Put yourself in Full Screen mode and then press Command-0 to zoom out so you can see the entire image on the screen. Click down in the gray area above the top-left corner of the image and drag out to the gray area below the bottom-right of the screen. This forces the entire dimension from top to bottom to be included. Now click in the center of the rectangle and drag it from left to right until it is centered and includes all the computers and books. Now press Return or Enter to crop the image to your 9x11.4x150 pixel size. Choose File/Save As and save this in Photoshop format as WhiteCanvas. You will turn this into your final canvas for this project.

STEP 3: Arrange WhiteCanvas and FinalAPDA on the screen so you can look at both at the same time. Set the Info palette to measure in inches.

STEP 3: Arrange WhiteCanvas and FinalAPDA on the screen so you can look at all of both folders at once. Bring up the Info palette (F9 with ArtistKeys) and in its Palette options, set its bottom measurement area to Inches. Double-click on the Line tool and set the line width to zero with no arrowheads. We will use the Line tool as a ruler to measure the distance from the bottom of the keyboard to the bottom of the FinalAPDA image. To do this, just click at the bottom left of the keyboard in the rightmost computer and drag to the bottom of the image area while holding the Shift key down, to force a vertical line. It should be about 1.812 inches shown as delta Y in the top-right panel of the Info palette. Now measure this distance on the WhiteCanvas image; it will be less. Figure out the difference between 1.812 and the distance on WhiteCanvas and write this down. Type M to get the Rectangular Marquee tool and use it to select the part of the WhiteCanvas image that was there originally, before we increased the height in Canvas Size. Select the full width. Type V to switch to the Move tool, then click and drag to move the selection upward. After starting the upward move, put the Shift key down to force the movement to be only vertical. Move it upward the calculated distance so the total distance from the bottom of the keyboard to the bottom of the image is 1.812 or very close to it. You can see the moved distance as delta Y in the Info palette. Delta X should stay zero; having the Shift key down after you start the move will force this. Press Command-D to drop the floating selection, and then press Command-S for Save.

STEP 3: Use the Line tool with the Shift key down to measure the distance from the bottom of the keyboard to the bottom of the image.

KNOCKING OUT THE BACKGROUND

STEP 4: Now you will use the Pen tool to make a selection around all the computers and other objects in the image. We want to knock out the background, and unfortunately, we can't do it automatically, because it is not a different enough color from the computers and equipment. Put yourself in Full Screen mode using the middle icon at the bottom of the Tool palette. Hit the Tab key to close all your palettes. Choose Window/Show Paths to bring up the Paths palette. Select the Pen tool from the Tool palette (P) and use Command-Spacebar-click to zoom into the top of the leftmost book at the left of the WhiteCanvas image. Start tracing the image around the edge between the books, computers, and other objects and the background. We want

STEP 4: Start and end your path here at the top left of the leftmost book.

to make a path that selects all objects, including the shadows but no background. Use the Spacebar to scroll, Command-Spacebar-click to zoom in, and Option-Spacebar-click to zoom out as you move around the edges of the objects making a path to eliminate the background. If you misplace a single point, you can Undo (Command-Z) to remove that one point and redo it. If you mess up several points, just continue and fix them later or hold down the Command key to temporarily switch to the Arrow tool and use it to adjust those points. Releasing Command will put you back in the Pen tool. Trace the path to the right across the books, up and around the leftmost monitor and down its right side getting the nook areas between the monitors. Don't forget to use click and drag around the corners and on curves to get an accurate path for each type of shape. Remember to use the Spacebar and mouse drags to scroll around the image as you work.

STEP 4: Make sure that you select the shadows below the keyboards, mice, and other items.

Trace up the left side of the rightmost monitor, down its other side, and over the tops of the books on the right side. Now come along the bottom of the mice and keyboards. When you are selecting shadow areas, include all the shadow in your selection. See the illustration here and make sure you select the shadows in the same way. This is very important! Move to the left along the front of the keyboards and then finally up the left side of your original book until you complete the path by clicking again on the first path point. When you get to that point, a little white circle will appear to the right of the pen nib to tell you the path has been completed. Choose Save Path from the Path palette's menu and name it Computers Outline. If you need a review of using Paths, see "Bob Goes to..." or "The Tool Palette."

STEP 5: With this path still active in the Paths palette, use the Pen tool again to add the two hole areas below and to the left of the leftmost monitor and below and to the right of the rightmost monitor. These areas will be holes in your final selection. Now type P to switch to the Arrow tool and click on the first big path you made around all of the equipment. This will bring up the points again and you should scroll around the screen looking carefully at each point and the adjoining lines and moving any points that need moving. Remember that you can get the Pen+ tool while using the Arrow tool by holding down Command-Option when on a line. You get Pen– with Command-Option when on a point and the Convert Direction Point tool with Control when on a point. Since you named your path, it and all its changes have been saved under the name we gave it in the Paths palette. When your path is completed, click with the Arrow tool on the image area outside the path to deselect any subpaths that could be selected.

STEP 6: Bring up the Layers palette (F10 with ArtistKeys) and rename the *Background* layer to Computers. Click on the background color in the Tool palette and set the CMYK values to 5,3,3,0. This is the white background that we want to use in the final image. Now Option-click on the New Layer icon in the Layers palette and name the new layer White 5,3,3,0. Do a Shift-Delete (Shift-Backspace in Windows) to bring up the Fill command and fill this new layer with this background color at 100% normal. We are using this particular color because it is the brightest white we can get and still hold a dot. We want the motion blur effects we are going to do later to slowly blend into a white that still has a dot, so that the blurs don't look pixelated around the edges. Drag this new layer down below the Computers layer in the Layers palette, then click on the Computers layer to activate it.

STEP 7: Here is the finished selection.

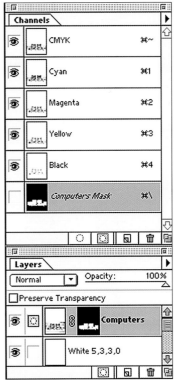

STEP 7: How the Layers and Channels palettes should look after clicking on the leftmost Layer Mask icon to create Computers Mask.

STEP 7: The WhiteCanvas with the selection loaded before the Layer Mask changes the background color.

STEP 7: The WhiteCanvas after the Layer Mask changes its background color.

STEP 7: Now, click on the Computers Outline name in the Paths palette and Option-drag down to the Load Selection icon (third from the left) at the bottom of the Paths palette to turn the entire path into a selection. Using the Option key when dragging brings up the Make Selection dialog box where you want to be sure that the feather is set to 0, Anti-aliased is on, and you are making a New Selection. Now click on the Layer Mask icon in the Layers palette to add a Layer Mask to the Computers layer selecting just the computers. The Layer mask should be black in the background area revealing the White 5,3,3,0 layer underneath. We are now going to blur the areas in Computers Mask that were shadows in the original image so the new background will blend into the original shadows.

BLURRING TO KEEP THE SHADOWS

STEP 8: Hit the Tab key to bring back the Tool palette if it is still hidden. Double-click on the Lasso tool and set its feather to 2 and make sure Anti-aliased is on. Select the shadow under one of the mice. Select very wide around the shadow where it blends into the white background, and then select more exactly the shadow edge where it meets the non-shadowed mouse. Look at the example selection here. You will use this selection to blur the mask. Press Command-H to hide the selection edges and then choose Filter/Blur/Gaussian Blur (Shift F5) and do a Gaussian

STEP 8: Select the shadow below the mouse with a selection like this.

Blur of 3 pixels on this selected area in the mask. Since you just created the layer mask, you are in the mode where you are changing the mask and seeing what those changes do to the image. While in Gaussian Blur, you can change the amount of the blur and see its effect on the image. Notice in the diagrams shown here what this does to the mask. Switch back and forth between seeing the mask and seeing the image, by Option-clicking on the Layer Mask icon in the Computers channel. In either case, when you modify anything, you will be working on the mask.

STEP 8: Here is the mouse before the blur.

STEP 8: Your final layer mask should look like this.

Now you need to repeat this process for all the shadows that occur at the bottom of the objects in the foreground. The shadows below the keyboards, the micc, the CD, and any other objects need to be done. The steps are: select the shadow area, press Command-H to hide the selection edge so you can

STEP 8: A Gaussian Blur of 3 pixels softens the shadow area below the mouse in the layer mask. This blends the original shadow with the new background color.

see if the blur looks clean, press Command-F to run the same Gaussian Blur of 3 pixels, and then select the next section. Don't forget about using the Option key with the Lasso tool to get straight sections. You can review this in "The Car" chapter. If you are not sure how the Computers Mask should look, compare it to the sample version in the Extra Info Files folder for this chapter on the CD. Press Command-S to save your completed WhiteCanvas file.

ADDING THE MULTIMEDIA OBJECTS

STEP 9: Now it's time to start adding the multimedia parts that are to be flying into the computer screens. Click on the Computers layer thumbnail to make the Computers layer, not its layer mask, active. When working on projects where you need to put important objects close to the edge of your image, you may want to use Guides to mark the trim area and live area in your image. In this magazine cover, the trim area was .3 inches in from the Bleed size of the image and the live area was an additional .3 inches in from that. Press Command-R to bring up the Rulers, and you will notice that each inch is divided into eight subdivisions. This does not help us if we want to set a Guide to .3 inches from the edge. Choose View/Show Grid (Command-") and set the Grid Preferences (File/Preferences/Guides & Grid) to have a grid line every inch with 10 subdivisions between each grid line. Now turn on Snap to Grid (Command-Shift-"), then create vertical and horizontal Guides that are .3 inches from each edge by clicking in either the vertical or horizontal ruler and dragging the guide to the third subdivision in the Grid along an edge of the image. You will have to zoom in closely to each image corner to accurately place these Guides. You can use the same procedure to place more guides .6 of an inch from each edge to mark the Live area. Now you can use Command-; to turn the guides on and off. You will probably want to turn the Grid off now using Command-". For more information on Grids and Guides, see "Navigating in Photoshop."

STEP 9: Set the Guides & Grid preferences as shown here.

STEP 10: Switch to the file PartsOrigScans and bring up the Paths palette (Shift-F11 with ArtistKeys). Since you have already had a goodly amount of exercise with the Pen tool, we won't make you outline all these parts. Notice that the path for each of the parts is already in this file. Just remember though, if you are trying to figure out how long it will actually take to do a job like this, each of these objects will have to be carefully outlined with the Pen tool. Click on the path called Video8 and you will notice it highlighted on the bottom right. You want to turn this into a selection, so click on it and drag it to the Load Selection icon at the bottom of the Paths palette. Now choose Edit/Copy to copy this first object. Switch to the WhiteCanvas, do Edit/Paste, and name this layer Video8. We will make each of the objects a separate layer, so that we can move them around and change them for the art director and even his or her boss.

STEP 11: This is what the distort parallelogram of Video8 should look like.

STEP 11: This is what the blur will look like when it is rotated, scaled, and lined up on top of the Video8 layer.

STEP 11: Look at the position of the Sony Video 8 cassette in the file FinalAPDA and then use the Move tool (V) to move the Sony cassette in the Video8 layer to the same location in WhiteCanvas. Choose Edit/Paste again and name this layer Video8Blur. Move this Video8 to the top-left corner of the image. Choose Layer/ Transform/Distort and distort the Video 8 cassette so that it is massively stretched along its longest axis but the shortest axis, the vertical, is not changed in size (see the diagram here). Press Return or Enter to finish the distort. Now choose Filter/ Noise/ Add Noise and add Gaussian noise of about 50.

Now choose Filter/Blur/Motion Blur and do a motion blur of Distance 32 whose Angle is parallel with the direction of motion of the cassette. You change the angle by clicking on the line in the circle and rotating it so that it is parallel with the direction of motion. The motion blur will cause the pieces of noise we just added to look like streaks. Now set the opacity of this layer to 50% and then use the Move tool to move the blur on top of the Video8 layer. With the opacity at 50%, you can see through the Video8-Blur layer to see if it is lined up and sized correctly with the Video8 layer. At this point, you will probably need to do Layer/ Transform/Free (Command-T) to get the scale and angle of the blur to exactly match the Video8 layer below. First, you grab the curved arrows just outside the corner handles to drag and rotate the blur the desired amount. If you wait a minute, Photoshop will give you a low-res prototype of the new rotated blur. If the angle doesn't seem correct, you can again click and drag to adjust the rotation amount. To scale the blur proportionally, Shift-click in one of the corner handles and drag to make it bigger or smaller. To move the blur, just click in the center and drag. When the low-res prototype seems correct, press Enter or Return to complete the rotate/scale and see it in hi-res. When the blur is lined up correctly, it should look like the diagram here.

STEP 12: The blur should be lined up on the Video8 layer so the white hub of the leftmost tape reel blurs off below and to the right. Set the feather on the Lasso tool to about 10 and use it to select the portion of the blur that is hanging off above and to the front of the Video8 layer. You want to select widely around this area so the 10 pixel feather doesn't affect the area you want to remove beyond the front edge of the Video8 cassette. The feather should cause the removal to slowly fade from a sharp front edge of the cassette on the Video8 layer into the blur caused by the Video8Blur layer. Once you make the selection correctly, Option-click on the new Layer Mask icon to remove this part of the blur by making a layer mask in the Video8Blur layer that is black in this area. Again, see the diagram here for details on how to make this selection. Now, for the final finishing touches, click back on the Video8Blur layer icon to activate the layer, not the mask, and set the opacity on it to about 60% and that on the Video8 layer to about 80%. I also did a Filter/Blur/Gaussian Blur (Shift-F4) of .5 on the Video8Blur layer to soften the streaking effect. You can use the same Lasso settings to select the back part of Video8 and blur it about the same amount, too.

ADDING THE SLIDES

STEP 12: Here is the selection, with 10 pixel feather, of the area we are going to remove from the Video8Blur layer.

STEP 13: This is the basic process for the effect of objects flying into the computer screens. The Video8 cassette is about the simplest object to do since it has a very symmetrical shape and it was easy to get a blur effect that looks good and also lines up with the original object. Many of the other objects presented specific problems due to their shape. The technique for the slides at the bottom left is about the same as Video8 but they need to be done in three different parts. First, do the single slide, called Slide in the PartsOrigScan Paths palette, and paste two layers like you did for Video8. One layer for the slide and one for its blur. To avoid too much distortion when you stretch the slide to make the blur, you may want to first rotate it so its bottom side is horizontal, and the left and right sides are vertical. You can then use Layer/Transform/Scale to stretch it straight down instead of using the Distort command. It can then be rotated back to the required angle. When the Slide layer and its blur layer look correct together, go back and do Slides in a similar way. Copy all the slides and paste them down as the Slides layer. Now edit that layer with the Rubber Stamp tool to remove the prop objects that are visible separating the front two slides from the back three. Now do one blur layer for the blur effect on the back three slides, and then do a separate blur layer for the blur effect on the front two slides. Once you have these slide layers looking correct together, you can merge them into fewer layers to reduce the total number of layers. Try these slides next, and then we will move on to some more complicated objects.

FADING THE BLUR

STEP 14: The Dat tape, diskettes, video tape, and cassettes all use some variations of the technique we used for the Video8 and the Slides files. The Dat tape is the simplest; just do the same thing again. The cassettes are difficult because the two blurs melt together awkwardly; still, I think you can figure this out. The video tape has a weird shape with dark holes in its bottom that don't blur very nicely. You will have to change their shape and remove some dark parts before you can get a blur that looks good. With the diskettes, the problem is getting the chrome sliding doors to look correct in the blur. One thing all these objects and the transparencies have in common (we didn't do this with the Video8 cassette) is that their blurs fade away as they get further from the object. The following steps cover a general technique to fade the blur (using the Dat tape as an example) that works with all the objects we have mentioned so far.

STEP 15: As in Video8, we start by making one layer called Dat in which we place the Dat tape copied from PartsOrigScan. Then, we create a second layer, called Dat Blur, where the blurred Dat effect was created. So far this is exactly like Video8 and here is what it looks like. To fade the blur, we need to use a layer mask in the Dat Blur layer. You probably already added a layer mask to remove the front part of the blur, as you did in the Video8 case. The layer mask should be highlighted, so we are editing the layer mask while watching the layer and all the layers below it. If it isn't already there, click on the layer mask once to put it in this state.

STEP 16: Here is the Dat tape with the blur effect as we fade the blur. To set up for fading, we use the Gradient tool with the Foreground to Background, Normal and Linear options and a layer mask. We click down in Gradient where we want the blur to be 100% gone and drag to where we want it to be 100% there.

STEP 16: The layer mask that caused the blur to fade, as pictured to the right. Wherever the mask is black, the blur is completely gone.

STEP 16: The blur after the Gradient tool fades it with a layer mask.

STEP 16: We need to double-click on the Gradient tool and make sure we are doing a Linear gradient from Foreground to Background at 100% Normal. Our foreground and background colors have been set to black and white by typing D for default colors and then X for exchange. We now click down on the far end of the blur where we want it to have faded completely away, and then drag parallel to the blur toward the Dat tape and let up where we want the blur to still be 100% there. Voilá, instant fade! It will have faded along the length of the gradient line. If you had already used the layer mask to remove the front part of the blur, as we did with Video8, you may notice that returning after you do the gradient since the gradient will turn that part of the mask to white. To resolve this problem, undo the gradient and then make a Marquee selection of the entire tail that you want to fade. Now, if you redo the gradient, only that selected part of the mask will change and the front of the fade should still be there. Try making longer or shorter gradients at different angles to see how they affect the tail of the blur.

VARIATIONS AND CLEAN UP

STEP 17: Remember, when you add a layer mask, the things that are black in the layer mask are removed from the layer. Pictured in Step 16 is the layer mask that removed the tail of this blur. If you are not happy with the length of the blur fade-out, you need to redo the gradient to make a longer or shorter distance in the transition from black to white. If you are not happy with the location of the blur fade-out, you can move the layer mask separately from the layer it is masking and change the location of where the fade starts and ends. To do this, click on the chain icon that separates the Layer thumbnail from the Layer Mask thumbnail. The chain icon goes away indicating that the Layer Mask and Layer are no longer linked. Now you can use the Move tool to move the layer mask without moving the layer. If you move the mask to the left, the tail on the Dat will get longer, and if you move it to the right, the tail will get shorter. Try it, but only do one adjustment at a time and each time use Command-Z to go back to your original mask location! You may notice that when you move the mask to the right, part of the tail appears at the left edge of the image. This is because when you move the mask, white fills this area in the mask. You

STEP 17: Click on the Chain icon between the Layer Mask and the Layer thumbnails to remove the icon and allow you to move each of them separately.

STEP 17: Click in the Link column to bring up the Chain icon and link the Dat layer to the Dat Blur layer. This way, when you move or transform one of them, the other will move or transform with it.

might also notice that the front part of the blur now also grows or shrinks when you move the mask. If you want to change the fade location by moving the mask, it would be best if you did the fade first, moved it to the correct location, then used the Lasso tool to remove the front part of the fade. If you do move the mask separately from the layer, click on the chain icon again when you are done to lock the layer mask and the layer back together again.

Anyhow, when you are happy with how the blur fades and the rest of the mask, an option is to click on the Layer Mask thumbnail and drag it to the trash at the bottom right of the Layers palette. You will then be asked if you want to Apply or Discard the mask. If you then choose to Apply the mask instead of Discard it, the areas that were removed from the blur by the layer mask will become permanently removed from that layer. They will become transparent, letting you see the layers below through them. You may not want to remove and apply the layer mask until the art director or person who needs to approve the project has seen it. That way, you can always change the mask to change its fade either in front or behind the object. You can always make a layer mask temporarily disabled by Shift-clicking on the Layer Mask icon. This would bring back the full length of the tail and the blur in front of the object in this case.

When you have completed an object layer and its blur layer, you could click on the upper of the two and choose Merge Down to combine them into one layer. This would make the file smaller but wouldn't give you the maximum flexibility if you later wanted to change the blur or the object by itself. In all cases, click on one of the two layers (either the object or its blur) to activate that layer, then click in the link column of the other layer to link each object to its blur. The link column is the column between the Eye icon and the Layer thumbnail. Now when you move either of these layers with the Move tool, the other will move with it.

MORE DIFFICULT EFFECTS

STEP 18: The most difficult objects are the CD, the video camera, and the microphone. Let's start out with the microphone. Go to the PartsOrigScan file and load a selection for the mike by clicking on it and dragging it to the Load Selection icon at the bottom of the Paths palette. Copy this as usual and do an Edit/Paste on top of all the other layers you have done so far. Name this layer Mike and use the Move tool to position the mike in the correct location based on the FinalAPDA file. The first thing you need to do now is straighten out the cord that leads from the end of the mike off the screen to the left. Set the Lasso feather to 0, and select the cord area and rotate it so it looks straight. I also had to copy a straighter part of it next to the mike and use that to lengthen the rest of the cord and also make it look straight. You will probably have to use the Rubber Stamp tool to do some cleanup when you are done creating the basic straight cord.

STEP 19: Here is the wire mesh selection we used to create the wire mesh blur.

THE BLURRED MIKE

STEP 19: To create the blur effect on the mike, we tried all sorts variations and the thing that looked the best was actually stretching out part of the wire mesh that you speak into on the head of the mike. To do this, select the wire mesh with the Lasso tool, as shown here. Choose Layer/New/Layer Via Copy (Command-J) and then move it to the top of the screen so you just see a white background. Call this new layer Mike Blur. Now do the following contortions to it to create the blur effect. Use Layer/Transform/Rotate to rotate it so it is vertical. Use the Option key with the Rectangular Marquee to crop it further so the vertical sides are straight. Now do

STEP 19: The wire mesh selection and the steps in distorting it to make the blur effect. The rotate step has already been done here.

Layer/Free Transform (Command-T) and Command-Option-Shift-click on the top right handle (this does perspective) to stretch the right side up and down at the same time, so it is more symmetrical to the left side. Click in the middle of it and drag to move this mesh object to the left side of the window and then click in the bottom right handle and stretch it all the way to the right side of the window making a long cylinder shape. Press Return or Enter to finish the Free Transform.

Now run Filter/Stylize/ Wind (Blast & From the Left) on it followed by Filter/Noise/Add Noise with Gaussian noise of 20. Run Filter/Blur/Motion Blur of 30 at 0 degrees two times. Type a 5 to set the Opacity on this layer to 50%. Now use Layer/Free Transform again to move this down on top of the Mike layer and then rotate and scale it so it's parallel with the movement of the mike in the Mike layer and the correct size to fit on top of the mike. Press Return or Enter to end the Free Transform, and then set the opacity to about 17%, which you can do by just typing a 17. Use the Lasso tool with a feather of around 3 to select, then delete the part of the blur that protrudes from the front of the mike. You can also delete this front part using a layer mask if you want to have the option of bringing it back or changing it later. Add a layer mask to the Mike Blur layer and use this with the Gradient tool to fade the blur toward the back of the mike.

You might also use the Paintbrush or Airbrush with a soft brush to edit the layer mask to fade the blur in toward the back of the mike and the cord. Have fun, you can spend hours playing with the possibilities! Press Command-S to save the file in Photoshop format when you are done.

THE FLYING CD

STEP 20: To create the effect of the CD flying into the computer screen, first load the selection of the CD from the Paths window on the PartsOrigScan file. Copy the CD and then switch to WhiteCanvas and do an Edit/Paste on top of your topmost layer so far. Use the Move tool to move the CD into position flying into the leftmost computer, and name this layer CD. While editing the layer mask, set the feather on the Lasso tool to 1 pixel and use it to make a selection of the right part of the CD that you want to remove. The edge of the selection on top of the CD should be straight.

STEP 20: This is the selection that deletes the front part of the CD by turning its layer mask black when you Option-click on the Layer Mask icon.

STEP 20: This is the selection that defines the area of the wave effect on the computer screen.

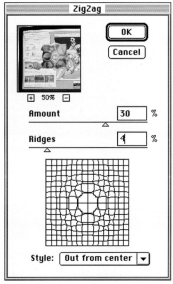

STEP 20: Here are the settings in the Zigzag filter to get the wave effect on the computer screen.

Option-click on the Layer Mask icon in the Layers palette to turn that area black in the mask you are creating and thereby remove the right part of the CD. Imagine that the computer screen is water and the CD is flying into the water. The image you see on the screen is just a reflection in the water. Ponder what would happen to that reflection when the CD creates a wave while flying into the water. We will use the Zigzag filter to create that effect.

First, use the Elliptical Marquee (type M until the top-left tool icon is the Elliptical Marquee) to make a selection that would be the area of the screen wave. Use Select/Feather to set a feather on this of about 5 pixels. Make the Computers layer, where the computer screen is, the active layer by clicking on it, and then press Command-H to hide the selection edges. Now choose Filter/Distort/Zigzag and go into this filter. Start by using Out From Center, Amount 30, Ridges 4, and then change the options until the wave looks correct to you. You may need to play with the options and/or your selection to get what you want.

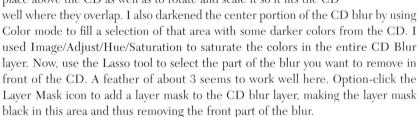

STEP 21: With the CD still in the copy buffer, do another Edit/Paste on top of the CD layer and call this layer CD Blur. Use Layer/Transform/Distort to stretch the CD out to make a blur. Use Filter/Noise/Add Noise to add about 20 Gaussian noise then Filter/Blur/Motion Blur to blur about 30 in the direction of CD motion. I did motion blur of 30 twice because a bigger value started to cause distortions in the blur. Set its opacity to 50% so you can see through to the CD. Use Layer/Free Transform to move the blur into place above the CD as well as to rotate and scale it so it fits the CD

STEP 21: The CD blur layer before its layer mask is applied to remove the black mask areas.

STEP 21: The CD blur layer mask which removes both the front of the CD blur to the right and the tail to the left.

well where they overlap. I also darkened the center portion of the CD blur by using Color mode to fill a selection of that area with some darker colors from the CD. I used Image/Adjust/Hue/Saturation to saturate the colors in the entire CD Blur layer. Now, use the Lasso tool to select the part of the blur you want to remove in front of the CD. A feather of about 3 seems to work well here. Option-click the Layer Mask icon to add a layer mask to the CD blur layer, making the layer mask black in this area and thus removing the front part of the blur.

Now use the technique described in steps 15 to 17 to have the tail of the blur slowly fade away. Since you have already used a layer mask to get rid of the front of the blur, you should Apply it before using it again to get rid of the tail, or do the work on the tail within a selection that includes only the tail area. If you don't do this, the white part of the gradient may extend across the mask and wipe out the work you just did to remove the front part of the blur. Look at the layer mask in my example WhiteCanvas file if you are not sure what the problem is here. The easiest solution is to fade the tail before removing the front of the blur. The final opacity I used for the CD blur layer was 40%. It is easier to see exactly what you want for opacity and saturation once the front and tail of the CD are removed.

THE VIDEO CAMERA

STEP 22: Load the selection and copy the video camera from Parts-OrigScan. Do an Edit/Paste of it on top of your topmost layer and call it Camera. Use the Move tool to position it appropriately. Double-click on the Lasso tool and set the feather to 3 pixels. We want to remove the piece of the tripod that is still attached to the bottom of the video camera. Use the Lasso tool to select a dark area from the bottom of the camera—above and to the right of the tripod. Now Command-Option-click and drag that area, and then move it to partially cover the tripod. Command-Option-click and dragging a selection makes a copy of the selection, in a floating selection, and leaves the original selection there. If you Command-Option-click and drag the copied area, it will make another copy of it, and you can use it over and over again to completely cover the tripod. You will also need to cover the white text that is partially obliterated by the tripod. Once all these areas are covered, press Command-D to drop the final

STEP 22: Underside of camera showing the tripod and the selection we used as a patch to cover the tripod.

STEP 22: The same area as above with the tripod now removed.

floating selection, and then use the Rubber Stamp tool to blend out any blemishes along the edges of the covering patches you put in. The feather of 3 should have done most of this for you if you selected the right dark area to use as a patch.

STEP 23: Make a copy of the Camera layer on top of the Camera layer by clicking on it and dragging it to the New Layer icon at the bottom of the Layers palette. Name this copy CameraBlur. Option-click on the Eye icon of this layer so you just see it for a while. Use the Lasso tool with a 3-pixel feather to delete the top and bottom of the

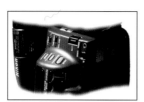

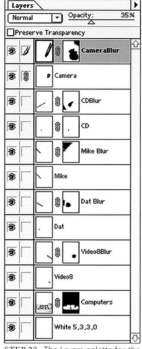

STEP 23: The cropped and rotated camera part before scaling it.

STEP 23: The final CameraBlur layer if viewed by itself without its layer mask.

STEP 23: The final layer mask for the CameraBlur layer.

STEP 23: The Layers palette for the layers we have added here in the directions.

camera in the CameraBlur layer so that it looks like the one pictured here. Since the camera has such a varied shape with varied light and dark portions, we get a better blur effect by just blurring this part of the camera. When we did this job, it took a lot of experimentation to discover this. Use Layer/Transform/Rotate to rotate this chopped camera so that the left and right edges are vertical. Use the Move tool to move this to the top of the window and then choose Layer/Transform/Scale and click on the bottom right handle dragging it all the way to the bottom of the layer. Make sure the delta X in the Info window stays at 0 so you know you are only scaling the object vertically. Press Return to finish both the rotate and the scale. Doing the Rotate first, and then the Scale separately, makes this process a little easier to control than if you were to try to do the entire thing in one step with the Free Transform tool.

We rotated the camera first so we could use Scale instead of Distort to stretch it. That way it keeps its shape when stretched. Use Filter/Noise/Add Noise to add 50 Gaussian noise then use Filter/Blur/Motion Blur to blur it by 30 at an angle of 90%. Do the Gaussian noise and motion blur steps a second time. Set the opacity of the blur layer to 50% for now. Option-click on this layer's Eye icon to turn on viewing of all the other layers again. Now use the Move tool to move the blur back on top of the camera in the layer below. Use Layer/Free Transform (Command-T) to rotate the blur back to the correct angle to match the camera and to scale the blur so it's the correct width to fit exactly on top of the camera. Move the blur back and forth by clicking and dragging in its center until you find the location that best matches the lighting paths from the camera body. Now press Return or Enter to finish the Transform.

Use the Lasso tool with an 8-pixel feather to circle the front part of the blur that you want to delete. Option-click on the Layer Mask icon to create a layer mask filled with black in the lassoed area masking out this front part of the blur. Now make a Lasso or Marquee selection of the tail of the blur to protect the rest of the layer mask from the Gradient tool. Use the technique described in Steps 15 to 17 to fade out the tail of the blur. I then set the opacity of the CameraBlur layer to 40%. Save this final WhiteCanvas in Photoshop format so that you can turn on and off individual layers, or layer masks, change opacities, or move layers until you and your client are happy with a final image. For more information on how to do these multi-layered projects, see "The McNamaras," and "Night Cab Ride in Manhattan." Here is the final Layers palette showing the layers for the objects we added here with detailed instructions. You can use the same techniques to add the rest of the objects to complete this magazine cover project.

LINKING LAYERS TO MOVE OR TRANSFORM THEM TOGETHER

STEP 24: One advantage to having each of these objects and its blur in a separate layer is that you can change or move each of these items separately while showing them to your client or just trying different alternatives for the final effect. If you want to move an item and its blur together to a new place on the screen, there is a way to link the two layers together and move them at the same time. First, click on one of the two layers (the item you want to move) to make it the active, highlighted, layer. Now click in the Link column, between the Eye icon and the Layer thumbnail, of that item's blur layer, and you will notice the Chain icon appearing where you clicked. Now you can use the Move tool to move this item and its blur together to the left, right, or up and down in your image area. If one of these layers has a layer mask, like the CameraBlur does here, that will also move in unison with the linked layers. You can link more than two layers simply by clicking in the Link column of additional layers. To unlink a layer, just click in the Link column again. Layers that are linked together will also ALL be transformed when using any of the Layer/Transform commands, including Free Transform. You can also drag and drop groups of linked layers from one document to another. This should be especially useful for Web designers and multimedia people, who often represent a particular element by many layers. You can now drag that entire element to another document in one step.

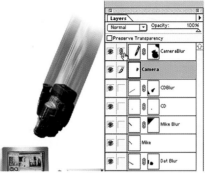

STEP 24: To move two layers at the same time, first click in one of the layers to make it active, gray. Then click in the Link column, the middle column, of the layer(s) that you want to move with this active layer. Now use the Move tool to relocate the position of these layers within your document window.

HANDS-ON SESSION: Creating Shadows

*Different techniques to create and refine drop shadows
and cast shadows, including objects
that cast shadows with irregular shapes.*

Here are a variety of techniques to add shadows to objects. This can be done in many different ways and people need to do it a lot. We believe at least one of these techniques will meet your needs. You should also check out the technique for preserving shadows we use in "The APDA Magazine Cover" and also the technique for doing automatic knock-outs using Difference in "Blend Modes, Calculations, and Apply Image."

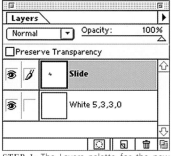

STEP 1: The Layers palette for the new Shadows file.

STEP 1: First, let's create an image that will be used in the next few techniques. Click on the background color square in the Tool palette and type in these values in the Color Picker dialog box: C = 5, M = 3, Y = 3, K = 0. This gives you a background white that still has a halftone dot. Choose File/New to create a new CMYK document of 500 pixels by 500 pixels at a resolution of 150 dpi with this Background Color, and name the file Shadows. Double-click on the Background layer and rename it to White 5,3,3,0. Now use File/Open to open the PartsOrigScan file from the Creating Shadows folder. Go to Window/Show Paths to bring up the Paths palette, then click on the path named Slide. Drag it to the Load Selection icon in at the bottom of Paths palette. This will turn this path into a selection. Edit/Copy the slide and then Edit/Paste it on the new Shadow document. Call this new Layer Slide. Choose File/Save As to save this file as Shadows.

DROP SHADOW ONE

STEP 1: This is the most generic and often used drop shadow technique and is similar to the Drop Shad Actions that can be accessed from ArtistKeys. Using the Shadow file that you created at the beginning of this exercise, make a another copy of the Slide layer and name it Slide One. Now make another copy and name it Slide One Shadow.

STEP 2: Go to Edit/Fill (Shift-Delete) and make sure that you turn on the Preserve Transparency option in the Fill dialog box. Fill this layer with 100% black or any other color that you wish to use as your shadow.

STEP 3: Click and drag the Shadow layer in the Layers palette to move your Shadow layer below the Slide layer. Now offset this layer in the direction of

STEP 2: Fill the Shadow layer with 100% Black.

the shadow using either the Move tool (V) or the Filter/Other/Offset filter.

STEP 4: Make sure that Preserve Transparency is off in the Layers palette. When you have your shadow in position, use Filter/Blur/ Gaussian Blur (Shift-F4) to soften the edges of the shadow. The amount of blur depends on how far from the original object you place your shadow—the further away, the softer the shadow. I used 4 pixels for this illustration. With the Preview button on in the Gaussian Blur filter, you see the shadow form and change with different amounts of blur.

STEP 5: Finally, change the opacity of the Shadow layer. Once again, this depends on how close the shadow is to the object. A short, sharp shadow will be darker than a shadow cast from a distant light source. I used 45% opacity here. Press Command-S to save the file.

DROP SHADOW TWO

STEP 1: Make a copy of the Slide layer by Option-dragging it to the New Layer icon at the bottom of the Layers palette. Call this new layer Slide Two and drag it to the top of the Layers palette. Turn off the Eye icons for the other slide and shadow layers. Use the Paintbrush or the Airbrush tool. For either tool, choose a large soft brush at about 25 to 30 pixels. The hardness should be set to 0 to give you the absolute softest edge. Now choose the color for your shadow, set the opacity of the Paintbrush to about 50%, or the pressure of the Airbrush at about 5%, and set the painting mode, in either case, to Behind.

STEP 2: Make sure that the Slide Two layer is active. Use either the Paintbrush or the Airbrush tool to paint your shadow. I prefer the Airbrush tool for its softer, more diffuse edge, but see what works best for your image. Begin inside the object that you want to shadow. Paint freehand or click with the Painting tool. Let go of the mouse button, move the cursor, and Shift-click with the tool to create straight lines. If you can draw the shadow with one stroke, you can undo it if you don't like the effect. If you don't like your shadow, just throw the whole layer away and start again by making another copy of the Slide layer. With a little practice you can create quick, cheap drop shadows at will. Press Command-S to save the file again.

STEP 3: Offset the Shadow layer.

STEP 5: Final version of the file using an offset and blurred layer described in "Drop Shadow One."

If you want your shadow to be only on the black printing plate, force the color of the shadow to 0,0,0,100 by clicking on the foreground color square and entering those CMYK values. The default black is a mixture of the four process inks. When you have a black shadow, sometimes creating it only on the black plate will avoid gradient color blending problems associated with using a combination of four inks. This is especially helpful when creating a shadow against a colored background. To try out a colored background here, just create another layer just above the White 5,3,3,0 layer and fill that new layer with another color, like red. If you are using the 0, 0, 0, 100% black color for your shadows, you will want to set the Blend mode for the Shadow layer to Multiply when this shadow is against a non-white background; otherwise, it will seem washed out.

STEP 2: Paint in the shadow with the Airbrush or Paintbrush.

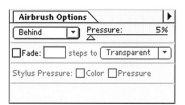

STEP 2: If you use the Airbrush, make its pressure about 5% and then slowly build up shadow density.

STEP 2: If you use the Paintbrush, lower the opacity to about 50%. Behind mode only paints on the transparent part of the layer. This brush works well right out of the palette.

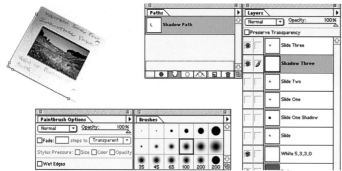

STEP 3: The setup for using the Pen tool to create your path and then stroking it with the Paintbrush to create the shadow.

STEP 3: Final version of Drop Shadow Three using a stroked path.

DROP SHADOW THREE

STEP 1: Make another copy of the Slide layer, call it Slide Three, and put it on top. Turn off the other Slide and Shadow layers underneath. Go to Window/Show Paths to bring up the Paths palette, then type P to get the Pen tool. Now make a path along the edge of the object where you want your shadow. Double-click on the Work Path name in the Paths palette and name this path Shadow Path.

STEP 2: Create a new Layer, call it Shadow Three, and place that new layer directly under the Slide Three layer. Select the Paintbrush tool with a large soft brush and set the Opacity to 100% and the Blend mode to normal. Type a D to make sure the foreground color is black, or set the foreground color if you want something other than a black shadow.

STEP 3: Go back to the Paths palette and drag your path down to the Stroke Path icon at the bottom of the Paths palette. If you are unhappy with the size or location of your shadow, Edit/Undo the stroke (Command-Z) and change the shape of your path or the size of your brush. Now do the Stroke again until you are happy with the size and location of the shadow. To change the Opacity, just use the Opacity slider in the Shadow Three layer. By initially painting this in at 100% Opacity, you can always lower the opacity to be whatever you want.

DROP SHADOW FOUR

STEP 1: Make another copy of the Slide layer and put it on the top calling it Two Objects. Turn off the Eye icons for all the other slide and shadow layers. Go back to the PartsOrigScan file and drag the Tapes path to the Load Selection icon at the bottom of the Paths palette. Copy the Tapes and then switch back to the Shadows file and do a Paste. Now you have the slide surrounded by transparency in the Two Objects layer, and the Tapes surrounded by transparency in the layer on top of that. To combine them, choose Merge Down from the Layers palette menu. They should now both be in the Two Objects layer.

STEP 2: Bring up the Actions palette, which we assume you have set up using ArtistKeys in "Automating with Actions." Click on the Drop Shad (Ob in Actv Lyr) button to run that action. The action will automatically make a drop shadow of both these objects. Work through the action and follow the directions on the screen. I used an offset of –7 to the left and 8 down and a Gaussian Blur of 4. The action created the layer called Two Objects copy, so rename this to Two Objects Blur. Change the Opacity of this blur layer until you like the darkness of the blur.

STEP 3: You may notice that there is a slight white ghost around the left and bottom edge of the Tapes object. This is caused by Tapes path actually including a few pixels from the white background in the PartsOrigScan file. Having some ghost pixels on the edge of an object is a common problem when compositing. Here are several solutions for getting rid of ghosts like this. Click back on the Two Objects layer to activate it. The easiest way to rid these ghosts is to choose Select/Load Selection and then load Two Objects Transparency as a new selection. Now choose Select/Modify/Contract of 1 pixel to pinch this selection in on the objects by one pixel all around. These white ghost pixels are all located within this 1 pixel. Now choose Select/Inverse to select the transparent area including these ghost pixels. Use the Marquee tool (M) to Option-drag a selection around the Slide excluding any pixels from being deleted there since there is not a problem with ghost pixels around the slide. Now use Command-H to hide the selection edges then hit the Delete key to delete one pixel of width from around the edge of the Tapes. This method works very quickly but sometimes deletes pixels that we wanted to keep. Choose Command-Z to undo this Delete, then choose Select/None (Command-D) and try the next method as another alternative.

STEP 4: A method that gives you absolute control is to click on the Layer Mask icon to add a layer mask to this Two Objects layer. Type a B to choose the Paint-Brush tool, and pick the third brush from the top left. Paint with black in the layer mask along the edge of the Tapes objects to remove the white ghost pixels along this edge. Also, paint black in the layer mask to remove the white middle of the tape spindles and other holes in the plastic tape container since you would normally see through this to the shadow below. Remember, that whatever is black in the mask gets removed from this layer. You can type X to exchange the colors and paint with white to bring anything back that you accidentally remove. Now that you have some ideas of how to create basic drop shadows, let's try some more interesting shadows.

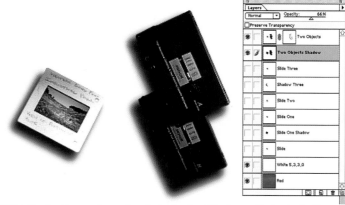

STEP 4: Our final layers setup and results for the Two Objects case. Notice the Red layer at the very bottom. If we turn off the Eye icon for the White 5,3,3,0 layer, we can now test any of our shadows against a red background. A shadow against a colored background may work better if its Blend mode is set to Multiply.

CAST SHADOW ONE

STEP 1: Open the Ball file from the Creating Shadows folder. Click on the Ball layer to make it active. Use Layer/Transform/Rotate to rotate the ball until the light source comes from above then press Return or Enter to end the rotate.

STEP 2: Make a copy of the Ball layer by Option-dragging it to the New Layer icon at the bottom of the Layers palette, and then name it Shadow.

STEP 3: Shift-Delete to Fill the Shadow layer with 100% Black (or other shadow color). Make sure that you turn on the Preserve Transparency option in the Fill dialog box. Next, use Layer/Free Transform (Command-T) to flatten and widen the shape of the ball's shadow. Click down and drag in the top middle handle to flatten, then Command-Option-Shift-click in the top right and bottom right handles and drag to

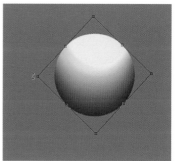

STEP 1: Use Layer/Transform/Rotate to rotate the ball so light comes from above.

STEP 3: Use Layer/Free Transform to flatten the shape and add perspective.

shrink the perspective on top and widen it on the bottom. Press Return or Enter to finish the transformation.

STEP 4: Now move this layer down in the Layers palette between the ball and the background. Filter/Blur/Gaussian Blur (Shift-F4) the Shadow layer by about 8 pixels, then change its opacity to about 60%.

STEP 5: Use the Move tool to position the shadow. Remember, the further away from the shadow the object is positioned, the larger and softer the cast shadow. An item further away from its shadow is also further from the plane on which the shadow is cast. Therefore, an item that casts a large soft shadow, which does not touch the shadow itself, indicates that the item "floats" away from the projection plane. Experiment with moving the shadow closer or further from the ball to see how this affects the depth perception of the object to its shadow. Save the file as Shadow Above.

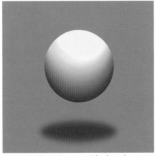  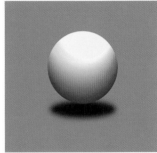

STEP 5: Experiment with the placement, opacity and softness of the shadow to achieve the effect of distance from the background and closeness of the light source.

CAST SHADOW TWO

STEP 1: Reopen the Ball file. Here we have an object lit from the upper right. Therefore, we will have a cast shadow that goes down and to the left at an opposite angle. Make a new layer of the ball by Option-dragging it to the New Layer icon at the bottom of the Layers palette and calling it Shadow. Press Shift-Delete to fill this layer with black, making sure Preserve Transparency is on. Use Layer/Free Transform (Command-T) to change the shape of the shadow to match the light source. You may have to try this transformation several times. Photoshop only gives you a rectangular shape to use as the basis for your distort, and it's difficult to get an accurate read on what your distorted shape will actually look like. With the Command key down to get the distort function, I brought the upper right point inside the shape of the ball, the upper left and lower right points in on a diagonal but still outside the shape of the ball, and the lower left point out and down in a diagonal in the opposite direction of the light source.

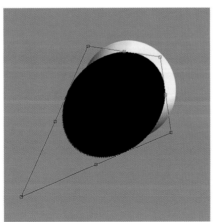

STEP 1: Use Layer/Free Transform to change the shape of the shadow.

STEP 2: When you get a shape that you're happy with, move the shadow layer below the ball in the Layers palette. Filter/Blur/Gaussian Blur the shadow layer,

then use the Opacity slider to change the opacity and the Move tool to position the shadow. Remember that the distance from the object dictates how soft the shadow should be. The closer the shadow, the sharper the shadow. If the rotation of the shadow doesn't match the direction of the light, use Layer/Transform/Rotate to get the angle that matches. Use File/Save As and name the file Ball Cast Shadow.

STEP 2: A hard, dark shadow seems to place the ball directly against the background.

STEP 2: A soft shadow with more offset gives the appearance of the ball floating above the background.

CAST SHADOW THREE

This technique is similar to Cast Shadow Two, but incorporates a fade from the front of the shadow to the back.

STEP 1: Make a copy of the shadow you just made in the Ball Cast Shadow file you were just working on and call the copied layer Shadow2. Turn off the Eye icon of the first shadow layer. Use Layer/Free Transform to change the shadow shape to make it wider and longer than your last cast shadow.

STEP 2: Click in the Layer Mask icon to add a new layer mask to the Shadow layer. Type G to access the Gradient tool, and then set the options to: Normal, 100%, Foreground to Background, Radial blend. Type a D for default colors, and then do a blend from slightly inside the shape of the ball and outward in the direction of the distort and beyond the bottom left end of the distorted shadow. You should get a shadow that is soft on all sides but has a more pronounced fade at the tail. You may want to experiment with starting and ending your blend at different points as well as further distortion of the shadow layer to soften or enlarge your shadow.

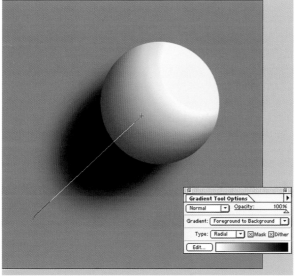

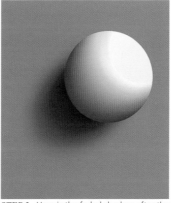

STEP 2: Here is the faded shadow after the Radial Gradient Blend.

STEP 2: Try your Gradient Blend in the Shadow2 Layer Mask from this position and with these options.

STEP 2: Modify the Tape Top path so the path is larger than the actual tape.

STEP 3: Initially, the shadow overlaps the tape.

CAST SHADOW FOUR

Occasionally, you need a cast shadow that is an irregular shape where neither Distort or Perspective gives you a realistic shadow. Try this technique in those instances.

STEP 1: Open the Video Tape file from the Creating Shadows folder on the *Photoshop 4 Artistry* CD.

STEP 2: Show Paths (Shift-F11) and use the Pen tool (P) from the Tool palette to draw the basic shape of the object creating the shadow. In this example, it is the top of the tape cartridge that actually casts the shadow. Look at the light source. It is coming from the upper left edge of the object; therefore, our cast shadow will be down and to the right. Also look at the bottom edge of the cartridge. Since it is totally in shadow, the cast shadow must start at the left edge of the cartridge to be believable. Save the path you create as Tape Top, and then use the Arrow tool from the Pen tools (P again switches to the Arrow) to modify the shape for the shadow. Make the shadow area for the tape wider than the tape itself. Click on the TapeTop path and drag to the Load Selection icon at the bottom of the Paths palette to turn this path into a selection.

STEP 3: In the Layers palette, click on the *Background* layer to make it active, then Option-click on the New layer icon to make a new transparent layer called Shadow. Use Select/Feather to feather the selection by about 9 or 10 pixels. Edit/Fill (Shift/Delete) this selection with 100% black. Make sure the Preserve Transparency option is off. Now choose Select/None (Command-D) and change the opacity of the Shadow layer to about 65%. You now have a basic shadow but there is shadow area on the left of the tape that needs to be deleted.

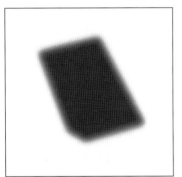

STEP 3: The Shadow layer before the layer mask cuts off the left edge.

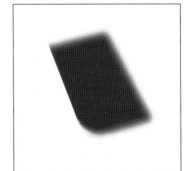

STEP 4: The Shadow layer after painting the layer mask to cut off the left edge.

STEP 4: Click on the Layer Mask icon in the Layers palette to add a layer mask to this layer. Now use the Paintbrush with a large soft brush and 100% black to paint out areas of the shadow on the left edge. You may need to change brush sizes or switch to the Airbrush tool to get the desired softness or sharpness to your edge.

STEP 5: Finally, for this image, I noticed a gray hairline at the bottom of the tape that interfered with the shadow, so I added a layer mask to the Tape layer and used a small brush with black in the layer mask to "erase" the edge so that the shadow layer would show through.

STEP 5: The final image with the modified shadow.

IMAGES FOR THE WEB

AND

MULTIMEDIA

DIFFERENCES IN CREATING FOR THE WEB AND 8-BIT COLOR

What is it that is different about the Web, and determining which viewers are most important.

WHY ARE THE WEB AND MULTIMEDIA DIFFERENT?

When I first started working with digital images in 1988, I was in the "Hypermedia Group" at Apple. This was a great research group that was doing all sorts of interesting things. We used to have the most fun in our weekly meetings, daydreaming about futures like digital virtual reality environments, sending color images over high-speed ISDN networks, computers that actually had built-in CD players as well as accelerated image compression and decompression, digital video and video conferencing, experiences like QuickTime VR, and many other things that were not really possible at the time with our slow Mac IIx computers. The only thing that was just barely possible then, for patient followers, was full-color printed output from a Mac or PC. I would bring large color scans up on my screen and love to work with them, and I could actually make color prints on Apple's Dupont 4Cast dye-sub printer. There was so much detail in these large images for print. This was important to me as a photographer. All the 8-bit color stuff seemed of low quality and of little interest to me. There was no Web, as we know it today, back in 1988.

In 1997, most of the things we dreamed about back then have happened and are old news. Now we have the Web and lots of multimedia applications where 8-bit color is important for speeding up digital delivery of images. Even for us photographers, who like seeing all the minute detail in a photograph, the current reality is that we will probably have to transmit digital comps to clients, we will often want to create a Web site to advertise our work, and clients will want both print and Web versions of their images. In making Web images for myself and my clients, I have realized that there is a real art to creating quality images for the Web and multimedia. Most of the techniques are the same that we would use in creating images for print, but there are some very important differences that will allow you to make the transition between okay Web images and great Web images.

The Web is a very rapidly moving and changing environment. There are constantly new features and possibilities, and on the Web you don't have to wait for a new book to be published or worry about the distribution channels to get the latest product. What I am telling you here in this book is based on what I know today and, in the world of the Web, that may easily change tomorrow or next week or a few months from now as new features appear. If you really need to always know the latest about the Web, the best place to find that out is the Web, because it can be updated any time. We will post the latest things we discover, as well as any corrections to this book, on our Web site (maxart.com). Please visit us there for any late-breaking news. Constructing our Web site will be the next project after we finish this book, so give us a few months to get it together. We will post what we learn there as we are creating it. You can send Wendy and me e-mail at wendy@maxart.com or barry@maxart.com. We always enjoy hearing from our readers. By the way, our 21-month old son's name is Max!

WHY IS 8-BIT COLOR IMPORTANT AND WHAT IS IT ANYHOW?

There are two reasons 8-bit color is important. First, many computer users have computers that can only see 8-bit color on their monitors. Second, 8-bit color images take up less space to store than 24-bit color images of the same monitor display size. In some cases, this makes them faster to transmit over the Web and also allows you to store more of them on a multimedia CD. They are also faster to read from a CD and put up on the screen.

To display color on a computer screen, you need a 24-bit digital value. Eight bits of Red plus 8 bits of Green plus 8 bits of Blue specify the exact color value of each pixel on a computer monitor. A 24-bit video card that places that color on the screen needs enough memory to store one 24-bit value for each pixel on the screen. The 24-bit color values from your 24-bit color image get placed in the video card's memory buffer to display the part of the image you are currently seeing on the screen. This allows each pixel on your screen to be any one of 16,777,216 colors (256 ° 256 ° 256). Until recently, computer memory was quite expensive, so many computer models were shipped with the cheaper 8-bit color instead. With 8-bit color, you can only see a total of 256 different colors on your entire computer screen at one time. Out of the possible 16,777,216 colors, you can only see 256, but you can pick any 256 of these 16,777,216 colors. Images that are 8-bit color store only 8 bits of information for each pixel in that image. Because of this, 8-bit digital images can have a total of only 256 distinct colors but each 8-bit image can pick the 256 colors it will have out of the set of 16,777,216 colors. The particular set of colors that is chosen is called the color palette for that image. A color palette is a table of 256 24-bit digital values.

When an 8-bit image is being displayed on an 8-bit monitor, the 8-bit values of each pixel in the image are used as an index into a table of 256 24-bit color values to drive the monitor. The monitor itself still gets 24-bit values from the 8-bit video card, it just gets only 256 different values at a time. When that 8-bit image is first displayed on the screen, this table is loaded from the color palette of that image. There are 256 24-bit values in a color palette and the index number (0..255) that represents each pixel in an 8-bit image is used to tell the video card which of those 256 24-bit values in the table to display for that pixel. If the pixel's value is 0, the first entry in the table will be used. If the pixel's value is 5, the fifth entry will be used, and so on. This table lookup and display of the color pixels on the

8-bit image with one byte (8 bits) for each pixel

2	2	99	99	82	81
2	17	137	122	17	17
17	2	36	38	36	2
36	137	126	122	17	17
245	27	65	33	89	88
55	84	56	24	17	12

8-bit value is used as an index (lookup number) into the color palette table

	RED 8-bit	GREEN 8-bit	BLUE 8-bit
0	27	59	222
1	69	159	38
2	122	161	16
3	65	16	200
4	47	58	166
253	56	17	8
254	197	22	78
255	56	147	59

256 entries in color palette

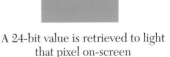

A 24-bit value is retrieved to light that pixel on-screen

screen generally happens at least 60 times per second for each pixel on the screen. This is just one of the many things the computer has to always do while you are just sitting there looking at it.

Eight-bit color files can be faster to load from a CD, or to transfer over the Web, because there are only 8 bits per pixel, verses 24, to load or transfer. One reason 8-bit video cards are cheaper is because they only require enough memory for 8 bits per pixel on the screen, plus the 256 entry 24-bit table, verses 24 bits per pixel on the screen. Now you know why the masses with color monitors have only had 8-bit color. They were cheaper to produce!

ABOUT JPEG AND GIF FILES

JPEG and GIF file formats are both used in compressing images. The GIF format assumes you start with an 8-bit image (or 7, 6, 5, or whatever). The trouble is that for photographs, a lot of loss occurs in converting from a 24-bit to an 8-bit or lower format. Once you have the 8-bit format, creating a GIF will compress that, but the user will get the same 8-bit file when decompressed on the other end. No further loss will occur, but the main loss in a photograph has already occurred in converting from 24-bit to 8-bit. For graphic images that have fewer than 256 colors in them to start with, GIF is great because the image can decompress back to the original with all its colors.

The JPEG format starts with a 24-bit image and compresses it to make it smaller. When the user opens it on the other end, they will also get a 24-bit image of the same opened size as the original but the quality will be less than the original due to the compression. The more compression you choose when you make the JPEG, the smaller the compressed file but the lower the quality when reopened again. For more information on these file formats, see "File Formats and Image Compression." JPEG is generally better for compressing 24-bit color photographs and GIF is generally better for compressing graphics. When you JPEG-compress graphics, the decompressed file will often not be as sharp as the original.

We will sometimes end up compressing photographs using the GIF format because GIF gives you the option of having a transparent area surrounding a knocked out photographed object. This transparent GIF format, when displayed on a Web page, shows the background of the Web page in all the transparent areas. This allows transparent GIF images to be placed on any background and still, in theory, look fine. For this to work in practice, as we will show you, you need to be careful how you make your transparent GIF. Another advantage of the transparent GIF format is that it also supports images that require even less than 8 bits of information per pixel to represent them. Many of the images I have created for commercial sites, like the Netscape online catalog, were GIF files that required only 5 bits per pixel. These files can be made very small and can also be transparent GIFs.

DESIGNING FOR THE VIEWERS YOU CARE ABOUT THE MOST

When you, or your client, create a Web site or multimedia CD, it is really important to consider who will be viewing it and what type of equipment those viewers may have. There is also the most important subset of those viewers, called the ones you really care about. Those are the ones you want to design the site/CD for. In creating your Web/multimedia images, you will want them to look best for these viewers, the ones you really care about. In creating the images for your project, you can choose to use all 8-bit images, all 24-bit images, some of each, save your images in JPEG format, save your images in GIF format, or further variations on each of these choices. Let's discuss how to simplify these decisions.

My general assumption is that the average American who is browsing the Web will have a browser that uses a cheaper computer, or even their TV set, as the monitor environment (these are both 8-bit color) and a modem that is 14,400 kilobits/second in speed. At this speed, it is taking them about one second to download 1K (1024 bytes) of information. The extra bits are taken up by software overhead, and the speed you actually gets depends on a lot of issues, especially the performance of your Internet provider and the number of other people who are also trying to access information on that same site at the same time. If you create a 14K file, it will take these average Americans about 14 seconds to download and view that image. If you are creating a site for the average American, say, the site for the Sears catalog, the person you care about is this average American Web browser. You can currently assume these people have 8-bit color systems. For them, you will want color photographs and color graphics to be mostly 8-bit GIF files. Eight-bit GIF files will look better on their 8-bit screens than 24-bit JPEG files, because 8-bit files generally look better on 8-bit monitors.

For our Web site, we will make a different set of assumptions. We will assume that the users we care most about are photographers, art directors, designers, and digital artists. These are the people who will be most interested in our books and services, and almost all of them will have 24-bit color systems, 28.8 or faster modems or ISDN access, and they will only be interested in seeing the best-quality images. For our site, we will save most images that started out as photographs in JPEG format. Anything that is a photograph of nature or people, or a commercial (for print) composite example, will be saved in JPEG format so it opens up in 24-bit color on the viewer's screen. We will probably be more concerned about showing the user a high-quality image on their screen than creating an image that opens a few seconds faster. We may even show them small, lower-quality versions and give them the option of waiting a little longer to see a higher-quality version. The only time we would use a GIF would be for a graphic or illustration that started with less than 256 different colors or for a small image that required a transparent background. Our set of assumptions about the viewers we care most about will be different than if we were creating a site for the average American Web surfer. When creating images for your site, or that of your client, you need to know the type of user who is most important for that site. Make your images look best for that user.

If you really want your viewer to always see the best images no matter what type of system they have, especially if your site has a lot of photographs, you may want to provide a choice on your home page to either view a set of pages created for users who have 8-bit systems or a set of pages created for users who have 24-bit systems. You could then optimize the images on each separate branch of your main site to make each type of user happy.

HANDS-ON SESSION: GIFs, JPEGs, and Color Palettes

This chapter deals with color palettes
(adaptive, System, and Web) and building
GIFs versus JPEG files.

GIFs AND JPEGs—HOW THEY LOOK ON DIFFERENT SYSTEMS

STEP 1: Open the files gc.psd, redac.psd, and macn.psd from the GIF JPEG and Color Palettes folder on your CD. The names are abbreviations for Grand Canyon in Photoshop format, Red Acura in Photoshop format, and McNamaras in Photoshop format, respectively. When you are creating images to use on the Web, you need to use file names that will work on any computer system. The names of your files will also be embedded in your HTML code for your Web pages, and that code needs to work on any system. Some Windows systems can't read files with names longer than 8 characters, and most Windows systems use the 3-character suffix at the end of the file name to decide what type of file it is. If you use file names with a maximum of 8 characters and a 3-character suffix, they will work on all Macs and all PCs. We will call this the 8.3 file name format. On Unix systems, it can be even more complicated, because they see a difference between upper- and lowercase letters in file names. If you specified a file name in your HTML code that was both upper- and lowercase but the file on the Unix volume was all in lowercase, when you ran that code on a Unix server, the HTML code may not find your file. To be safe when creating images and HTML for the Web, make all your file names lowercase and all the names in your HTML code also lowercase. That way, the code and the files will work together correctly, no matter what type of server your Web pages end up on.

STEP 2: Choosing the JPEG format and a 8.3 name that reflects what you are saving.

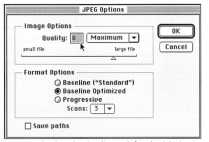

STEP 2: Setting the Quality to 8 for the Maximum quality setting. Also, make sure that Baseline Optimized is on and Save paths is off.

STEP 2: For each of these three open files, choose File/Save A Copy (Command-Option-S) and save one Maximum quality JPEG version and one Medium quality JPEG version. Set the Quality number on the Maximum to 8 and the Quality number on the Medium to 3. Give each an 8.3 format file name that reflects what you are doing in each file. For example redacmed.jpg and redacmax.jpg are the names I used for the Red Acura file. Open all six of these files into Photoshop and compare them at 100% zoom factor to the original three files that are on the screen. Viewers of a Web site or a multimedia application are going to be seeing the images at 100%. You will notice that all of these, even the medium-quality JPEG ones, look pretty good at 100%. Now compare each to its original when zoomed in to 200%. The acura emblem in the center of the hood really breaks down in the medium-quality JPEG version. You will also notice more posterization in the faces of the McNamaras as the JPEG quality gets lower. The Grand Canyon image just looks a bit softer and more posterized at 200%. But hey, at 100% these JPEG mediums look pretty good and they are much smaller than the originals. When I am working on a commercial file for a client, I often send the client a digital comp over the Net by first resampling a copy of my image to about 5Mb in size, and then saving that as a medium-quality JPEG. This is usually a file, about 200–400K in size, that will quickly transfer with my 28.8 modem and then open up on my client's screen to a nice screen comp about 5Mb in size. Notice that all the originals are 928K in size in Photoshop format. With the Maximum JPEG setting, the McNamaras comes in the largest at 288K, where it takes only 192K to compress the Grand Canyon image.

All these images started out with a pixel resolution of exactly 640x480 pixels. When you open them back up from JPEG compression, they will still be 640x480 pixels, their file size just gets smaller for saving on the disk and transmitting over the network. The amount of compression you get depends on the contents of each individual image. The more complex it is, the less compression you get. The

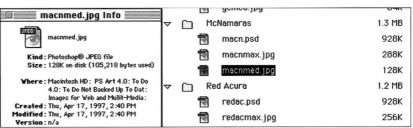

STEP 2: Different files sizes in Photoshop versus JPEG format.

Medium JPEG-compressed images are getting pretty small, with the Grand Canyon one the winner at 64K, Red Acura comes in second at 96K, and the McNamaras are the biggest at a whopping 128K. Notice that all these files sizes are in multiples of 32K. That's because 32K must be the smallest parcel of disk space the driver for this hard disk will allocate for a file. That means all files will

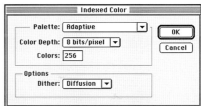

STEP 2: On the Mac, you need to choose File/Get Info (Command-I) from the Finder to see the real file size. In this case it is 105,218 bytes, instead of the 128K the Finder displays.

show up as being at least 32K in size. To see the real size of any file, the size that will actually get transferred across the Net, you need to first click on that file in the Finder, then choose File/Get Info (Command-I) to bring up the Info dialog box for that file. The rightmost part of the Size line will have the actual bytes used in parentheses. You want to set File/Preferences/Saving Files to Never Save Image Previews, and then the size displayed by "bytes used" in the Get Info box will be correct. With Windows and DOS, the file sizes displayed are quite close to the actual file sizes.

STEP 3: Now we are going to create GIF versions of all these images and compare them to the JPEG versions you still have on your screen. For each of the original of the three images, use the Window menu to bring up the version saved in Photoshop format. Its file name will end in .psd. Choose Image/Duplicate (F5) to make a copy of the image, then choose Image/Mode/Index Color and convert it to Index Color using the settings shown here to the right. Now choose File/Save As and save this file with the Format set to CompuServe GIF. Give it a file name that shows this; for the McNamaras, we used macn8mi.gif. Macn tells us it's the McNamaras, 8 tells us it's 8 bits per pixel, mi tells us we used Mode/Index to do the conversion, and .gif tells us it's a GIF file. Now click back on your original Photoshop version of the file and choose File/Export/GIF89a Export (F3) and set things up as shown in the dialog box to the right, to make an 8-bit GIF file using this better filter. The file name we used here was macn889.gif. The 89 before the .gif shows us that we used the GIF89a Export plug-in to generate the file. Open this file and you will notice that it looks just as good as the other 8-bit file on the screen, but if you look at its file size, you will notice that it is smaller than the file you created the other way. Now go back to the original Photoshop file one more

STEP 3: Here are the settings to create an 8-bit Index Color image using Image/Mode/Index Color. To save this as a GIF file, you then need to choose File/Save As and set the Format to CompuServe GIF. You can use the Color Depth pop-up to create 7-bit, 6-bit, or smaller index color images. Setting Dither to None will make the file smaller but it may not look as good.

STEP 3: Here are the settings to create an 8-bit GIF file using File/Export/Gif89a Export. This is a one-step process to convert your 24-bit RGB file directly into a GIF file on the disk, and you can choose the number of Colors while you are at it. 128 colors = 7-bit, 64 colors = 6-bit, 32 colors = 5-bit, and so on. The GIF89a export approach is faster, and generally creates a smaller file that is just as good or better in quality than the above Index Color technique.

time and again choose File/Export/GIF89a (F3), but this time, set the Colors to 32 instead of 256. Name this file macn589.gif. The 5 tells us it's a 5-bit image, using 5 bits of color information for each pixel. Open up this smaller 5-bit image and compare it to the others. In most cases, you will prefer the medium-quality JPEG-compressed file to any of the 8-bit images and certainly to the 5-bit image on a 24-bit color monitor. The 8-bit GIF file may look a bit sharper in some cases than the Medium JPEG-compressed version. Now look at the file sizes again. The Medium JPEG is always a lot smaller than any of the GIF versions, even the 5-bit GIF version. Even the Maximum quality JPEG is about the same size as the 8-bit GIF files and certainly a lot better quality on a 24-bit monitor. So if the intended client has a 24-bit monitor and the image is a continuous tone photograph, the file format of choice is JPEG. The only exception to this right now would be if you are going to create transparent GIF images as you will in the next chapter.

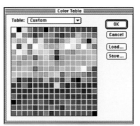

STEP 4: The Adaptive palette for the Red Acura image.

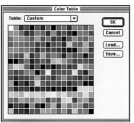

STEP 4: The Adaptive palette for the Grand Canyon image.

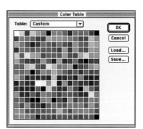

STEP 4: The Adaptive palette for the McNamaras image.

STEP 4: Now switch your monitor to 8-bit color. To do this on the Mac, choose Control Panels/Monitors from the Apple menu, and then choose the 256 Colors option in the Monitors dialog box. Different video card software and different Mac systems have other alternative ways to do this. On Windows 95 or NT you do this by accessing Display properties with your right mouse button. Go through and look at all the files we have created on the screen in 8-bit color mode. You will notice that the 8-bit images look better than the 24-bit ones when viewed on an 8-bit screen. To see an image properly on an 8-bit screen, you need to click on its window to activate it. This will load the adaptive palette for that particular image. This will make that image look good, because we are displaying it using a palette that was optimized for it. Notice, however, that the other images on the screen will not look so good. When looking at the 8-bit version of the Red Acura file, the Grand Canyon and the McNamaras files will not look as good. This will be true for each of these images because everything on the screen needs to be displayed using the palette for the active window. Each time you activate a different image, the entire screen is viewed using its palette. To the left are the adaptive color palettes created by the GIF89a Export filter for each of these images. If you need to display more than one 8-bit image on an 8-bit monitor at a time, which you will often need to do for a Web page or in a multimedia application, you will need to use the same palette for both images; otherwise, one of them will look bad. The palette also controls the colors used to display the menu bar and other system items or items from the application. By the way, you can display multiple 8-bit images on a 24-bit monitor and they will all look their best because all the palettes can be seen at the same time in 24-bit color.

CHOOSING BETWEEN SYSTEM PALETTES AND CUSTOM ADAPTIVE PALETTES

STEP 5: There is a palette, called the *system palette,* that was created to deal with the differences between adaptive palettes of images that need to be displayed on the same page of an 8-bit monitor. A system palette contains a broad range of colors from all over the spectrum so that you can display any image and it will look okay. It won't usually look as good as it would with its own adaptive palette, but using the

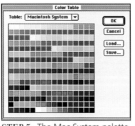

STEP 5: The Mac System palette.

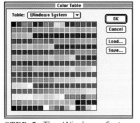

STEP 5: The Windows System palette.

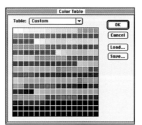

STEP 5: The Web palette.

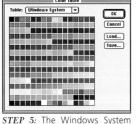

STEP 5: Built-in Photoshop 4 palette choices.

system palette, you can display many different images at the same time with reasonable results. The problem for Web developers is that the Mac and Windows OSs each have different colors in their system palettes. Fortunately, there are 216 colors in common between the two palettes. The palette with these common colors is called the Web palette. Photoshop 4 now allows you to choose any of these palettes when creating 8-bit images using Image/Mode/Index Color. Creating images using the Web palette allows them to display well in 8-bit color on the Mac and on the PC when using Netscape or Internet Explorer to browse your images.

STEP 6: Here you see the three images pasted together in one so you can create a common adaptive palette. Once this is done, you can separate each image again.

STEP 6: When creating images for a multimedia CD where you have absolute control over your palettes, you could also create a custom palette for each group of images that would be on the screen at one time. To do this from Photoshop, with these three images, choose one of the three original 24-bit images (let's do the Grand Canyon), type D, for default colors, and then go into Image/Canvas Size (F8). The width of each of these images is almost nine inches, so make the new width 27 inches and choose OK. Put this image into Full Screen mode, then choose one of the other original RGB images from the Window menu. Press V to switch to the Move tool, then drag and drop this image on top of the new wider one below. Move it to one end or the other, then use the Window menu again to find the third image. Drag and drop the image on the other end of your new wider image, then choose Flatten Image from the Layers Palette menu. Your image should now look like the figure at the top of this page. It doesn't really matter which of the three images is in which position. Choose Image/Mode/Index Color and pick the same Adaptive, 8 bits Per Pixel, 256 Color, Diffusion Dither options you chose last time you used this dialog box, to create an adaptive palette. Choose OK to convert to 8-bit color, then type C to get the Cropping tool, and crop this back to the same Grand Canyon image you started with. Save this as gcall3.gif in CompuServe GIF format. Switch to one of the other two original 24-bit images and choose Image/Mode/Index Color, but this time, set the Palette type to Previous. This will use the same palette we created when all three images were together. Save this with another appropriate "all3" name like macall3.gif, then do the same thing with the third image. You now have all three images created with the same adaptive palette that was custom-developed for just these three images. You'll notice that, in 8-bit color monitor mode, you can switch back and forth between these three images with no flashing. That's because the color palette is the same for each. Go into Image/Mode/Color Palette and look at this common palette. It is a mixture of the three you saw on the last page. Click on the Save button and save this palette as All3Palette. Now you can load this palette from the Color Palette dialog box and also from the GIF89a Export plug-in. By loading this palette, you could use GIF89a to create your GIF files and they might be a little smaller. I tried it and it does make smaller files from the export. Now you know some palette magic! If you need to make a lot of common palette images, create an action to do it to all the files in a folder, or get a copy of DeBabilizer, which has a lot of software features for making custom palettes to work with groups of images.

I went back and created 8-bit images for all three of these using the Web palette. The All3Palette looked better for the McNamaras and Grand Canyon images, but the Web palette actually looked a little better for the Red Acura.

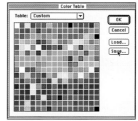

STEP 6: The All3Palette that works for all three of these images. Click on the Save button then you can later Load this into the GIF89a export.

When creating an adaptive palette, to bias the color table toward particular colors in an image, make a selection of those color areas before the mode conversion to Indexed color. The color table will be more weighted to the selected area.

HANDS-ON SESSION: Creating Small, Transparent GIF Composites

These are the techniques I used with the GIF89a Export filter to create images for Netscape's site.

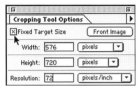

STEP 1: Set the Cropping tool to Fixed Target Size with these dimensions.

STEP 1: The initial crop before color correction.

STEP 1: The initial layer setup with Jacket and Collar.

STEP 1: The initial Collar crop.

One of my first experiences creating images for the Web was to create some images for Netscape's General Store Bazaar. The specs for these images called for a final size of 180 pixels high by 144 pixels wide. They wanted non-interlaced transparent GIF files. Here, using some similar images, is how I produced those GIF files. The images in this example were shot by Frank Bevans Photography, 2164 Old Middlefield Way, Mountain View, CA 94043, 415-694-4640. Even though images for the Web end up small, it is still important to start out with a high-quality photo. Frank is the best!

First of all, if you have ever tried to do a scan that is 180 pixels by 144 pixels, you know that most scanners don't do a great job scanning something that small. You are better off doing a bigger scan and then resampling down to the small size after color correcting, compositing, and sharpening the image. In this example, we shoot a model, me, wearing a jacket. The jacket is the item that will end up in the catalog, but we shoot it with a person in it because the client wants that "invisible man" look—that is, the jacket is filled out as though an invisible man were wearing it. I have not figured out how to make myself invisible yet, so we shoot a second shot of the collar without anyone in it. It will be composited with the jacket; my head, hands, and body removed.

THE SCANS, CROPS, AND COLOR

STEP 1: Do some bigger scans of each image. This project was shot with 35mm because that gives plenty of detail for the creation of Web images. Each image was scanned using a Nikon Super Cool scanner (the LS 1000), which is a great scanner for this type of project.

I actually did the original scans at full-size, full-frame, without any resampling by the scanner. This scanner attached to my Power PC 9500 132 does the full-size 26Mb scans very quickly with interpolation turned off. For you, open the Jacket and Jacket-Collar files from the Small Transparent GIFs folder of the CD. Type C to get to the Cropping tool, then press Return to bring up its options. In the options, turn on Fixed Target Size and set the Height to 720 Pixels and the Width to 576 Pixels. This is four times the final required pixel dimensions of 180x144. Doing all your work at this larger size and then resampling down at the end gives better results than trying to work with a 180x144 image. Crop the image as tightly as you can on the jacket without actually cutting out any of the jacket. Do a similar crop on the collar image; the same size but tighter around the collar area. Type V to get the Move tool then Shift-drag and drop the collar on top of the Jacket image. The Shift key forces the collar layer to be centered. Name this new layer Collar, then double-click on the *Background* layer and name it Jacket. Drag the Collar down underneath the Jacket layer in the Layers palette.

STEP 2: You now want to do the Basic Overall Color Correction on the Jacket layer. Review "The Grand Canyon" session if you don't know how to do this. The background was actually white here and the Jacket is a neutral gray, so both of these need to be close to balanced in RGB to look correct. I found that exactly balancing them makes things look too yellow. Anyhow, you can load my Levels settings (JacketLevels) from the CD if you like. I ran these levels settings and increased the Saturation by 10% in Hue/Saturation. For Web images where I composite two images of the same object together, I find that the color balance on the collar, after correcting the Jacket, will get pretty close by clicking on the Collar layer and then doing Command-Option-L to run the same Levels settings in the Collar as I ran on the Jacket. I did the same thing with the Hue/Saturation settings on the Collar.

MAKING THE KNOCK-OUT

STEP 3: Now we want to create a knock-out of the jacket from the background because this composite is going to become a transparent GIF. It will help automate this process better if we first sharpen the image. We will want to sharpen it before downsampling anyhow, because there will not be enough pixels after downsampling to do a full sharpen. Click back on the Jacket layer to make it active, then choose Filter/Sharpen/Unsharp Mask (F4). I did a sharpen of 100% Amount, 1.0 Pixels, and 0 Threshold. Click on the Collar layer and press Command-F to sharpen it by the same amount. Now press Command-Shift-S (File/Save As) and save this file as JacketLayers. Click back on the Jacket layer, then bring up the Channels palette (Shift-F10), and look at each of the Red, Green, and Blue channels to select the one with the most contrast between the Jacket and the rest of the image. I picked the Red one because it had better contrast between my hands and the jacket than the others did. Click on that channel and drag it to the New Channel icon at the bottom of the Channels palette. This makes a copy of it in Channel #4. Choose Image/Adjust/Threshold (Shift-F7) and adjust the threshold slider until you have the best edges on the jacket mask, and then click on OK. Press L to get the Lasso tool, and use it to clean up your mask by either filling holes with black or areas on the outside with white. For a review of using threshold to make masks, see "Bob and the Kestrel" or "Bryce Stone Woman." Option-click on the New Layer icon to create a new layer and name it Red. Use the Color Picker to pick a new bright red as the foreground color, then use Edit/Fill (Shift-Delete) to fill this new layer with 100%, Normal of this

STEP 3: The Layers setup for clean up of the jacket.

STEP 3: The jacket after mask clean up.

Foreground color. Drag the Red layer to below the Jacket layer but above the Collar layer. Now Command-click on Channel #4 in the Channels palette to load a selection of the mask you just made. Click on the Jacket layer to make it active, then Option-click on the New Layer Mask icon at the bottom of the Layers palette to make a new layer mask with the selected area removed from this Jacket layer. You should now see a Jacket with a red background. Use Shift-F4 to Gaussian Blur the mask by about one pixel. This will blend the edges of the jacket with the background. Type D for default colors, B for PaintBrush, and 0 for 100% Opacity on your brush. Use the left and right bracket keys ([and]) to scroll through the brushes until you find a medium-sized hard edge brush. Shift-[gets you to the top left brush, and then a few]s will get you to a brush that will work here. Use the brush to clean up the edges of your mask. Painting with white adds more of the Jacket layer, and painting with black deletes from the Jacket layer revealing more of the Red layer underneath. You can type X to eXchange between white and black.

BLENDING THE JACKET AND COLLAR

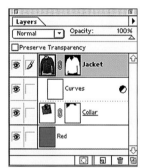

STEP 4: The Layers setup for the final Jacket composite.

STEP 4: When your Jacket mask is clean, click on the Red layer and drag it to the bottom underneath the Collar. You will now see the collar behind the jacket. Click on the Collar layer to make it active, then choose Layer/Free Transform (Command-T) to scale the collar. Shift-click and drag the corner handles to scale the Collar layer proportionally. Click in the middle of the handles and drag to move the scaled down collar up where it belongs behind the jacket. Continue to scale and move this until it seems to be in the right place, then press Return or Enter to finish your transform. Command-click on the New Layer icon to create a new adjustment layer of type Curves that is Grouped with the previous Collar layer. Use the curves to adjust the contrast and color of the Collar layer to best match that of the Jacket layer. Choose OK when it is as close as possible. Because this is an adjustment layer, we can tweak it again later with no quality penalty. Now click back on the Collar layer and then click on the Layer Mask icon at the bottom of the Layers palette to add a new layer mask to the Collar layer. Use the Paintbrush again to remove the parts of the collar you don't want to see. Remember that the Collar is behind the Jacket, so you don't have to be too careful in areas that the Jacket layer is going to hide anyhow. You will now have to switch back and forth between painting in the Jacket layer mask and the Collar layer mask to blend these two layers together properly. You will also have to use a soft brush and less than 100% opacity to seamlessly blend the edges between the two. I also used the Rubber Stamp tool to add a little to the right side of the inside of the Collar layer where I needed a little more blue ribbon and gray inside of jacket. Check out my JacketLayers file on the CD if you are having problems getting this to look right. Pres Command-S to save this version.

STEP 4: Using Free Transform to scale and rotate the collar so it fits behind the jacket.

THE FINAL TRANSPARENT GIF

STEP 5: Now we are going to downsize the Jacket. The trick here is to get the smaller version, when looking at it at 100%, to look similar to the big version. This jacket is harder than most because it has that soft fuzzy texture. The first step is to choose Image/Duplicate (F5) to make a copy of the image; call the copy JacketSmall. You want to copy all the layers, so don't check Merged Layers Only. Now go into Image/Image Size (F7) to scale the image by 25%. Change either the Width or Height Print Size setting to read as a percent, then type in the value 25. Since Proportions is locked, both dimensions will scale the same and you should see the "180 x 144 pixels" at the top in the Pixel Dimensions section. This is the final size we wanted. You will notice that the image now looks really blurry. While viewing it at 100%, choose Filter/Sharpen/Unsharp Mask (F4) to sharpen first the Jacket layer and then the Collar layer by the same amount. To get the look I wanted, I sharpened the layers by 100, 1.0, and 0 again before resampling them down, and then sharpened each of them by 200, 1.0, and 0. Most images don't require that much sharpening, but to get the fuzzy jacket look, that is what I did here. It really won't look right unless you are viewing at 100% while doing this. Zooming in to 200% won't help you here because you are used to looking at sharpening for print and this look is entirely different. Just sharpen it so it will look the best at 100%; that's what people will see on the Web site.

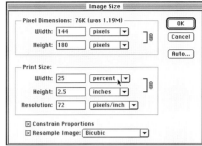

STEP 5: The settings to scale LayersSmall.

STEP 6: Since this is a transparent GIF file, the Red background you see here will actually be replaced by whatever background the Web page has. It helps if you know the background color that is intended. On the other hand, if that background color is likely to change, you should test out different ones now. Option-drag the Red layer to the New Layer icon and make a copy called Gray. Pick a gray from the Color Picker, Netscape Gray is 192, 192, 192, then use Shift-Delete to Fill this new layer with that gray. You will now see that background instead of the Red, but you can turn off the Eye icon on this Gray layer and the Red background will re-appear. You can test out as many background colors as you would like using this process.

STEP 7: Turn off the Eye icons for all your background colors. The image, and the Layers palette, should match the illustration here. Whatever is transparent now will be transparent in your transparent GIF file. Choose File/Export/GIF89a Export (F3) to create the GIF. We want this file to be as small as possible, so we are going to try 128, 64, and 32 Colors for our adaptive palettes. Turn off the Interlaced option and set the Colors to 128 with the Palette set at Adaptive. Click on the OK button and call this file jack128.gif. Use the export again (F3) with the same settings, but this time set the Colors to 64 and call it jack64.gif. One more time with Colors set to 32 and call it jack32.gif. Use File/Open to open all of these images in Photoshop. You will probably notice that the 32-color version doesn't look that different from the 128-color version. Look at the file sizes on each one (use Get Info on the Mac). You'll see that the 32-color one is a lot smaller. I got about 10K for the 32 colors, 13K for the 64 colors, and 16K for the 128 colors. The 128 colors is not worth the extra six seconds a Web surfer would have to wait to see it.

STEP 7: The settings to use in Gif89a Export to create these transparent GIFs. The Colors setting will change depending on the bit depth you want.

STEP 7: Here is how the image and the Layers palette should look in preparation to make the transparent GIFs.

TESTING AND FIXING THE BACKGROUND

STEP 8: Now we want to test out the actual background color you are going to have on the Web page. This is the secret to getting these to look the best. If you are developing your Web site on your system, you could just bring the image up in your browser and see how it looks. In Photoshop, though, there is an easy way to preview any solid color background. Let's use the jack32.gif image, but you could do the same procedure with any of them. While in the jack32.gif image, choose Image/Mode/ Color Table (Shift-F3) and click on the one gray color by itself at the bottom left. The color at the left in the bottom row is always the transparent background color. This color will be replaced by the background of your Web page. When you click on it, that brings up the Color Picker, which allows you to pick any other color for that color. Pick a very bright red color, then choose OK to the Color Picker and OK to the Palette Editor. You will now see the image as it would appear against a bright red

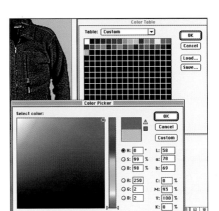

STEP 8: Editing the Color Table to test a background color with your GIF file.

STEP 9: The correct setup for doing the Merge Visible.

STEP 9: jack32.gif on the left, before the edges are fixed. The fixed version is on the right.

background. You may notice some white edges around the jacket and also around the edge of your image. These didn't show up against a gray background, and probably wouldn't show up against a white background but they glare at you from a red background. To make a more perfect GIF file that will work against any background, you need to get rid of these.

STEP 9: If you see white edges around the jacket, they could have been caused by your layer masks not being perfect or as the result of the Gaussian Blur you did on the layer mask in the JacketLayers image. When working for print, Gaussian Blur of a mask edge is a good way to blend the edge with the new background and get rid of the jaggies. Since every pixel counts, and shows, on the Web, blurring the edge of a mask will only get rid of the edge jaggies if the background color for your site is similar to your original background color. With a totally different background color, it may be better to have masks that are not blurred, or not anti-aliased, on the edge. You might also notice that the very border of your image area, one or two pixels around the border, is not a solid red background color. To solve both of these types of problems, go back to the JacketSmall image. Turn on the Eye icons for the top three layers only, then choose Merge Visible from the Layers Palette menu. This will merge the Jacket, Collar, collar color correction, and their layer masks into one layer, called Jacket, with a transparent background. Choose Select/Load Selection of Jacket Transparency as a New Selection. Now click on the Layer Mask icon at the bottom of the Layers palette. This will add the transparency as a layer mask that we can modify while looking at the results. Now turn on the Eye icon for the Red layer, and then choose Image/Adjust/Threshold (Shift-F7) to adjust the threshold of this new layer mask. With the Preview option on in Threshold, you will notice that when you move the slider to the right, the mask will cut away a few pixels from the edge of the jacket. Using Threshold will also force the mask to be either completely white or completely black. It will remove any gray values from the edge of the jacket area and from the edge of the image. I found that moving the Threshold slider slightly to the right solved the problem for me. You might want to Option-click on the layer mask thumbnail, to just see the mask, and then do Command-Z over and over again to see the difference Threshold has made to your mask. Click back on the Jacket layer thumbnail so it is active and turn off the Eye icons for all your background layers. Now you are ready to try the GIF89a Export again. Use File/Export/GIF89a Export (F3) and re-create the 32-color image, calling it jack32f.gif (the fixed version) this time. Open this image and again choose Image/Mode/Color Table (Shift-F3) to bring up the Color Table and change the background color. If you made the right modifications to the mask, your improvements should look similar to the illustration on this page. All my versions of the files are on the CD in the area for this chapter. I re-saved the fixed versions, calling them JacketSmallFixed, jack32f.gif, jack64f.gif, and jack128f.gif. For more information about creating images for the Web, see Lynda Weinman's *Designing Web Graphics.2* published by New Riders. Also, check out the bibliography of *Photoshop 4 Artistry* for information on some more great Web books.

BIBLIOGRAPHY

PUBLICATIONS

Adams, Ansel with Mary Street Alinder. *Ansel Adams: An Autobiography*. Boston, MA: New York Graphic Society Books, 1985.

Adams, Ansel with Robert Baker. *Ansel Adams: The Camera*. Boston, MA: New York Graphic Society Books, 1980.

Adams, Ansel with Robert Baker. *Ansel Adams: The Negative*. Boston, MA: New York Graphic Society Books, 1981.

Adams, Ansel with Robert Baker. *Ansel Adams: The Print*. Boston, MA: New York Graphic Society Books, 1983.

Black, Roger, with Sean Elder. *Web SitesThat Work*. San Jose, CA: Adobe Press, 1997.

Blatner, David, and Bruce Fraser. *Real World Photoshop 4: Industrial Strength Production Techniques*. Berkeley, CA: Peachpit Press, 1997.

Blatner, David, Phillip Gaskill, and Eric Taub. *QuarkXPress Tips & Tricks: Industrial-Strength Techniques, 2nd Edition*. Berkeley, CA: Peachpit Press, 1994.

Booth, Sara, ed. *Step-by-Step Electronic Design*. Peoria, IL: Step-by-Step Publishing.

Burns, Diane and Sharyn Venit. *The Official QuarkXPress Handbook, Macintosh 3.2 Edition*. New York, NY: Random House Electronic Publishing, 1994.

Cohen, Luanne Seymour, Russell Brown, Lisa Jeans, and Tanya Wendling. *Design Essentials*. Mountain View, CA: Adobe Press, 1992.

Cohen, Luanne Seymour, Russell Brown, and Tanya Wendling. *Imaging Essentials*. Mountain View, CA: Adobe Press, 1993.

Dayton, Linnea and Jack Davis. *The Photshop Wow! Book*. Berkeley, CA: Peachpit Press, 1993.

Hamlin, J. Scott. *Photoshop Web Techniques*. Indianapolis, IN: New Riders Publishing, 1997.

Haynes, Barry and Wendy Crumpler. *Photoshop Artistry, A Master Class for Photographers and Artists*. Alameda, CA: Sybex, 1995.

Lawler, Brian P. *Photo CD Companion*. Rochester, NY: Eastman Kodak Company

McClelland, Deke. *Macworld Photoshop 4 Bible*. Foster City, CA: IDG Books Worldwide, 1997.

Rich, Jim and Sandy Bozek. *Photoshop in Black-and-White: An Illustrated Guide to Producing Black-and-White Images Using Adobe Photoshop*. Berkeley, CA: Peachpit Press, 1994.

Siegel, David. *Creating Killer Web Sites: The Art of Third-Generation Site Design*. Indianapolis, IN: Hayden Books, 1996.

Tapscott, Diane, Lisa Jeans, Pat Soberanis, Rita Amladi, and Jim Ryan. *Production Essentials*. Mountain View, CA: Adobe Press, 1994.

White, Minor, Richard Zakia, and Peter Lorenz. *The New Zone System Manual*. Dobbs Ferry, NY: Morgan Press, Inc., 1976.

Weinman, Lynda. *Deconstructing Web Graphics*. Indianapolis, IN: New Riders Publishing, 1996.

Weinman, Lynda. *Designing Web Graphics.2*. Indianapolis, IN: New Riders Publishing, 1996.

Weinman, Lynda, and Bruce Heavin. *Coloring Web Graphics*. Indianapolis, IN: New Riders Publishing, 1996.

Wilhelm, Henry with Carol Brower. *The Permanence and Care of Color Photographs: Traditional and Digital Color Prints, Color Negatives, Slides, and Motion Pictures*. Grinnell, IA: Preservation Publishing Company, 1993.

WEB SITES

Atkinson,Bill. *Natureimages.com*. Bill Atkinson Photography

Haynes, Barry and Wendy Crumpler. *Maxart.com*. Imaging consultants and *Photoshop 4 Artistry* authors.

Lawler, Brian P. *Callamer.com/BPLawler*. Graphic Arts Consultant

Weinman, Lynda. *Lynda.com*. Web books and information.

INDEX

Symbols

2.5 file format, 21, 31
8-bit colors, 289-290
8-bit video cards, 290
24-bit video cards, 289
32-bit addressing
 (Macintosh), 18
[ ] (brackets), sizing brushes, 45, 172

A

About This Macintosh command
 (Apple menu), 17-18
Accented Edges filter, 263
accessing palettes, 7-8
Actions
  ArtistKeys, 12
  batch processing with, 16
  editing
    adding breakpoints, 14
    copying commands, 15
    stop commands, 14-15
  menu items
    disabling, 15
    Load Actions, 12
    recording, 13-14
    Replace Actions, 12
  shortcut keys, setting up, 13
Actions folder (drop shadows),
 creating, 14
Actions menu commands (Insert Menu
 Item), 13-14
Actions palette, xxi-xxiii, 12
  Batch, setting up files, 16
  Button mode, 12
  compare to Commands Palette, 12
  shadows, creating, 282-283
  shortcut keys, 11
activating layers, 77
Active channel (Channels palette), 72-
 73
Adams, Ansel
  duotones, *see* duotones
  influence, 82
  Zone system, *see* Zone system
Add mode (blending), 238
Adjust command (Image menu), 176
Adjust Hue/Saturation command
 (Image menu), 124
Adjust menu commands
  Equalize, 245
  Posterize, 251
  Selective Color, 159
Adjustment layers, xxii, 76
  changing colors, 62

color correction, xxii, 206-208
  Curves, 76
  dodging (burning), 144
  grouped levels, xxii
  grouped adjustment layers see:
    McNamaras, 210, Versailles, 192,
    Bryce Stone Woman, 173, The
    Band, 200
  histograms, xxii
  McNamaras example, 211-214
  New Adjustment Layer options, 76
  Versaille example, 194-196
Adobe Photoshop 4.0 Prefs, 27
Airbrush tool, 45-46, 171
Al example
  blemishes, removing, 172
  color correction, 169-170
  oversaturation, 170-171
  sharpening, 172
  whites, brightening, 171
Aldus Gallery Effects filters, xxv, 263-
 264
aligned cloning (Rubber Stamp tool),
 46-48
aligning text (Type tool), 51
Amount parameter, sharpening images,
 114, 151
anti-aliasing
  dodging (burning), 143
  tools, 41
  postscript preferences, 19
  Type tool, 50-51
APDA Magazine Cover example, 266-
 279
  creating a magazine cover, 267-268
  knock out and keep existing shadows,
   268-271
  linking layers, 279
  motion blur of objects, 271-273
Apple menu commands
  About This Macintosh, 17-18
  Desktop Pattern Desk Accessory, 91
Apply Image (Blend mode), 228-229,
 234-235
Apply Image command (Image menu),
 175, 226
Arrange menu commands (Send to
 Back), 249
Arrow tool (paths), 181-182
ArtistKeys
  Drop Shad, 14
  loading, 12
  replacing, 12
  shortcut keys, setting up, 13
Async I/O, 23
audience considerations, 290-291
auto erase option (Pencil tool), 45

Auto Levels command, 67

B

B&W (Black & White) digital images
 (duotones), *see* duotones
Background layer, 77
backgrounds
  changing, 180-181
    Bob Goes To example, 186-187
    Layer mask, 184-185
    paths, 181-184
  colors, changing (Gradient tool), 54
  GIFs, 299-300
  layers, 77
    adding layers, 78
    Bryce Stone Woman example, 174
    Kansas example, 149
  monitor calibration, 91
ball file (Actions folder), 14
Band example
  color correction, 203-205
    adjustment layers, 206-208
    Levels, 205-206
  combining images, 200-201
    blending, 203
    Gradient tool, 201-202
    removing elements, 202-203
  flattening, 208
  sharpening, 209
Bas Relief filter, 263
Batch (Actions palette), 16
Batch dialog box, 16
beeping preference, 20
Behind mode (blending), 231-232
bicubic interpolation, 19
Bike Ride in the Sky example, 242
  blending (Multiply mode), 243-244
  text
    configuring, 245-248
    glow text and text from Illustrator,
     244-249
    placing, 249
Bitmap command (Mode menu), 251
bitmaps
  blurring, 252-253
  diffusion dither, 250-251
bits, 99
  8-bit colors, 289-290
black points
  finding (Video LUT Animation), 169-
   170
  monitor calibration, 92
blend modes, 226-227
  Add mode, 238
  Apply Image, 228-229, 234-235
  Behind mode, 231-232

blurring bitmaps, 252-253
Calculations, 229-230
Clear mode, 232
Color Burn mode, 240-241
Color Dodge mode, 240-241
color mode, 239-240
Darken mode, 237
Difference mode, 237-238
Dissolve mode, 231
Exclusion mode, 238
Fill, 227
Hard Light mode, 236
Hue mode, 239-240
layers, 227-228
Levels, 227-228
Lighten mode, 237
luminosity, 239-240
Multiply, 232
Normal mode, 231
Overlay mode, 236
painting tools, 227-228
saturation mode, 239-240
Screen, 233
Soft Light mode, 233, 236
Subtract mode, 238
Wave filters, 257
Blending
Band example, 203
GIFs, 298
Gradient tool, 53-54, 190, 242-243
layers, 78, 171
Blue channel (color corrections), 112
Blur command (Filter menu), 256
Blur menu commands (Gaussian Blur), 176
Blur tool, 49-50
blurring
Gaussian
bitmaps, 252-253
Bryce Stone example, 176
masks, 195-196
motion blur filter, 255
Radial blur filter, 256
Wave filter, 256-257
Bob and the Kestral example
images
combining , 190-191
cropping, 188
Gradient tool, 190
masking, 189
Bob Goes To example, 180-181
backgrounds, changing, 186-187
Layer mask, 184-185
masking hair, 185-186
paths, 181
creating, 182-183
editing, 182
selections, converting, 183-184
brackets ([]), sizing brushes, 45, 172
brightness
Buckminster Fuller example, 161-163
color corrections, 112, 130-131
Color Picker, 58

Grand Canyon example, 122
brightness/Contrast tool, 65, 175
brushes, sizing, 45, 172
Brushes palette
Airbrush tool, 45-46
Car example, coloring, 141
Eraser tool, 46
keys, 45
options
customizing brushes, 44-45
fade, 45
opacity, 45
setting, 44
stylus pressure, 45
Paintbrush tool, 46
Pencil tool, 45
Rubber Stamp tool, 46-48
Bryce Stone Woman example, 173
blurring (Gaussian), 176
CMYK conversion, 178
color correction, 174-175
Highlights, replacing, 177
images, merging, 177-178
masks
editing, 176-177
unsharpening, 178
thresholds, masking, 176
Buckminster Fuller example
brightening, 161-163
colorizing, 164-165
dodging (burning), 163
luminosity, 164-165
removing bandage, 164
sharpening, 163
burning, see dodging, 143
BurnleyGraveyard example
duotones, see duotones
tritones, creating, 134-135
Button mode (Actions palette), 12
bytes, 99

C

cache
histograms, 23
image preference, 23
see also disk cache
Calculations (Blend mode), 229-230
Calculations command, 226
calibration, 88
monitors, 90
backgrounds, 91
black point settings, 92
color balance, 92
gamma settings, 91
output settings, 93-94
white point settings, 91-92
testing, 89-90
Canvas Size, changing, 24
Canvas Size command (Image menu), 267

Car example
colors
correcting, 140
matching, 166-168
feathering, 142
Paintbrush tool, coloring, 141
Quick Mask mode, 140-142
selections
Lasso tool, 138-139
Magic Wand, 138
saving, 139-140
cast shadows, creating, 283-286
CD ROM, 2-3, 36-37
ArtistKeys, 12
Extra Infor Files, 36
GrColOrPur file, 52-54
PS Artistry Small Compressed images
set, 37-38
ChainMap, 262
Channel Options dialog box, 70
Channels, 69-75
Blend mode
Apply Image, 228-229
Calculations, 229-230
Gradient tool, 243
color corrections, 112, 204-205
Kai Krause's helpful tips, 244-245
layers, 74-75, 171
layer masks, see Layer Masks
loading selections, xx
mask channels, 70
deleting, 71
editing, 70-71
moving, 72
replacing, xxi
selections & channels, 69-75
RGB, 174
Channels palette, 69-75
Active channel, 72-73
Bryce Stone Woman example, 175-176
Eye icons, 72-73
Night Cab Ride example, 216
oversaturation, 170-171
Channels palette menu commands
(Duplicate), 72
Clear command (Edit menu), 232
Clear mode (blending), 232
clipboard, exporting, 19
Clipping Path command (Paths Palette menu), 187
cloning (see Rubber Stamp tool)
aligned, 46-47
non-aligned, 47
patterned, 47-48
snapshot cloning, 48
CMYK (Cyan, Magenta, Yellow, Black), xxx, 56
black ink, 57
color corrections, 115
converting
Bryce Stone Woman example, 178
Car example, color matching, 167-

168
  duotones, 136
  Kansas example, 154
  RGB, 57, 115
  Yellow flowers example, 158-159
customizing separations, 28-29
preferences, 21, 25
saving, 115-116
Selective Color tool, 64-65

CMYK command (Mode menu), 136, 158

CMYK Preview command (View menu), 153

Color (Blend mode), 239-240

Color Balance tool, 65

Color Burn mode (blending), 240-241

Color Channels in Color preference, 21

Color Correcting Al, *see* Al example

color correction tools
  Auto Levels command, 67
  Brightness/Contrast tool, 65
  Color Balance, 65
  Color palette, 61
  Curves, 63, also see Curves
  Desaturate command, 67
  Eyedropper, 61
  file modifications, 61-62
  Hue/Saturation, 63-64, see HSL
  Info palette, 61
  Levels, 63, also see Levels
  preview button, 62
  Replace Color, 64
  Selective Color, 64-65
  Variations tool, 66
  Video LUT Animation, 62-63

Color Dodge mode (blending), 240-241

Color match spot, 166

Color Merged layer, 170-171

Color palette, 59
  color corrections, 61, 110-111
  HSB mode, 166
  picking for Web, 292-295, 299-300
  shortcut key, 169

Color Picker, 19, 58-59

Color Range command (Select menu), 153, 155-158

Color Settings command (File menu), 19, 24

Color Table command (Mode menu), 60, 292-295, 299-300

Colored Pencil filter, 263

coloring shadows, 281

colorizing (Buckminster Fuller example), 164-165

colors
  8-bit, 289-290
  B&W (duotones), *see* duotones
  backgrounds (GIFs), 299-300
  balance
    Grand Canyon example, 122-123
    monitor calibration, 92-93

changing
  adjustment layers, 62
  Gradient tool, 54
CMYK, 56-57
Color Picker, 58-59
corrections, 110
  adjustment layers, xxii
  Band example, 203-208
  brightness/contrast, 112
  Bryce Stone Woman example, 174
  Car example, 140
  channels, 112
  CMYK, 115
  color management systems, 95-96
  Color palette, 110-111
  Grand Canyon example, 118-128
  highlights, 111-112
  Hue/Saturation, 113
  Info palette, 110-111
  Kansas example, 130-131, 149-151
  RGB format, 114-115
  scans, 88, 111
  selections, 113-114
  shadows, 112
  Versaille example, 194-195
duotones, adjusting, 134
HSL (Hue, Saturation, Lightness), 57-58, see HSL
Lab color space, 58
matching, 166-168
merged layers, 170
oversaturation, fixing, 170-171
printing preferences, 25-26
RGB, 56
setting preferences, 21
Swatches palette, 60
separations
  customizing, 28-29
  digital imaging, xxx
  Highlight settings, 26
  preferences, 24-25
  Shadow settings, 26
tritones, adjusting, 135
whites, brightening, 171

columns (Marquee tool), 41

Command key, xx

commands
  Actions menu, 12-16
    Insert Menu Item, 13
    Insert Stop, 14
  Adjust menu
    Brightness/Contrast, see Brightness/Contrast
    Curves, see Curves
    Equalize, 245
    Hue/Saturation, see HSL
    Levels, see Levels
    Posterize, 251
    Selective Color, 159
  Apple menu
    About This Macintosh, 17-18
    Desktop Pattern Desk Accessory, 91
  Apply Image, 226
  Arrange menu (Send to Back), 249

Blur menu (Gaussian Blur), 176
Calculations, 226
Channels palette menu (Duplicate), 72
Control Panels menu (Monitors), 294
Edit menu
  Clear, 232
  Define Pattern, 48
  Fill, 51, 227
  Stroke, 204
  Take Snapshot, 48
  Undo, 138
File menu
  Color Settings, 19, 24
  Get Info, 18, 293
  Revert, 127, 255
  Save, 30
  Save As, 30
  Save a Copy, 223-224
Filter menu
  Blur, 256
  Distort, 256-257, 261
  Fade, 262
  Noise, 255-256
  NoiseAdd, 197
  Other, 281
  Pixelate, 75
  Render, 260
  Sharpen, 163, 172
  Stylize, 255
Image menu
  Adjust, 176
  Adjust Hue/Saturation, 124
  Apply Image, 175, 225
  Calculations, 226
  Canvas Size, 200, 267
  Crop, 40
  Duplicate, 178
  Map, 257
Layer menu
  Free Transform, 184, 211
  Merge Visible, 170-171
Mode menu
  Bitmap, 251
  CMYK, 136, 158
  Color Table, 60
  Duotone, 133
  Indexed Color, 60, 293-295
  RGB, 136
Navigator Palette menu (Palette Options), 11
Paths Palette menu (Clipping Path), 187
Preferences menu, 17-29, see Preferences
  General, xxvi
  Image Cache, xxii
  Memory & Image Cache, 18
  Save Palette Positions , 8
Select menu
  Color Range, 153, 155
  Feather, 69, 171
  Grow, 42
  Inverse, 69, 163
  Load Selection, 68-73
  Modify, 283

None, 80
Save Selection, xxi, 68-73, 140
Similar, 42
Settings menu (Control Panel), 91
View menu
CMYK Preview, 153
Gamut Warning, 153
Hide Edges, 150
New View, 9
Zoom, xxiv
Window menu
Show Action, 12
Show Brushes, 189
Show Channels, 70
Show Color, 61
Show Layers, 74
Show Navigator, 10
Show Options , 39
Commands palette (Photoshop 3.0), 12;
see also Actions palette
composites (Band example)
blending, 203
color correction, 203-208
combining images, 200-201
flattening, 208
Gradient tool, 201-202
removing elements, 202-203
see also APDA, Night Cab Ride, Bob,
McNamaras, Creating Small
transparent GIF composites
examples
sharpening, 209
compression
GIFs, 290
JPEGs, 34-35, 290
lossy, 31
LZW, 34
Context Sensitive menus
brushes, 44
control key, 11
eye dropper, 55
layers, 80
see The Tool Palette chapter, 39
selections, 40, 41
zoom tool, 55
contrast (color corrections), 112
Control key, xxiii
see Context Sensitive menus
tool options, 39
see also shortcut keys, 6
Control Panel command (Settings
menu), 91
Control Panels menu commands
(Monitors), 294
converting duotones, 136
copying layers, 79
copying commands, 15
corner points (paths), 181-182
Corner/Curve tool (points), 182
Crop command (Image menu), 40
Cropping tool, 43
Fixed Target Size, 296

Curve points (paths), 181-182
curves
color correction, 63, 204-205
dodging (burning), 145
duotone, 133
Grand Canyon example, 125-128
Kansas example, 150
McNamaras example, 210
scanning histograms, 105
The Band example, 200
Curves Adjustment layer, 76
Curves dialog box, 126
cursor tool settings, 22
Custom Colors picker (duotones), 134
customizing
brushes, 44-45
Color Picker, 58
color separations, 27-29

D

Darken mode (blending), 237
DCS (Digital Camera System), xxix, 33
Define Pattern command (Edit menu),
48
deleting
layers, 77, 79
mask channels, 71
option key, xx
points (Pen tool), 182
Desaturate command, 67
deselecting (Lasso tool), 139
Desktop Pattern Desk Accessory
command (Apple menu), 91
desktop publishing, xxx
desktop scanners, xxviii
destination folders (Batch), 16
Dialog boxes
Batch, 16
Channel Options, 70
Color Range, 155-158
Curves, 126
Duotone Curve, 133
Duotone Options, 134
Duplicate Channel, 189
Duplicate Layer, 75
Edit Image, 107
EPS, 136
EPS Format, 32
Fill, 280
Filter, 176
Hue/Saturation, see HSL
Image Cache, xxii
Image Size, xxiv-xxv
Indexed Color, 60
Insert Menu Item, 13
Layer Options, 80, 253
Levels, 169
Make Selection, 183
Monitors, 294
New Adjustment Layer, xxii, 76

Nikon scan, 103
Paint Style, 249
Preferences, 19
Record Stop, 14
Replace Color, 64
Selective Color, 159
Separation Tables, 26
Units and Rulers Preferences, 24
Dicomed digital camera, xxix
Difference mode (blending), 237-238
diffusion dither, 21, 250-251
Digimarc watermark filters, xxvi, 263-
264
digital imaging
adjusting images, xxx
color separations, xxx
delivering, xxxiii-xxxiv
desktop publishing, xxx
direct digital, xxix-xxx
duotones, 133
Kodak Photo CD system, xxviii-xxix
printing, xxxi-xxxiii
scanning, xxviii
Zone system, 87
direct digital imaging, xxix-xxx
disk cache (Macintosh), 18
displacement maps, 261-262
Dissolve mode (blending), 231
Distort command (Filter menu), 256-
257, 261
dithering
diffusion, 21, 250-251
Gradient tool, 53-54
document Sizes option, 23
dodging (burning)
Blend mode, 240-241
Buckminster Fuller example, 163
Grand Canyon example, 143, 146
adjustment layers, 144
Curves, 145
Eyedropper, 145
feathering, 144
marquee tools, 144
scratch removal, 147-148
sharpening, 146-147
spot removal, 147
Dot Gain preference, 25
dots per inch, *see* dpi
downloading graphics, 291
dpi (dots per inch), 99-101
Draft mode (Radial Blur filter), 256
Drop Shad ArtistKey, 14
drop shadows, creating, 14, 280-283
Duotone command (Mode menu), 133
Duotone Curve dialog box, 133
Duotone Options dialog box, 134
duotones, 133
adjusting colors, 134
CMYK conversion, 136
creating, 133-134

curves, 133
Levels, 133
measuring (Eyedropper), 135
Monotype setting, 133
output
  calibrating monitors, 135-136
  EPS format, 135-136
RGB conversion, 136
see also tritones
Duplicate Channel dialog box, 189
Duplicate command (Channels palette menu), 72
Duplicate command (Image menu), 178
Duplicate Layer dialog box, 75
Dye sublimation printers, xxxi

E

edges (filters), 259
  finding, 257
  inverting, 257
  minimizing, 258
Edit Image dialog box, 107
Edit menu commands
  Clear, 232
  Define Pattern, 48
  Fill, 51, 227
  Stroke, 204
  Take Snapshot, 48
  Undo, 138
editing
  actions
    copying commands, 15
    stop commands, 14-15
  layer masks, 76
  layers, 79
  mask channels, 70-71
  masks, 176-177
  tools
    Blur, 49-50
    Gradient, 52-54
    Paint Bucket, 51
    Sharpen, 49-50
    Smudge, 48-49
    Type, 50-51
editors (Gradient), xxiv, 53-54
Enable Async I/O, 23
EPS (Encapsulated PostScript) files, 32-33
  duotones, 135-136
  saving, 116
EPS dialog box, 32, 136
Equalize command (Adjust menu), 245
Eraser tool, 46
Exclusion mode (blending), 238
exposure values
  latitudes, 83, 86
  Zone system, 84-86
extensions, changing, 20-21
Extra Infor Files (CD ROM), 36

Eye icons (Channels palette), 72-73
Eyedropper tool, 55
  color
    corrections, 61
    settings, 25
  duotones, measuring, 135
  Replace Color tool, 156-158

F

Fade
  brushes, 45
  filters, 262-263
Fade command (Filter menu), 262
Feather command (Select menu), 69, 171
feathering
  a selection, 69
  Car example, 142
  Grand Canyon example, 144
  Marquee tool, 40
  Night Cab Ride example, 220
File menu commands
  Color Settings, 24
  Color Settings , 19
  Get Info, 293
  Revert, 127, 255
  Save, 30
File menu commands (Get Info), 18
files
  Actions palette (Batch), 16
  color correction tools, 61-62
  formats, see formats
  naming, 292
  saving, 20-21, 30
  sizes, 100-101, 293
Fill command (Edit menu), 51, 227
Fill dialog box, 280
Filter dialog box, 176
Filter menu commands
  Blur, 256
  Distort, 256-257, 261
  Fade, 262
  Noise, 255-256
  NoiseAdd, 197
  Other, 281
  Pixelate, 75
  Render, 260
  Sharpen, 163, 172
  Stylize, 255
filters (examples of usage), 254-255
  Aldus Gallery Effects, 263-264
  displacement maps, 261-262
  edges, 258-259
  fade, 262-263
  finding edges, 257
  Lighting Effects, 259-261
  motion blur, 255
  Night Cab Ride example, 219
  Pointillize (layers), 75
  Radial blur, 256
  Unsharp Mask filter, 114, 151-152

Versaille example, 197-198
Wave, 256-257
Zigzag, 276-279
flatbed scanners, xxviii
flattening layers, 208, 224
floating selections, 80, 218
fonts (Type tool), 50-51
foreground colors, changing (Gradient tool), 54
formats
  2.5 Format Compatibility option, 31
  comparing, 31
  EPS (Encapsulated PostScript), 32-33
    DCS (Desktop Color Separation), 33
    duotones, saving, 135-136
  GIFs, 33, 290
  JPEGs, 30-31, 34-35, 290
  LZW compression, 34
  Photoshop, 30-32
  PICT, 33
  SCITEX CT, 33-34
  TIFFs, 30, 32
formatting text (Type tool), 50-51
Free Transform command (Layer menu) xxiii, 184, 211-212, 298
Fugi Pictrography printers, xxxii
Full Screen mode, 5-6
fuzziness
  Color Range tool, 157
  Replace Color tool, 64

G

Gamma output calibration
  duotones, 135-136
  monitors, 24, 91, 93
Gamut Warning command (View menu), 153
gamuts, 23, 153-154
garbage in, garbage out, scanning, 104
Gaussian Blur
  bitmaps, 252
  Bryce Stone example, 176
  Night Cab Ride example, 219
  Versaille example, 195-197
Gaussian Blur command (Blur menu), 176
General command (Preferences menu), xxvi
Get Info command (File menu), 18, 293
GIF89, 33, 293
GIFs, 33, 290
  creating, 296
    backgrounds, 299-300
    blending, 298
    scanning, 296-297
    separating images, 297-298
    sizing, 298-299

transparent GIFs via GIF89a Export, 298-300
JPEG comparison, 293-295
transparent, 299
Gradient Blend tool, 52-54, 242-243
  Band example, 201-202
  Bob and the Kestral example, 190
Gradient Editor, xxiv, 53-54
Gradient Tool Options menu commands (Reset Tool), 201
Grand Canyon example
  brightness/contrast settings, 122
  color balancing, 122-123
  Curves, 125-128
  dodging (burning), 143, 146
    adjustment layers, 144
    Curves, 145
    Eyedropper, 145
    feathering, 144
    marquee tools, 144
    scratch removal, 147-148
    sharpening, 146-147
    spot removal, 147
  highlights, 120-121
  Hue/Saturation, 124-125
  Levels, 117-120
  shadows, 120-122
  Video LUT Animation, 123
graphics
  audience considerations, 291
  GIFs, 290
    backgrounds, 299-300
    blending, 298
    creating, 296
    JPEG comparison, 293-295
    scanning, 296-297
    separating images, 297-298
    sizing, 298-299
    transparent, 299
  JPEGs, 290
    GIF comparison, 293-295
    quality, 292-293
gray balance controls, 25
GrColOrPur file (CD ROM), 52-54
Green channel, 112
grids, xxiii-xxiv, 9
  preferences, 23
  snapping to, 10
Grouped levels adjustment layers, xxii
Grouped adjustment layers, see Adjustment layers
grouping (palettes), 8
Grow command (Select menu), 42
guides, xxiii-xxiv
  creating, 9-10
  preferences, 23

H

Hand icon (Zoom controls), 7
Hand tool, 55

handle bars, 181-182
Hard Light mode (blending), 236
hardness settings (brushes), 44
Hardware monitor calibration device, 24
Hide Edges command (View menu), 150
Highlight Eyedropper, 26
highlights
  color corrections, 111-112
  scanning, 102-103
  settings, 26
  tritones, 135
histograms, 101-105, 108-109
  cache settings, 23
  color corrections, 110
  layers, xxii
  scanning, 101
    comparing originals, 104-105
    Curves modification, 105
    Levels modification, 105
    Photo CD, 106-107
    troubleshooting, 108-109
HSB mode (Color palette), 166
HSL (Hue, Saturation, Lightness), 57-58
  Al example, 170
  Bryce Stone Woman example, 174-175
  Car example (changing an objects color), 140
  color
    correction, 63-64, 113
    matching, 167
  Grand Canyon example, 124-125
  Kansas example, 131-132, 150
  whites, brightening, 171
  Yellow flowers example, 160
HTML, naming files, 292
Hue mode (blending), 239-240
Hue, Saturation, Lightness, see HSL
Hue/Saturation Command, see HSL

I-J

Illustrator (text)
  configuring, 246-248
  placing, 249
Image Cache command (Preferences menu), xxii
Image Cache dialog box, xxii
Image cache preference, 23
Image menu commands
  Adjust, 176
  Adjust Hue/Saturation, 124
  Apply Image, 175
  Canvas Size, 267
  Crop, 40
  Duplicate, 178
  Map, 257
Image Size dialog box, xxiv-xxv

images
  adding (Night Cab Ride example), 220-221
  B&W digital (duotones), see duotones
  combining
    Band example, 200-202
    blend modes, see blend modes
    Bob and the Kestral example, 190-191
    McNamaras example, 212-214
    Night Cab Ride example, 216-217
    Versaille example, 193
  dividing (Zone system), 83-84
  merging, 177-178
  Photo CD, scanning, 105-107
  previewing preference, 20
  rotating, 221
  separating GIFs, 297-298
  sizing, xxiv-xxv
  Web, see Web images
imagesetters, xxxiii
Impressionist mode (Rubber Stamp tool), 48
Indexed Color command (Mode menu), 60
Indexed Color dialog box, 60
Info palettes, 9
  color corrections, 61, 110-111
  displaying, 24
  measuring, 268
  shortcut key, 169
Ink setup (printing), 25-26
Input controls (Levels), 118
Insert Menu Item command (Actions menu), 13
Insert Menu Item dialog box, 13
Insert Stop command (Actions menu), 14
interpolation preferences, 19
Inverse command (Select menu), 69, 163
Iris printers, xxxi-xxxii
ISDN digital services, xxxiii-xxxiv

Johnson, Stephen, xxix
JPEGs, 30-31, 290
  compression, 34-35
  GIF comparison, 293-295
  mask channels, 38
  quality, 292-293

K

Kai Krause's helpful tips, 244-245
Kansas example
  brightness/contrast, 130-131
  CMYK conversion, 154
  color correcting, 149
  Curves, 150
  gamuts, 153-154
  hiding edges, 150

highlights, 129-130
Hue/saturation, 131-132, 150
Levels, 129
Rubber Stamp tool, 150-151
shadows, 130
sharpening, 151-152
spot removal, 152-153

keyboard shortcuts, *see* shortcut keys
KnownOutputTest, 89, 97
Kodak Digital Camera System (DCS),
see DCS
Kodak Photo CD system (digital
imaging), xxviii-xxix

L

Lab color space, 58
laser printers, xxxii
Lasso tool, 41-42, 69
Car example, 138-139
keys, 139
selecting, 171
latitudes (Zone system), 86
Layer Masks, 75-76, 78-79, for
examples of use see the Grand
Canyon Final Tweaks, Kansas Final
Tweaks, Yellow Flowers, Fuller, Al,
Bryce, Bob, Versailles, Band,
McNamaras, Night Cab Ride, APDA,
Shadows and GIF Composites
examples
Linking a layer mask with a layer, 191
Step 15 caption
Layer menu commands (Free
Transform), 211
Layer Options dialog box, 80, 239-240,
252-253
layers, 74-76
activating, 77
adjustment layers, xxii, 76
Curves, 76
McNamaras example, 211-214
Versaille example, 194-196
backgrounds, 77
adding layers, 78
Bryce Stone Woman example, 174
changing, 181
Blend mode, 78, 227-228
Apply Image, 228-229
Calculations, 229-230
context menus, 80
Control key, xxiii
copying, 79
deleting, 79
duplicating, 75
editing, 79
flattening, see flattening
layer masks, see layer masks
linking 78, 279
masks
activated layers, 79
adding, 78

Bob Goes To example, 184-185
creating, xxi, 75-76, 175-176
editing, 76
Night Cab Ride example, 218-219
merging layers
Sample Merged, 42, 51
Versaille example, 196
Night Cab Ride example, 223-224
moving, 78-80
Night Cab Ride example, 217, 222
opacity, 78
Pointillize filter, 75
selection conversion, 80
Shadow layer, 280-281
transparencies, 77
Layers palette, 74-75, 169
blend modes, *see* blend modes
floating selections, 80
Highlights, replacing, 177
Merge Visible, 177-178
opacity, lowering, 171
Layers palette menu commands
(Merge Visible), 170-171
leading (Type tool), 51
Levels
adjustment layers, xxii, 194-195
Auto Levels command, 67
Blend mode, 227-228
color correction, 63
duotone, 133
Grand Canyon example, 117-120
input controls, 118
masking hair, 185-186
output controls, 118
scanning histograms, 105
see McNamaras, Al, Kansas, Fuller,
Bryce, Versailles and The Band
examples
Video LUT Animation, 169-170, 174
Zoom controls, 6-7
Levels dialog box, 169
light meters (Zone system), 83
Lighten mode (blending), 237
Lighting Effects filter, 259-261
lightness, 57; *see also* HSL
Line tool, 54
linking layers, 78, 279
Load Selection command (Select
menu), 71, 68-73
loading
actions (ArtistKeys), 12
channel selections, xx, 71
path selections, 183
lossy compression, 31
Luminosity (Blend mode), 239-240
LZW compression, 34

M

Macintosh
32-bit addressing, 18

disk cache settings, 18
memory requirements, 17-18
PC, compared, 3-4
RAM disk, 18
Virtual memory, 18
Magic Wand tool, 42
Car example, 138
changing selections, 69
Kansas Tweaks, 149-150
Replace Color tool, 64
Make Selection dialog box, 183
Map command (Image menu), 257
Marquee tool, 40
anti-aliasing, 41
columns/rows, 41
dodging (burning), 144
feathering, 40
keys, 41
sizing, 40
Masks, 70
blurring, 195-196
channels
deleting, 71
editing, 70-71
moving, 72
editing, 176-177
hair, 185-186
JPEGs, 38
Layer Masks, see Layer Masks
layers
activated, 79
adding, 78
creating, 75-76, 175-176
editing, 76
Quick Mask mode, 140-141
saving selections, 70
Unsharp Mask filter, 114, 151-152
thresholds, 176
Master mode, brightening whites, 171
McNamaras example, 210
grouped adjustment layers, 211-214
combining images, 212-214
Levels, 211
memory requirements
Macintosh, 17-18
PCs, 18-19
Memory & Image Cache command
(Preferences menu), 18
Menu Items (actions)
editing
copying commands, 15
stop commands, 14-15
recording
disabling, 15
multiple, 13-14
single, 13
Merge Down (Layer Menu), 221
Merge Visible command (Layers
palette menu), 170-171, 177-178, 224
merging layers, 170-171, 177-178, 221,
224
for color, 171

Metric Color Tags, saving, 21
midtones, 102
    color matching, 166
    scanning, 102-103
Mode menu commands
    Bitmap, 251
    CMYK, 136, 158
    Color Table, 60
    Duotone, 133
    Indexed Color, 60
    RGB, 136
Modify command (Select menu), 283
monitor settings, 90
    backgrounds, 91
    black point, 92
    colors, 24, 92
    duotone output, 135-136
    gamma, 91
    output, 93-94
    white point, 91-92
Monitors command (Control Panels
    menu), 294
Monitors dialog box, 294
monotone type (duotone), 133
Motion blur filter, 255
Move tool, 43, 78
multimedia images, 288
    8-bit colors, 289-290
    GIFs, see GIFs
    JPEGs, see JPEGs
Multiply mode (blending), 232

N

names
    files, 292
    short PANTONE preference, 20
Navigator palette, 10-11
    view box, 11
    zoom controls, xxiv, 10-11
Navigator Palette menu commands
    (Palette Options), 11
Neon Glow filter, 263
New Adjustment Layer dialog box, xxii,
    76
New View command (View menu), 9
newspaper settings, 28-29
Night Cab Ride example, 215, 223-224
    adding neon images, 220-221
    cab, adding, 216
    Cab colorizing with a layer, 222
    combining images, 216-217
    feathering, 220
    filters, 219
    floating selections, 218
    layer masks for cleanup, 218-219
    using layers to make choices, 222-224
    using Screen to drop blacks, 217
    working on layer verses mask, 219
Nikon scan dialog box, 103

Noise command (Filter menu), 255-256
NoiseAdd command (Filter menu), 197
Nonaligned cloning (Rubber Stamp
    tool), 47-48
None command (Select menu), 80
Normal mode (blending), 231

O

opacities
    Blur tool, 49-50
    brushes, 45
    Gradient tool, 53-54
    layers, 78
    lowering, 171
    numbers, 172
    Paint Bucket tool, 51
    Rubber Stamp tool, 172
    Sharpen tool, 49-50
opening multiple windows, 9
option key
    deleting, xx
    Lasso tool, 41-42, 139
    Marquee tool, 41
    selection tools, 42
Other command (Filter menu), 281
output
    calibration, 88
        monitors, 93-94, 135-136
        separations, 90
        testing, 89-90
controls (Levels), 118
    gamuts, 153-154
    printing, xxxi-xxxiii
Overlay mode (blending), 236
oversaturation, 170-171

P-Q

Paint Bucket tool, 51
Paint Style dialog box, 249
Paintbrush tool, 46
    coloring, 141
    editing masks, 176-177
    quick mask mode, 141
Painting tools (Blend mode), 227
Palette Options command (Navigator
    Palette menu), 11
palettes
    accessing, 7-8
    Actions, xxi-xxiii, 12, see Actions
        shadows, creating, 282-283
        shortcut keys, 11
    Brushes
        Airbrush tool, 45-46
        customizing brushes, 44-45
        Eraser tool, 46
        fade, 45
        keys, 45
        opacity, 45

        options, setting, 44
        Paintbrush tool, see Paintbrush
          tool
        Pencil tool, 45
        Rubber Stamp tool, see Rubber
          Stamp tool
        stylus pressure, 45
    channels
        layers, blending, 171
        mask channels, 71-72
        oversaturation, 170-171
    Color palette, see Color palette
    Commands palette (Photoshop 3.0),
        12
    grouping, 8
    Info, see Info palette
    Layers, see Layers palette
    Navigator, 10
        view box, 11
        Zoom controls, xxiv, 10-11
    Paths, 181-182
    positioning, 8
    preferences, 20
    Swatches, 60
    Tool, 39
        Blur tool, 49-50
        Brushes palette, see Brushes
          palette
        changing options, 39
        Color palette, see Color palette
        Color Picker, see Color Picker
        Cropping tool, 43
        Eyedropper tool, 55
        Full Screen mode, 6
        Gradient tool, 52-54
        Hand tool, 55
        Lasso tool, 41-42
        Line tool, 54
        Magic Wand tool, 42
        Marquee tool, 40-41
        Move tool, 43
        Paint Bucket tool, 51
        Photoshop 4.0 changes, xxv
        Sharpen tool, 49-50
        Smudge tool, 48-49
        Type Mask tool, 50-51
        Type tool, 50-51
        Zoom tool, 55
PANTONE (short name preference),
    20
paths
    Bob Goes To example, 181-184
    making knock-outs, 268-269
    saving, 187
    shadows, creating, 282
    Text, 247-248
Paths palette, 181-184
Paths Palette menu commands
    (Clipping Path), 187
patterned cloning (Rubber Stamp tool),
    47-48
patterns
    creating, 47, 51, 250
        blurring bitmaps, 252

diffusion dither bitmaps, 250-251
   posterizing, 251
   streaked patterns, 251-252
Paint Bucket tool, 51
PCs
   Macintosh, compared, 3-4
   memory requirements, 18-19
   RAM, 19
   shortcut keys, 7
Pen tool
   options, 181-183
   paths
      APDA example, 268-269
      Bob Goes To example, 181
      creating, 182-183
   points, adding, 182
Pencil tool, 45
Photo CD images, scanning, 105-107
PHOTOS40.PSP, 27
Photoshop 3.0 (Commands palette), 12
Photoshop Separation test, 90, 98
PICT files, 33
Pixelate command (Filter menu), 75
pixels, xxiv-xxv, 69-70
Plug-ins preference, 22
Pointillize filter (layers), 75
points
   adding (Pen tool), 182
   Corner/Curve tool, 182
   paths, 181-182
Posterize command (Adjust menu), 251
Posterize, Bitmaps and Patterns
  example (cool stuff, check it out!),
  250-253
postScript imagesetters, xxxiii
preferences
   antialiasing postscript, 19
   beeping, 20
   CMYK, 21
   Color Channels in Color, 21
   Color Picker, 19
   color separations, 24
      Eyedropper Tool, 25
      Highlight settings, 26
      Monitor Setup, 24
      Printing Ink Setup, 25
      Separation Setup, 25
      Shadow settings, 26
   diffusion dither, 21
   exporting clipboard, 19
   file saving
      2.5 file format, 21
      extensions, changing, 20-21
      Metric Color Tags, 21
      previewing images, 20
   gamuts, 23
   grids, 23
   guides, 23
   image cache, 23
   interpolation, 19
   palettes, resetting, 20
   Picker sliders, 20

plug-ins, 22-23
printing, 25-26
saving, 26-27
Scratch Disk, 22-23
Short PANTONE Names, 20
system palette, 21
Tool cursor settings, 22
Tool Tips, 20
Transparency, 23
Video LUT animation, 21-22
Preferences dialog box, 19
Preferences menu commands
   General, xxvi
   Image Cache, xxii
   Memory & Image Cache, 18
   Save Palette Positions , 8
previewing images, 20, 62
printing
   calibration, 89-90
   digital imaging, xxxi-xxxiii
   dpi (dots per inch), 99-100
   duotones, see duotones
   ink setup, 25-26
   sizes, xxiv-xxv
Pro Photo CD scans, 106
ProofPositive printers, xxxi-xxxii
PS Artistry Small Compressed images
  set (CD ROM), 37-38

quartertones, 102-103
Quick Mask mode
   Car example, 140-142
   Color Range tool, 157

R

Radial blur filter, 256
radius parameter, sharpening images,
  114, 151
RAM (Random Access Memory)
   Macintosh, 18
   PCs, 19
Record Stop dialog box, 14
recording actions (menu items), 13-15
red channels, 112
Red mode (Color Picker), 59
Reds layer (masks), creating, 175-176
Render command (Filter menu), 260
Replace Color dialog box, 64
Replace Color tool, 64, 155-158
Reset Tool command (Gradient Tool
  Options menu), 201
Resolution, 99-101
Revert command (File menu), 127, 255
RGB (Red, Green, Blue), xxx, 56
   color corrections, 114
   converting
      CMYK, 57, 115
      duotones, 136
      HSL, 58

RGB command (Mode menu), 136
rotating images, 43, 221
roundness setting (brushes), 44
rows (Marquee tool), 41
Rubber Stamp tool, 46-48
   blemishes, removing, 152-153, 172
   removing scratches, 147-148
   spotting, 146-147
rulers, 9-10, 24

S

Sample Merged, 42, 51
saturation, 57
   Blend mode, 239-240
   Bryce Stone Woman example, 174-
   175
   Car example, 140
   color corrections, 131-132
   color matching, 167
   Color Picker, 58
   Desaturate command, 67
   Grand Canyon example, 124-125
   Kansas example, 150
   oversaturation, fixing, 170-171
   whites, brightening, 171
   Yellow flowers example, 160
   see also HSL
Save command (File menu), 30
Save Palette Positions command
  (Preferences menu), 8
Save Selection command (Select
  menu), xxi, 68-73, 140
saving
   CMYK format, 115-116
   duotones (EPS format), 135-136
   EPS/DCS format, 116
   files, 30
   GIFs, 293
   JPEGs, 292-293
   palettes, 20
   paths, 187
   preferences, 26-27
   selections, 68-73, 139-140
scanning, 88, 103-104
   color correction, 88, 111
   digital imaging, xxviii
   dpi, 99-101
   GIFs, 296-297
   highlights, 102-103
   histograms
      comparing originals, 104-105
      Curves modification, 105
      Levels modification, 105
      troubleshooting, 108-109
   histograms, 101
   Photo CD images, 105-107
   Pro Photo CD scans, 106
   resolution, 99-101
   shadows, 102-103
   sizes, calculating, 100-101
   Versaille example, 192-193

SCITEX CT files, 33-34
Scratch Disk preference, 22-23
Scratch Sizes option, 23
Screen mode (blending), 233
Scrolling (Navigator palette), 10
Select menu commands
    Color Range, 153, 155
    Feather, 69, 171
    Grow, 42
    Inverse, 69, 163
    Load Selection, 71
    Modify, 283
    None, 80
    Save Selection, xxi, 140
    Similar, 42
selection tools, 68
    anti-aliasing, 41
    Cropping tool, 43
    feathering, 40
    Lasso, 41-42, 69
    Magic Wand, 42, 69
    Marquee, 40
        columns/rows, 41
        fixed size, 40
    Pen Tool, see Pen Tool
    Move, 43
    selection modifier keys, 41
selections, 68
    changing, 69
    channels, 69-70
    color correction, 113-114
    Color Range, 155-157
    converting (layers), 80
    feathering, 49, 69
    floating, 80, 218
    inverting, 69
    load selection, 68-73
    mask channels, 70
        deleting, 71
        editing, 70-71
        moving, 72
        see also masks, 70
    pixels, 69-70
    Quick Mask mode, 140-141
    Replace Color, 155-158
    saving, 68-73, 139-140
    thresholds, 189
Selective Color command (Adjust menu), 64-65, 159, 168
Selective Color tool, 64-65, 159, 168
Send to Back commands (Arrange menu), 249
Separation Tables dialog box, 26
separations
    printing preferences, 25-26
    calibration test, 90, 98
Settings menu commands (Control Panel), 91
shadows
    APDA Magazine Cover example, 270-271
    color corrections, 112, 130

coloring, 281
creating
    cast shadows, 283-286
    drop shadows, 280-283
Eyedropper, 169
Grand Canyon example, 120-122
layer, 280-281
preferences, 26
scanning, 102-103
Sharpen command (Filter menu), 163, 172
Sharpen tool, 49-50
sharpening images, 114
    Band example, 209
    Buckminster Fuller example, 163
    Grand Canyon example, 146-147
    Kansas example, 151-152
    unsharp mask, see Unsharp Mask
    Versaille example, 196
Shift key
    brushes, 45
    Marquee tool, 41
    selection tools, 42
Shortcut keys, xx-xxi
    actions, setting up, 13
    Actions palette, 11
    Airbrush tool, 45-46
    Blur tool, 49
    Color palette, 169
    Control key, xxiii
    Eraser tool, 46
    Eyedropper tool, 55
    Gradient tool, 52-54
    Hand tool, 55
    Info palette, 169
    Lasso tool, 139
    Line tool, 54
    Marquee tool, 40
    Navigator palette, 10
    Paint Bucket tool, 51
    Paintbrush tool, 46
    PCs, 7
    Pencil tool, 45
    Rubber Stamp tool, 46
    Rubber Stamp tool opacity, 172
    rulers, 9
    save, 30
    Sharpen tool, 49
    Smudge tool, 48-49
    threshold, xxiii
    Tool palette, 39
    zoom, xxiv, 6-7, 55
Show Action command (Window menu), 12
Show Brushes command (Window menu), 189
Show Channels command (Window menu), 70
Show Color command (Window menu), 61
Show Layers command (Window menu), 74
Show Navigator command (Window

menu), 10
Show Options command (Window menu), 39
Similar command (Select menu), 42
Sine waves (Wave filter), 256
Sizing
    brushes, 45
    calculating scans, 100-101
    Canvas Size, 24
    GIFs, 298-299
    images, xxiv-xxv
    Marquee tool, 40
    see Cropping Tool
sliders, 20
Smudge tool, 48-49
snapping to grids, 10
snapshot cloning (Rubber Stamp tool), 48
Soft Light mode (blending), 233, 236
source folders (Batch), 16
source images, 228
spacing text (Type tool), 51
Spectrophotometer, 29
Square waves (Wave filter), 257
stop commands for actions, 14-15
storage (Scratch Disk preference), 22-23
streaked patterns, creating, 251-252
Stroke command (Edit menu), 204
styles (Type tool), 51
Stylize command (Filter menu), 255
stylus pressure (brushes), 45
Subtract mode (blending), 238
Swatches palette, 60
System palette preference, 21

T-U

Take Snapshot command (Edit menu), 48, 161-162
target audience considerations for Web sites, 290-291
target images, 228
testing
    backgrounds (GIFs), 299-300
    calibration, 89-90
text
    glow and Illustrator text effects, 244-248
    formatting (Type tool), 51
    Kai Krause's helpful tips, 244
    placing Illustrator text, 249
Text Path, 247-249
three-quartertones, 102-103
threshold
    masking, 176, 186, 189
    parameter, 114, 151-152
    selections, 189

shortcut keys, xxiii

TIFF files, 30, 32

tolerance (Magic Wand tool), 42

Tool palette, 39
Arrow tool (paths), 181-182
Blur tool, 49-50
Brushes palette, *see* Brushes palette
changing options, 39
Color palette, *see* Color palette
Color Picker, 58-59
Cropping tool, 43
Eyedropper tool, 55
Full Screen mode, 6
Gradient tool, 52-54
Hand tool, 55
Lasso tool, 41-42
Line tool, 54
Magic Wand tool, 42
Marquee tool, 40-41
Move tool, 43, 78
Paint Bucket tool, 51
Photoshop 4.0 changes, xxv
Rubber Stamp tool, 46-48
Sharpen tool, 49-50
Smudge tool, 48-49
Type Mask tool, 50-51
Type tool, 50-51, 247-248
Zoom tool, 55

Tool Tips, xxvi, 20

tools
cursor settings, 22
Free Transform, see Free Transform
Paintbrush, *see* Paintbrush tool
Rubber Stamp, *see* Rubber Stamp
   tool
selection, *see* selection tools

Transparency preference, 23
Gradient tool, 54
layers, 77

transparent GIFs, 299

trashing actions, 15

Triangle waves (Wave filter), 257

tritones
creating, 134-135
highlights, 135

troubleshooting (scanning histograms),
108-109

Type Mask tool, 50-51

Type tool, 50-51, 244, 247-248

Undo command (Edit menu), 138

Units and Rulers Preferences dialog
box, 24

UNIX, naming files, 292

Unsharp Mask filter, 114
Bryce Stone Woman example, 178
Kansas example, 151-152
see sharpening
Versaille example, 196, 198

V

Variations color correction tool, 66

Versaille example
color correction, 194-195
combining images, 193
foregrounds, 195-196
Gaussian noise filter, 197
masking, 193-194
merging layers, 196
opacity, 198
scanning, 192-193
sharpening, 196
spot removal, 196
Unsharp Mask filter, 198

video cards
24-bit, 289
8-bit, 290

video digitizers, xxix

Video LUT animation, 21-22, 62-63
finding white/black points, 169-170
Grand Canyon example, 119, 123
Kansas example, 131
Levels, 174

view box (Navigator palette), 11

View menu commands
CMYK Preview, 153
Gamut Warning, 153
Hide Edges, 150
New View, 9
Show Grids, 9-10
Show Guides, 9-10
Zoom, xxiv

views (Full Screen mode), 5-6

virtual memory (Macintosh), 18

visualization, 83

W-X-Y

watermarks (Digimarc filters), xxvi,
263-264

Wave filter, 256-257

Web images, 288
8-bit colors, 289-290
creating, 296
backgrounds, 299-300
blending, 298
scanning, 296-297
separating images, 297-298
sizing, 298-299
transparent GIFs via GIF89a
   Export, 298-300
GIFs, 290
JPEGs, 290

Web site (Author's), 289
audience considerations in creating
   your Web site, 291

white points
monitor calibration, 91-92
finding (Video LUT Animation), 169-
170

whites, brightening, 171

Wind filter, 219

Window menu commands
Show Action, 12
Show Brushes, 189
Show Channels, 70
Show Color, 61
Show Layers, 74
Show Navigator, 10
Show Options , 39

windows
Full Screen mode, 5-6
opening multiple, 9

Windows menu (palettes), 5
accessing, 7-8
grouping, 8
positioning, 8

Yellow Flowers example
adjustment layer for more control,
   160
changing colors, 159
CMYK conversion, 158-159
Color Range selections, 155-156
   fuzziness, 157
   quick mask mode, 157
Hue/Saturation, 160
Replace Color selections, 155-158

Z

Zigzag filter, 276-279

Zone system, xvii, 82-83
dividing images, 83-84
digital images, 87
exposure values, 84-86
light meters, 83
Zone V exposure, 84

Zoom commands (View menu), xxiv

zoom controls, xxiv, 6-7, 10-11, 55

COLOPHON

This book was produced almost entirely by the authors on two machines: first, a Power PC 9500/132 with 2 Gb internal and a 2 Gb ProMax disk array (for Photoshop Scratch Disk), 128 Mb RAM, Radius Thunder 30/1152 video board and PressView 21 SR monitor, Bernoulli 230 Mb transportable drive and an Iomega Zip drive; and second, a Quadra 900 accelerated with a Daystar PowerPro 601 Power PC board, 112 Mb RAM, Radius/SuperMac Thunder/24 video board and 20" Trinitron Dual Mode monitor, Micronet Raven disk array, Bernoulli 230 Mb transportable drive and a Micronet CD drive. CD backups were burned using a Micronet Master CD Plus 2x4 CD burner, and tape backups were made to a Micronet DAT tape drive using Retrospect.

Each chapter of this book was set up as a separate document in QuarkXPress. The text was input directly into Quark using a template document with Master pages and style sheets. Charts were done in Adobe Illustrator and color correction and separation was done, of course, from Photoshop using the methods and settings described in this book.

Screen captures were done with Screenshot™, and occasionally with the Mac's Command-Shift-3 command. Low res RGB captures were placed in the original documents and sized in Quark. After design decisions were made as to final size and position, the resolution was changed to 350 dpi and photos were resampled, sharpened, separated, and saved as CMYK TIFFs in Photoshop. They were then reimported into Quark at 100%.

Most photographs in this book, including the cover, are from Photo CD or Pro Photo CD scans from 35mm slides done primarily by Palmer Photographic in Sacramento. Several were from scans done by Robyn Color on a Howtek D4000 drum scanner and the McNamaras scans came from a Leafscan-45.

Film output for Match Prints was done by Shepard Poorman on a Scitex Dolev 200 imagesetter. Most pages were output at 2400 dpi using a 175-line screen. Critical color proofing was done using 3M Match Prints and less critical color was proofed with Fuji First Look proofs. We used the techniques covered in this book with the Gamma control panel that comes with Photoshop, as well as our GTI Soft-View D5000 Transparency/Print Viewer (a great product) to calibrate our PressView 21 SR monitor to color proofs for critical color pages and the cover.

Transfer of files was done primarily using CDs and Bernoulli Zip disks which were sent via Airborne Express between the authors and the printer. Files were sent as Quark documents with high-res photos in position. We sent a FileMaker Pro document which delineated the names of each chapter, and the page start and length of the document. Film was set in signatures of 16 pages starting with the most color critical signatures first. In some instances, images and Quark files were sent via internet between the authors and the publisher.

Printing was done by GAC Shepard Poorman in Indianapolis, direct to plate with a Creo platesetter, then printed on Heidelberg Speed Master sheet fed presses. The book is printed on 80lb Productolith Dull and the cover is 12pt C1s with a lay-flat gloss laminate.

Typefaces are New Caledonia, New Caledonia SC&OSF, Frutiger, and, on the cover, Industria, all from Adobe.

PHOTO CREDITS

Adobe Systems Incorporated *(415-961-4400)*
© 1989, Adobe Systems Incorporated, All Rights Reserved
Olé No Moiré: 89, 92, 97

Bruce Ashley *(408-429-8300)*
© 1995, Bruce Ashley, All Rights Reserved
Bob: 180, 183, 184, 188, 254, 191
Kestrel: 188, 191
Fuller: 161, 163, 164

Frank Bevans *(415-694-4640)*
© 1997, Frank Bevans, All Rights Reserved
Barry in Jacket: 296, 297, 298, 299, 300
Jacket Alone: 296, 298, 299, 300

Will Croff
© 1995, Will Croff, All Rights Reserved
Wine Grapes & Checkerboard: 89, 92, 97, 265

Wendy Crumpler *(408-338-4569)*
© 1995, Wendy Crumpler, All Rights Reserved
Men In Boat: 47, 48
Boats In Harbor: 225

Marita Gootee
© 1995, Marita Gootee, All Rights Reserved
Cardline: 265

Barry Haynes *(408-338-4569)*
©1997, Barry Haynes, All Rights Reserved
Wave at Sunset: 81
My View: 137
McNamaras: 210, 214
San Leone Pizza: 287
All other photographs in this book and on the cover:
© 1995, Barry Haynes, All Rights Reserved

Susan Holland
© 1995, Susan Holland, All Rights Reserved
Hands: 265

Jeffrey Myers *(713-661-9532)*
© 1995, Jeffrey Myers, All Rights Reserved
ChessQueen: 265

Marc Simon *(415-864-5606)*
© 1992, Marc Simon, All Rights Reserved
Flying Books: 89, 92, 97
Headland: 230, 233
Computers: 266, 267, 268, 269, 270, 272, 273, 276, 279
Multi Media Parts: 266, 267, 268, 272, 273, 274, 275, 276, 277, 278, 279, 281, 282, 283, 286

12 Free Photo CD Scans. . .

Not All Photo CD Scans Are Created Equal

Join the thousands of satisfied customers nationwide using PALMER'S. 25 years in the imaging business and pioneering Photo CD, we unconditionally guarantee the quality of every Photo CD scan.

Excellent service and support... just a few of the reasons Photoshop users, designers, photographers, and publishers choose PALMER'S. Your image is taken seriously whether you need one scan or thousands.

Introduce yourself to the PALMER'S difference. We'll scan 12 - 35mm negatives or slides for free* (*a $36 value*) with an order of $36 (12 Repro scans) or more. That's it! You'll find PALMER'S is America's premier Photo CD service.

P A L M E R ' S

MOUNTAIN VIEW	**SACRAMENTO**
650 Castro Street	2313 C Street
415 969 1950	916 441 3305
415 969 1956 *fax*	916 441 1157 *fax*

SMART SOLUTIONS
800 735 1950

Yes!
I Want 12 Free!

Name _____ Title _____

Company _____ Telephone _____

Address _____ Fax _____

City _____ Business Type _____

State/Zip _____ Scans Per Month _____

How did you hear about us? _____

* This offer is good for **35mm film** and **one time only**, although pass it along to your friends.
(does not include disc and offer subject to change)

PSA

USE YOUR INFLUENCE

Have you ever said, "If only there were a book that…" or "I'd like like to have a book that told me how to…" If so, we want to hear from you.

We're thinking of possible topics for our next book and we'd like to know what kind of information you've been looking for and can't find. Here's a couple of ideas that we have, but send us your wish list. You may not be the only one who's looking.

THE PHOTOSHOP, LIVE PICTURE, PAINTER CONNECTION. This book would be a manual for learning Live Picture or Painter if you already know Photoshop. It would point out the similarities and differences and give examples of when you might want to use each program. Or, would you rather see, Photoshop, Painter, and Illustrator?

TWO-COLOR AND THE COMPUTER. This book would explore the problems and solutions of creating two-color documents on the computer. It would cover simple Quark documents, Illustrator or Freehand graphics and trapping issues, and duotones versus using two process plates for bitmap graphics.

GO AHEAD, PUSH US AROUND!

You bet! I'd race right out to find a copy of:

☐ **THE PHOTOSHOP, LIVE PICTURE, PAINTER CONNECTION**

☐ **TWO-COLOR AND THE COMPUTER**

Actually, I'm more interested in a book about _____

_____

and if you want to talk about it, here's my important information.

Name _____

Address _____

City _____ *State* _____ *Zip* _____

Phone _____ *Fax* _____ *E-mail* _____

Barry Haynes and Wendy Crumpler
820 Memory Lane
Boulder Creek, CA 95006

Hey, I'd also like to know more about

☐   THE PHOTOSHOP FOR INSTRUCTORS COURSE

☐   THE PROJECTS FOR DIGITAL ARTISTS CLASS

☐   PHOTOSHOP 4 ARTISTRY DEMOS ON CD

Check our Web site at Maxart.com for details on these and upcoming projects.

Fold this side up first, staple or tape the edge, and send it on!

REGISTRATION CARD

Photoshop Artistry

Name _____ Title _____

Company_____ Type of business _____

Address _____

City/State/ZIP _____

Have you used these types of books before? ☐ yes ☐ no

If yes, which ones? _____

_____

How many computer books do you purchase each year? ☐ 1–5 ☐ 6 or more

How did you learn about this book? _____

Where did you purchase this book? _____

Which applications do you currently use? _____

_____

Which computer magazines do you subscribe to? _____

_____

What trade shows do you attend? _____

_____

Comments: _____

_____

_____

Would you like to be placed on our preferred mailing list? ☐ yes ☐ no

☐ **I would like to see my name in print!** You may use my name and quote me in future New Riders products and promotions. My daytime phone number is: _____

New Riders Publishing 201 West 103rd Street ◆ Indianapolis, Indiana 46290 USA

Fax to 317-817-7448

Fold Here

- -

BUSINESS REPLY MAIL
FIRST-CLASS MAIL PERMIT NO. 9918 INDIANAPOLIS IN

POSTAGE WILL BE PAID BY THE ADDRESSEE

NEW RIDERS PUBLISHING
201 W 103RD ST
INDIANAPOLIS IN 46290-9058